# WAKE UP WARRIOR

# WARRIORBOOK

# WAKE UP WARRIOR

# WARRIORBOOK

## A Modern Man's Doctrine to Having It All

NEXT CENTURY
PUBLISHING

**WarriorBook**

Published by Next Century Publishing
Austin, TX
www.NextCenturyPublishing.com

ISBN: 978-1-68102-527-8

Printed in the United States of America

## This Book of Warrior Doctrine is Dedicated to

My Queen Danielle K White,
and my three amazing children: Parker, Bailee and Ruby.

Without you this book would not exist.

Without you this doctrine would not matter.

I Love You No Matter What.

You are the reason I choose the live the Warrior's Way.

# TABLE OF CONTENTS

## SECTION #1: THE FOUNDATION

## SECTION #2: THE CODE

## SECTION #3: THE STACK

# SECTION #4: THE CORE

# SECTION #5: THE KEYS

# SECTION #6: THE GAME

# SECTION #7: THE SUMMARY

# SECTION #8: THE APPENDIX

# INTRODUCTION
## By Garrett J White

Dear Reader,

Here are the FACTS:

I don't know who you are.

I don't know what circumstances brought this book into your life at this time.

I don't know what the situation was that you were born into.

I don't know why you have chosen the life you have.

I don't know what your family life looks like.

I don't know what your financial life looks like.

I don't know what your Body looks like.

I don't know if you are a man reading this book for yourself or a woman reading it to find something more out in your own life.

I don't know if you are gay or straight.

In the end?

None of that matters.

SO, WHAT DOES MATTER?

That you are Human.

That you are alive on this earth.

That you are doing the very best you can to figure the Game of Life out every single day.

That you have to wake up every day and face the reality you have created for yourself.

And let's face it.

Some days that is not very fun at all.

Some days it would seem to be more acceptable to not get out of bed.

In 2012 I invited fellow entrepreneurial men to Laguna Beach to start what became known as Warrior Week, and in early 2015 I launched a podcast series called "Warrior On Fire."

The intention of Warrior Week was to share the message that I had been learning for the past few years so that I could establish a Brotherhood of other men that wanted to better their bodies, their spirituality, their family life and increase their revenue, which we call the Core 4 (Body, Being, Balance and Business).

The message took hold, and I was no longer the only one going through this journey of waking up the KING I was always meant to be.

It became so successful, I decided that the best way to spread this doctrine of living the Warrior's Way was through a podcast which was to serve men and woman around the globe with a Daily Message of FIRE.

This Daily Message of FIRE became known as the DAILY FUEL.

It quickly rose to #1 in iTunes and garnished nearly 1 Million Downloads in the first 6 months of the show.

It was working.

Tens of thousands of men and women around the world subscribed to the podcast and started listening daily.

More and more men were arriving to Warrior Week and leaving with a new outlook on how to live life.

People started asking, "Where are the books that teach the Warrior's Way?"

There were none.

Towards the end of 2015, I knew that for this message to continue to spread, we needed to have it in written word.

So, I published the first edition of *WarriorBook* within the Warrior program as an exclusive book for a select group of men.

It sold out the first day.

We realized that we might be on to something here.

When I arrived at Episode 350 in my podcast, I had someone pose another interesting question to me:

"Garrett, why haven't you turned these Daily Fuels into a book that someone could study every day along with the audios?"

I replied, "I have no idea."

I had never thought of myself as a writer. I didn't have any text for others to read about the Warrior's Way, which I created from reading multiple books, spending hundreds of thousands of dollars on training (yes, you read that right), and making my own revelations about life.

I knew I could publicly speak and share a message in a way that spoke to me based off of my own experiences, which is why I created the podcast.

There's a need for men to stop sedating themselves and redefine what it truly means to be a modern man in today's world.

But they didn't know the Code.

It had been forgotten.

A second edition of *WarriorBook* began taking shape in early 2016 with footnotes and a topical guide, dictionary of common Warrior vernacular, and additional resources for those that could not get enough of living the Warrior's Way.

That version was shared at a Warrior Mastermind, but still not available to the common man.

We were making connections between the spoken and written word, breaking down and simplifying the documents created to living as a Warrior King.

Men were waking up from the fog of sedation.

Within a few weeks, *The Manual* became the next book breaking down the document tools used in the *Wake Up Warrior* program, showing how simple it is to live the Warrior's Way, as long as it is maintained on a DAILY basis.

*Warrior On Fire* continued to air on iTunes, which eventually had 84 hand-selected episodes made into a book, *The Daily Fuel,* available for men within Warrior.

This podcast became a guide to both men and women, providing support in experiencing the DAILY FIRE needed to begin down the path of living the Warrior's Way to Having It All.

Over 450 episodes were shared in the public domain, and I continued to teach the doctrine of *Wake Up Warrior* from audio, video, and now written form within the program.

The Warrior's Way to Having It All continued to spread.

But I still hadn't created a book for the public.

An amalgamation of the videos, audios and written word became the state of the art *Warrior Book*, an interactive magazine.

For the first time, *Wake Up Warrior* became available to those that wanted to learn more about what is taught inside Warrior without attending a Warrior Week.

But it was still missing something.

And that's when we broke the Code with the Warrior Stack, which is Section Three in this book.

What you have in your hands is the 4th Edition of *WarriorBook* inside Warrior, the 1st Edition available to the public.

Within one year, we have already created four editions and revision to the tome that you now have in your hand, and it has already changed lives.

My hope is that this message becomes a Key to giving you new perspective daily and inside of that new perspective you are able to ACT differently.

It's not for the faint-hearted.

The Wake Up Warrior Movement is committed to expanding the lives of Men just like you and the few Brave Warrior Women who choose to join us on this journey.

Having it all is not a theory.

Having it all in Body - Being - Balance - Business is a reality for hundreds of men and families around the world and I am excited for you to experience the beginning journey to this reality leveraging this tool.

So off you go.

The End,

**Garrett J White**
Creator, Warrior Week
Founder, Wake Up Warrior

# FOREWORD

## By Jeremy T Finlay

Ten years ago, I sat in an office building in Salt Lake City, UT waiting for an appointment with who I'd hope be my mentor.

Legs crossed, clock ticking, a few fake plants to lighten up an already modern-looking lobby, furry rug and all.

I'm 16 years old. Homeschooled. And infatuated with business, I tell my sweet school teacher one day, "Hey mom, I think I should focus more on real life stuff, rather than this school work stuff."

She's a believer in said path, partially because of who I'm about to meet with.

Back to the lobby.

The man I'm waiting for is Garrett White... and I'm on a mission.

I'm sporting a dirty suit. The only suit I have, and I don't have money to Dry-Clean it. It's too big, but I go with it. Thick pin-stripes, because the movie "Wall Street" was my fashion inspiration - sans the suspenders. Trying to act like a 30 year old at 16 is a science I thought I'd mastered...

In reality, I was a baggy-suit-wearing bean-poll with horrible acne. I was decidedly blind to that reality, and only saw "Protege" when I looked in the mirror.

"Crossing your legs shows confidence, Jeremy. I like it."

Garrett walks in. Clean-shaven. Smiling, seemingly half-annoyed, half-entertained.

"Dude!" he says as I stand up and shake his hand... "You're thinner than I remember, I didn't think it was possible. You skinny bastard. Come on back."

This is my second meeting with Garrett. At this point, I'm in full-on stalker mode, on the hunt for what someone suggested for me months ago to "Go find a mentor."

I had met him four weeks back at one of his "Rich Dad, Poor Dad: Cash Flow" events, selling mortgages like they were hot dogs at a baseball game. You know how they throw the hot dog to you over like 20 people? Same visual. People were hungry, and he had the lip-smackingly delicious goods.

In a room of 400 people, he was still the world-class speaker he remains to be today. Just a bit fake, and no profanity. But boy, could he still get the room laughing one moment, and in tears the next. Even in his "showiness," he was still inspiring as hell.

That's when I knew he was the dude who'd be my mentor.

Whatever a mentor did, I had no clue. I just knew I needed one.

Afterwards, I waited until everyone left to get a moment alone with him. No idea what I'd say, but I knew something would come out. It's about 10 pm, and he's in a group talking. Looking down at his phone, his wife is texting and calling him. He looks uneasy, but willing to talk.

"You guys are awesome. Thank you for coming. My wife needs me home; I swear she'll leave me if I don't leave right now," he says jokingly. People laugh, but little did anyone know he was actually telling more truth than he wanted to admit.

I followed him out.

"Garrett, I'm Jeremy. I'm 16, and I'm gonna start a real estate business when I'm 18. I want to learn from you. You inspire me."

I said something to that effect, I don't remember exactly.

He looked me up and down, grinned a little (even in his uneasiness), and said, "Here's my card, call my assistant, meet me in a couple weeks."

And he zoomed off in his brand-new M6.

This was the beginning of an unlikely relationship that has now proven to unfold in a miraculous way.

Garrett, along with a handful of others, mentored me over the next two years and I eventually became that 18-year-old success I had dreamed of. Passionate about young success and teen mentoring.

Until one year later, while he was losing his ass, I lost mine in a very small way, comparably.

We lost touch, and as you've heard Garrett's story, the rest is history...

Little did I know, eight years later, I'd be at the helm with Garrett helping him steer a movement destined to change the world.

Who am I?

Jeremy Finlay. Warrior Week 5 graduate.

Story Teller for Wake Up Warrior.

You see, any film you've watched, any marketing or message you've seen in the marketplace is something I helped create with Garrett.

I've been behind the scenes and behind the lens, capturing the stories and moments which may have inspired you to become part of this Brotherhood.

And through it all, I've seen Garrett's most vulnerable moments of uncertainty and bleeding for the Warrior Movement to grow and reach men who need to hear its message.

Witnessing Garrett pour his entire life and everything he has into this Movement, sacrificing more than anyone will ever truly know, has changed my own life as a result.

Why do I tell you this?

Because in the pages which lay before you are years of research, learning and discovery of a peculiar kind of map - born of blood, sweat, pain, and thousands of hours - with which Garrett has dedicated to fine-tuning and preparing for you, right now, a map that has the power to change your life.

But Garrett is a man. No super hero. No savior. No angel. He's a mere guide to helping you discover and realize a life you were destined to lead.

It's with true honor that I've been at his side the last three years dedicated to his vision of the world being blanketed by men committed to living a four-dimensional life.

I've seen men thriving as liberated fathers, husbands, businessmen and leaders: as beacons in this world.

But none of Wake Up Warrior, nor this Movement, nor this message, is about Garrett.

It's about you.

It's about the Brotherhood.

And in your hands, you hold more than this book...

In your own hands, you also hold the keys to your liberation.

Get ready brother, your journey is about to begin.

With love,

-Jeremy T. Finlay

CMO, Wake Up Warrior

# WAKE UP WARRIOR

# WARRIORBOOK

# THE FOUNDATION
## Chapter 1: THE PIT

At some point you will find yourself in the Pit of Despair playing the Sedation Game. Your Liberation will come through your ability to hear and act on the Voice inside of you.

# SECTION ONE
# THE FOUNDATION

## CHAPTER ONE
# THE PIT

"Through me you go into a city of weeping; through me you go into eternal pain; through me you go amongst the lost people."

**-Dante Alighieri**
The Inferno excerpt from The Divine Comedy
[Late Middle Ages Italian Poet, 1265-1321]

---

1. New Year's Eve, 2007. As the rest of the world went about celebrating the dawn of a New Year heading into 2008, I lay in my bed, inside my large home that we had acquired not two years before. My wife sat up next to me and I can still remember the current of wind from the ceiling fan that I had become so addicted to, blowing down upon us.

2. We had these huge shutters over the left side of some giant windows that filled the master bedroom. I could see the moon reflecting through these giant shades off my wife's face. She turned and looked at me, with tears pouring down her cheeks: "I did not sign up for this. How are you going to fix it?"

3. I lay down and put my hands back behind my head, closing my eyes. My mind raced back to the summer, six months before, of me sharing the stage with Tony Robbins at the Mortgage Planner Summit in Las Vegas, Nevada. My mortgage empire was expanding and we were dominating, and yet, here I lay, heading into 2008, with everything crumbling around me. My marriage was about to be exposed for the shell that it was.

## Exposed During Low Tide

4. What's interesting about the tide is that when it begins to go out, it exposes everything that was hidden. At low tide, it exposes realities like rocks that you can't see when the tide is high; they're always there, whether you can see them or not.

5. When the financial tide in my life began to roll out, it exposed a painful reality inside of my life within my marriage, spiritual truth, physical body and business that I had been ignoring for years. That reality was simply this: my life was not working, but because the money had been so good for so long I was able to simply ignore the painful issues.

6. The fact was that no matter how much I hustled every single day, my life had become a Sedation Game filled with quicksand that was constantly filling in every single hole that I attempted to dig. No matter how much I tried to wrap my mind around what was happening, wanting to blame my wife for the pain I was feeling, the loss of all three of my businesses, and the implosion of my entire life, I wouldn't have had my rebirth without it.

## Reality Bites

7. You never hear people shout,

"Hey, you know what? I'm so glad that my life is burning down to the ground right now. I'm so glad I'm selling my bullshit big boy toys that I spent top dollar on so that I can try to put groceries in the fridge and diapers on my babies."

8. No, that's not the part of the story anybody actually wants to experience, or even acknowledge, let alone write in a book that matters. They don't want to experience the reality of me sitting in the basement with a bottle of vodka in one hand, drinking myself stupid every afternoon, trying to figure out how in the hell I got here, and how in the hell I was going to get out.

9. Reality bites hardcore when in the Pit.

10. I reached out to many people while I was in the Pit but most of them simply thought the answer was, "Read this scripture, pray, and life will just work itself out." Although I could appreciate where they were coming from, at the same time it was not assisting me at all. Day after day, the

Darkness of Uncertainty filled my veins, slowly killing all creativity and confidence I had.

11. Inside that pain, the drinking continued and the drugs soon followed. Because of the stories I lived in at the time, I felt that I couldn't truly expose my reality to anyone and so the cover-ups began. I would button these exposing parts of myself up every single day as I put my suit jacket on, and I would go out into the world and pretend. Pretend that my life itself hadn't faded into oblivion; that I wasn't hurting. What I didn't realize at the time was that I was slowly committing suicide.

12. I couldn't see that what I was creating were even greater problems stacked upon the problems I was already facing. Perhaps as you are reading this book of Warrior Scripture you might be sitting there with the thought, "Garrett, I don't drink, I don't have marriage problems, my life is really good; I just want *more*."

Or

13. "Garrett, my life is good, maybe even great, but I'm bored out of my mind and feel like I am about to burn it all to the ground."

## Not Thinking Outside of the Burning Box

14. There are two ends of the same burning wick. You see, your kingdom can be destroyed equally from one of two directions.

1-Boredom

2-Burn-Out

15. I know it sounds ridiculous to some, but I have watched more men burn their lives to the ground out of boredom when life was good than I have seen men over the years destroy everything because of burnout.

16. In my life I have experienced both and 2008 was not a Boredom game; it was a Burnout Game. As my world was burning to the ground, I was left with the greatest challenge that a man faces when shit is not working: Shift.

## No Easy Way to Shift

17. You would think that shifting would be easy when something is not working at the level you know it could and should, but the challenge is the fact pointed out by Albert Einstein,

18. "A man's mind lacks the capacity to solve the problems it has created at the same level of thinking that originally created the problem."

19. I was stuck. My mind was closed and I was stuck in a suicide mission of thoughts. I wanted out of my burning world but I had no idea how to do that, and the possibility of accessing my own liberation based on where my mind was, sat at about zero.

20. I was stuck; I felt like a slave to my own mind. I tried religion, fitness, marriage counseling, talking to my parents; none of it was working. It seemed to me that I was doomed to a painful death, convinced that I was fast on my path to becoming another Entrepreneurial Statistic of Failure.

21. When I fell, everyone disappeared and I was alone. The hundreds of people I had employed, all of the individuals I had supported over the years, gone. There I sat, alone, trying to find the answers in my own insane mind. Why does my life hurt so much? Why am I so angry? Why do I feel so helpless? Why do I have all these questions? What are all these desires that I am feeling? There was no one to ask; nowhere I could go to find these answers.

22. I started searching desperately, trying to find an answer (any answer) that would give me some kind of direction. After hundreds of conversations with the leaders at church, the individuals in my neighborhood, the people who were supposedly my friends; I started to realize that they were also stuck in many of the same problems that I was, but they lied and suppressed and weren't willing to acknowledge them yet, so our conversations would end up fruitless.

23. I was so sick of the flat, shallow conversations I was having. Nobody, it seemed, was willing to talk about *real* Shit: The Panic, the Pain or the Problems they were facing.

## Looking For Support In All The Wrong Places

24. "How do I fix this painful reality called my life?" I asked myself.

25. Unable to find freedom through this internal conversation, I began to blame my wife for everything. The Blame Game became the easiest move making my wife a target. I blamed her for my pain. I blamed her for my confusion. I told myself a seductive story that supported me in casting her as the character of my destruction.

26. As I assaulted my wife with my verbal venom, I had become completely ignorant to my role in my own pain. I ignored the fact that I had shown up like an idiot for almost a decade in our relationship; the more I told myself this insane story that it was all her fault, the more I believed it.

27. In my darkest pain I was alone. I had no WarriorBook. I had no Brotherhood. I had no Warrior's Way to Having It All. There was no CODE to live by. I was alone, frustrated, hurt and deeply confused.

28. By the end of 2009 I was weighing in at 172 pounds because my solution to all of this pain was to start running every single day. For most people this would mean a three to five mile jog. But for me, this meant 20-30 miles every single morning. I was literally, physically, running myself to death. I looked sick and unhealthy. I would run and run and drink and drink, trying to find some connection inside of this pain.

29. Fueled by the story that my wife was the problem and the cause of my pain, I began to search for emotional support from other women in my life since I didn't feel I could get it from her. I was convinced that another woman was what I needed: one who could love, embrace, and accept me as I was.

30. This led me to an affair and that's when I finally hit rock bottom. The day after the Affair, I stood in front of the bathroom mirror, looking into my sunken eyes after returning from a 32 mile run exhausted and ready to go back to bed. I could not recognize the man that stood in front of me. What had happened to me in less than 18 months? Where was Garrett?

31. I wanted to die.

32. Some men speak of their affairs as this glorious experience, that they learned a lot and even enjoyed it. Not me. Mine was a one-time event, and it was the opposite of everything that my fantasies had told me it would become. After that experience I felt more alone than I had ever felt in my entire life. I felt like God had left me just as my wife and family were leaving me. I was going to fucking lose everything, and for what? A one-night fling trying to escape who I was.

33. I was convinced that I had become cursed, and that God and the Universe had conspired against me, set out to destroy this shell of a man that I had become because somehow I had missed the turn in the road. That is, until I heard something. At the bottom of that painful Pit, all alone, there was a Voice that entered into my experience. It wasn't loud; it just simply said,

34. "Will you listen to me now?"

## It's Not The Size Of The Pit That Matters

35. I don't know what your Pit looks like: it could be a small one, or it could be a massive crater like mine was. You could be in a situation in which life is painful, or you could be in a situation in which life is just numb. You could be in a situation in which life is filled solely with pleasure but you know there's something more out there, and guess what?

36. Inside of all of that is going to come the same experience for you that I had; at some point, you will need to become humble enough, beaten-down enough, to listen to the Voice inside of you.

37. On that day, mine said,

"Are you ready to listen? Are you ready to hear what I have to say?"

38. As I rose from that place, I was very aware that I would likely lose my wife, my family; everything. I would become the second-time divorced man, children with two ex-wives, and a walking billboard for "*How To Fuck Up Your Life*, now playing in the douche bag next to you." The craziest part of these years? On the outside, everyone thought at some level I was just fine.

39. I knew I could no longer sustain the lies or the façade. I refused to continue to maintain the energetic resource necessary to mask, suppress

and pretend that I actually believed what I believed in church; that I felt what I felt in life.

40. I was tired of pretending and believing the lies inside my own mind. I was sick of being a believer in God; I wanted to Know Him. I wanted to find and discover my Divinity, but the only way to do this was to have the courage to put my entire life on the line, and in that place, say, "If I lose it all, that is fine, because I am going to start from a foundation that is built upon Truth."

## The Necessary Difficulty of Building A Foundation On Truth

41. Little did I realize how difficult this would be, and how much society does not support men like you and I to tell the truth. Not in business, not in marriage, not in life. We are surrounded by people every day who truly can't handle the full truth we have to share with them. These same people have told us to calm down, relax, or tone it down. They have asked us to be quiet. They have told us to shut up. They have demanded that we not share everything even if it means we die. The world is so politically correct these days that it's almost impossible for a human being to actually express what they are feeling.

42. For powerful men like you and I, this becomes our downfall. It becomes our casket. My life went to the place it went to, my affair happened, all because I couldn't tell the truth to my wife. I couldn't speak about how much I was hurting and about how big of a failure I felt like I was. I couldn't be honest with her or colleagues in business. Literally, the Truth would have set me free but I was unable and unwilling to speak it.

## How Do You "Be The Man"?

43. One night, deep inside another fight with my wife, with tears pouring down her cheeks she screamed, "Just be the man!" It was the same fight we had every night about the same topics: sex, money, the kids…take your pick.

44. But in that night's fight, for some reason the phrase she screamed echoed in my soul:

"Just be the man."

45. The Problem arose in me for the very first time:

"I don't even know what the fuck 'Be The Man' means."

46. Here is the reality: My dad was never around to teach me how to be a man. He was gone all of the time providing for the family, and I appreciate his commitment to make sure that we had food and shelter. But because my Dad was gone all the time, do you know who was teaching me to be a man? My mom.

47. My mom is a total badass and I love her to death. I love my dad as well and know he did the very best he could, but he was not an example of what it was to be a whole man in our home. He was an example of what it was to be a sedated one, a one-dimensional father who could make some money but was not emotionally and physically around. I didn't grow up with mentors and guides and examples who truly taught me, "Garrett, this is what it means to be a man."

48. So, I started looking. I thought maybe there was somebody who was doing this. Maybe there could be someone who had figured out how to train me to be a man. I Googled "how to be a man" (true story) and all kinds of crazy shit came up, none of which had any semblance of what I was truly seeking.

49. Inside of that, I started searching and reading, going to events and programs, and figured out that part of my problem was that I had not been able to actually see the truth inside of me. I could fundamentally not answer what should seem like the simplest questions in life:

Who am I beyond the roles of husband, father?

Who am I beyond the experience of this religion?

Who am I beyond this political system?

Beyond all my labels, who was Garrett?

Who am I?

I had no answer for this. I didn't know.

## Searching for the Key

50. Then I started to have these other conversations enter into my mind. I went to a workshop where this guy was talking about these 12 categories of life. I looked at him: fit with a really beautiful wife. I'm hearing how they talk about sex and intimacy, while I'm sitting in this disconnected relationship in which things are not working out at all with my wife.

51. I'm looking at them as a couple. They're making money, they're fit, and all of this shit seems to be working in their life. They've got great kids. I'm like, "Oh my God, they must be full of shit. There's no way, no way possible, that these 12 areas they talk about could actually be real for them." And yet, they were.

52. I wanted to say, "Bullshit," because it seemed so impossible in my own life. Much like it might have seemed impossible to you to Have It All before Black Box. I couldn't believe it, yet deeply wanted it to be true for me also.

53. You might be having the same thoughts.

54. "Dude, I don't even know if this is possible. Can I truly have it all in my Body, Being, Balance, and Business, Garrett? I don't know. It seems like a concept that resonates as truth for me at the Core, but I don't know if that's possible."

55. If you're like I was, there's likely a part in you that is scrutinizing and part of your mind is listening, just searching for a reason to tell me to fuck off. I wouldn't be upset with you, because guess what my mind would have done? The exact same thing, because when I was in that state of wanting, it seemed so unreal, improbable, and impossible, that I could have it all. The blinders were painfully small through which I saw the world.

## An Empty Search

56. After searching and searching to find this, it came down to one simple truth; there was no training for what I was seeking. There was no comprehensive program on what it was to be a man, let alone a four-dimensional modern man facing modern problems in a modern society. The best that could be delivered up was a series of one-dimensional men who could train you on one, maybe two dimensions.

57. Most men that I had ever worked with, been in business with, or had as clients, were very good at two things: making the money and maintaining their body for the most part. When it came to spirituality, parenting and marriage, it was a nightmare. Occasionally I would meet men who were very, very good as fathers and amazing husbands, but they couldn't bring home the money; they struggled financially.

58. Or maybe they could make the money and they were very good at being a parent, but they were physically falling apart with diabetes, having to give themselves injections every day because their body was fat and had become a cage instead of a weapon.

59. I found some who were very, very spiritual, but the rest of their world was in complete disarray. They would sit and meditate all day, yet not be able to pay their cell phone bills let alone fund anything that would really change the world.

## Systematic Sedation of A Modern Man

60. It was confusing to me, because inside of each one of their specific focuses they were amazing, but the moment it went comprehensive, they were left wanting. In the end, like myself, I recognized they were nothing more than one-dimensional douche bags that knew how to be good at one thing only.

61. Good for you, you're powerful inside a meditation room. Good for you, you're powerful inside a conference room at a meeting. Good for you, you're beautiful, amazing, and powerful with the weights inside the gym. Good for you, you're amazing when it comes to your kids. Good for you.

62. I was like, "Dude, how is it possible that we have defined being a man as a guy who just makes the money?" That seemed to be the only conversation that was consistent, that the role and goal of "being a man" was to make money. As long as that happened, sex should follow, and everything else should just take care of itself. Yet this was not my experience because I had made the money and still was left wanting: I knew that was a lie.

63. So I went on a journey to figure out why. Along the way, I uncovered something so massive it was hard to believe at first. My reality, which was what most modern men were facing, had been manufactured over 100 years ago to systematically destroy mankind by sedating the Kings. The results

of living we were experiencing today had come on the wake of a series of world-altering shifts over a century that made it almost impossible for men like you and I to ever have it all.

64. My brother,

All great revolutions began with a simple question.

My question was,

"How in the hell did we get here as men?"

65. The answer that I found I now call the Systematic Sedation of a Modern Man, but you're going to have to read on to the next chapter to learn how it all came to be.

## Chapter 1:
## POINTS TO PONDER FROM THE GENERAL'S TENT

- **POINT #1:** Your kingdom can be destroyed equally from one of two directions: boredom and burn-out. It requires a Shift to get out of either of these mindsets.

- **POINT #2:** At some point, there comes a time inside of us all in which we will need to become humble enough, and beaten-down enough to listen to the Voice inside.

- **POINT #3:** It is difficult for society to accept men like you and I to tell the truth. We are surrounded by people every day who truly can't handle the full truth we have to share with them because they have become too comfortable with the lies.

- **POINT #4:** Meeting successful men becomes confusing because inside of each one of their specific focuses they were amazing, but the moment it went comprehensive, they were left wanting.

# WARRIOR WITNESS:

## P.P., Alberta, CANADA:

*"I will never forget the first time I started listening to the Pit. The realization that I was burned out stung horrible! I thought no fucking way. I'm burned out: what the fuck?! Only weak pussies burnout. That as I continued along, the fact that I was now a very bored burnout brought me to tears. I'm getting ahead of*

*myself now and should back up to where I am in life and what brought me to Warrior. Bottom line I was on a path of self fucking destruction.*

*I have a lot of realizations and self-assessments written down and getting ready to talk about them; but I feel so fucking ashamed it's hard at times. I'm grateful to have Brothers to share with. Can't wait to discuss more tomorrow!*

*The biggest realization that came for me this morning happened while listening to Jeff. I realized we DO have choices and brothers to help us stay strong and there's a safe place to share feelings! And then I saw the above on the Black Box! Liberation Brothers! Make the choice!*

*It really struck hard after listening to the Pit that I realized how deep I was in it. I would preach to my friends that finding women elsewhere made my marriage better because it relieved the sexual tension, but it was all a lie. My marriage went to shit, I would power over my team and blow up. I had some power behind."*

---

## B.L. Ohio, USA:

*"For the first time in my life, I have acknowledged the pits that I have gone through in my life. My own father had wanted to be more, but didn't know how to do that. I told myself stories that the debt I took on for my businesses was to become more real.*

*I've struggled with just about everything, including lack of commitment, showing up, infidelity, sedation. I'm in a fight for my life and I need to figure out who's going with me. This isn't easy, is it? But what other choice do we have? Continue with the sedation we've been doing or choose a different path.*

*I'm taking my wife in for surgery this morning after they found a golf ball sized mass in her abdomen. I'm in my Pit but I think I can figure a way out of it.*

*The world and our society has been built to keep great men down. It only takes one or two to not let them get them down. The world's not going to keep you down; only you will, so decide to be different."*

---

## L.B. UK:

*"I've found myself lying and showing the world that everything's ok and it really isn't. I see men walking around looking half dead and I don't want that myself."*

---

## D.C., Seattle, Washington, USA:

*"The last 10-years have been very hard on me. I said goodbye to so many, each time that I did I felt like a quitter for not being there with them anymore. So many times I just felt incredible rage, anger, hatred. I wanted vengeance so badly. Each time I lost one of my bros I had to put on my best face even though i felt like giving up. The sadness has taken to some very dark places. On the surface I created a successful business. I created my business to help others but the joy and passion I once had began to fade. Helping others still makes me happy but the ownership and the worries of running a massive operation began to break me over time. Last week I sold my business and i went to my car and I broke down. I told my wife I could no longer put our family into the financial and emotional ebbs and flows the business brought upon me. Owning my gym was a dream come true. I created it in the park from a set of dumbbells and a med ball. In a few weeks my 25,000 sqft dream will belong to someone else. I was sad for a long time while i thought the pro's and cons of selling or keeping it. When I went to my car I broke down not just because of sadness but also relief. Until that moment i had no idea how much stress I was holding onto and how tight I was holding it. I knew i was suffering but I just had no idea how much. Listening to you speak just a few moments ago made me understand I am not alone."*

---

## T. M., Georgia, USA:

*"When I started this Warrior process, when I had my first conversation with Sam, I talked about how there was this massive pit that I was circling the rim of. That I was teetering on the edge of falling into a hole too big to climb out of and that I needed to make changes to make sure that didn't happen. But after I started going through the Black Box and the Warrior process, I came to understand that I wasn't on the edge of falling into a pit, I was already face-down in the mud of a pit far larger than had ever imagined. That the stories I was telling, was keeping me from seeing the truth. The reality of how broad and deep my own pit was. It was, and still is terrifying."*

---

## G. P., Maryland, USA:

*"My pit began long ago. The problem is that I've lied to myself about being out of it at times. I think I've always been there but at times I could see over top and fooled myself into thinking I was elsewhere. For as long as I can remember I've never been satisfied! I've always wanted more. No matter what it is, money, women, nicer car, bigger house, etc...because of that I have busted my ass working*

*since I was 14 yrs old. That's fine when you're single but when my life changed and I met my wife and had kids, life had to change. I could no longer work as long as I needed or do things I wanted. So I blamed my wife. And not just for that, but just about everything. Last year the pit got deeper when my asshole meter pegged the scale and I more or less missed our 5th anniversary because of work. At the time I had excuse after excuse why it wasn't that big of a deal. It turned out I was just lying to myself the same as I have been for years. Our marriage began to decline rapidly and things got pretty dark for awhile. She finally agreed to counseling. And in the process I took off 3 months while my wife ran the business. In my spare time I was able to think for me for once. I felt all alone, like no one understood me. I looked everywhere to talk to someone, to find that leadership I so desperately needed. But I found nothing. Until Labor Day. And I watched this video for an hour. And I sat there in tears while this stranger talked about my life and my feelings. And light bulbs went off. And here I am to save my marriage and my business from who else but myself."*

# THE FOUNDATION

## Chapter 2: THE PAINFUL PROBLEM

Long before we were born, the Systematic Sedation of Men was set into motion.

# SECTION ONE
# THE FOUNDATION

## CHAPTER TWO
# THE PAINFUL PROBLEM

"The Industrial Revolution has two phases: one material, the other social; one concerning the making of things, the other concerning the making of men."

## - Charles A. Beard
[Influential American historian in first half of 20th century, 1874-1948]

---

1. As much as I wanted to blame my dad for not raising me to be a man, the truth was, my father (like me) had been born into a Game of Sedation that had been gaining momentum for generations before he was born.

2. The Sedation Game was created long before my father and I were born, spinning out of control, taking men from a place of power and thrusting them in a place of powerlessness. This dark system was literally destroying kings and turning them into peasants.

3. By the time my father was born, this was all the men around him knew. He didn't understand the disconnect behind why, how, or what he was experiencing and feeling. The last thing in the world he was able to do was to actually talk with anybody about it. Why had this happened? See, I wanted to know and understand how we as men had gotten here. Every man I looked around at, and came into conversation with, far and few between were those who were willing to beat the drum the way that I believe a four-dimensional modern man living the Warrior's Way should.

## Living Contrary to Society

4. Living in Power as a man these days is almost impossible with the current set up of rules and guidelines that we are supposed to follow according to what society has dictated. There is an [1]epidemic of disconnected teenagers and men in their 20s and 30s who are literally becoming dysfunctional at everyday living of the most basic human skills. This problem is not only apparent in the younger generations, but is showing itself in massive ways for men who are in their 40s and 50s, with suicide rates that have gone through the roof for men in their 60s.

5. Divorce rates are running rampant as men scramble to try to figure out "How to Be the Man" while women grow tired of the pussies their husbands have become and would rather raise their children alone *and* fulfill both roles as Mother and Father than to be married to dead wood.

6. There's an alarming rise of divorces[2] that we're experiencing inside of the United States being filed by women in their 50s: the moment the kids graduate from high school and move out, they look at the man they have tolerated for nearly three decades and say,

7. "Forget you, my kids are out of the house so I'm out of here to finally live my life."

8. Men are left hollow and alone, and don't know why because they were acting like what they thought a man was supposed to act like. The truth is, there are tons of programs that help women, but when was the last time you saw one to help men? It didn't exist. I couldn't find one, which is why I launched Wake Up Warrior in 2012 and built the Black Box System in late 2015. Over the past seven years, I uncovered the facts about the Systematic Sedation of Men including the *why* and *how* it happened. I discovered that history can teach us more about our own lives and how to course correct them when things are off than what I ever imagined.

---

[1]   This has been referred to as extended adolescence, gone into more detail in 2:43-47

[2]   Divorce After 50 Grows More Common" internet article by Sam Roberts from *The New York Times*. Retrieved 11 February 2016: http://www.nytimes.com/2013/09/22/fashion/weddings/divorce-after-50-grows-more-common.html?_r=o

## Solving Systematic Sedation

9. In order to understand how my dad and I got to this place (and how you did too), we've got to go back to the late 1800s and early 1900s, on into the beginning of what became known as the Industrial Revolution. There was a fundamental shift in the way that living occurred here inside the United States and around the world at this time. The shift would affect everyone and literally change the way the world worked.

10. Before the Industrial Revolution, the majority of society existed in what has been labeled an agrarian existence. This way of living occurred in the following reality: Dad, mom, and child co-creating together. They were feminine and masculine equals, yet at the same time distinct and different in their roles with the man as the head of the household. A typical day for Dad would be waking up in the morning then going to work on the farm minutes from the house and at the core of his Community. Guess who also got to watch and participate in this same work every single day?

11. Johnny. Little Johnny would go to work with his dad side by side, literally, every single day. Little Johnny was seeing through example on how being a man worked. Dad didn't disappear for the day and then return home to guide the children at night. From breakfast to lunch to dinner, dad was actively role modeling to children respect, education, hard work, fear of God, connection to the queen, respect and responsibility. Every single day, dad was demonstrating to his sons the answer to the question,

## "How do I be a Man?"

12. That same question is still asked today, yet a massive shift in mentality led to a different answer. What does this have to do with the Industrial Revolution? Everything, my friends. Until the 1800s, the majority of society lived in self-sufficiency this way. There was a co-parenting relationship: Dad was not sent away; mom was not sent away. There was this home-base Core Connection where family mattered and was valued, where each individual knew his and her role in running a household and land.

13. This way of thinking and living had been a part of society for centuries, so surely a cataclysmic event caused this great shift in thinking, right? It did, a plague came about, but not as a natural disaster. The Promise of More

caused us as a society to shift from this agrarian age in which mom and dad co-parented and co-raised the children to one of limitless possibilities.

## The Big Promise

14. The Industrial Age offered up a Big Promise. The promise itself was an interesting one, very appealing to Mom and Dad. How do we know? Because it changed the entire world from what it was to the way that we know it now. Some people feel it was a bad, horrible, and an awful promise that caused the rich to grow richer and the poor to grow poorer. Although the rapid growth of industrialization did have its upsides in building a powerhouse nation in America, the downside as to what this did to the family was hard to ignore. The Industrial Revolution wasn't seen as a problem; it was a Solution to a Problem. With that solution came a "cost" many were willing to pay, which also brought with it a new series of problems that we could not have anticipated. This is the crazy catch-22 part of all blessings: we can't have them without the downside curse of natural consequences.

15. So, what was the solution to the problem? The Industrial Pitch was essentially this: Move in order to [3]progress forward. Literally, let go of the Farm and move your family from the country to the city. No more blood, sweat and tears with the back-breaking work of the farm. No seasonal issues with weather, or dealing with a starving family if the crops failed. Men were enticed to venture forth into the new possibilities awaiting them within the city with more certainty in the future there for what? More money. All at the low cost of simply leaving the home during the day for the factory and office.

16. Instead of Dad working side by side with little Johnny, he would be required to leave the home every morning, travel miles away to and go to work in the factory, a place that Little Johnny would not be allowed to work side by side with his father.[4] It was no longer a possibility to have hands-on schooling side by side while performing chores and working on

---

[3]   See Appendix, Resources: Progressive Era

[4]   Child Labor Laws came about during the Progressive Era in which children were also sent to work in factories, resulting in a whole generation of children uneducated as well as extremely unsafe working conditions. See Walter Trattner, *Crusade for the Children: A History of the National Child Labor Committee and Child Labor Reform in America* (1970) in Appendix Resources: Progressive Era.

the farm with dad, but that felt like a justifiable loss in order to give the family more, right?

17. What had not been considered along with this commute was the distance between this separate place of work and home, and that's where several other things began to shift in men. Before the Industrial Game, Dad was rewarded for playing the Game of Life on the farm by using his creativity, innovation, and ability to solve problems. This game play was worked out of a man with rote actions specific for one job. Men were punished in the marketplace for innovation because there was a systematic way of doing things that were not to be disrupted. He was required to sell his Crown for cash, taken from his position as a king and compelled to become a cog in a machine. A significant percentage of males in society went from being a king in the home, praised in admiration by his children and his wife, where the family unit all worked alongside each other, to a disposable tool. Sometimes he would not even see the sun as he would leave for work early in the morning, enter the office while it was still dark, returning home late after long factory hours and commuting after sunset.

## An Exhausted Reality

18. On the odd nights that this industrial man got home before Little Johnny was asleep, he was so exhausted from the relentless grind that any attempt to fulfill a role as a father was mediocre at best in such a fatigued state. He still wanted to be there for his kids, but little by little as he started to climb the corporate ladder towards the Industrial Revolution's American Dream, priorities shifted more and more from the influence he once had while on the farm.

19. All of this was justified under the belief that the money was the most important gift he could offer his children: a future brighter than his own with opportunity to experience a "better" and easier life. What didn't he account for, however? The time he was gone from little Johnny and the impact of having mom fulfill both the Father and Mother roles meant that little Johnny wasn't learning how to be a man, *by* a man.

20. Dad thought in his mind that at least they weren't living in tenements like some of the immigrants that had come over from the Mother Land

where the whole family had to work.[5] There was more money, so mom and the kids were actually having the opportunity within the city to experience some things they didn't get to experience out on the ranch and on the farm. They wore better tailored clothes made from textile mills, and eventually moved up into a better house, therefore gaining more social networks and friends.

21. Dad looked at this overall experience as good. "This was beautiful," he decided. Slowly, though, the game was different, and Mom shifted as well, saying, "It's okay, Love. I know you're tired. You're doing everything you can to provide for this family."

22. Over one generation span (around 20 years) boys were no longer working side by side with Father anymore. They were no longer being raised by both parents. They had a father who only saw them for one hour, maybe two, at night; this is what they saw and so they figured that's how it's to be done. It became the norm to be raised by Mother. This may not seem like a big deal, but just like all journeys that we take, if we shift just one degree, we split in a completely different direction. Look how quickly thousands of years of fatherhood had shifted within just one to two generations as the agrarian life was replaced by the factory and office life.

23. In the beginning, it doesn't really look like too much. After all, our whole purpose in life is supposed to be progress and expansion, right? And that's exactly what the Industrial Age and Progressive Era consisted of.

24. This simple shift declared, "Fathers, your job is to be a cog and bring home the bacon. Become a tool of production by being a cog in a system, inside the factory of the Industrial Revolution; that's how you hunt the buffalo now." Not a king with council to provide for your family the emotional, financial, social, spiritual support that you were once required to live and teach. That's outdated. Now we just need you to go produce in the office: "Go, make the money." The Progressive Era[6] then came in to rectify the unsafe and unlawful working conditions, but any thought on the mental progress of the working man became even more sedated.

---

[5]  Refer to footnote 4 which talks about Child Labor
[6]  The Progressive Era was a period of widespread social activism and political reform across the United States, from the 1890s to 1920s.

## Progressing Towards World Wars

25. Part of that was due to outside events, when the world experienced a Great War[7] to end all wars, which further solidified this mentality that man serves society best by being away from the home. We had all of these boys that saw their Dad working in the factory and office become men as soldiers in World War I, learning firsthand in the trenches further "progress" that war brings. A nation-wide Depression[8] occurred as we were slowly reminded that it requires hard work to bring in the paycheck within an office or factory, but because jobs were so few, men didn't know what to do. Countries were invaded and declared war on others as World War II[9] then ensued, providing drafts and opportunities for men to continue to go out and not only provide for their family, but for their nation's freedoms and liberties.

26. In the military, there is no room for feelings. We needed to take those feelings and suppress them because they'll get in the way of killing another man. Now, men have been killing each other since Cain found a rock, so none of that was new; what was new was that war had been created with industrial strength, and it required industrial men to execute it. To defend the truths that we hold self-evident here in the United States of America, men declared, "We've all got to go fight the wars of old men."

27. So, Johnny who was disconnected from Dad already has now learned to shut his feelings down. Entire generations of men were taught that their role was to not only hunt the buffalo, but at the same time, to not even feel. Feeling was not safe because you could die if you did, and so this global lie became truth. The message became: Feeling + showing emotion = death, so if you want to live, operate like a machine and act on what you're told,

---

[7]  The Great War occurred from 1914-1918. See also The Great War in Appendix.

[8]  A time of great economic hardship in America between 1929-1939, but many countries were also facing economic hardships as well post WWI. Many other parts of the world also faced troubling times within their government, such as Germany electing a nationalist named Adolf Hitler to make their war-torn and depressed nation great again.

[9]  WWII: 1939-1945. America joined the war after the bombing of Pearl Harbor, December 7, 1941, known as a "Day which will live in infamy" according to President Franklin D Roosevelt.

not how you feel. This created what we have come to know in society as The Greatest Generation.[10]

## The Greatest Generation

28. While the men were gone to War, the women were back on the home front, trying to figure out their new place in this new Age.[11] Society still had to continue, after all. For the first time inside the United States, we began to see a significant rise inside the capacity of employment for women. Women replaced the men who were called out to war in the factories AND were still required to raise the children. I'm going to have you consider that these events could have gone a different way in bringing the family structure back to where it was less than 50 years earlier, but instead this then led to its own movement for women, shifting roles within society which we will discuss in a few moments.

29. Mixing the Industrial Mindset with the War Mindset, entire generations of men were told to stop feeling, stay disconnected and don't you dare show any feelings or fucking bitch about how you might feel inside. Just get the job done. Don't talk about your feelings, don't talk about your emotions: men were taught to not feel. That being a man means you go get shit done regardless of how you're feeling at the time. You come home, and you don't bitch about it. You don't talk about it and you don't get emotional about it. You hold this stoic position of Emotionless Power. In doing that, you are a great man.

30. That was my grandfather, Colonel in the Air Force for 30 years. Beautiful, powerful man. However, in the final years of his life here on this planet, the truth started to come out about the pain of what it was to be him; how hard it was for him to be the Man society told him to be.

31. And yet, for his entire life he had been taught, trained, and educated not to be real, raw and emotional with his wife, his kids or his grandchildren. He literally stayed in the Game of War that feelings could get him killed. When he came back for his last 30 years, he didn't know how to operate

---

[10] A term phrased by Tom Brokaw in describing the men and women that grew up during the Depression and faced further hardships in the form of World War II and the resiliency that came from those events within human nature. See Appendix, Resources: World War II

[11] http://www.history.com/topics/world-war-ii/american-women-in-world-war-ii

any other way but Focused Fire on the outside with a Chaotic Emotional Circus occurring on the inside.

## Twisting Feminism with The Feminist Movement

32. And then in the 1960s things inside the United States began to take another massive shift. From finally gaining the right to vote in 1920, women created a small door and opened it slightly during World War II as men who were fighting in the war were replaced by women in the workforce, but it was the '60s and '70s that this Feminist Movement door fully swung open. Inside was a twisted, bastardized version of the feminist suffragists which declared: "We don't need men. We're not just equal, we're superior and they are unnecessary. We can do for ourselves anything that a man can do for us."

33. What started inside of feminism with votes for women and this first declaration at the door that said, "We want to have a voice" then shifted to the twisted feminist version which threw that door off its hinges with "We want our voice to scream out the equality we demand because we are the same." Equality became: we are the same, and in being the same we don't need you.

## Depolarization of Couples

34. This became the Giant Rift, a depolarization of couples; men who were now having to compete with masculine energy with their women and intimacy was slowly being replaced with Competition.

35. Thoughts in Dad's mind started to become,

> "It's hard enough that I have to go fight these assholes all day at the office. I then have to come home and battle for a voice inside my own home. I can't talk about my feelings anywhere because society told me I'm not supposed to in order to be a man. If I'm completely honest, I already feel slightly castrated because I'm married to a feminist. I'm not sure what I'm supposed to do."

36. Let's clarify what it means to be the same by recognizing what isn't. A penis and a vagina will never be the same thing. A woman and a man are not the same thing. They never will be. I don't care if you are gay or you

are straight or whatever the hell your fucking sexual orientation is: There is Woman and there is Man. They are not the same.

37. They can be equal, but they will never fucking be the same. One is not superior to the other. This became another subtle insertion of a lie into our society as masculine traits of hunting buffalo began to rise in women and men began to get confused at levels they'd never been confused in before.

38. How do I actually show up as the man when I'm confused about what being the man means? I'm looking at this woman but she's kind of being the man, showing up like a dude right now. Confusion is running rampant for men because it's completely misidentified.

39. We don't even know what being a man *is* anymore because everywhere we turn men are being disappointed, disjointed, and disconnected. They're being told, "Shut up, go get the money, don't talk about your feelings, and just so you know, we don't need you because we're the same."

## The Confused Information Age

40. What quantifies this at an even bigger level? The Information Age.[12] This technological boom began in the late 1990s and then took off into warp drive after the early 2000s. For the first time ever, information proliferated globally through the World Wide Web, where information was no longer only found in books but at the ease of our fingertips. Men and women began to search out insight through the onslaught of information as it became mobile through cell phones and various electronic devices within a few short years.

41. And yet, all of this unlimited access to information was drowning us. Men and women were searching for answers only to receive contradictory opinions masked as fact; that if it's posted on the internet, it *must* be true. We think that information will actually liberate us, when it has enslaved us. We are becoming robots, plugged in to various electronic devices day in and out.

42. Five to six generations later from the men that left the agrarian lifestyle, boys are being born into a world that makes no sense. The lessons from these past generations of men and information doesn't liberate us, nor does

---

[12] See Information Age in Appendix

it address the fact that we now have 75 plus years of patterns being built and ingrained.

## Boys Never Becoming Men

43. This confusion has become something known by psychiatrists as "extended adolescence." Divorce rates are running rampant (if a couple even chooses to marry) and we have more single moms with children than we have ever had in our planet's history. As we've been able to vaccinate certain diseases that plagued society, we now have super viruses, more physical dis-ease and dysfunction than we have ever had. More disappointment and exodus from religion than we have ever experienced. More governments being toppled and confusion inside of political regimes than we have ever seen. Information has not made all things better, despite what the marketing claims. Information has merely accelerated the inevitability of the implosion in the world as we know it.

44. Inside of all of this there's this exposed reality of boys who are staying boys long into their 30s and 40s now, never leaving home. They're saying, "You know what? I don't know how to even play this Game called adulthood let alone know how to win. I don't know what it is to be a man. Nobody is teaching me. The men I see on reality television, YouTube, and social media are not teaching me. Governments and political officers aren't teaching me how to be a man. Everyone's getting divorced. Nobody is staying married. Families are becoming smaller. The entire landscape of making money is changing.

45. This Game called "Being A Man" is a goddamn nightmare.

46. Inside this confusion, single and divorced men simply choose to Not Grow Up. And why would they? What incentive is there except the miserable life that they saw their fathers live? "Eat, drink and be merry for tomorrow we die" has become the mantra of the Modern Boy Man who has forgotten he is a King.

47. Hell, at 30-40 years old, if you can still run around like a 22-year-old frat boy, play *World of Warcraft*® every single night and *Call of Duty*® on your gaming system, get laid with girls that are 10 years younger than you, and consume an unlimited amount of porn, why in the world would you want to grow up and move out of your parent's basement?!

## Shifting the Foundation of Our Society

48. The Foundation of our society is driven by kings and men. The way they lead nations comes down to how they lead from the inside of their own families, and that family dichotomy is being destroyed. The boys that are being born into the Game have been given no clear path and so they choose to remain boys. Where does this lead?

49. A society that no longer wants to raise families. Pornography and quick promises of sex on social media platforms like Tinder have replaced any attempt to work on any form of lasting relationships, because that requires work. A lot of it. Over 35 percent of all content consumed on the web is pornographic in nature by men, so why are they buying porn? Why are they masturbating daily? Why is this occurring? Because men are lost without a roadmap. They have no idea what it is to truly be a man. And it is not their fault.

50. The message has become so confused with the only maps women have to offer titled "Read My Mind" or "Be the Man" which when opened has no Key to decipher the content inside.

51. Women are not to blame in all of this either. They are simply playing the Game they were also taught. Trying to play two sides of the equation, the first as the old school tactic of being a woman which says "Be the man" to their masculine counterparts yet even they don't know what that fucking means; they just know it's what they need. And then there's the other side of the equation, in which most of these women have become just as confused as men about what it actually means to be feminine resulting in a daily emotional castration of is it on or of? with the man they are with.

52. Nobody in society seems to have the Key to the MAP.

53. This is why my marriage was plummeting to divorce. Some people were like, "Well, that's because you cheated, dumbass" which is definitely part of the equation in my own life. My Life was plummeting to divorce because neither one of us had an answer on what it meant to "Be the Man." Do you think my dad had an answer? No. Do you think my church leaders had an answer? No. Their answer was, "Pray to God." Nice. Fuck off. I appreciate your little Sunday School answer but it's not cutting it. It's not cutting it

with me nor with any of the thousands of men that I'm engaged with on this topic every single week.

## Finding the Definition of Being A Man

54. We needed something *more*. What even is the definition of a man pursuing a life of having it all? We knew what the one-dimensional man looked like: go make some money and workout. Hopefully inside of that you can get laid a couple of times so you feel good about yourselves. If your wife doesn't want to put out, no problem. Porn is just a few mouse clicks away and you can just jack off for free without making any deposits. If that doesn't cut it, then you'll cheat.

55. Inside of this, men were left with no guidance system at all. This isn't about women attacking, being wrong, or doing something stupid. Women were just as oblivious in the Game as we were (though we'd never tell them that).

56. Our entire society is plummeting into Chaos because kings—men—are not leading. Men are not standing. How is terrorism running rampant? Because even our political systems are not being led by kings anymore. Sedated jerks hold the seats. What runs rampant inside our body when it is not healthy? A virus. Cancer cells become activated and begin to build without us even realizing it. We are getting destroyed from the inside out, both male and female. It's happening everywhere. *Everywhere.*

57. When I saw this, I realized it wasn't even our fault. I was sharing this information with a friend one day and I was like, "Dude, we're all messed up. I don't even know what we are supposed to do with this. How do we fix this?"

58. My friend responded, "Dude, why don't *you* fix it?"

"Pffft."

59. Feeling a lot like most leaders do when it comes to attacking a giant problem, I questioned my capabilities and capacities: Who am *I* to do this? Who am I to be great and lead this movement? Who am I to start this conversation and define what a man is? What a Modern Warrior Man is?

# If Not You, Then Who?

60. Long before society started questioning my validity of who I am, and whether or not I'm qualified, I was asking myself those questions. Who am I to lead? I've burned a lot of shit to the ground.

61. Why not somebody who at least has their shit together? Pick one of the clean cut guys. I'm a bit of a maniac. Why me? Why me?!

"Listen dude, if it's not you, then who?"

If not you, then who?

62. "Who is more qualified than a guy who has genuinely fucked everything up, to build the map on the way out of the Gates of Hell to the Place of Power? You speak about this 'have it all' situation, but you don't have it. So why don't you figure out how to build it?"

# The Warrior's Revolution

63. This one idea began a Revolution. When I looked around at the results in our society on one dimensionality training, what I saw were men who were alone, depressed, hiding, sick, suffering, struggling, hurting, confused, frustrated, suicidal, homicidal, addicted, dying, and alone.

64. I knew what it was like because I have felt all of those things as well. I took that on and said, "If it's not me, then who? I don't know who else it could be, so I'm going to give it a shot. Not to lead other's lives. No. I just want to liberate mine."

## Chapter 2:
## POINTS TO PONDER FROM THE GENERAL'S TENT

- **POINT #1:** For generations the Sedation Game for men has been in place, spinning out of control, taking men from a place of power and thrusting them in a place of powerlessness.

- **POINT #2:** There was a fundamental shift in the way that living occurred here inside the United States and around the world during the late 19th and early 20th century with the Industrial Revolution in full swing.

- **POINT #3:** Both men and women have become fundamentally confused on the role of a male and female because we have been told the confusing inaccuracy that we are the same so therefore we are equal. Men and women are not the same, but they are equal.

- **POINT #4:** Most beginnings to a Revolution come down to one question when faced with an onslaught of confusion: "If not you, then who?" This led Garrett to build a map on the way out of the Gates of Hell to the Place of Power in pursuit of having it all.

# WARRIOR WITNESS:

## P.P., Alberta, CANADA:

*"The first time I learned about little Johnny, I saw myself in that place and it hit me right between the horns. The problem is me, so who else to better fix it than ME. As I looked at the numbers along each paragraph, it was like looking at my life transpire, slowly falling into more of a sedation."*

## B.L., Ohio, USA:

*"A huge revelation I had was coming out of my wife's surgery, not knowing if my wife was ok sitting in the waiting room. I can't even tell you the flood of emotions that came over me as I looked at my wife, heavily sedated and in a lot of pain, and it made me realize how much she needed me, and I knew that our relationship was not something that I could do without. I hope it doesn't take a surgery to give you a perspective, and that you find that in an easier way. I found God in me and I found God in her.*

*The Problem really spoke to me because of my job; I'm supposed to make the complex look simple as a strategist. To have Garrett unpack the problem in such a way and back to the way that society has changed, it helped me to understand this. My dad wasn't a guy that was gone a lot, but he never figured out how to get more. What I've allowed is having the people around me tell me that I already have it all. There's no way to get this correct without Warrior.*

*It pisses me off to be told that I have it all because they're small thinkers and how small they think. I think I've allowed them to influence me and convince me that nothing needs to change. What The Problem has helped me see has told me that "good" is not OK."*

### BH, Oklahoma, USA:

*"The Problem opened so many thoughts in my head of how I was raised and how I was taught to never show emotion and to never address any "issue," just ride it out, shut up, and it will pass. Evaluating marriage, my parent's marriage, and looking in my 10-month old son's eyes, realizing and having the Revelation I have to be the One, the generation to change it all, to stop sedating, start showing up, being present….To have it all. I have never in my life thought of it like Garrett put it, and thank God I was able to hear it and obtain that perspective of this before it's truly too late. Time to go to work NOW, not tomorrow but right NOW!"*

---

### T.M., California USA:

*"I've always known instinctively that something wasn't right. Nobody ever showed me how to do this shit. I've had to figure out what I know by fucking up mostly. Education helped. My parents helped. Friends and experience helped. But after childhood, nobody really had any answers. I realized that everyone else was as clueless as me, or worse. My dad would say, "you have a family now, your life is over". Sarcastically of course, implying that life sucks now so get used to it. It's the same for all of us.*

*God was always there but has somehow always been out of reach to me.*

*Since we started having kids 17 years ago, things started getting progressively more unsettling and confusing to me. I haven't felt like the king of my castle since then."*

---

### M.K., Oregon, USA:

*"**Revelation:** The problem is multi-generational. I didn't start the fire, but shit am I burning up in it. I always thought that everyone could just get 'a little better' and that was enough. You have to decide. Make your choice, because if not you, then who?*

***Reaction:** Enough already. I will not lay this upon my children. It's time to break the chain."*

---

### J.M., Western Cape South Africa:

*"I know my dad did the best he could but he came from a system and life of where sedation was a way of being. Being influenced by so many factors here in*

*South Africa with the indoctrination of the previous regimes mandatory military service and the then daily economic functions of this country. My heart was confused and crying as a child not understanding that this is the way life is and the way men should be. I went opposite avoiding the conflict and not wanting to hurt people and wanted to ease people's pain. All giving up my power to create to rule my kingdom and unleashing my power for the man that's inside."*

### J.R., San Diego, California USA:

*"Blown away by this epidemic. Hard to walk around now and see things the same. Like the Matrix, I see past the BS and a world full of well meaning men who are neutered. This is not a call to be some fake alpha male dick but a call to be multi-dimensional and be a servant warrior king, put here to add value, conquer biz, love and engage family, meet the needs of those who are in pain and hurting in society. I am realizing that how compelling this vision is and I am fueled more by fear instead of pulled toward my mission."*

# THE FOUNDATION

## Chapter 3: THE POSSIBILTY

Your Worldview drives your reality. Even though you had no control over how you were born, you can dictate how you're going to live.

# SECTION ONE
# THE FOUNDATION

## CHAPTER THREE
# THE POSSIBILITY

"But when a long train of abuses and usurpations, pursuing invariably the same Object evinces a design to reduce them under absolute Despotism, it is their right it is their duty, to throw off such Government, and to provide new Guards for their future security."

### -Declaration of Independence

---

1. A worldview is nothing more than the world that we believe is real to us. It doesn't mean that that World is actually real to anybody else; it just means it's real to us. Now, can you and I be influenced by the world around us and the worldviews of people around us? Absolutely. Are we affected by this with social media? Absolutely. Are we affected by this with television and the churches that we go to? Absolutely.

2. The people that you associate with more often than not are the people who share a common worldview with you. Most of us do not spend time with somebody who has a conflicting worldview because when you have two opposing worldviews they collide and cause conflict.

3. One of the great demises inside of this "sedated man experience" is that:

- Conflict itself has become something that is politically incorrect
- I shouldn't actually take a stand for a new worldview or the truth the way I see it
- I shouldn't take a stand for truth the way I see it
- Ultimately, unless you collapse yourself down into the politically correct worldview, then it's impossible for you to actually be accepted.

- Most men find it significantly easier to surrender their opinion about the world that they want and just collapse it down into the worldview of what is, not recognizing that in doing so they are continuing the insanity to the next generation.

## Founding Father Bad Asses

4. At some point You Must Take A Stand. A Stand just like the [13]Founding Fathers of the United States of America who said, "You know what? Your taxes are too high. We don't want to be part of this sovereignty anymore. We don't support your worldview about how we should live here in this country, nor do we support your governance anymore. We're going to create a document called the Declaration of Independence. We're going to unroll it and sign this bitch, all of us together."

5. This small band of men, prominent leaders only within their own communities and not yet known to the Crown, knew they were committing high treason putting this document together. And yet, they proceeded in signing it like the wig-wearing bad asses they were, declaring their independence, liberating themselves from what the English crown thought to be true. They said, "We declare our independence. Our worldview is free of the worldview that you say is true. We reject that worldview. Not only that, we pledge our lives, our liberty, and our fortunes upon this land to say 'Fuck you' and your worldview." Well, they were a little more eloquent than that, but the feeling behind the declaration hasn't changed.

Where are the men willing to make declarations like that today?

Do they even still exist?

6. These were men of integrity; men who listened to the Voice inside of them, willing to take a stand and be comprehensive men. You don't find much of that anymore in leadership after a century of this sedation cycle we saw in detail within Chapter 2. What we have ended up with is a bunch of weak boys; men who never grew up, that cannot take a stand.

## Social Media Opinions; It's Not Working

7. Social media and the internet has given every asshole an opinion. "Keyboard Vigilantes" run rampant around the world. Disconnected,

---

[13] See Appendix Additional Resources: "Founding Fathers"

unconscious assholes whose opinion, in some twisted reality, some actually think matters. All of a sudden, we have become influenced in our worldview by people that we don't know, who we don't give a shit about, and yet their opinions are dictating our lives. The Media World has become a den of thieves and a band of liars. Social Media is forming your Worldview every single day, in some of the most twisted and distorted ways.

8. In some ways, it is beautiful and in others it is destroying you and everything that you hold dear. So the question I have for you is this,

## "Is Your Life Working?"

9. If it is, then the Worldview you are living through is working and you can continue living the way you are with no issue. But if your life is not working and you are searching for more, then you are left with only one reality:

## CHANGE YOUR WORLD VIEW.

10. Damn straight. The only solution is to destroy the worldview that guided you to create the reality that you desire to change. Figuratively speaking, it is time for you to sign your own Declaration of Independence that compels you to no longer live as a man that society has decided to tax us with by declaring,

11. "I will no longer live the one to two-dimensional lifestyle as a sedated modern peasant king who lives in the shack and rejects his crown. I reject this doctrine, and I say, 'Forget you, world doctrine. Forget you, century of tradition. Forget you, political correctness. Forget *you*.' I choose to live."

## What Does Living Mean?

12. But what does living as a modern man mean? What is the current world's view of a Modern Warrior King? You see, I had to begin to define this inside my own life. I didn't start doing this because I knew you existed, or saw a Revolution ahead of me that was going to change millions of families' lives. What I saw was a life that wasn't working, and it was mine: *my* life was not working. My Worldview was destroying me and I had to change or die. To hell with anybody else; I wanted to wake up with a Desire to live and I knew this was going to require me to change the world I saw.

So, what does it mean for me to ultimately have it all?

What do I want my life to look like?

What do I want as a man?

13. I wanted to feel Harmony, waking up in the morning and mentally feeling like I was on fire. As an athlete, I had moments, even after my athletic career was over, where my body felt just like a weapon, which exuded this powerful confidence because of the way I was eating and the way I was training my body. There was this confidence that seemed to affect everything else around me.

14. I also wanted to feel like God and I were on the same page, fucking tattoos and all. I wanted to feel like I could hear the Voice inside of me, that as soon as I woke up, I knew my life mattered because this Higher Source, this power called God, this Universe around me, confirmed that it did.

15. But, you know what? That's not enough. I looked into my home and saw the relationship with my wife and children, and said,

16. "I want to be done with all this guilt and shame. I want to be done with these inabilities to communicate and to speak my truth; when I'm fired up, I want to be able to speak it, and when my wife is fired up, to be able to allow her to speak it as well."

17. I needed to learn how to communicate and be real inside that relationship. I needed to learn how to be a parent: babies don't come with goddamn instruction manuals. I wish they did.

## Not Knowing How to Be A Husband

18. Sexuality, spirituality, communication and intimacy inside of a relationship are all categories within marriage, yet I realized I didn't know how to be a husband. These topics were all a blur to me and I had no true map to make them work at any level.  I came to a very clear reality that I didn't know how to be a husband.

19. I seriously did not know. It was the greatest and craziest day of my life when I came to truly realize:

20. "I don't even know how to be a husband, because I've been trained by disconnected douche bags. I don't even know what that looks like."

21. I grew up seeing men who would come in after being gone all day golfing on a Saturday, and feel entitled to dinner ready right at the time he walked through the door, food on the table with the kitchen already cleaned, and then sit down on his throne, the couch, to watch football, waiting for the dinner bell to ring. Then, he'd rise up from one throne to the next one, eating as the fucking Lord of the Land at the head of the table, and promptly leave the food and plates to go back to the couch throne, watching more football on TV while the women cleaned. I would watch these men talk and play pool, and then they would go to their royal bed chambers, still entitled as a king. If they felt like they needed to get laid, the wife better perform her marital duties. This was the example I was being given; what I saw happening all around me. Now, there is absolutely nothing wrong with playing golf, watching football on Sunday, having your wife cook for you or SEX.

22. But what I saw behind these actions was an unconscious series of patterns that were creating marriages filled with Suppression and Secrets. A vast majority of the marriages I saw like this were ending in divorce or worse; complete apathy.

## Looking For The Man I Knew I Needed To Be

23. So the question is: Who are the role models to follow on how to be a man? A husband and a father? Most of us were not raised with fathers who taught us this. In fact, we are now experiencing generations of men who were raised in fatherless homes. We were not trained on how to be the man that we knew we needed to be. I knew I had to take my responsibility as a father in a completely different direction than I had seen my father take with me, or how my grandfather had approached fatherhood with him.

24. I knew I needed to be a better lover and a more seductive player inside my wife's life. I needed to be more supportive, emotionally available, and able to communicate better. I needed to be able to allow her space to grow and become, yet not be triggered by my own ego when doing it.

25. I knew I needed to find a relationship with God, but I was so stuck in my religious patterns I was raised with that I couldn't get it; it didn't make

any sense to me. I couldn't connect inside that space, and so I had to ask myself better questions that ultimately had me leave the church.

26. I knew I needed to make money, but I also refused to build businesses that I didn't feel had made a difference. Not that the mortgages, insurance and financial services that I came from had no value and importance; I just wanted to create and build businesses that mattered. I didn't want to be a capitalist for capitalism's sake. I wanted to have it all, but I didn't know how.

27. One day I was talking with some friends about this concept of "having it all" and I shared with them, "Well, I think we could be fit, I think we can be spiritually on point, I think that we can be deeply, passionately, lustfully desiring and connected to our wives, and, at the same time, completely passionate, almost aching to return  home to be with our kids instead of trying to avoid parental duties by remaining at the office, hoping they're in bed by the time we get home. And I believe that in business we can 10x our revenue while covering all of these other areas in our life at the same time, not mutually exclusive."

"Dude, have you been smoking something, bro?"

"How the hell are you going to pull all of that off?"

I don't know anybody who's pulled all that shit off."

I said, "I know. I'm going to be the first one."

"Good luck with that."

28. I leveraged his doubt and the doubt of many others, leaping into what most considered to be a total suicide mission. Had I known how much work and how painful it would have been, to this day I am not sure I would have taken the leap, but thankfully my ignorance fueled my fire.  Over the next couple of years, I would die and be reborn a hundred times emotionally, leaving behind the old me and awakening to a new version of myself.

## The Pursuit of Having It All

29. In my pursuit to having it all in Body, Being, Balance and Business I came to realize that I was going to need a shit load of training in each area. Trying to find this kind of training was going to require me to hire coaches, mentors, attend masterminds, read books, articles, newsletters,

etc… inside of each one of the four domains of Body, Being, Balance, and Business. And, if that wasn't enough, I was going to have to learn how to put them all together, gluing the conversation into a comprehensive yet simple system that would allow for a man like myself to actually get, implement, and maintain the game longer than a weekend or even a couple of months.

30. I knew any asshole could do something awesome for a weekend, we can all be Weekend Warriors, but I was interested in rebuilding my life permanently. To do this, I needed to change the trajectory of my reality and information, in which guidance and counsel was going to be mandatory.

31. Although I intellectually understood the price that was having to be paid emotionally, things were 10 times more complicated; I had no fucking clue how much work it was really going to take. Just like most parents admit when being honest about having and raising children, "If I'd known this shit was going to be this hard, I probably wouldn't have had kids." And yet, you're grateful you did because in that ignorance, you started having babies. Same goes for pursuing down the paths with Business, and you're like, "Dude, if I knew it was going to be this hard as an entrepreneur, I don't think I would've done it."

## Are You Ready to Pay the Necessary Price?

32. If I knew how much work, money, literal blood, sweat, and tears it was going to take for me to uncover the Code I call The Warrior's Way to Having It All, I am promising you I would have not taken the journey. I wouldn't have had the courage, and that is why journeys of a thousand miles begin with just one simple step.

33. I have spent millions of dollars (yes, you read that right) and tens of thousands of hours, pouring my heart and soul into building and perfecting The Warrior's Way as a predictable System. It took me four years to discover its use in my life and another three years proving the concepts of this game with 200+ ELITE high level clients who invested $10-$100k to train directly with me. I had to prove that this system could work in the lives of other men, and in order to do that, I needed years of research and proven data. The possibilities at the end of the seven-year journey are mind-bending.

# The Results in My Own Life

34. I eventually went from a place in which sex and intimacy in my marriage was only happening once every two to three months to frequently happening two, sometimes three times a week or more. Not only was it happening, but my wife was actually wanting and desiring me in ways I had never experienced before, and sex was no longer a hunt for a quick vaginal masturbation session. My life in this area had become un-fucking-recognizable for me, particularly knowing the things that I had chosen and the things I had done.

35. I went from a disconnected, chaotic relationship with my kids who barely knew their father the banker to wanting and longing to be with my children as much as I could every single day. These days I work out with them in the morning in our home CrossFit gym before I take them to school.. I pick them up in the afternoons after school several nights throughout the week. I stay up late with them doing homework and end 90% of my nights lying in bed with each of my babies tickling their backs while we tell stories, pray and listen to meditation music. My kids want to be around dad; I want to be with my kids. There is almost never any guilt because I know when and how to choose fatherhood with my children daily so that I gain power from that relationship.

36. I became the guy who went from complete disconnection as a believer in God to knowing my purpose. I shifted from following old school religious routines that didn't matter to me while faking my way through the conversation of purpose and Divine Power. In this state of being, I rarely heard the Voice of Revelation and constantly felt as if my life was not on purpose. Today, I am a man who knows his life is on purpose and when it gets off how to listen to and trust the Voice inside of me that is guiding me to specific actions. I have the courage to make decisions that I can't see the end result of, clearly and simply guided by Faith, with a knowing in my heart that when the Voice Speaks it always sees the path clearer than I do.

37. I went from Business destruction, failure and empty bank accounts to rebuilding an Empire in three different industries while at the same time acquiring Elite Level Skills in Marketing, Selling, Technology, Sequencing, Systems and Leadership. I am no longer a victim to an industry changing

or a marketplace shifting. The Warrior's Way has literally allowed me to guide myself through any dark times in business because the "have it all" lifestyle demands that I see myself as a King equipped with the mindsets and skillsets of Modern Business Mastery. Truly, for the first time in my life I know my businesses and bank accounts are under my control and that I am the one determining my destiny.

38. Within my body, I initially started out as a tired, worn-out shell of a man coming off of three major surgeries, cancer, and 14 months on crutches while shifting several major addictions. This up and down, year to year roller coaster with my body went from over a decade to a body at 39 years of age that is more defined, more shredded, more functional, and more powerful than it was in my early 20s as a high-level elite athlete. My mindsets and skill-sets in fighting, fitness, endurance, strength, power, performance, consistency and nutrition are at levels that make my life feel bulletproof most days as I stand naked in front of the mirror or walk clothed down the street anywhere in the world.

And all this you just read?

Yea, it's happening every single day.

This is the Life of Kings.

This is the Life of Modern Businessmen.

This is the Warrior's Way to Having It All.

39. Many Warriors have come to The Black Box Brotherhood on the brink of divorce, some of them with divorces filed, marriages that are numb, families that are falling apart, businesses that are burning to the ground and watch them not only turn them around but take them to levels that seem to only exist in the movies.

40. Many Warriors have come to the Black Box Brotherhood with bodies that were jacked up and beaten down from years of abuse, yet have been able to take those shells of abused bodies and turn them into healed weapons of destruction and creation inside their life. They are more Fit and on Fire in their 30s, 40s, 50s and 60s than they ever were in their 20s.

41. Many Warriors have come to the Black Box Brotherhood confused about God, their church and beliefs about the system of ideology on the

purpose of life, only to level up their understanding with the Divine while experiencing power and purpose at levels they never knew existed. I would then watch these same men (who had no concept of spiritual leadership in their home) return home to tears of gratitude streaming from their queen's eyes as they stand as spiritual presiders in their homes.

42. These men don't sit back like the sedated motherfuckers that we see all over the place who don't take a stand on a damn thing; who allow the media, church leaders, and the schools to teach their children.

Warriors who are Waking Up are saying,

"I am the Creator and the Dictator of my Life."

## A Sacred Legacy

43. Of all the responsibilities in my life that I hold sacred, it is my calling as a Father that I hold the most dear, the king inside my own castle to lead my legacy. If you are able to hear that call as well, why would you return to the shack and live with the peasants and hang out with the whores when you can stand at the top of the Game you've been called to? As a king with a queen standing by your side and children who love and adore you?

44. It is natural to want to place the Crown upon your head and to raise the Title of Liberty[14] in your own life, declaring your desire and intention to Have It All in Body, Being, Balance and Business. This single declaration will awaken in you a desire to defend and protect the kingdom and to expand the empire in your world with a Fire that will be difficult to control.

45. The possibility I speak of inside this Brotherhood, inside this conversation, is the Game of Awakening into the life of a Modern Warrior King. It is not to become, but *awaken* what you always were.

---

[14] The Title of Liberty is a phrase declared by the Nephite commander, Chief Captain Moroni, from an event in the Book of Mormon that states "In memory of our God, our religion, and freedom, and our peace, our wives, and our children" (Alma 46:12-13). This was written on a piece of ripped cloth (it's what he had at the time on the battlefield) and strung up as a banner showing his why behind fighting against his enemies; for the sake of his religion, his nation's freedom, and his family (wife and children). See https://www.lds.org/scriptures/gs/title-of-liberty?lang=engfor more

46. Two of the greatest words used in all spiritual writings across all traditions are these:

"Awaken"

and

"Remember"

47. Brother, before you and I were even born the nightmare of Systematic Sedation had begun. You had no choice with the reality that you were born in the Pit, a hole of male conditioning in which there's nobody to blame and no reason for shame, but you have got to change the game.

48. And that game starts with you.

So how do you change the world, Brother?

You change one man.

If you change a man, you change a marriage.

If you change a marriage, you change a family.

If you change a family, you change a community.

If you change a community, you change a city.

If you change a city, you change a state.

If you change a state, you change a country.

If you change a country, you change the world.

49. And so it all starts with one man.

Brother, that man is you.

50. Welcome to the revolution of the Wake Up Warrior Movement.

## Chapter 3:
## POINTS TO PONDER FROM THE GENERAL'S TENT

- **POINT #1:** At some point we must all take a stand for what we believe in and not be scared of the Revolution that may ensue with this new worldview. Embrace the change as you become what you want to see in the world.

- **POINT #2:** Warrior is about creating Modern Warrior Kings that are seeking their own individual path towards harmony in having it all.

- **POINT #3:** The Core 4 (Body, Being, Balance & Business) was created for men interested in rebuilding their lives permanently by changing the trajectory of my reality, posterity, and to ultimately make a difference in the world with my life.

- **POINT #4:** There is a Game of Awakening into the life of a Modern Warrior King as men remember what they were always meant to do. Learn to change the One Man inside yourself to create a series of events that will eventually lead to changing the world.

# WARRIOR WITNESS:

### J.M., Oklahoma, USA:

*"For me, personally, I'm looking back at everything I'm going through in my past and there's a lot of repetition. I suck at communication. I was raised that men don't voice their opinions and it just makes matters worse. Every time we get in a conversation it ends in a fight, making us not want to communicate.*

*It requires change. I decided to be brave in my conversation with her, not really knowing what I was going to say, but one deep thing from that conversation was About conversation. I needed to learn how to create a different conversation, and Warrior is the tool that's going to help me.*

*I'm already getting a ton from it. Growth is uncomfortable at times but that's what it takes to expand. It's a privilege to take this journey with each and every one of you in the Brotherhood!"*

### A.C., California, USA:

*"The Voice inside me has said it's time to take a stand. Fuck political correctness… MY worldview matters! "Does my life work right now?" Yes, but barely…I'm*

*only giving it about 40%. What kinda asshole only gives 40% to his life and expects great things to happen? For the past 2 years I have....*

*I know what 100% dedicated effort looks like. It's fucking amazing. Right now I'm wandering, lazy, and skating by. Time to destroy the present mind trapped in my head..."*

———————————————

## J.F. South Carolina, USA:

*"Had to take some time to think on this one....Still not sure 100% that I've cleared my thoughts on it...but as of right now, my takeaway from the Possibility is:*

- I am a motherfuckin King of my world.
- I have been called upon as a leader of my:
    - family
    - business
    - body
    - life

*Do not shy away. Man up. Own it. Conquer these challenges. It can be done. I can't wait to learn more about how because I'm fired up but still cloudy as to how the hell we actually pull this off."*

# THE FOUNDATION

## Chapter 4: THE PATH

Where are you and where do you want to go? The Doctrine of the Warrior's Way is distinct and different from anything else you have ever imagined.

SECTION ONE
# THE FOUNDATION

CHAPTER FOUR
# THE PATH

"Two roads diverged in a wood, and I—
I took the one less traveled by,
And that has made all the difference."

**-Robert Frost**
"The Road Not Taken" excerpt

---

1. By this point in the book you have likely asked yourself the following: "What the hell is it that I've stepped into?" The Doctrine of the Warrior's Way is distinct and different from anything else you had ever imagined, and yet, it's refreshing to have the truth that you feel inside this conversation. Am I right? Only now you're wondering,

"How am I going to pull this shit off?

How am I going to actually have it all?"

## The Warrior Domino Effect

2. This was what I wanted to know too when I first started down this path. It seemed to be like a series of dominoes as the Warrior's Way Doctrine unfolded for me. I was reminded of the impact that one man could truly have on an entire nation: any great movement we have ever known at any time began with just one man.  What if *you* are that man that will change the direction of your posterity's path for the next 300 years?

3. Inside the Wake Up Warrior Brotherhood we have proof of the impact one man can have on literally hundreds of people over a very short period

of time. These Warriors have become beacons of the Warrior's Way. Their impact, like yours when you start to live it, will spread the Doctrine of 'having it all' as an influence to tens of thousands, until the Wake Up Warrior Movement revolutionizes the way businessmen operate all over the world.

4. Anytime that we start a journey there are two crucial points, asked as questions, that must be uncovered. If either of them is not clear, it becomes impossible to actually change anything in your life. Point #1: Can you see where you are right now? and Point #2: Can you see where you want to go from here?

## Mirror Assessment

5. Looking in the Mirror is the key to beginning this journey. I like to call it "The Mirror Assessment." It is literally and figuratively a way of assessing the reality of Now across Body, Being, Balance and Business. What does the mirror reflect back to you in facts? What are the stories that cloud those facts as you see them in the Mirror? Oftentimes, when we attempt to see where we are, it is impossible because our stories make it so difficult to clearly see the reflection.

6. BODY: Where are you at today with your Body?

7. Where are you at now physically? When you stand naked in the mirror, looking at yourself; the energy, fat and/or muscle that you have or don't have, what do you see? How do your energy levels and vitality feel as of today? What is the current state of affairs with your Body?

8. This same process is followed across the rest of the Core 4 Dimensions of Being, Balance and Business within yourself as you look to answer the following questions:

9. BEING:

Where am I at today with my spirituality?

Who am I?

Who do I believe myself to be?

Who do I believe God to be?

What is the purpose of my life?

What does that path look like for me spiritually today?

You don't just stop there,

## 10. BALANCE (Marriage):

Where am I at today with my Balance?

What does my marriage look like?

How is my sexuality & intimacy?

What does my communication look like?

How is my spiritual connection with my Queen?

What does that currently look like?

## 11. BALANCE (Children):

How is the relationship with my Children?

How much time do I get to spend with each one?

What connection is had during that time?

How present am I during those interactions?

## 12. BUSINESS:

Is my business profitable?

Are my Bank accounts full?

Do I have a three to six month reserve of cash?

How effective are my marketing & sales systems?

What is the reality of my teams?

How much am I working compared to being at home?

What do my operations look like?

Do I love what I do?

Does my lifestyle exist or am I slave to the business?

## Starting The Journey from What Is

13. The current reality of [15]"What Is True?" for you is the foundation upon which you will uncover and commit to what you want next. If you cannot see what today consists of then it's impossible for you to declare a commitment to some new way.

14. Imagine this: If I say I want something new inside my marriage relationship but I'm not real about where my marriage currently is, then what I say I want in that relationship is a lie. Why? Because whatever you say you want you are saying from a foundation of fantasy, hence anything you say you want will only be half a fantasy.

15. "Well, Garrett, I want my marriage to look like this. I also want my body to look like this. I want my business to look like this and spiritually I want to feel like this."

16. My first response to you will always be the same:

"Great. So where are you *right* now? What does your world look like today?

17. If you struggle to answer truthfully where you are today or you don't even know, I can guarantee that there is nothing I can do to assist you except slap you in the face and make sure you do the hard work of getting clear about reality today.

## The Birth of The Code

18. Reality. The Truth. These seem like such simple terms to me today, but a few years back that was not the case. I was a man who had been raised to not deal with reality or to seek the full truth. This is why your first deep dive training inside this book is learning to live by The Code.

19. Developing an understanding of the theory behind Warrior will help eliminate any confusion you may have about content within this book. Take, for example, if I'm doing knee surgery on an individual: having a hammer might not make a lot of sense. Although I may have this tool called the hammer inside my toolbox, if the context of what I need to have

---

[15] Taken from Byron Katie's principle teachings by asking "Is it true?" based off of her book: Katie, Byron, and Stephen Mitchell. *Loving What Is: Four Questions That Can Change Your Life.* New York: Harmony, 2002. Print.

happen is surgery on my knee, then I won't need that hammer; I'm going to need a scalpel. That hammer will be the tool necessary for nailing pieces of wood together to make a storage shed later on though, after my knee surgery healed and I was ready to tackle a home project. Different tools are applicable for different situations, even if you know how to use each one of them. The proper use of the Doctrine will be discussed in further detail later on in this book.

20. The Code is the foundation and the fuel of the "have it all" lifestyle; a mandatory requirement to live the Warrior's Way. The Code is not something that we interpret, pontificate on or conceive as a possibility; it is a reality that you must choose to live by. If you don't, or you choose to violate the Code, everything else that I will teach you here in Warrior will mean very little.

21. The Code has four simple steps:

> Step #1:  Be Real: to tell the truth and to deal with the Facts of your Life.
>
> Step #2:  Get Raw: to be emotionally connected to the facts and truth
>
> Step #3:  Stay Relevant: to have direct focus of the facts and the feelings.
>
> Step #4:  Ruthless Results: to achieve a measurable and attainable outcome.

## "We Live By A Code!"

22. We openly declare on a daily basis, "We live by a Code!" within Warrior. It is the foundation of our kingdom and yours. Your clean-up phase of our reality is found inside The Code. This is the place where you can access with clarity the Truth.

## Core 4 Power

23. We stand for The Core. We choose to live (and so will you) the Warrior's Way within our Body, Being, Balance and Business. Measurable success in

each of these dimensions daily is the Game and the framework for scoring the "Core 4 Daily War:"

(1 point) Body:  Fitness & Fuel

(1 point) Being:  Meditation & Focus

(1 point) Balance:  Partner/Posterity

(1 point) Business:  Discover & Declare

TOTAL POINTS DAILY:  4

24. We will break these down in extensive detail within Section 3: The Core, but the overall emphasis we want to make here is that while the Code gives us a Foundation, the Core 4 gives us Fuel by strategically allowing us to make deposits and withdrawals daily from all areas of our lives.

25. Think of the Core 4 like a Spartan military force creating the phalanx, step by step, linked together and moving forward, not as one individual but as 4 harmonious dimensions. It is where you as a modern man and Warrior move forward in a systematic and gamified daily war with yourself to win every single day the Game we call Core 4:

26. In summary, we commit to "Hit our 4 before the door, prepared to go to war."

## Unlocking The Keys of Production

28. "Create with the Keys."

29. This simple statement is the gateway to channeling the power and purpose you have accessed in the CODE and the CORE into a simple-strategic-system of execution daily and weekly.  The Keys become the sniper rifle "site-scope" to allow you to zero in on the most crucial and profitable moves every single week during your business execution.

30. When it comes to executing powerfully within Business, most men are in total Chaos which comes down to one of two reasons:

1- They simply lack the capacity and energy to execute consistently.

2- They have very little clarity on the Key Moves that need to be made every single week in order for the profits of the business to explode.

31. Key 4, unlike Core 4, is a Production "Business Only" Focus. While you will track and record all your actions with Core 4 Daily across Body, Being, Balance and Business, Key 4 is a weekly metric assessed inside your General's Tent, specifically within your Business.

32. As a Man, a King and an Entrepreneur, you are under a serious mandate to provide abundance and prosperity to all those who live in the kingdom. This does not mean that this is your exclusive role as King, and it is very clear that you were not called exclusively to become an ATM and a penis with some testicles to make babies.

33. You're a king, and part of that mantle is managing the wealth of the kingdom, unlocking the powerful results of financial resources in order to fund the "have it all" lifestyle.

34. Only YOU are able to hold the Keys to your kingdom because only you are able to hear the Customized Voice's instructions that come from within in regards to the maintenance and expansion of the walls in your Kingdom. If you "Live by the Code" and "Stand for the Core" but lack the ability to produce financial results, your kingdom will be destroyed. The queen will leave. The children will perish and this entire dream of having it all will crumble to the ground.

35. Key 4 is a specific science; a game of weekly production with a specific emphasis on increasing financial results in your life with 4 simple points:

1. What is the target?
2. Why does that target matter?
3. When will you accomplish it by?
4. How are you going to do it?

36. Key 4 is the assault rifle; the missile or hand grenade. It becomes the weapon through which your newly-accessed power is demonstrated so that you can obtain the stability of living when you know production is now a clear Center Stage Conversation.

## Setting Up the Pieces To Play The Game

37. We "Live by the Code" and "Stand for the Core," while expanding prosperity in the kingdom by "Creating with the Keys," but it is the GAME that makes everything harmonize together in living the Warrior's Way.

38. Brother, we're not stupid here at Warrior. We are not encouraging you to run around like blood-thirsty maniacs with a machete randomly hacking away towards creating a kingdom and expanding an empire. It's a systemized game and you are a key player. *This* is why the Keys only make sense in regards to the emphasis we have in Warrior on Business inside of the system we call The Game.

39. Life is frustrating; not necessarily because it is inherently difficult, but because most men have no idea what questions to ask in order to know if they are actually winning the Games they have chosen to play.

40. The following questions are not just asked broadly over life with the faint hope of getting answered. They are asked inside of each Dimension of the Core 4 every single day:

"Am I winning?"

"Am I winning this Game of life?"

"Is it worth it to play?"

"What are the targets I am searching to hit today, this week, this month, this quarter?"

"How do I know if I'm winning?"

"How do I simplify my life down to a game of metrics?"

41. The Game is played in metrics, not concepts, theories, or principles. This is exactly how I knew it would have to be, a game of numbers that I could play and win every day. The Game of Warrior is literally a gamified science that takes all the power from The Code, The Core and The Keys, which then strategically inserts the tools, techniques, tactics and theories into a transformative game:

There is a Daily Game.

There is a Weekly Game.

There is a Monthly Game.

There is a Quarterly Game.

42. The Brotherhood is part of the equation and is the support network of men, like you, who are playing the Game every single day, week, month and quarter from around the world. The game allows for transparency through software and apps that give you the gift of connection and competition with the brotherhood from around the world.

## Transforming Lives from 4 Pillars

43. Upon these four pillars rests the Doctrine and the transformation of your entire life. Although the game is simple, it is far from easy. Any asshole can create something complex; it took me years to figure out how to make it simple enough for you to actually live in life.

44. There are plenty of people who have attempted to create great solutions for men like you and me using a series of very complex scenarios and formulas that don't make any sense long term and are totally impractical for us to live for a month, let alone a lifetime. I'm going to have you consider that the simplicity in the Game of Warrior IS its power.

45. You are receiving the refined Game placed before you today, a system that hundreds and hundreds of men invested 10s of thousands of hours perfecting in the trenches of real lives, not laboratories of theory. It is upon their results and mine that we have proven the Warrior's Way works. They are living examples of it. It is undeniable that the Game works, but only if you are ruthlessly committed to take it on *every* single day.

## Conceive The Possibility

46. Phase number one inside this book is for you to *conceive* the possibility of having it all. This will require you to study the content for Concept first and then follow it up with Creation and actual Execution of the entire Game of Warrior.

47. I can't emphasize enough the importance of giving yourself several weeks to study the Warrior's Way Doctrine and to allow it to distill on

your soul. Once your mind has begun to open up and make the Shift, things will get really exciting as you begin to actually execute on the truth you will find here.

48. This is when you leave the Land of Theory with Warrior and enter the Land of Real Results. Everything you learn here will always come down to your willingness to do the work. There is a specific phrase we use inside this Brotherhood and it is "Do the Fucking Work."

49. No one is coming to save you here.

50. Only you can do that. This doctrine will not liberate you if you do not live it; the Game is so simple but the decision to invest money into it was not enough; you must be willing to live it ALL IN.

## Final Thoughts About Your Family

51. My prayer for you, your queen, and your children is that you're 100% clear about what you're fighting for.

52. Your "Why" is the difference between whether you live or you die. I could never in a million years have imagined my life would have become what it is today. From those dark moments inside the basement of my own home all alone, I didn't see you. I didn't see the Warrior's Way Doctrine. I just saw a pathway out of my own pain.

53. What you are about to embark on in this journey inside the Black Box is not something I created to fix the world. It's something I created to fix *my* world and when it worked, I knew I had to bring it to other men like you around the world.

54. Today, this week, next month, this quarter and this next year you have an opportunity to change everything in your life, to become a Brother with us and bleed black while ushering in a new doctrine, a new worldview, a new curriculum of living for Modern Men. A Warrior at the soul and a King who is under control. May you have the success in this journey that you are about to embark on at the level of your commitment. No more, and no less.

55. I'm going to say it again: If there is only one thing that you take from this it's to realize that no one is coming to save you. The only thing that stands between you and what you want is the work.

56. Brother, do the fucking work.

57. On the other side of that work will be the glory, power and a reality of Having It All because you chose to reclaim your crown.

### Chapter 4:
### POINTS TO PONDER FROM THE GENERAL'S TENT

- **POINT #1:** There's a domino effect of living the Warrior's Way, which has transformed hundreds and hundreds of men forever, living this as a Doctrine inside their lives.

- **POINT #2:** The Code is simply your ability to Be Real: to tell the truth, Get Raw: to be emotionally connected to the truth that you are seeing and the truth that you are feeling, Stay Relevant: meaning to have a focus of those facts and the feelings that you're having, all for Ruthless Results.

- **POINT #3:** Upon the four pillars (Body, Being, Balance and Business) rests the Doctrine and the transformation of your entire life.

- **POINT #4:** Although the game is simple, it is far from easy. Having already seen hundreds of transformations within Warrior, it is undeniable that the Game works, but only if you are ruthlessly committed to work at it, every single day.

# WARRIOR WITNESS:

### C.T., Louisiana, USA:
*"I feel like I'm in a pretty good spot and not relying on stories, but I've GOT to be clear about where I am.*

*There's nothing in me that doesn't believe that this works. It's humbling to be aware of the effort this will take, building up over time which will take incredible focus, being clear.*

*In regards to direction, I don't really know where I'm going, like Christopher Columbus, so I want to get clear about where I'm going. What do I want? I don't fucking know! I expect and demand from myself that that changes."*

## M.M., California USA:

*"Everything is coming to a point. When I listen to the path, the part of it that rings the loudest to me is that Garrett has a plan, a proven strategy for big ass results.*

*The way I think about the game and the way I think about what I do daily is shifting around the code. It's the culture of who we are together as brothers, who Garrett, Sam, Steve, and all of the brothers before us built this brotherhood to be.*

*When I listen to the path, I feel like we had just had the directions read to us and now we are pulling out the game board and it's all making a little more sense."*

## B.L., Ohio, USA:

*"I've been really struggling with this, because it has forced me to look myself in the mirror and identify where I'm at right now across the Core 4. My body is strong but it is not a weapon. If I put half the energy I do for Business into Balance for my family and Being for myself the possibilities are endless."*

## R.L., Wondonga, Australia:

*"When I look at the world I see fake people everywhere just trying to fit it and find acceptance. The teaching around the Code of just be real is liberating yet also quite challenging. I thought I was pretty genuine but the more I listen to Garrett and his teaching, the more I realise that at times I'm no better. One of my goals with Warrior is to just go deeper again into being Real as I believe its the foundation of liberation."*

# THE CODE
## Chapter 5: OVERVIEW

The Code is the foundational doctrine of all that you will learn inside the WarriorBook. Nothing else that you read here will matter if you do not live by The Code's Real, Raw, Relevant Results.

# SECTION TWO
# THE CODE

## CHAPTER FIVE
# OVERVIEW

*"If you tell the truth, then you don't have to remember anything."*

**-Mark Twain**

---

## Context Precedes Content

1. There are two aspects to a Painting: 1- Content and 2- Context. The actual picture is the focus or the content. The outside of this Picture is the frame or the context. Without this, the eyes have a more difficult time focusing on the Painting and experiencing it for the power that it is. The Code operates like a contextual frame that allows you to focus on the Painting, which consists of The Core of Warrior.

2. Without The Code, the Warrior's Way would be nothing but confusion, so let me start off with how I define and describe The Code.

3. Back in 2005, I was standing there in front of what was almost 1,000 people in Las Vegas, Nevada,[16] where I'd been brought in to speak and train at an event on the keys to my marketing and business success. It was a room full of entrepreneurs and business men and women wanting to understand more about how to take a message that mattered to them to the market place.

---

[16] Mortgage Mastermind Summit, 2005

## Anchor Point of the Code

4. The host of the event announced my name, and I walked out ready to share with the room my key statement that stands at the center of The Code. As I got on stage, I walked to the middle, stopped and then went to the edge, not yet speaking. Standing on the edge, I gazed out on the audience, took a couple deep breaths and still said nothing. I just stood there, looking at them. After 45 seconds people were sitting on the edge of their seats thinking, "What the hell is this guy doing? Why is he just standing there?"

5. Just as they were feeling the discomfort in the silence I slowly and clearing declared the following:

"Stop...fucking...lying."

6. I said those three words once; several people clapped and shouted.

7. I repeated the same statement a few seconds later and as I finished there was more cheering from the audience and people began to give me a standing ovation.

8. Literally, I said three words and got a standing ovation.

9. So when people ask me,

"Garrett, what is the Power of the Code?"

10. My reply:

"The Power of the Code is a standing ovation on stage, in your home, in business and life."

## Living a Life Written by Lies

11. The Code was not something I was trying to uncover after some glorious success. It came about because I was living a life that was written by lies, stories and half-truths. The Code declares that the only way that you and I can truly experience a life that matters and is full of power is to stop lying. The Have It All lifestyle of the Wake Up Warrior Movement demands a life free of lies.

## Lies of Omission Vs Lies of Commission

12. Growing up, the words of *omission* and *commission* were used by my preachers to teach the conversation of Sin. There were sins of *omission* (things I didn't do that I should have) and there were sins of commission (things I did do that I shouldn't have). After taking a little creative license here in applying these concepts to the Warrior Doctrine, let's replace Sins with Lies.

13. When I commit a Lie of Commission I say:

14. "Hey, you know what? I'm going to make up a fucking story and I'm going to tell someone else this story and I'm going to pretend like it's true when I know that it's not."

15. Then there are Lies of Omission. Lies of Omission are the single greatest threat to businessmen like you today. Your unwillingness to tell the truth about what you feel, where you are and what you truly want is literally killing you.

16. Lies of Omission are a loser's game of Suppression and Sedation. It says:

17. "Who I am is not enough and I can't tell you what I'm actually feeling and thinking because if I do, you are going to reject me. You will not be able to handle all of what I'm feeling and what I'm thinking. So instead of telling you the truth, I'm going to fucking lie."

## Taught to Lie and Suppress Feelings: The Teeter-Totter Effect

18. If you can't see it, it doesn't exist right? This is a Lie, but this is how many of us choose to operate because this is how we were raised. You and I were taught, trained and educated as young boys to lie. As a Grown Man you have been taught to suppress how you feel and what you think about everything.

19. As you continue down the path of Suppression, it will create a Life of Chaos...period.

20. So here's the question:

Why?

21. Why has lying about how you feel, what you're thinking, who you are, and what you want out of life become so normal? Why is it such a difficult task for men like you and I to come to grips with such a simple truth? In my experience, it comes down to what I call the teeter-totter effect of lying.

22. On one side of the teeter-totter you have the Truth: the "right" way to do it, which is the good way to do it. Then on the other side you have what? The "wrong" way, and of course that's the "lie" or bad way to do it.

23. With this way of thinking, we're completely stuck. Depending on who we recently hung out with at the time, there was an Unspoken Code, and inside that Code was: "here is the wrong way and right way to do shit." We were constantly trying to figure out as kids what was the right and wrong way to do life; this has not changed as we have gotten older.

24. You and I are still stuck on a daily basis riding the Teeter-Totter of Right and Wrong. In any room or situation we find ourselves in, we are faced with the same dilemma: How we are "supposed" to behave and not behave. And inside of that question, we begin to suppress how we actually want to behave in order to fit in.

25. So, if this is how the Game of Life has evolved to be for us, how in the hell did I liberate my life by getting off the Teeter-Totter 90% of the time? Well, I did this crazy thing called The Shift and *took* myself off. In its place, I decided to focus on my Freedom rather than simply trying to be Right.

## Black Box: Before and After

26. Before the Black Box and the Warrior Doctrine, you saw the world a certain way. Inside that perspective, you experienced the possibilities of your life. Along the way you have seen this world has worked. What you did up to this point in life was the best that you could do, and how do we know this to be true? Because it's what you did. Yep, it's that simple. Where you stand today is simply where you are today and it truly is not Good or Bad; it just is what it is.

27. This concept was very hard for me to accept. Around almost every action of my past for most of my life, there was shame, blame, guilt and complete self-doubt based upon what I considered to be "Bad" behavior. I was stuck in The Drift. When I looked into my past, all I could see was

that I couldn't do *it* right. No matter what I tried to do, I found myself more often than not in a game of doing it wrong.

28. Everything that was ever said about me by others or to myself, I put in this tiny little box, tucking it deep inside as I stuffed away all my feelings. After my first divorce, I decided to hide those feelings for good, putting on a suit jacket with a white shirt and a red tie for the next decade. Yep. I buttoned that shit up like a politician, and would look people in the eye, shake their hands and said, "Brother, how are you today?"

## A Decade of Pretending Takes Its Toll

29. I pretended for the first 10+ years of my life as a businessman. It was exhausting as I was trying to cover up my Darkness and My Stories.

29. Do you know the feeling?

30. You're trying to be pumped on the outside while you are slowly dying on the inside, in which pounding down the energy drinks aren't enough to keep you standing anymore.

31. So people ask you on a day-to-day basis, "How are you?"

32. And your suppressed, sedated response is likely, "I'm good."

33. But this is bullshit most of the time and you know it.

34. The truth is, inside you really want to say, "I fucking hate my life some days, but I can't tell you that. I can't tell you about the desires, cravings and thoughts that I'm having. I can't tell you that I'm questioning my religion, my marriage or being a father. I can't tell you that I'm questioning my business because I've got 100 employees that I feel the weight of responsibility for. Why in the world would I tell you this? It is not safe."

35. We've been conditioned from the start that it is not safe for a man to tell others how he really feels.

36. And so, we become Kings of Unreality. Perpetual liars. Lying to ourselves; lying to the world, pretending like everything is okay.

37. For me? While I played this game, the part you didn't see was the closet drinking, lying to myself, cheating on my wife, doing all this shit and pretending like I was all right.

38. On the outside I had the appearance of having it all together. Yet, on the inside was the truth: I was falling apart. "How did I get to this small, dark, fucking hole?" I would ask myself. I didn't live by the Code in those years, that's for sure.

## The Gateway to Freedom

39. There was nobody in my world calling me out, telling me that the gateway to my freedom existed through my capacity to tell the truth.

40. In order to do that, I had to *stop fucking lying*. See, for some human beings they could just make this decision. They could simply switch it up, change it up, and they can just make it happen. I, on the other hand, required the universe to compel against me, nearly destroying my life in order to be reborn into a new way of seeing.

41. This rebirth was to be born again into seeing that the fastest path to living my life was to be all of me: the darkness *and* the light. My Purpose of life shifted from "Do It Right" to "Expand Every Single Day." It was to become something more than I was when I got here.

42. As we dive into the Code conversation, I want you to understand: I don't care what religion you come from or if you come from no religion. I do not care if you are spiritual or not, if you feel like you have purpose or not. I don't care.

43. The only thing that I'm going to have you consider is that it might be more useful for you to shift the story you have around the purpose of your life. The only way that you can expand is to step off the teeter-totter of Right and Wrong, Truth and Lies, and start asking better questions.

## Discovering Expansion

44. The question is not "Why am I broken?" or "Why am I a wretched man?"

45. It is simpler than that and far less judgmental, yet insanely useful to having it all in life.

46. Instead, ask yourself "Is my life working? Yes, or No?"

47. It's not a complicated formula.

48. Just a simple question: "Is my life working or not working for me right now?"

49. Simple doesn't mean easy, however. And it's a lot more difficult to explain how you or I would know if it's working or not. Here is one thing I know for sure though; if you're here in this program and reading this book, at some level you're searching for more out of your life because some or all of your life is not working at the level that you know it could be.

50. So, here are a couple of other things to consider:

51. If the purpose of your life is expansion, then this means that it does not simply happen once or twice a week; it is something that must occur every single moment of every single day.

52. Every single day in every single way, you and I are searching and looking for this Game inside of us to find the balance between our darkness and our light.

53. You are here to have a conversation that's Real. A conversation that's beyond the fucking stories. Beyond the lies, the misinterpretation of who you truly are and the misinterpretation of who you've been called to be.

54. The Code is simply this:

"Stop fucking lying and start telling the truth."

## Moving Beyond the Storytelling Liar

55. So as I started trying to "Tell the Truth," I recognized very quickly that I was not prepared to be radically honest. I had become a storytelling liar, so afraid of my life looking bad and not acceptable, that I believed the lie I told to myself and to the world.

56. I rejected everything about me, hence I couldn't accept anything about you. Inside of that, I still wondered why my life was not fucking working.

57. I needed help, just like you. I needed guidance. In a trained society of liars, it's difficult to tell the truth as a man, so I started down this path of searching for what it would mean to tell the truth and how I would practically do it. I had an epiphany as a businessman to name one of my businesses *The Authentic Entrepreneur* as a daily reminder.

58. To this day, *The Authentic Entrepreneur, LLC* is still the foundational business during this transition that we do *DBA, Wake Up Warrior*, and a series of other businesses.

## The Authentic Entrepreneur

59. Long before anybody thought it was cool to be real and authentic, long before everybody was willing to be so open on social media, I started down a path in 2008 that was a journey to discovering the Authentic Truth inside of me, free of as many lies as I could get rid of.

60. You see, I knew I was a liar and in an effort to offset this reality, I named my business and created a personal brand that matched the truth I was searching for. Every day I would stand up and say, "Hello. My name is Garrett White. I am The Authentic Entrepreneur coming at you real, raw and relevant."

61. Don't believe me? Go type it up in YouTube and click search: you'll find videos on it.

62. There I was, trying my best to preach to the world the truth. Really though, I was just reminding myself,

63. "Hey, Garrett! Your brand is *The Authentic Entrepreneur* so you should probably stop fucking lying."

64. It worked, as crazy as that may seem, and evolved into this place of power which became Warrior text within the exclusive *Black Box* experience of the Wake Up Warrior Academy program, as well as the book that you are reading right now.

65. You see, I started to recognize that when I lived by the Code regardless of what was going on around me, or what people thought about me, or what I thought about myself, in that moment I found Power. This unseen power rose when I was able to simply declare,

66. "Here is *what is* for me. It's not good and it's not bad; it's not right and it's not wrong; it's not righteous and it's not wicked; it simply is WHAT IS for me and what I AM."

67. I realized very quickly that armed with the Code I became the most powerful man in any room I walked into. I was willing to say what other people would never give themselves permission to even write down, let alone express verbally to another human being.

## The Evolution of the Code

68. So began the evolution of this sequence we call The Code, which is broken down into four phases. This introductory section sets up the four-part discovery of the Code as:

> Conversation #1: Be Real
> Conversation #2: Get Raw
> Conversation #3: Stay Relevant
> Conversation #4: Ruthless Commitment to Results

69. Real, Raw, Relevant, Results. I've set this context and story around this point of Doctrine. We're going to cover all four of those one at a time in their own chapters, getting practical reality for what this all means to you within the Black Box Brotherhood. What does it mean to stop fucking lying? How do I make the Shift?

### Chapter 5:
### POINTS TO PONDER FROM THE GENERAL'S TENT

- **POINT #1:** The Have It All (Body, Being, Balance, Business) lifestyle of the Wake Up Warrior Movement demands a life free of lies. Lies of Omission (things I didn't do but should've done) are the single greatest threat to businessmen like you today.

- **POINT #2:** In order to stop pretending, we need to shift the story for the purpose of our life from "Do It Right" to "Expand Every Single Day."

- **POINT #3:** Every single day in every single way you and I are searching and looking for this Game inside of us to find the balance between our darkness and our light.

- **POINT #4:** Is your life working? Yes or No. Be Real, Get Raw, Stay Relevant to get Ruthless Commitment to Results

# WARRIOR WITNESS:

## M.A., Washington, USA:

*"I've listened to this many times, and I get something different from it every time. Today, I was caught by a line early on that says for the Code to work, we have to not only want to live by a Code, but we have to understand the consequences of NOT living by a Code. For me, that's huge. I've always admired those who live by a "code" and are good people (at least on the outside, who knows what is going on underneath because they don't tell you), but it takes me understanding that there has been a big consequence in my life of NOT living by a Code. That's actually huge. I realize I have no code or character to pass on to my kids, especially my son. I have secrets and haven't been real. I have shit in my life I am ashamed of. That's my consequence of not living by a code. That shit is NOT acceptable!"*

## B.C., Texas, USA:

*"I am uncovering lies about my identity. Rules I created about life and who I am when I was 8, 10, 17 years old. I've followed this "code" and it's had some pretty fucked up results. So many lies we tell ourselves are so hard to uncover since we have been repeating them for so long. We need a Brotherhood that has the balls to challenge our BS."*

## B.F., Tennessee, USA:

*"If I'm to stop lying to myself then I need to admit that I've been a FUCKING PUSSY my whole life. I've been successful just by showing up and being there (which is more than 90% of the population), but I want a life that's on FUCKING fire. It starts with being Real about where I am, and how that's made me feel my whole life, and the focus on my goals, so that I can achieve big ass results.*

*The lies of omission discussion really hit home because the little voice in our head lies to us all fucking day and gives reasons instead of results. It's time to turn that fucker off and start connecting to our purpose."*

## <u>M.M., California USA:</u>

*I realized by watching this for the 3rd time that it took Garrett years to figure this out. In other words the deep truths had to get dug up and relentlessly sought after. I can't just comb through this black box while I'm driving or watching the football game. I'm not going to get real results unless I get raw and not allow give myself permission to be a phony. I am only going to get out what I put into this and I now waking up that I need to get a whole lot more serious if I'm going to get what I came here for.*

————————————————

# THE CODE
## Chapter 6: REAL (FACTS)

Being Real comes down to the Facts and is the first principle of the Code. When we tell the truth, we lay the foundation for liberation in everything else.

SECTION TWO
# THE CODE

CHAPTER SIX
# REAL (FACTS)

"Facts are stubborn things; and whatever may be our wishes, our inclinations, or the dictates of our passions, they cannot alter the state of facts and evidence."

**-John Adams**
[2nd President of the United States of America]

---

1. The first principle inside of the Code is "Be Real." You see, "Being" is a function of who you are at this exact moment. Accept me, reject me, I don't give a shit. *Here* is who **I Am.** This is my Light and my Darkness,[17] which are the aspects of me that you enjoy and the aspects of me that you reject. Blend all of them together and what you have are the simple FACTS of who I am being.

2. The challenge that you likely face at this point in your life is the fact that you can't even see the facts any more. The hard-core Truth stares you back in the face every single day about your Body, your Marriage, your Family, your Connection with GOD and your Business.

3. Can you look at the Facts of your life?

---

[17] For more on this concept of Light and Darkness within ourselves, Debbie Ford's *The Dark Side of the Light Chasers* shares some invaluable input on moving beyond our Darkness by openly acknowledging it, thus no longer allowing it to rule our lives as a hidden and ignored dictator. See Bibliography for ISBN info.

# The Facts About Being Real

4. Right now, in this exact moment, you have and are experiencing a reality about your life in the form of feelings and results. These feelings and results are not inherently Good or Bad, they simply *are* the facts of your life:

Here is what I'm feeling: ***Facts.***

Here is what's going on for me: ***Facts.***

Here is my thought process: ***Facts.***

Here is a checklist of things that I did: ***Facts.***

Here is a checklist of things that I want: ***Facts.***

5. Facts are data points.

6. Your Target is to be able to back away from them in the most neutral position possible and say okay, here are the facts and the truth according to the way I see it today.

7. I recognized about eight years into my marriage that I couldn't tell my wife what I was truly feeling or what I was even thinking. If I had a sexual thought, I couldn't tell her. If I had an emotional desire, I couldn't tell her. If I had a fear, I couldn't tell her. If I thought about maybe doing something different, I couldn't tell her.

8. This led me to create a small little box into which I started living inside. Doing this, I became the least attractive human being on the planet to my wife. I sat there longing, wanting, searching and hoping to have a connection with my Queen and yet I couldn't. Why? Because what stood behind me, between us, was a stacking series of lies and suppressed truths that I was terrified to actually share with her.

## Living in Fantasyland

9. Brother, you and I both have our coping mechanism for ignoring the Facts and "Reality" of our lives which plummets us into the depths of fantasy and illusion.

10. This is why so many men in their 30s and 40s are wrapped up in mind-numbing activities such as video-gaming, porn and social media

surfing. Get off the goddamn game systems and your cell phone, Brother! You're living in a fantasy land!

11. Men & women today have become so used to lying and so used to not dealing with the facts, the average person can't even take a picture of themselves without filtering it 75 fucking times and then posting it on Instagram as if they had just taken it on a whim. Then we take this over-filtered image and declare:

"This is ME!"

No, it's *not YOU*. It's a filtered version of you.

12. Then the real problems begin when you start to put those filtered images out into the marketplace and the marketplace begins to fall in love with this fantasy-filtered version you…which of course is not YOU.

13. Hey, I did this too. For years I was Business Suit-Guy. During the Suit-Guy years I would see people at church or the office, and then I would go to the grocery store and run into the same people without even recognizing them because I didn't have my suit on and neither did they.

14. We didn't recognize each other because we became radically different people at the office and church than we were in our "normal" day-to-day lives.

## The Reality of the Unreality

15. Reality television was initially created as an attempt to bring realness to the marketplace, yet it's turned into scripted bullshit meant to look unprompted when it's just as scripted as any other sitcom or movie you have ever watched.

16. Social media was built as a platform for us to "Be Real" with each other, giving us a deeper look into reality in each other's lives throughout the globe. Yet even with that being said, software creators have given us a ton of other ways to filter the shit out of what is real and deliver up to the social media world more Un-Reality.

## Un-Reality has Become the New Reality

17. We're such liars to ourselves and to each other because we can't even see ourselves anymore. We have become so filtered as men, we cannot tell what's real or not. When we've told ourselves the heavily edited story for so long, it becomes almost impossible for us to see the facts.

18. I was in the mortgage banking world for years. We would get people that would call our offices all the time with the following dialogue:

"I'm about to lose my home to foreclosure, can you help?"

"When are you scheduled to be foreclosed on?"

"Friday."

"Dude, it's Wednesday. There's nothing I can really do for you this late in the game."

"But I'm gonna lose my house by Friday. Isn't there something you can do?"

"No. Dude, how long did you know you were having financial problems with this?"

"Well, for, like, a year."

"Why didn't you call us like three months ago, or six months, or a year ago?!"

"I was too embarrassed."

19. This situation parallels what most men I run into these days are facing: they stay stuck in unreality until it's too late and the Foreclosure of Life is impossible to stop. The marriage is going to divorce, the business is going to bankruptcy or the kids are so far gone that the last semblance of a conversation you had with them was, "Fuck off, Dad."

20. These are the Men that are pretending like their marriage is "good" even though the reality is that it is sexless and disconnected. If you're in a marriage right now that you're having sex once every two to three months or longer, you are in a sexless marriage. I am also certain it is not her fault but it is how you as a man have chosen to show up: Sedated.

## The Facts We Pretend to Ignore

21. Think of a situation you have continued to ignore in your life. I had an aunt like this; she would ignore how much marijuana my cousins were smoking. She was like "Oh my kids, my kids are so great. They're just so great." But then I was the jackass pointing out the reality that both her sons were potheads who were lazy as shit instead of going along with her ignorant oblivion. Of course it was easier for her to call me an asshole than to deal with the reality of her sons' drug problems.

22. For most men, it's easier to pretend like you don't see the problem. We think it's easier to avoid the facts today. Men look in their bank accounts and they ignore what they see. We generally don't want to look at the facts of how "off" life results have become. It is not unusual for a man to refuse to Wake Up until life literally hands his ass to him financially, through disease or divorce.

23. I was talking with a fellow Warrior in my program a while ago about how his wife had been cheating on him for the past ten years. Big businessman and his wife was cheating on him for *ten years*. As we were sitting there at dinner the conversation went as followed:

24. "So, your wife has been cheating on you over ten years with multiple partners yet you're telling me this is a surprise and that you didn't know?"

"No, I didn't know."

25. "Okay. First off, fuck you for lying. Now, I don't believe that you didn't know. You might have decided to ignore the signs that this shit was happening, but don't sit here and pretend like you didn't know. You did know. You run a hundred million-dollar a year empire and somehow this one just slid past the goalie? Come on, man. You're not a dumbass. What are you not clear about? How about we address the real issue: you knew your marriage wasn't healthy and yet you ignored all the late nights she was gone and the weekend getaways with her 'girlfriends.'"

26. He looked at me all offended, in his early sixties, and I knew what he wanted to say but he was stuck between his own story of Victimhood and the Truth. He also realized that we were sitting down for dinner because he had invested in me to slap the shit out of him and he was getting his money's worth.

## Getting Shit-Slapped

27. So now I'm going to slap the shit out of YOU, Brother. This is why you're reading this book. I slap you not because I hate you; it's actually quite the opposite. If you cannot deal with the facts of your own life, then you can't deal with reality, and if you can't deal with reality, you can't create a new possibility. It is impossible to create a new reality without a clear picture of your current reality.

28. The ONLY way you can have it all and live the Warrior's Way is to learn to love Reality. Not because it makes you spiritual or become some type of Personal Development Guru, but because it is crucial to creation.

29. Many men don't want to go to the doctor's office for a check-up because they know they've been abusing their body and are afraid to hear what the results may be.

30. They're like,

"Doctor, don't give me the facts. Please. I just want to stay in unreality because if I can stay there in my story in this game, somehow I'm convinced that this is going to turn out for me by some miracle."

31. And it never does. Put a Band-Aid on the truth all you want, but it will eventually get exposed after rotting within you. All you'll be left with is a festering sore and a mountain of Pain.

## Facing Facts

32. So let's say you are willing to look at the Facts and peel back the Band-Aid. What do you do with these facts once you've acquired them and are able to take out the War Map (journal) and deal with the infection?

33. Write down the facts from within the Core 4:

Here's where I really am today.

Here are the facts about my Body.

Here are the facts about my past behaviors.

Here's how I've abused it.

Here's what I've done.

Here are the drugs I've taken.

Here's the way I've eaten.

Here's the fitness I've done or not done.

34. Trust me, at either extreme: you can beat the shit out of yourself where you don't do enough or end up doing too much. In your Being & Balance:

Here are the facts about my spirituality.

Here is how I feel about my relationship with God.

I don't know if I believe what my parents believe.

I don't know if I feel these things that they say they feel.

I don't know.

Or, I do know. But I'm scared to say because that might cause conflict inside these social agreements of my relationships, so here's where I really am.

Here are the facts about my spiritual purpose.

Here are the facts about my religious experience.

Here are the facts about my relationship with God.

35. Here are the facts. I'm going to write them down. This is how I've shown up or how I've not shown up. They're not good or bad. They're not right or wrong. They're not righteous or wicked. They're just simply the facts. And I'm going to stop omitting the facts from my life. I'm going to look at the numbers. These are the words my CFO gives me constantly. "Look at the numbers and live, my friend. Look at the numbers and live."

## The Foundation of the Warrior Games

36. Every marketing, sales, and fulfillment system in my businesses requires me to look at the facts. Many times these facts are the numbers which tell a story of their own and have the power to guide me to Big Time Results.

37. Inside of the Game we call the Warrior's Way, you must be willing to look at the facts and investigate the story that they are telling you.

38. If you can't start looking at the facts, then you will never look at the numbers which leads to the natural consequence of never telling the true story. You will tell a story that destroys; not a story that empowers.

39. And so we start with this foundational idea as we continue through the Core:

What are the facts about my Business?

Where am I at financially right now?

What does my bank account look like, for real, today?

What do my marketing skills look like?

What do my sales skills look like?

What do my leadership skills look like?

What are the facts?

40. You have *got* to become absolutely committed to the truth inside your life in which you must create the story that says "I can deal with reality, but what I *can't* deal with is unreality. What I can't manage are the stories. What I can't manage are the assumptions. What I can't manage are the fucking lies. I can't manage that shit because that's not real; it's fantasy."

41. Reality is staring you in the face every single day. If you're like me, and how I was for so long, it is so scary because of the stories you and I have told ourselves in our mind about being bad, awful, wrong, and broken, which have all twisted our reality.

42. Most men just choose to close the book on the truth and pretend like the facts don't exist. Then they wonder why their marriage never works out. Why the people around them never stay. They wonder why their relationships have no depth.

43. Well it's simple. Because you're a fucking liar.

## The Social Media Façade

44. Here we go with contradictions in social media again. I see couples go within weeks of sharing how amazing their life is being married to each other only to reading a post out of left field from one of them a few weeks later stating:

45. "I really want to thank all of my friends out in social media for supporting my family through this rough time as I'm going through this divorce."

What the hell?!

Three weeks ago:

"Oh, we're best friends. We never fight, I just love you."

Now:

"Forget you, bitch, I'm out."

Whoa, dude.

Wait a second.

How did this happen

How did this *happen*?!

46. Maybe it wouldn't have gotten to "forget you bitch, I'm out" if you had actually just told her the truth. Maybe if you made your reality more of what you had been mimicking on social media you wouldn't be alone. If you had looked at the facts, you would see that you were an asshole. You were a douche bag, not showing up, when you should have been taking her on actual dates instead of posting about that one date you did years ago that someone else tagged you on. You weren't spending time investing in her. You were trying to make withdrawals every single day, yet you deposited nothing.

47. Not on her, my friend.

That's on you.

48. Inside of Warrior, the fact is this:

You are at cause for your life.

49. No one—not your wife, kids, friends, clients, business partners, the government, nobody—is responsible for your facts but you. Inside of Warrior, you will fail the Game if you try to blame somebody else for your facts.

## The Facts Will Set You Free

50. Deal with the facts.

The facts will set you free.

They say the truth will set you free.

51. Well, the truth is called the facts. The facts will set you free. *The facts will set you free.* The facts will set you free because the facts allow you to be. To be what? To be clear. Here's what is. These are the facts. No bullshit. No hiding. I'm standing naked before you here. Here's the truth: If I cut all the stories away, here's what's really going on.

52. From that foundation of facts comes the fury of freedom.

## Chapter 6:
## POINTS TO PONDER FROM THE GENERAL'S TENT

- **POINT #1:** Facts are data points. Your Target is to be able to back away from them in the most neutral position as possible and say okay, here are the facts and the truth to me the way I see it today.

- **POINT #2:** It is impossible to create a new reality without a clear picture of your current reality.

- **POINT #3:** Make a list about your Facts through journaling on your War Map. Acknowledge your realities as what they are, which then gives you an opportunity to move forward with an honest approach towards reality.

- **POINT #4:** No one is responsible for your Facts but you. When you realize this, where they had before held you captive, the facts will now set you free.

# WARRIOR WITNESS:

## M.M., California USA:

*"Took a stab in the dark and listened to this earlier this morning. I felt a huge spotlight on something I do that until now I would have never even thought of as not looking at the facts. For example, my wife will say, 'Hey, we went in the red 20k last month personally,' and my first response is anger, like she fucking did something wrong. Next is a thought of "Shit!!! Then I ask to see all of the expenditures and justify the FACTS."*

*Saying shit like, 'Well, we paid taxes, we went on vacation, the dog needed veneers, you get the point.*

*Justify the facts = Life*

*Instead of looking at the facts and understanding that regardless of what they say, they are the facts.*

*I would say that I spend more time in a justification place disappointing my body, being, balance, and businesses, than I ever do basking in the facts…Scary."*

---

## J.F., South Carolina, USA:

*"Be Real—I have a dark side that gets pissed off and can't let shit go. It festers inside of me to the point where I villainize people and begin to hate/resent them….*

*It's happened with my queen, with "friends" with family.*

*My pride doesn't let me go first to them and say "hey I'm fucking pissed at you and I'm not even really sure if it's fair or if you deserve it, but it is true nonetheless."*

*I also catch myself dreaming of how my life should be but not actually putting pen to paper and making it happen.*

*I resent my queen for not seeing me as the man I WANT to be…Even though I am not him. I want the credit and appreciation he deserves even though I have not put in the work to BE HIM.*

*People tell me all the time how successful I am and how I'm killing it at life… And I tend to let them think that…but it's a lie. I don't make much money, my body is so-so, and my relationship is on the brink.*

*Spirituality is a 1 out of 100.*

*I can fake being a 2-3 dimensional douche bag but I'm really 0-1…And I need to figure this out fast or I'll be looking back wondering what the fuck I was thinking and how I could possibly let it all slip through my fingers."*

---

## A.C., California, USA:

*"If it was easy, everyone would do it…everyone would have it all…but it's not easy and it's going to be hard as fuck!!!! It's going to be hard as fuck to retain your mind to think in a different way…to process in a different way. If your shit is upside down right now YOU are the only one who can make the decision to change. So if you are 'in the drift' hang half of your body off the life raft into the water, hold on with both hands and kick like hell until you land on your own private island YOU created. One foot at a time, Brother…"*

---

## A.L., Meridian, Idaho, USA:

*"The fact is that I am so fucking tired of being what I think everyone else wants me to be. I want to just be me. I want to be a warrior king and I know I cannot be any fucking thing near it if I don't stop spinning the plates that are so unnecessary. I am so overwhelmed and disappointed with my current state. I know I am here for more than this and I am committed to DOING THE FUCKING WORK!*

---

## E.M., Bothell, Washington, USA:

*"As a lifetime liar… digging deep into the facts of my life is painful beyond words. I see the truth in it that I have no shot of finding my way out of hell if I don't first admit that I am actually in hell. Getting REAL , down to the most guarded secrets and lies I've held onto in my life required something of me I wasn't sure I had two days ago. Courage to crush the fears of rejection and self loathing I've held inside for years!!"*

---

## T.M., Georgia, USA :

*"Truth is, I don't want to look at the facts of my life. They tell a story that I don't want to listen to. They expose me as a fraud and they are a suffocating burden. No one's fault but my own. My facts are a direct result of my story, but that doesn't mean I want to look in the mirror and acknowledge them. That doesn't mean that I have the emotional fortitude to deal with them and the*

*dark realities of my life that they illuminate. Besides, I've gotten REALLY good at ignoring them. Fuck this is hard."*

## I.M., Medina, Washington:

*"What do the facts make you do? The facts simply make you stop lying and most importantly- they make you stop lying to yourself. It is the brutal honesty to the most important person that I am responsible for- and that is me. I have had every reason to shift that responsibility internally. Externally- I would stand-up and take responsibility for my team and for my actions. Internally- I would be seething- looking for every reason not to look at the hard facts about myself! Gentlemen- I really think this is the underpinning of the entire Code. Being Real is being brutally, radically honest with myself. Without the anchors of judgment, guilt or shame- the brutal honesty is the key to shedding the dysfunctional and long-standing defense mechanisms- and owning who I really am and taking sole responsibility for who I want to be. Empowering!"*

# THE CODE
## Chapter 7: (RAW FEELINGS)

Part Two of the Code is to get Raw with feelings. It's what begins the journey to power and the feelings linked up to those facts discussed in the last chapter.

## SECTION TWO
# THE CODE

## CHAPTER SEVEN
# RAW (FEELINGS)

"It matters not how strait the gate,
How charged with punishments the scroll,
I am the master of my fate,
I am the captain of my soul."

**-William Ernest Henley**
"Invictus" excerpt

---

## Separating the Feelings and Facts

1. Here are several of the facts in my own life. My first marriage lasted a year and a half; my now ex-wife and I got married and divorced within 18 months. During that short time, I got cancer, she had our son Parker, and we got divorced. All Facts. The Feelings around these facts have been *very* different, however.

2. It's one thing for me to say, "Well, you know what, our first night we had sex seven times. I broke the record out of all my friends. We had sex *seven times* on our wedding night!"

3. Yeah, that's a fact. And then there's the feelings that are linked up to that as a man now looking back asking himself, "What was I thinking?! What kind of asshole turns his wife into a sex slave the first night of marriage and doesn't even begin to consider how she's feeling?"

4. She was young (only 19), neither one of us had had sex before we were married so the Game was new for both of us and yet here I was in this married relationship hurt, confused and so was she.

5. The day after that first night my young bride looked at me and I looked at her; we both thought, "What have we done? We should never have gotten married."

6. Yes, I can relate to you the facts of the number of times we were separated and the number of times we got back together. I can tell you the fact that I laid there in my hospital bed, coming out of my first cancer surgery of almost 10 hours, alone, while my ex-wife was shopping with her mother, not really caring if I came out of surgery alive or not.

7. I can write about that final fight we had when I drove away from her home in Calgary Alberta, Canada. My nine-month-old son, who is now a teenager, was leaning up against the screen door with his hands pressed up against the frame as I pulled away.

8. Yes, I can speak of a drive that took 12 hours to go to my parents' home in search of support only to end up as a crumbled emotional mess, lying on their front doorstep in the middle of the night, not wanting to bother them until they woke up in the morning.

9. I can tell you what it's like to be married again and to be in a relationship with a woman a second time that is so painful. Lying in the same bed as her, night after night and feeling so helpless to connect and longing for her touch and yet never receiving it.

10. Yes, I can share all those facts with you, but what becomes difficult to describe are the *feelings* attached to all of those facts.

## Shame to Express Myself

11. Truth was, I didn't share much with anybody. I was too ashamed that I had feelings.[18] Even if I could muster the courage to share the facts, I was so emotionally disconnected, that I couldn't actually differentiate the facts from the feelings that were connected to those facts. Instead, I would just suppress and ignore those feelings I was having.

---

[18]  Refer back to Chapter 2: The Painful Problem as well as WD Systemized Sedation of Men

12. So yes, I would *tell* the truth (Real) but I wouldn't *feel* the truth (Raw) and so my life continued to not work.

13. I wouldn't talk about how I felt with my wife, my family or my friends. I wouldn't talk about how alone I felt as I stood at cocktail parties with my wife who was so beautiful, everybody looking at us thinking "you two must be the happiest couple on earth." I couldn't tell them how it felt to have two to three months go by at a time without sexual intimacy between my wife and me.

14. I couldn't tell anyone what it felt like at the time when my business began to implode and I took it upon myself to find other jobs for my key players, which in 2007 included my brother-in-laws and all my sisters who worked for me, only to have several of them turn their backs on me when I was in deep pain and struggling months later in 2008.

15. Nobody knew how I felt when I had no money and struggled to even get enough in the bank account to pay for the groceries.

## My Breaking Point

16. One day, it all became too much. Every day that went by, ignoring the feelings inside my soul, the questions and the emotions and the frustration and the anger and the rage grew inside of me. And it was quite literally killing me.

17. Although I didn't know what would happen or what the proper way was to do anything, I just knew that I could not keep this emotional shit inside me anymore.

18. I didn't speak about how much it hurt inside to watch people I had given my life to for years not give a fuck about me when I was a crumbled mess on the floor in tears. In the most crucial moments when I needed fucking help to climb out of the goddamn hole I was in, no one was there. Many of these people I had given hundreds of thousands of dollars when they needed help, and yet when I needed a lifeline there was no rope thrown down to aid me. They weren't there.

19. I couldn't tell you how it felt to be accepted as a "brother" inside a church as long as I said and did the right things, but the minute I had problems,

questions, or concerns, I was ostracized, an outcast no longer accepted as a brother anymore. What was once praise for my Voice became persecution.

20. You want to be my conditional friend?

21. You want to be in my life conditionally?

22. This is how I really feel…

Fuck you.

## Crashing Waves of Stacked Up Feelings

23. So all of that had to come out somehow, right? And it would; at all the wrong times. Something would happen (and it was always something small, too), which would blow the recipient of my Rage away. All of this fire, fury, rage, sorrow and pain would come out in the craziest situations.

24. I couldn't see anyone anymore for who they were. My wife, my kids, business partners, clients, nothing. I just became this blood hungry maniac who would vomit these emotions onto the marketplace triggered by something small, unleashing as my response massive amounts of Large Pain, yet never releasing anything of worth.

## Waiting to Explode While Trying to Free the Dark Warrior

25. In my world there were these moments of explosion that would come up because I wasn't giving myself freedom to be free about what I felt. So, every single day I wouldn't tell anyone how I felt; I would just wait a few months and unleash. Some people blow up and they destroy themselves; I blow up and I start emotionally murdering everyone.

26. This Dark Warrior inside me was a gateway to my power, but see, his job was to sustain life. When I was unwilling to sustain my own life he would come out and destroy everything in order to set me free.

## "I'm Doing Awesome!"

27. I was taught a powerful lesson one day while walking down the street. We were on our way to the church house for Sabbath service and there was this young teenage girl who was passing by us on the sidewalk. We engaged in the typical interaction and exchange people have with each

other, but this young girl changed my life forever. As she was walking by, I asked out of common courtesy, "How are you doing?" and she replied, "I'm doing awesome!" What? What do you mean you're doing awesome? I thought. My mind had no way to compute with "Awesome" because all it was programmed for was "I'm good."

28. Why did I want to kill everybody? Well, because my life was "good;" i.e. I was a fucking liar. And then here was this girl who says, "My life is awesome."

29. Her reply inspired an idea that decided that I'm going to be honest about my feelings and about where I'm at. I'm going to stop apologizing for how I feel, even if I'm angry, or feeling happy; I'm going to stop apologizing for being excited. I'm going to stop suppressing my excitement just because everyone around me fucking hates their lives.

## Absolutely Shitty Feels Pretty Good

30. If I'm really angry, I'm not going to pretend I'm really happy, even though this might offend people. No, I'm actually going to be pissed and I'm going to try on this idea of being completely honest about how I feel.

31. It was quite an interesting journey; the first experience occurring when I walked into the local grocery store. It was a horrible morning from the start after getting in a fight with my wife, and things were continuing to go downhill.[19]

32. I went into this grocery store and as I was checking out in the line, the cashier asked me the typical question all cashiers ask customers: "How are you doing?"

33. My response?

"Absolutely shitty."

34. Everybody in the line froze…Like I had just spread a virus, or cancer had just been dropped from my mouth in the line, and anybody within a 10-foot radius of me was going to be infected. So, people started moving

---

[19] Fun tip about Garrett if you didn't already know: no morning workout = formula for disaster.

out of the line, not knowing what to do with themselves. And yet, I was standing there watching it and thought,

35. "I actually feel a lot better now that I told you guys that I feel pretty shitty and yet now all of you guys are feeling pretty shitty and I'm feeling just fine."

36. Wait a second! There might be something to this shit of telling the truth about how I'm feeling! So I continued to practice this Raw truth-telling. One day I saw the reflection of my wife changing from a mirror hanging on the closet door, and she was looking amazing, but I thought I was supposed to pretend like I wasn't horny out of my mind seeing her nearly naked. As if somehow experiencing the feeling that my wife is amazingly sexy is a sin.

37. So you know what I did? I said to myself, "Forget it. I'm just going to tell her how I'm really feeling." I was like,

"You are so hot."

38. She stopped and looked at me so I stated,

"I would love to make love to you, right here, right now."

39. Now, just because I got Real it didn't mean that anything actually changed in that moment. I got passionately denied by Danielle sexually because we were not quite at the point in the reconstruction of our relationship for that to happen, but it also helped me move further down this journey of "Raw."

## Learning to Honestly Feel

40. I remember the day I declared to myself in the mirror:

## "I'm going to allow myself to be my feelings, whatever they are."

41. So this journey began; a discovery about these feelings linked up to the facts. I started to see this interesting connection, that the stories that I told were directly linked to the feelings that I was having.

42. For the first time in my life, I started to see that my stories were driving my feelings about the Game I was living. My facts were clear or unclear,

based upon the stories I was telling about them. The feelings I was feeling linked up to the stories I was telling.

43. This trifecta between my Feelings, my Stories and the Facts worked together somehow and I was just at the beginning on my road of discovery. As the second piece of this Code, Being Raw became about separating my feelings from the facts. Playing the game of Letting Feelings Out isn't an easy one to pick up on as it becomes something we all have to learn, shifting the mentality of what it means to be a man and hide our feelings which have been programmed within us since birth. Our children are always doing it, and yet we punish them for having feelings and displaying them.

## The Teeter-Totter Effect Revisited

44. I have three children. Maybe you have children, maybe you don't, but I can tell you right now most of us were not raised to say "it's okay to have feelings."

45. We were programmed that we can have some feelings while out in public, but if we have these other feelings, those are NOT OK and you don't ever say or express them in public. There were certain feelings that were okay, that if you have these feelings it's acceptable, but if you have these other feelings, you're punished and sent to your room or disciplined for being inappropriate.

46. So there we are back on the teeter-totter again. We'll have feelings that end up on the acceptable list according to one group of people, so therefore we can talk about them. Especially as men. Then within that same group of people they will have another list of unacceptable feelings that must be suppressed. These are the ones that we're supposed to pretend don't exist and that no one else has them…

Right?

47. Not if you live by the Code.

48. I am going to guide you through the process of how to let those emotions out productively.

49. If you can't be honest about the Facts, then you can't be honest about the Feelings. If you don't get your feelings out, they become weapons of destruction and instead operate like a ticking time bomb waiting to explode.

50. Once you release these percolating feelings—that aren't bad or wrong—life gets exciting because you are no longer in your own way of getting what you want in order to have it all.

## Honestly Reversing Your Feelings

51. The feelings you're having, once investigated, might be challenged and altered and leveraged to allow you to get what you want out of your marriage, body, business and life. But if you can't be honest about what you're feeling right now, then you literally have nothing to work with.

52. If you have no palette to paint on, if you have no clay to mold, you've got nothing to work with except a fantasy. You can't do shit with that because it's not real, therefore you can't change it. You can't build anything if you don't have something tangible to work with in the first place. If you can't fucking look at reality, you cannot build a new possibility.

That is it.

The End.

53. So you decide to look at your spirituality and say,

"Okay, how do I feel now?"

54. You see, six years ago when I was sitting inside the church I was raised in, I wanted to vomit in my mouth; I just couldn't be there anymore with this new honesty of the Code in my life. I just couldn't pretend anymore. It didn't mean that the church was wrong or broken, or the people there had a problem. It just meant for me, it was no longer working.

55. Going to church every week angry, wanting to fucking punch everyone in the face was not the greatest feeling and seems a little contradictory. This is probably not a healthy pattern and it definitely wasn't going to give me what I wanted, but I had to be honest about my judgment, how I felt and where I was.

## Just Being Honest

56. My marriage was broken in 2009; it was completely broken. It hurt to be in a second marriage, failing for a second time knowing that it was all on me. It hurt. But somehow I didn't recognize that just being honest about those exact thoughts were the gateway to my freedom: being honest about how sad I was and owning the reality that I had created it was the start to my liberation, even if I didn't quite realize it yet at the time.

57. I knew I honestly didn't know how to be a husband. I was scared to death of my wife, and I didn't know how to be honest with her. I was more than just a little intimidated by her. I know; seems weird. I'm an athletic 6'2, 200 pounds and my wife is a petite 5'3, 105 pounds.

58. How the hell should I be intimidated by her?

Like she's going to whoop my ass or something?!

59. Well, I was scared of her emotionally because I was lying and knew that wasn't a place of any kind of power.

## When Business Is Not Working

60. In Business, I hated doing what I was doing but I couldn't be honest about what I felt. I was a horrible businessman because I couldn't deal with the truth of my feelings and definitely ignored my gut instincts and the Voice inside. Even though I was able to create really big shit, it never really lasted because I couldn't Get Real or Raw about any of it.

61. I would have employees that were on board, or partners that I knew needed to go, moves that needed to be made, but I was scared so I wouldn't make them. The Voice inside of me was drowning in my Suppression, hence the actions I was taking were weak.

62. I would be looking at the numbers financially and knew we were having problems, but lacked the balls to actually speak the Real, Raw truth about what I was seeing, let alone do anything about the bloodbath that was coming.

63. This was a completely bipolar time in my business life: on one side of the equation I was feeling focused and on fire, while on the other side

I wanted to torch everyone and everything to the ground. The confusion came when I simply did not acknowledge what I was feeling.

64. Occasionally I would release:

"Ah, that felt nice to get it out."

And when I did I always felt the same reminder:

"What was I worried about?"

## Linking Feelings to Facts

65. So, in summary, my feelings are linked up to the facts and there's a tool that we're going to introduce that will allow you to possibly adjust and be able to see the story that's driving the feelings. You may find, as I did, that the stories that you're telling about the feelings are triggered *by* the stories that you're having about the facts. The Code is to #1: Be Real as you tell the truth about the Facts, while #2 is to Get Raw by letting your feelings flow with connection to the facts.

### Chapter 7
### POINTS TO PONDER FROM THE GENERAL'S TENT

- **POINT #1:** Facts (Real) and Feelings (Raw) both occur, but are also VERY different parts of any experience. The feelings within a situation are much harder to define.

- **POINT #2:** We all have a Dark Warrior that wants to be unleashed. If you can't be honest about the Facts, then you can't be honest about the Feelings. If you don't get your feelings out, they become weapons of destruction and instead operate like a ticking time bomb waiting to explode.

- **POINT #3:** There is a trifecta that occurs between our feelings, stories, and facts, in which the stories that we tell are directly linked to the feelings that we have; all three are separate yet linked together.

- **POINT #4:** We will remain confused if we don't acknowledge the feelings that we are feeling in any situation we encounter.

# WARRIOR WITNESS:

## R.C., Illinois, USA:

*"Lesson learned on Raw: Results will always speak for themselves but without addressing your feelings, results can be masked by reasons. Get raw, abandon the reasons; reasons are excuses. Fuck the excuses….Face the feelings and you can face the facts!*

*My truth: I rarely tell anyone how I feel. Life is always fucking wonderful… But it's not. Some days it sucks shit but I smile, laugh and say I'm living the dream. Holding it in is fucking killing me. I'm done holding it in."*

## A.S., USA:

*"This is probably my hardest lesson to be learned for me. Since my childhood and through my adult life I have always been in a role of leadership. I have always been the example and source of strength and enlightenment. This was taken to the extreme when I was presented a Superman cape by my friends who refer to me as SuperSplaver. So I was never given permission; I never gave myself permission to express my feelings and get Raw. When I almost lost my wife to the hemorrhagic stroke that uncovered her tumor, I was the Rock and guiding force that brought my kids and my community forward. When she underwent her dangerous surgery to remove the tumor in the center of her brain several years ago, then too I had to suck it up and be the man. I can tell you Thank God she has pulled through, Thank God she is a fighter, Thank God that operation and radiation didn't kill her. But I've been dragging this shit around for way too long and I have been self-medicating by immersing myself in my work, community work as well as CrossFit. It has pulled me away from all that I have fought so damn hard for over the years and it's my fault I didn't give myself permission to get raw.*

*This past week when my friend died, it brought back many of the emotions I had undergone during this trying time. It threw me back to the black pit of emotions and loneliness. I know I need to do the work. I know I need to get real, raw and relevant. I know I need to deal with all that I have bottled up inside for so much time.*

*I think for the first time I found myself bawling my eyes out while sitting in my car reciting Invictus this morning. Not a pretty sight but kinda made me feel better knowing that I can and will overcome.*

*There is much that must be done.*

*I am the master of my fate. I am the captain of my soul!!!!!"*

## M.A., Washington, USA:

*"For the first time I'm listening to "Raw" and am completely lost. I've been through it several times before and it always evoked a strong response, knowing that I have felt that suppressed feeling forever. But for the first time today, I realize I don't know HOW to get to those feelings. I mean, I can relate to some superficial sadness and anxiety about Facts when I think of them and review my list, but I've been so numb to them for so long, with the feelings coming up randomly (and intensely). I don't know how to access them "on demand." It's like they just sit way down deep waiting for the wrong time to pop up and overtake me. In those cases, the feelings rule over me, not the other way around. I need the ability to access and acknowledge them on my terms, not when they come out on their own at all the wrong times. I now know that they are creating the stories in my head and that those stories are limiting my actions. And that if I can get to them, I can control my stories instead of the other way around."*

## A.P., Victoria, Australia:

*"Ok…getting Raw. Here's where I'm at.*

*I'm out of shape and my body is no longer working for me. I've had 3+years of chronic pain that I've allowed to impact just about every area of my life.*

*I have no assets - gave away 75% of my wealth to my x wife because I felt guilty because I couldn't fix the relationship.*

*I constantly put other people's happiness before my own.*

*I don't feel connected to anything greater, I have no real passion in my life*

*I've lost my love for my current work and the practice is slowly but surely dying.*

*I've spent the last 15 years covering over all my emotions and I'm scared what will come if I let out the rage and anger that is just beneath the surface."*

## G.V.D, California, USA:

*"This whole 'feelings' chapter really got me thinking today. Why is it that we tend to hold on to this notion that sharing feelings is something women do,*

*kids do? I too have been convinced of this, not necessarily because I thought I needed to suppress certain or all feelings because it was not manly to do so, I have actually always considered myself to be a pretty emotional guy, but more so because I didn't think analyzing, sharing or even just exhibiting feelings was very practical. It didn't lead to anything. It was a waste of time. Women do that shit. We are supposed to be more pragmatic.*

*But I was wrong. What I think I come to realize now is that I have been omitting a great source of power and have missed great opportunities to plant seeds for growth and expansion. It's easy to call yourself 'emotional' when all you do is be selective in the feelings you exhibit. The only way I knew and the only way I was comfortable with."*

# THE CODE

## Chapter 8: RELEVANT (FOCUS)

What you focus on, you feel. In this chapter we go over the third pillar
of the Code: Relevant, which is a function of Focus.

SECTION TWO
# THE CODE

CHAPTER EIGHT
# RELEVANT (FOCUS)

*"When you can't make them see the light, make them feel the heat."*

**-Ronald Reagan**

---

1. We have now reached component number three of the Code: Relevant. You have Real, Raw, and now you have Relevant. Relevancy is a function of Focus. Real was a function of Facts and Raw was a function of Feelings, but your relevancy becomes the Focus of those facts and feelings.

2. Your Focus dictates what you Feel.

3. Your Focus is what drives your Perspective.

4. Your Perspective drives all your Actions.

5. Your Actions deliver results.

## A World of Perspectives

6. Your perspective is the way you see the world; an inside view of the facts and rules about how life is. This perspective rotates on an axis of your focus. Most men that I meet day-to-day do not go around with a strategic focus about anything. There's literally no focused strategic action in life, just a series of decisions driven by reaction from what is happening to them.

7. Wait, I take that back. There *is* one focus: "How do I continue to tell the stories that other people want to hear so that I can continue to be accepted?"

8. There is a driving desire inside of all of us as human beings to be accepted for who we are and feel significant to others, even if it requires lying. We lie so that we fit in, to assure that we are part of the group and accepted.

9. So we tell people the stories we think they want to hear, not realizing that they were lying to us also. I was lying, they were lying, neither one of us were telling the truth. Therefore, what kind of relationship did we actually have except for some fantasy bullshit?

10. We will never have relationships that matter when they are built on lies.

## Wandering Generalities Vs Meaningful Specifics

11. The reality of your life with this worldview focus also inserts this other concept that a friend of mine, years ago introduced to me. It goes like this: if you do not have a plan, (Focus) for your life, don't worry, someone else will plan it for you.

12. Most men that I know are wandering generalities, a phrase I first heard from the badass personal development trainer Zig Ziglar. I like that idea: Wandering generalities versus meaningful specifics.

13. So how does a Wandering Generality Man operate? He simply reacts like a dog to the day.

14. He wakes up and says,

"Well, I think I'm going to. you know, I'm going to go do this...stuff.... over....here."

15. Or you talk to a Wandering Generality Businessman and ask,

"What's your goal?"

16. "We're going to be a billion-dollar company."

"Why do you want to be a billion-dollar company?"

17. "Well, because we want to show that we can do it, yeah."

"Nice. How much have you done?"

18. "We made $1200 dollars last week."

19. Well, shit. You've got a long way still to go.

20. Focus isn't just about what you're wanting. Focus is about being honest about where you want to go, driven by what you are seeing ,and about where you actually are today.

21. As I was starting to uncover this Code and the conversation of sharing my truth, I would say,

22. "Hey, listen! Here are the facts—here are my feelings."

23. The problem was, I had no focus. Instead of being a sniper rifle with a clear target, I had no real focus for my feelings and the facts that I was seeing, except that I wanted to be free.

## Relieving the Emotional Constipation

24. In the beginning, you're just going to feel amazing simply by telling the truth after being so suppressed. It's like being constipated and finally taking a big crap. Total relief. You're like this big ass emotionally constipated Man and once you release the constipation everything feels amazing.

25. Once you get used to it, Emotional Release will feel absolutely awesome. This is very much like being physically constipated. Imagine you have this huge piece of poo inside you. I'm going to name him Bob. Hey everybody, meet my poo baby, Bob. The problem is that Bob is actually killing you and when you finally let him out, he's so massive that he often clogs the toilet.

26. Emotional constipation is no different than physical constipation. While you may not be walking around with a big ass poo baby named Bob inside your intestines, I can tell you right now you're walking around with a big ass emotional poo baby called Bob all day long.

27. In the beginning, sometimes, you're just going to have to let it out. We can't even try to have a conversation about adjusting your emotional diet because you've got such a big ass poo baby demanding all of your attention until it comes out, which may require an adjustment in order for that to happen.

# What Do You Want?

28. Then what? We know that you don't want a big, emotional poo baby again, so what do you want?

"What do you mean by that Garrett? Could you be a little more specific?"

29. "Okay, okay, let me go ahead and slow this down for you one more time:

"What. Do. You. Want?"

30. How do most men respond?

31. "I don't know. I don't know what I want."

32. Can you see the problem here?

33. If I came to your house with a GoPro® camera strapped on my forehead and followed you around for a day, what would I see?

34. Could you show me what it is you want?

35. Can you clearly and metrically-based tell me the outcome you are moving toward to create over the next 90 days? Over the next 60 days? Over the next 30 days? Over the next 7 days? Can you tell me? Can you tell yourself?

36. The reality is, you can't.

37. But don't worry; most men cannot. Hell, I couldn't. I had no idea. It wasn't even on the radar of the worldview that said, "Garrett, you should probably have some focus in your life." People told me this all the time, trying to get me to take pills in order to focus all of my wandering attention into one, boring zombie. Good thing I didn't. I told everyone to fuck off and that I was never going to take their pills. I'm crazy and I'm going to stay that way; leave me alone.

# Focusing On Your Light

38. You're crazy and that is awesome in my book. My only suggestion is to learn how to be relevant with your crazy. See, relevancy becomes the focus of your energy. I can sit here with the lights on in the video recording studio, shining bright but they are not burning me. They're just lights; and

the light shining from them is focused enough to let me see but not so focused that they burn me.

39. But if I take all of the light from these bulbs and begin to focus them down into a small laser, that same light that didn't burn or do much does something now. The bulbs that were simply providing light become a heat that can cut. If you have no focus, if we have no relevancy to what we're saying and what we're doing in this Real and Raw conversation, then it doesn't really matter.

## Adding Focus to the Circus Act:
## Bringing About Relevant Change

40. Life will not change as you find yourself in a karmic cul-de-sac, continuing to loop and loop until you find relevancy in the Real and Raw experience. So, what brings about change then? What brings out the possibility from being a one-dimensional (maybe two-dimensional at best) man to a Four-Dimensional Liberated Warrior King?

Relevancy in your life.

41. This means that when you wake up today, you have a focus for where you're trying to go today, tomorrow, next week, next month, and this quarter. You have a focus for your Core 4: Body, Being, Balance, and Business.

That is it.

42. So when shit gets in the way, when my feelings come to play and my facts stand in the way of getting me what I want, I can internalize and investigate my feelings about those facts and then channel both of those into a sniper rifle weapon of relevancy to focus on the target of getting what I truly want.

43. The moment I saw this connection, I went from this scatterbrained dude who was just doing drive-by shootings of the mouth, to having Real and Raw strategic conversations that allowed me to take out specific targets.

44. In the beginning, I was a bit of a circus act with it: I'd go into networking events, we'd sit down and Jimmy would be like, "All right. Now we've gotten to the time where we're going to introduce ourselves. We're going to go

around the room and take a moment to just say 'Hello, my name's Jimmy. I'm a real estate broker and I like to sell real estate. Today I'm looking for a few good referrals that you might send my way.'"

45. So, Jimmy would stand up there and talk about his real estate and I would stand up there and I would say, "Hello, my name is Garrett, I was sexually abused as a kid, I cheated on my wife, and I have had alcohol problems most of my life. I built and lost several really big businesses. I had to fire my mom and all my sisters at the end of one of those business failures and I just left my church. I have no idea what I'm doing in business right now. I don't have very much money; I just sold my $12,000 Ironman bike for $2,000. That was awful. The most sexual interaction I've had with my wife in the last six months was a hand job."

BOOOM!

46. I would do this at these networking events and oh, the poor people at my table. I would just randomly share facts and more than anything, it started to become a circus game for me of power through intimidation. I knew I could get a reaction out of people the more edgy my Speak was.

47. I wasn't lying about my facts: I was just being super real and not relevant about it. I'd be like sitting there and people would walk by and ask me, "What do you think about that girl?"

48. And I'd say,

"I think she's amazing. I think she's totally hot."

49. They'd be like, "Dude, aren't you married?"

"I'm totally married, but I can still think she's totally hot. Look at her!"

50. It just became this weird game of trying to be a one upper. So, somehow I managed to mess up Real and Raw just like you will if you're not careful. What changed it for me and must be added by you is the Relevancy. This gave me a Focus that in business at those networking events I could have a Real and Raw conversation that will ultimately be Relevant in getting me what I want.

## Releasing the Poo Baby for Good

51. Some of you cannot think straight about the Doctrine we've been discussing here in the Black Box yet because you have been emotionally constipated for so long. We have got to get that large emotional poo baby out of you before you ever have a chance to change your diet or the way you live or operate. You cannot see clearly, so when I ask, "What do you want?" you're like, "Oh, the poo baby!"

52. Get it out! In order for some of you to release, you have to be in a colonic environment where you can just yell and scream and break shit and shoot guns and beat things and just be like "Ahh. Poo baby…" Just let it out because you've held it in for so long. This is why we created environments like Warrior Week and Warrior X, allowing a space for men to get out the shit and say,

53. "Here I am! I am a King! I am ready to return to the throne. I am going to get this crap out and flush it away forever."

## Focused Relevancy

54. This rage that we're feeling—it has to be released so we have the ability to see. We can take the facts and feelings, focusing them on what we want. We can say with these outcomes what we're searching towards in our Body, Being, Balance, and Business, "Here's where I'm going."

55. Relevancy is what brought the Focus; it's what brought the Focus to the Facts and to the Feelings.

56. I want you to take a look at your world right now. As we're having this conversation of the Code, it's just as much about being able to be honest about where you're going and what you're wanting as it is about being honest about the facts and feelings of how big you want your life to be.

## Living a Big Life

57. We talk about how big and great we want our lives to be while the people around us look at us, thinking we should learn to be content with a good life. Tell them to fuck off. These are the facts and here's how it feels

to search for these things but you know what? If we don't live by the Code, then we can't deal with the crap that occurs in life.

58. So, part of the Code empowers you to deal with the stuff that might have been painful from the past or is currently painful in the present. The Code helps channel the relevancy that you want so deeply and passionately. Most guys are not around individuals where they can be fully honest about this, which is why we have the Black Box Brotherhood inside Warrior.

## Getting Honest in Our Relevancy

59. Learning to be Real and Raw helps us get honest about where we are, but the third stage, Relevant, is what brings it all into Focus. It gives our statements a purpose, no longer just random people running around, dropping off emotional poo babies everywhere.

60. Oh well, I just dropped off my feelings, here you go.

61. Oh, I just blew up on you emotionally, here you go.

Why?

62. Not because it's wrong, bad or broken. It's one simple reality: randomly dropping off your emotions does not get you what you want. It will never get you what you want.

63. You must be committed to the following conversation:

·   I am willing to do the work about being honest with what I want.

· I'm going to set clear targets that allow me to move towards something so that when I'm feeling things, and I want to look at the facts, I can look at the facts of where I'm at and assess whether or not I'm on track.

· I want to be honest about the feelings that I have. I can do that because my feelings are either accelerating or decelerating.

64. In the end, our feelings are either empowering or they're dis-empowering us to focus and move towards what we want or away from what we want.

# Bringing the Chaotic Circus
# to An Emotional Focus

65. And so the third component of the Code is Relevancy. It's what brings all this chaotic circus—this emotion—into a direct and functional push forward.

66. It says: here is my Focus, this is where I'm going, this is my challenge and I'm going to be honest about my Facts and Feelings at the level that they will support me in getting what I want.

67. Relevancy becomes the Focus of my Facts and for my Feelings.

## Chapter 9:
## POINTS TO PONDER FROM THE GENERAL'S TENT

- **POINT #1:** There is a driving desire inside of all of us as human beings to be accepted for who we are and feel significant to others, even if it requires lying. We lie so that we fit in, to assure that we are part of the group and accepted.

- **POINT #2:** Focus isn't just about what you're wanting. Focus is about being honest about where you want to go, driven by what you are seeing about where you actually are today.

- **POINT #3:** In order to realize what you want, you have to define what is relevant in your life. Recognize that relevancy becomes the focus of your energy.

- **POINT #4:** Your feelings are either empowering or they're dis-empowering you to focus and move towards what you want or away from what you want.

# WARRIOR WITNESS:

## W.T., Salisbury, Maryland, USA:

*"Do I want a second chance? The man said get off the boat, I got off the boat. In early 2000, I was a Marine and I was proud. In 2004, I went into the car business and lived a party life and was in prison for a few years thinking about how my business got mismanaged. I'm in my 4th marriage with the only lady that I've had kids with. I have two kids, and I'm very emotional about the experience with Warrior and coming to become a better man and father."*

### Z.G. Arizona, USA:

*"Being Relevant is a function of Focus. Of course, I cannot lie and so there are times that I need say to a group to be real and raw but relevant is the glue. I have fucked it up many times because I was not being relevant. I'm continuing to drain myself, showing up not being present with my wife, kids and God."*

### E.M., Alberta, Canada:

*"I really get how I need to drop off my poo baby so I can be clean and clear to get what I need done; nothing can come out of the funnel without getting all of that shit out, and that laser focus is key to getting the results that I want."*

### T.M., Georgia, USA:

*"It's funny to me how amazingly obvious this is, but at the same time profound. I've been waking up every day working towards and end I haven't defined, across most of these areas (and on some days, none of them). My challenge is that in the past even when I have had a goal or set of goals, once they were achieved, they did not provide the satisfaction that I wanted. The goal itself did not deliver the result I wanted. I'm now taking my time with this to figure out what I need to do differently to truly understand what it is I want and to have confidence I'm on the right path to get it."*

### S.W., Arizona, USA:

*"This video/content really ties a lot together for me - but, it also exposes another blind spot for me. I am that guy who is not clear on what he wants. I have no fucking clue and it sounds pathetic when I say it to myself, but it is true. And, it is 100% b/c I have that emotional poo baby stuck backing me up - and I do not have the skill set (currently) to cleanse myself."*

### M.S.,Virginia, USA:

*"I am a "wondering generality". Look it up - my picture will be there. Not sure how in the hell my business is where it is today. I have lacked focus for so long. Great ideas will suck the energy right out of you without focus. I have been experiencing this for years. It's exhausting. Not seeing or thinking straight. Waking with no direction. Sure I have a to-do list and "plans" - but they are all over the fucking place with total disregard to what I really want. Why? Because I don't know what I want. Since the first time I listened to this video I have been asking myself that question - WHAT DO YOU WANT? WHAT*

*THE FUCK DO YOU WANT? I've made my lists, changed them, thought they were too shallow, changed them again, made more. Truth - I don't know what I want - yet. Maybe my mind is not yet big enough to understand what I want. Definitely making progress by learning more about and understanding my facts and feelings, but have a long way to go. It's going to take releasing the rage for me to truly understand what it is I want. Release the rage so I can release this emotional constipation that is holding back my power. I do know this - I am done with letting anyone else plan my life for me."*

# THE CODE

## Chapter 9: RESULTS (FRUIT)

Results are all that matter in the end. Your actions will always speak
louder than you words.

SECTION TWO
# THE CODE

CHAPTER NINE
# RESULTS (FRUIT)

*"Insanity: doing the same thing over and over again and expecting different results."*

## -Albert Einstein

---

1. Results. They are all that matter in the end. You can argue all day long over the processes, systems, ideology, worldviews and about what a man is or is not. But the one thing that you can't argue away? A man's Results.

2. Results are the great divide between the fakers and the players in life every single time.

### Did You Do the Work or Not?

3. That's why I love them, because Results say,

"Yes, I did the work." or

"No, I did not do the work."

4. In the Christian Bible it says simply this: by their fruit (results) you shall know them. You can know a lot about a Man, but in the end, his results will always tell you the true story, not his words or his feelings.

5. I had a friend of mine in college, funny little guy. Here is what he used to do: "Oh, I've been working out really hard dude. I've been working out really hard but I'm still fat."

"Yeah, I know. I can tell, dude. What's going on?"

"I don't know, dude. I'm just like ... I'm trying really hard, it's just not working."

"Well, whatever you're doing is clearly not working. How about I train you?"

"Really?! Okay, cool."

6. We created this training regimen, and we decided we were going to show up to the gym every single morning at 5 am. Initially, I was impressed that he started showing up at the gym even earlier than I would.

7. He would show up at the gym early, but see, he started pulling a little, subtle game: he would show up early, turn the treadmill on, and then stand on the sides of the treadmill, allowing the belt to flow between his legs for about ten minutes before I even got there.

8. Once I arrived, he would tell me that he only had ten minutes left in his treadmill total workout before we started our weights. Now, I bought his story for about a month. How was I supposed to know? I would show up and he would still be running on the treadmill right at five o'clock.

9. Along with that we also started adjusting his diet. But, like the treadmill, I wasn't around 24/7, so I didn't know what he was eating, not eating, etcetera, except that I knew that I gave him the tools, which he told me he was following perfectly.

10. Two and a half months the road and he like, didn't look any different at all, so I knew it was time for me to call out the bullshit.

11. One day after a session I asked him:

"Dude. What are you doing?"

"What do you mean? I'm following the exact plan you created for me."

"Bullshit you are."

"No, dude, I am! I'm following exactly what you told me."

"If you were following exactly what I told you to do, you would have results, period. But your results tell me right now you're a liar."

## Karma Served On a Silver Platter

12. Now, he didn't admit that he was a liar at the time, but a day or two later, karma served itself up on a big, silver platter for me, my friends.

13. I decided to show up at the gym a little bit early that time. Instead of 5 am, I showed up at the gym at roughly a quarter to five. And I happened to see my friend sitting over on the side drinking a coffee. He walked over to the treadmill, turned it on, put his legs on both sides of the belt, and the belt began to move between his legs. I sat and watched him for the next ten minutes as he watched the news, not moving as he drank his coffee with the treadmill going between his legs.

14. I was thinking, "There is no way he's been pulling this crap off the entire time. You've got to be kidding me!"

15. This reality confirmed 100% in my mind what I knew was true about his commitment (or the lack thereof) to the program.

"I don't look any different, I'm still overweight."

These were the words he shared with me the night before.

"How is this possible?"

16. Well, standing there and watching him, I had my answer.

17. So, I walked up on my friend. He's holding his coffee, treadmill was running between his legs, and he thought he was still pulling one over on me.

"What in the hell are you doing?!" I demanded.

"Gah! Oh, I was just taking a break, dude. I was just taking a break."

18. He's stumbling and holding his coffee, spilling everywhere, getting back on the treadmill. We had the concluding conversation:

"Listen, I've been standing over there watching you for ten minutes: you are full of crap. How long have you been doing this?"

"I just started today, I promise. This was just today, dude."

"Don't lie to me. How long have you been doing this?"

After pausing a few seconds, he admitted, "…The whole time."

"Let me get this straight. You spent more time and energy trying to create this sadistic little plan of yours to avoid doing work? It would've taken just as much energy *doing* the work as it took you to avoid the work, but you would've seen different results. I knew you were lying."

## Fun Fitness Facts

19. Fitness is a fun place because your facts are what they are. You're either fit or you're not; that's what's so fun about it.   Business and your bank accounts are the same. You either have money or you don't, and your business is either profitable or it's not. This is not up for negotiation and no matter how you try to spin it, NO money is NO money. This is why I love the scale, and this is why I love Profit and Loss Statements (PNL). The scales and PNLs just don't lie.

20. Here's the fun part about working out: you cannot get to power unless you get through pain.  This is the Truth with business, marriage, parenting and spirituality.  In every one of these areas, the Pathway to Power is through the Valley of Pain. That is it.

## Discovering the Pathway of Power by Traveling Through the Valley of Pain

21. Listen, Brother, having sex with your right hand (masturbation) is not having sex. Just like your fantasy vision boards are not what? They are not Results. Your Results might align with your vision boards; if they do, that's great, but if your Results do not align with them, then something is not working. As mentioned above, I'm going to have you consider that the Pathway to Power is always through the Valley of Pain. And that through the Valley of Pain, all that you have to gain comes down to the story that you tell in that Valley.

22. Having the courage to look at the Facts of our Results has the power to transform the world the way we know it to be.

23. If you don't like the fruit you are eating in your life, it does not mean that you are a Bad Man or a total mess up; it just means that whatever you have been doing is just not working to produce the life and the world that you truly desire.

## Ruthless Commitment to Radical Results

24. See, you have the power inside of you to create everything that you choose to create, but it is going to require you to have an Honest, Ruthless Commitment to Results. Results are Radical. Why? Because Results cut through the façade of Fantasy and bring a man straight back to Reality.

25. Let's use marriage as an example, shall we?

## Tracking Marriage

26. On a scale of one to ten, (ten being you're a god in the relationship, one you're an asshole) how would you currently rate your marriage? Where do you think you are as a husband to your wife inside the relationship?

27. Most guys would be like, "Oh, I'm like a seven."

"Okay, cool, now let's go ask your wife."

"Wait. What?"

"You said you act like you are a seven, so I'm going to go ask your wife now."

28. On average, over the last four years that I've done this, the scale gap is approximately four and a half points different.

29. And it's not in the positive direction.

The husband: "I'm like a seven."

The wife: "You're a two."

30. You're an actual two, but in your mind you're a seven and so you live in a fantasyland that continues to get smaller and smaller and smaller.

## Busy Doesn't Mean Productive

31. Or you're a businessman, and it's like showing up at work being busy, busy, busy without anything to show for it. Or you're an entrepreneur that's distracted, spending three straight weeks trying to create a logo.

32. There was a phrase introduced to me a number of years ago, and the phrase goes simply as follows:

"You don't get what you want. You don't get what you deserve. You don't get what you are entitled to. You get what you are ruthlessly, fucking committed to creating."

33. See, amidst all this conversation of feelings, we can be *honest*, but when we begin to *investigate*, we are going to find out really quickly that oftentimes our feelings are lying to us.

34. And so, all of a sudden, we start to show up to the party of life with Reasons instead of Results. Our society has become a group of men willing to hand out reasons in ready supply when they should be providing tools for results. And so we fall victim inside our own hell-bent story that says "my reasons are equal to my results."

## Reasons = Results

35. If my reasons are equal to my results, then what I actually live in is a world that is driven upon *reasons,* not upon *results* and this kind of life will NEVER work out in the long term.  EVER!

36. The CODE is simple.

Real

Raw

Relevant

**Results**

Notice the formula is not…

Real

Raw

Relevant

**Reasons**

37. This latter Formula will never work, and yet it is the fastest way to mess up the Game when we  stay committed to our reasons and "righteousness" rather than our ruthless drive to produce the results we say we want.

## If You Don't Feel Fear, You Can't Have Courage

38. This is why I love to measure results. Measurements and numbers take the emotion out of the game like clockwork. This is possible because with a number I can say "Yes I did" or "No I did not accomplish it." A feeling on the other hand can become a story which will create complete confusion, leaving me in the land of "Maybe" as I attempt to hit my target.

39. For many men it feels easier to just not look at the numbers, as if somehow the results will be easier. The only numbers they want to look at are ones that support their current behavior. If the numbers they are looking at tell them they are failing and that behavior modification is mandatory, these are the numbers they will ignore or blatantly change so they don't have to change themselves.

40. "Well, Garrett, I'm feeling a lot of fear around my numbers when I look at them and they don't say what I want them to say."

That's okay.

41. If you don't feel fear, you can't have courage, so just go find courage and let's get to work course correcting the Reality you had the courage to look at.

42. "Oh, Garrett, it's very nerve racking. It's stressful to me to make this jump from my current patterns to my new ones."

No shit, are you serious?!

43. Did you think it was just going to float down from heaven in a little cute box full of manna? Here you go: here is your "I don't have to do the work to get results of manna."

Are you kidding me?!

44. That's not how life works.

45. You've got to do the work, facing the feelings telling you to stay down and shrink instead of remain standing up and expanding.

## Lives Driven by Reasons

46. A life driven by reasons is a life also governed by lies. This is the lie that we're always going to *feel comfortable* doing what is necessary to change.

47. Some of the most intense, invigorating decisions I've ever made in my entire life did not bring with it peace until after traveling through the Valley of Pain to the Promised Land. The Peace did not come and the Power was not acquired until I was willing to put myself into a decision that didn't make any sense as I leapt into the Void of the Unknown. I had no desire to leap. Yet, I knew I needed to do it in order to get the Results that I wanted.

48. Society has told you that you're supposed to feel really good all the time, and if you don't, something's wrong with you and you need to stuff those feelings down. What I'm going to have you consider is you can feel really good all the time, but you've got to change your story of what that entails. Sometimes, for me it feels really good to hurt as much as it does to feel pleasure.

## Where Are You Trying to Go, Brother?

49. Some of us have become so addicted to telling stories about our lives that we  simply lack even the basic creativity to create stories that even excite us anymore.

50. This barrage of stories has begun to kill our drive and focus, which ultimately has left us stuck in a place that we never want to end up: in a boat without a rudder.

51. No guidance.  No clarity.  No direction.  No ability to see a vision beyond this exact moment that keeps us suppressed and hell bound.

52. If I asked you face to face where you were trying to go today, tomorrow, this week, this month, this quarter or this year, what would you likely say?

53. "I don't even know where I'm trying to go."

54. What you must *drive home* in the six inches of real-estate between your ears is this:

55. You aren't entitled to a damn thing. You were born into this world endowed by God our Maker with a gift called Agency.  This Agency is literally the Power of the Divine locked within you that, when accessed, will allow you to unleash the power of the Heavens on Humanity.  It is the Gateway to Having It All and the Key to all Creation.

56. Don't you dare fall into some kind of little drama story inside your head that says somehow your story is different. That somehow, your childhood was harder and that your path has been different. Guess what I'll do with your little box of story-based justification to ignore what I am saying?

57. I'll drop kick that crap to Timbuktu.

58. You want to come to me with results even if they are ugly as HELL? Great! In that place you have a shot.

59. Give me Reality, not Reasons.

## A Society of Disempowered Men

60. We live in a society of men who have been dis-empowered: taught a story, trained and educated to believe not only that lying is okay, but that feeling pain is not part of the process of growth. That it's okay to be a one-dimensional douche bag, excusing away all the results in life except for the ones that society thinks matters: make money to buy a free pass while the rest of it can go to hell.

61. How many of you think this is total bullshit? That it's not the way it is, it's just the way you *think* it is because that was how you were taught it was? What if reality was different and being one-dimensional *isn't* the only option?

62. In the Bible, the concept goes in this form: "If a child asks of his father for bread, does he give him a stone?"

63. Your kid can't eat stones, Brother. And neither can you.

64. When your wife asks for results, don't tell her: show her. Don't tell her you're going to change: BE the change. It is a function of priorities, telling a better story all while questioning the stories that you've been currently telling yourself.

65. You can be right about your story or you can get results, but you can't get both. And if this is too intense, hardcore or too much for you to face, then run right back to your little group of friends and family who have allowed you to continue to show up for years with Reasons rather than Results.

## Creating a Four-Dimensional Man

66. Here in this conversation within the Brotherhood, we hold you to one standard, and that is the Code. That is the foundation of this Movement, to create a four-dimensional human being; this superhuman we know lives inside you who can become a superhuman. You, Brother, are so much more powerful than you've ever given yourself permission to be.

67. But it's going to require you to come down from this place of fantasy into reality, and inside that place to live and die by Results. That is it.

67. My Results will do my talking while my Reasons will do the walking. If you don't feel like it today (or tomorrow), forget your feelings. I'm going to do the work down through the Valley of Darkness and Pain, and I'm going to search inside of that for the gain that I know. I know it's possible for me, and therefore it's possible for you, Brother: you *can* have it all.

68. But if you don't get this piece, if Results, metrically based and tracked, don't start becoming the reality of your life (through Core 4 = Body, Being, Balance and Business), you're screwed.

## By Your Fruit You Will Be Known

69. If it is not Result driven, it is Reason driven. And in reason we find unreality. It starts with the questioning of the stories. The stories that you've been running and telling, speaking inside your own mind. And so the fourth part here to the Code is very simple: It is a Ruthless Commitment to Big Ass Results, where ultimately by your Fruit we will know you.

### Chapter 9:
### POINTS TO PONDER FROM THE GENERAL'S TENT

- **POINT #1:** Results are the great divide between the fakers and the players in life every single time. You can know a lot about a Man, but in the end, his results will always tell you the true story, not his words or his feelings.

- **POINT #2:** You cannot get to the Path of Power unless you travel through the Valley of Pain, which is true across the Core 4 (Body, Being, Balance and Business).

- **POINT #3:** You have the power inside of you to create everything that you choose to create, but it is going to require you to have an honest, ruthless commitment to radical results.

- **POINT #4:** You get what you are ruthlessly, fucking committed to creating. There is no entitlement as a way to avoid the unknown. If you don't feel fear, you can't have courage. You've got to do the work, facing the feelings telling you to stay down and shrink instead of standing up and expanding.

## WARRIOR WITNESS:

### J.F., South Carolina, USA:

*"Since the beginning of my path on the Warrior's Way, one of the big things I've been doing I wake up early. I hear Garrett yell, "Do the fucking work!" as an alarm clock notice.*

*I've begun jogging on the beach in the mornings, which is the closest thing that I have for spirituality right now. I've also begun conversations with my estranged queen; we're separated, but I'm starting to see how I can do better. I want to be actively aware and there with my daughter. I know that I'm just scratching the surface."*

### G.B., Australia:

*"It was amazing to listen to how the mind creates excuses to not listen to the voice. I love the concept of metrics as we take the feelings and emotion out of everything; either the results are there or they're not. I'm looking forward to sinking my teeth into what I need to do in my Core 4.*

***Body:*** *I hired a trainer and find my body craving the green smoothies.*

***Being:*** *I'm starting to review scripture*

***Balance:*** *Texting my wife has allowed my wife to be more open and she's opened up as well, so it's helping us both ways. Reflecting on patterns and stories I've been telling myself for such a long time.*

***Business:*** *I'm sharing the concepts with my team, especially over metrics. I tell them that I don't want to hear the stories; let's look at the results."*

## M.K., Oregon, USA:

*"I shoot like a shotgun. My results are all over the board. My results look good initially, because I put a lot of points on the board early. However... I am never consistently after the same target. I'm already firing at other places. It's a fucking lie. It looks exciting as hell - I've got a lot of holes into the target before most people even realize what we should be aiming at... But I don't stick with it, I move onto the next thing, and so my results at the end of the day suck. Boom. Boom. Boom. I'm all over the place putting holes into everything I think is going to impress SOMEBODY. However, everybody else ends up with more points on the board because they are consistent. I just run from one target to the next without any long term success because it's more important to me to be seen as a leader, as someone who achieves in every area, then it is to actually make some real results that matter TO ME. I live in fantasy of achievement because I can always impress someone with those quick results. I'm done with that lie. I'm here to achieve, consistently, like a fucking sniper. It's going to be MY target and fuck all else... I'm doing the work."*

---

## J.E., Illinois, USA:

*"It's 10:39 pm at night and I am tired today. I'm experiencing pain just listening to this video and not because it is not "real, raw and relevant". My feelings are betraying me because I have not wanted to face my reality & "reasons". Wow, tired or not I am NOT going to let the pain keep me from getting results. This code just keeps leveling up on me and calling me on my Bullshit."*

---

## M.S., Virginia, USA:

*"As most, I've been trying to get results my whole life. The the results I have been working for have been based on my reasons. Reasons lie. Thus, the results I've been working toward have been based on stories and lies - not facts. I've had no system of metrically tracking results, with the exception of my business (money in the bank or not). I don't know yet the precise results I want in my body, being, balance or business. It's easy to say I want to get better in each area. Easy to say I want to be in better shape. Easy to say I want a better relationship with my wife. Easy to say I want to make more money. Mapping this out - the details - is fucking hard. As I do map it out - I am consistently brought back to the same thought - ETERNAL EXPANSION! This is what I am ruthlessly committed to. Expanding in each of the core four. Doing the work, knowing the facts, understanding my feelings, getting results and expanding beyond what I currently know is possible."*

---

# THE CODE

## Chapter 10: SUMMARY

If a man desires to Have It All in Body, Being, Balance and Business, he MUST begin with laying the Foundation of the Code. The Code will set you free, but it is also the one thing that if you let go of it, nothing else matters.

# SECTION TWO
# THE CODE

## CHAPTER TEN
# SUMMARY

*"Do you wish to rise? Begin by descending. You plan a tower that will pierce the clouds?
Lay first the foundation of humility."*

**-Saint Augustine**
[Christian bishop and theologian, 354-430 CE]

---

1. The Code is not something inside the Brotherhood that simply sounds nice; it is not just a way of operating—it is the **foundation** of our Game in living the Warrior's Way. It is the gasoline inside our Ferrari; the fuel that allows us to continue to go. The Code is the one thing that if you let go of it, nothing else matters. Nothing else you create will ever truly work at the level it could. It will always support you, lead you and guide you to the place you need to be. The Code itself is a light: a beacon in the darkness and lighthouse in the middle of the storm.

2. The Code will set you free into your humanity and unleash your Divinity in ways you have never experienced before. So let's recap what it means to Live by a Code.

### Be Real

3. What does it mean to Be Real?[20]

4. We have to be willing and have enough courage in our lives to look at the Facts of our experience. It was difficult for you to be able to look at "what

---

[20] Code 5:68-69, See Chapter 6: Real (Facts)

is" because of your stories around "what is not," which is our good and bad, or right and wrong, or righteous and wicked. These checklists of fury and of fire that we have built that say, "This is okay and this is not okay."

5. We said we're going to strip all that back inside The Code. Being real, we're going to commit every single day to stop lying and start looking at the facts of who we are, where we've been and where we're going.

## Get Raw

6. What does this mean?

7. Our Facts link to Feelings, which means that it's just as important to get our feelings out as it is to write down the facts. Feelings are either blinding us or empowering us to reach our full potential of Having It All. My feelings are fuel—fire—which is either burning me to the ground or empowering and inspiring me to move forward, so they *do* matter. Being just as honest about my Feelings and not lying about what I'm feeling is just as important about not lying about the Facts.

## Stay Relevant

8. What does it mean to Stay Relevant?

9. After we learn to Be Real, learning to be Free is going to require the Facts to be on the table. Mixing the Feelings and Facts together become the sauce for Focus (relevance). Without relevance that comes from Focus, my Fire found within the confines of my Raw and Real conversation doesn't have much power unless it's been given some direction. My reactions would be random in nature like an unmanned field fire, moving all around, focusing on whatever they choose to focus on, becoming all-consuming until we bring in Relevancy.

10. My Relevancy, for the first time, brings Focus. It takes all this fractured light that's all over the place and turns it into this laser-focused Energy that's being pushed out in the Facts and in the Feelings. "Here's what I want, here's where I'm going. This is where I'm headed to."

11. Without the Facts and Feelings lined up with a Focus, there would be no outcome that could ultimately be created. Then all you would experience is

this karmic cul-de-sac running around and nothing would ever change. Our lives will become nothing more than they are today unless we have a Focus.

## Ruthless Results

12. The fourth and final piece of The Code is Results: Fruit. "By their fruit ye shall know them.[21] "Amidst all the Facts, Feelings and Focus, our Fruit is the only thing that truly matters. Conversations on being Real, Raw and Relevant, all occur in order to show our ruthless commitment to Results. Feelings are going to betray us, therefore the commitment to the results is the only thing that can allow you to move forward from a land of living in reasons to a life of living in results.

13. We're now asking the right questions:[22] Is it true what I'm feeling right now?[23]What is it that I want? Is there another story that I could tell that would be more productive in helping me get what I want? How can I shift it? See, when you become a man who lives in a land of Results, your Fruit matters.

14. Then this weird thing starts to happen: your life becomes simpler. You start to realize there's a lot of crap out there in the form of stories, especially inside your own head. The stories may continue to come up, but you've learned how to turn, adjust, and how to refocus them. Inside of that refocus we're beginning to operate as one, harmonious heartbeat. This is your foundation inside of you as a Warrior: a modern man learning to have it all. This heart gives you the ability to breathe and live, to expeditiously expand the possibilities of having it all. Not as a fantasy, but as a reality.

## Receiving Simple Tools

15. How do we practically pull this off, though? How do we go about this process? Inside this Game called Warrior we've searched long and far. I have read hundreds of books, hired literally over 50 different mentors, attended over 100 mastermind groups and various workshops over the past 15 years searching for answers to these questions we've culminated down to three simple tools found inside the Armory of the Black Box: Release the Rage,

---

[21] Matthew 7:20 (KJV, NT Holy Bible)
[22] Foundation 4:13-17. See also Byron Katie's book Loving What Is, Appendix Bibliography.
[23] Code 8:28-29 (28-37)

Power Focus and Positive Focus, which I will go into more detail later on in the book.

16. Here, as we conclude The Code, I'm going to simply give you an overview of each one of them, letting you understand that these three simple tools, if you will fucking master them, can guide you towards living a life of having it all.

## Unraveling the Stories

17. The Code is the work that has to be done to unravel the stories and the lies that hold you choked, struggling for breath. We can now recognize the half-truths and fantasies that we've begun to worship as reality. The simplicity of your liberation is upon you, but do not take the simplicity in it as not worth your time and energy. Don't tell yourself another story that says, "Well, it's too simple. Having it all is supposed to be complex."

18. Inside of The Code there are two daily devices: one on demand and the other as needed. All three of these tools (Release the Rage, Power Focus, Positive Focus) can be used every single day if necessary. Some of you will need to use all three on a daily basis, some won't.

## Gateway Out of Incarceration

19. These three simple devices are the Gateway out of your Incarceration from within as if you are receiving a new pair of eyes. Inside of that new perspective you will see, for the first time, a glimpse of the Divinity that's inside of you, manifested in front of you at all times, which you weren't aware of until now. I love it when people tell me that God is disconnected from them; God is not disconnected from you or me at any time. The Universe is constantly plugged into the power of who we are, but it is you and I who sit and begin to mess with the lights. We turn the lights off and say, "I don't want to listen. I don't want to feel this anymore. I want to choose to fall on my sword and die instead."

20. One of the ways we do this is by making simple acts complex.

21. Men tell me all of the time, "Well, Garrett, it's got to be complex because if it's not complex then it's probably not going to work. Can you please just make it hard for me? Can you make it complex? Can you make

it difficult? Can you tell me to do 1,000 things, Garrett? Don't just tell me three. It's too simple, Garrett. It's too simple. Can you make it harder?"

22. No I can't. I won't. These simple tools have been perfected inside this Brotherhood for years. And before that, for years inside my own life. These tools have been used for nearly three decades by a [24] woman who was inserted into my life, changing my reality forever in 2009.

23. I couldn't see shit prior to this time. Just like many of you reading, you can't see right now. You're hurting so bad, and you have no idea how to change, tell a different story, or how to question the fantasy that's become your reality.

24. In my life, it started with one simple question by a beautiful woman named Byron Katie, first through audio and then in person. She asked me one simple thing:

25. "Is it true? Is the thought that you're having true?"

26. I can't explain the freedom that began to open up in my life by just one simple question, full of three powerful words: Is it true?

27. Two of these Warrior Action Documents (Release the Rage and Power Focus) have been inspired by "The Work" of Byron Katie, the author of the book *Loving What Is,* which has been modified and renamed in Warrior terms and systems to support you daily on your journey to having it all.

28. The third document, Production Focus, was inspired by [25] Dan Sullivan, the creator and founder of Strategic Coach. [26] Like the other two Action documents, this one has been modified and expanded into Warrior Terms to support your journey to Having It All.

29. Little did they realize that when they inserted two different ideas into my mind seven to eight years ago, these ideas would evolve into the powerhouse version used exclusively today inside of the Black Box Brotherhood and Wake Up Warrior.

---

[24] Bibliography: Katie, Byron (also applicable for v 27). See also *Appendix Resources*

[25] Sullivan, Dan. See Bibliography for full citation in Appendix

[26] Strategic Coach is a program designed to bring about gradual, transformational change for entrepreneurs' businesses.

30. These Actions Documents found in the Warrior Stack, Section Three of this book are:

1. The Dark: Release The Rage
2. The Drift & Lift: Power Focus, Parts 1 & 2
3. The Lift: Production Focus
4. The Light: Revelation Road Map

## The Dark Release of Rage

31. You will find "Release the Rage" listed in the back of this book with breakdowns of exactly how to use this tool on demand as often as you need it. Sometimes you'll use it multiple times a day. Sometimes one time a day. Sometimes once a week or you'll find that you won't use it for weeks. It is to get rid of the emotional constipation around scenarios and situations to allow you to see clearly.

## The Drift and Shift of the Power Focus

32. The second and third (accompanying) document we call The Power Focus documents. Use of these tools is in the following order: Release the Rage and then Power Focus. The experience from The Power Focus is going to take us from a place of powerlessness, where we are not living in reality, to living a new option of possibility. To figure out how I can change my story in a different way. How can we look around what we're currently looking at? If I can only see one perspective, how do I get more? There's access from another angle, but if I don't know the tools, how I can access that empowerment to get the thing that I want? It's going to move me forward, unlocking, uncovering and discovering inside of my life the power that I'm actually searching for. In order to do this, I've got to learn The Power Focus.

## The Lift: Production Focus

33. The last document tools, Production Focus and Walk the Block, were inspired by Dan Sullivan and *Strategic Coach*, which has been evolved and morphed into something more exponential we call the "Exponential Production Focus."

34. This allows me to be able to cause relevancy from the breakthroughs and experiences I'm having in life and in my Power Focus action documents.

From Production Focus, Power Focus and Release the Rage, these three documents, systems, and processes—three daily regimens—will allow us to literally change the world that we see. They will allow us to see the Light, which is to have a revelation or an epiphany which we call Walking the Block.

35. Without this foundational work and daily commitment to the Power Focus and the Production Focus experiences, nothing that you do here will work. They must become new addictions; new ways of living.

## Creating New Addictions for Living

36. Release The Rage must become a document, a process and a system that you use when life is going sideways and you can no longer see. Everything inside The Warrior's Way is fighting for perspective. Without perspective people die; without vision men commit suicide.

37. The Warrior's Way is simple. Here, as we conclude this first section of the doctrine we call The Code, it comes and is equipped with the Drift, Shift, Lift and Light Model, and we have powerful tools that we must use every single day: Release the Rage, Power Focus, Production Focus and Revelation Road Map. All of these will lay the foundation and create the favorable conditions for you to have it all inside of what we call The Warrior Stack.

## Chapter 10:
## POINTS TO PONDER FROM THE GENERAL'S TENT

- **POINT #1:** If a man desires to Have It All in Body, Being, Balance and Business, he MUST begin with laying the Foundation of the Code. If you let go of it, nothing else matters.

- **POINT #2:** Feelings are going to betray you, therefore commitment to the results is the only thing that can allow you to move forward from a land of living in reasons to a life of living in results. We do this by learning how to ask the right questions.

- **POINT #3:** There are four simple tools found inside the Armory of the Black Box categorized as the Drift, Shift, Lift and Light Model: Release the Rage, Power Focus, Production Focus and Walk the Block are all used to help us stand by the Code.

- **POINT #4:** Everything inside The Warrior's Way is fighting for perspective, without which the Warrior dies into sedated oblivion.

# WARRIOR WITNESS:

## R.C., Carson City, Nevada, USA:

*"I came to Warrior Week to find myself and it seems like a generic statement, but I feel in the world I had lost my heart, I had lost my soul. And coming here, really, the only word I can think of is liberating. Not only did it connect me back to my inner being and who I am but it freed my fucking soul, and it's amazing too, to come through here with all these brothers and walk away knowing that not only did you do it, but you have a connection to your heart and to your soul and a group of men that have your back. It's fucking amazing."*

## S.W., Arizona, USA:

*"The simplicity of this does make it ridiculous to not be able to do - yet, here we are all struggling with making it happen. It is simple, but not easy to maintain. That is the challenge for me is to stay consistent with the simple things."*

## M.K.,Oregon, USA:

*"It's too simple. That's going to be difficult for me to overcome -- not looking for "the next thing". I won't sparkle and fade at this. I am committed and strong. I'm not going to live a sedated life. I'm done fucking lying and living by other's expectations."*

# THE STACK
## Chapter 11: THE DRIFT & SHIFT MODEL

We all get stuck in a Karmic Cul-de-sac of cyclical behavior, as explained in what we call here at Warrior as the Drift & Shift Model.

# SECTION THREE
# THE STACK

## CHAPTER ELEVEN
# THE DRIFT & SHIFT MODEL

"You come to the point in your life when you can't pull the trigger anymore."

**- Evel Knievel**
(American motorcycle stunt and jump performer, 1938-2007)

## Finding the Right Formula

1. For the past ten years of my life, I have searched to figure out the formula. The formula that made my life tick, but more than anything, the formula that would help me uncover why I seem to fuck things up so frequently. Now brother, if you're here reading this book, it means that you are one of those men. Congratulations! Yes, *you* my friend, you fuck it up too.

2. Well, guess what? There's not a human being on the planet that doesn't.

3. Over that time of fuck ups I have found tools, techniques, and tactics to help. I have found a series of mentors, masterminds, gurus, and guidance from people outside of me to the Voice inside of me, helping me uncover piece by piece and line upon line this formula for why I fuck it up.

## Drift and Shift Model

4. Now this formula of why I fuck it up has become known as the Drift and Shift model. It helps us really have a container to place inside of it all, the tools and the tactics and the methodology of what works for you and for me inside of living the Warrior's Way.

5. We have to understand that the process of life comes down to one simple belief system. Here inside Warrior, the purpose of your life is one simple thing. What is it, you ask? No matter who you talk to, they're going to have an answer for you. Different religious belief systems are going to have a philosophy for you and different scientific belief systems will give you a philosophical stance on what you could believe about the purpose of your life.

6. Here at Warrior I'm going to have you consider the purpose of your life as one simple thing, and it is expansion. That your life and my life is driven by this reality, that who we are today is less than who we will become tomorrow, and that the purpose of our expansion is life, and that the purpose of our life is expansion, constantly pushing, becoming more and more and more than we were yesterday, today.

## Finding the Fire of Expansion

7. This model right here, the Drift and Shift, gives an explanation to what I have experienced in my own life and have watched in the lives of literally thousands of men who have followed this Warrior's Way belief system, the same psychological and tactical way for expanding. It also helps you and I understand why we fuck it up and how fucking it up was never the fuckup. Fucking it up was part of finding the fire that you and I needed, the desire deep inside of us to push and to grow and to become something more than we ever imagined before.

8. Inside of this, we're going to notice some points. The first thing we're going to discuss is the current path and the trigger.

## The Status Quo Path

9. Your current path operates as what we might call the status quo. Status quo is who you were in your patterns before you picked up this book or first heard about Warrior. Your patterns will continue day-to-day because no matter how much you expand and how much you grow, where you are today *is* the status quo. It's the status quo for who? It's the status quo for you, and it's the status quo for me. Our status quo patterns are different and distinct.

10. Here they begin with an identification that all growth and expansion first precedes itself with a status quo pattern for the way you operate physically, the way you operate mentally and spiritually. The way you operate in your marriage or with your children. The way you operate with business, marketing, sales, systems, money and bank accounts across the

game of Warrior. How you operate today is your new status quo and how you operate tomorrow will require you to grow.

## Interrupting Triggers

11. What interrupts this pattern is a Game we call Triggers. Triggers are the interrupters of life. These triggers are the moments in which the status quo becomes interrupted. It becomes acted upon. Who you are moving into within the status quo receives a collision from a circumstance, a relationship, or from something that you see that triggers inside of you a different experience of your humanity. It pushes you to see something you couldn't see before. It pushes you to knock on different doors and it pushes into a place that maybe even you would abhor finding out to be true about even you. So triggers are amazing, because triggers awaken in you and I Stories.

12. These Stories become the reason for the trigger, at least for us. They become the justificational frosting on top of a cupcake. They become the reason that the trigger exists. The trigger happens and then inside that stimulus comes the story. From that story comes our feelings. These feelings drive you and I every single day.

13. Sometimes we fly and sometimes we die. It depends on you and me and how we operate inside our humanity. When it comes to seeing the feelings and seeing the stories for what they truly are.

14. So this Drift and Shift model is a model that takes us along the current path to a trigger. This triggers an event that opens up for us these stories and these feelings. These stories and feelings are calling towards me and you and they're teaching us something every single day. See, the fire is found at the bottom of your desire inside of the fuckups. The fuckups are actually where the fire is found. It's not outside; around the land of all that is perfect and beautiful inside your life that you find all of the teachings that will actually cause you to expand. I'm going to have you consider that the fire at the bottom of that fuckup desire is the truth that will set you free, but it's going to require some discovery by you and me, to search inside our humanity, to find this place. We might just see some possibility beyond the reality that we currently see.

15. So the universe calls into play, into your life and into mine, a trigger that is sent by the divine to push you and I to a place that we couldn't ultimately find without the drift into this place called the Pit.

16. Now you've got a chance to hear some of that inside of this WarriorBook, inside of this conversation of my story into that place. But see, this magical place begins to open up as we look at this stacked experience of the triggers, the stories and the feelings. There is a moment for all of us in which we begin to experience what I call the Drift.

## The Gift of the Drift

17. The Drift is again the gift. The drift is when you and I begin to digress in our expansion from these triggers, stories, and feelings. We begin to collapse down and become less than we were before. If I continue down this path of the Drift, I'll ultimately find myself at the bottom inside of what I call the Pit.

18. Along this Drift, this place where I begin to compel my life because of a trigger that interacted with me in the path that I was going, I am no longer found in the status quo. I've pushed to something different than I knew before. I'm now pushing beyond the stories and the feelings and the triggers into this place of darkness, this Drift, this divine gift that has been given to me, but for most of us we don't see it this way.

19. We don't see that this Drift into the depth of this traumatic place known as the Pit, we don't see this place as a gift. Hell, most of the time on the way down we scream, we cry, we grab on to every branch we can find, almost as if this entire Drift on the way down, we're reaching back to clamber onto the weeds and the bushes and the trees and rocks and dirt and anything that we could pull on ourselves to not fall into the Drift, but see, that's the problem: our gift is in the Drift, but our eyes tend to look at something different. We tend to look back.

20. So most of us find ourselves stuck in this dilemma of not understanding the Drifts, not understanding that the Drift itself can take us all the way to the Pit, or it can open up for us an opportunity to search for something over here at the Peak. But the Pit and the Peak, both are found from the triggers that begin the drift. When and where and how we decide to lift to that Peak, or to lift from that drift, or to return back to the place that we

began in what I call the karmic cul-de-sac will come down to the ability for you and I along this drift at any given time that we choose to begin to awaken and to Shift.

## Shift the Drift

21. The Shift requires you to see the Drift from a different place. It requires you to be able to analyze that the trigger from your wife, your children, your boss, employees, clients, or even the trigger from the person at the gas station. *All* that these triggers are teaching you. They're guiding you; the Drifts are the Gifts that are trying to help you find the deeper truth inside of you. That you and I inside that trigger, if we peel it back just little bit, just like peeling a Band-aid off the top of our wound on our arm, we may find something inside that wound that will let us live.

22. With the tattoos on my arm sleeve, they become the symbolization of this entire conversation. To not understand the Drifts is to believe that inside those Drifts, we are going to die, which is why I have the skull on the lower part of my arm, yet inside that Drift is what we truly find are the eyes to fly. Our eye begins to expand, like what I have tattooed on the upper part of my forearm.

23. When one has the ability to turn on the Light inside the Night, everything changes. What becomes terrorizing to others in the form of death becomes light and sight to those who choose to see the gift of the Drift. Nonetheless, it's going to require a Shift.

24. This Shift itself is a decision to begin to learn from the Drift at any one of these checkpoints along the way, I'm drifting, I'm drifting, I'm drifting, I'm drifting, I'm drifting, I'm drifting, I'm drifting, I'm drifting, I'm drifting, I'm drifting.

25. Lift says, "Follow the Voice." Shift says, "The Voice." Like exits on a freeway, we begin to miss them. Exit one, exit two, three, four, five, six, seven, eight, and for some of us, we just don't hear until we hit the rock bottom of trauma. In a world that's fucking burning to the ground, we can't find any way around the pain inside that Pit.

## Worshiping False Peaks

26. Most of us, we've been taught this very fucked up way of seeing the fuckups. From this place we don't see this Peak up here, this new path. We don't see this light available for us up here. We don't see the purpose of our life expansion. We begin to see another path that doesn't make any sense, and yet we do it so damn often.

27. Instead of learning from our Drift we will begin to worship the past before the Drift began, and we will say things like "Listen, I don't want to go to this Peak. My story of the Peak is to come back here to the false Peak, to actually choose to pursue a return to what was before the trigger," believing that if I can return back to this false Peak and I can experience this false lift, then life itself will improve, but it cannot.

28. If my life is filled with triggers cascading me with stories and feelings that never change, to a Pit of fire and drama and trauma that exists down here at the bottom, only to desire my life to be back to what it was before, if I could just go back and take back what I said. If I could go back before the mistakes. If I could just take my life back to what it was. I listen to men who come to this place saying "If I had just done this, this and this, then I could go to things the way they were before I fucked up with my wife. I could go back to the way things were before I had said the things that I wish I had never said to my children. If I could go back before I made those massive fuckups inside my business, if I could just go back…."

29. That is the problem inside the path; looking back becomes your own destruction. Your freedom comes in seeing and having faith in the fire that comes from the fuckups. Inside that fire of the fuckups comes the truth. Many men will stay inside of this loop of constantly being triggered by the same shit, telling the same stories, having the same feelings constantly drifting, hitting the bottom in the Pit, then experiencing what I consider to be one of the most dangerous aspects of the game called life, is the belief that one is growing through the false lift of death.

30. There is no progress in this. This False Lift experience sits over on the side of the Drift, inside of this Game. This represents a decade of my marriage, stuck inside of a karmic cul-de-sac, pushing along, pushing along, triggered by the same bullshit every single time with my wife: drifting, missing the lessons, missing the lessons, missing the lessons, filled with shame and blame

and guilt. No learning. Then a deep desire filled with regret and remorse and personal blame and shame of my wife, desiring to return back to what wasn't, feeling like "Oh my God, yes, we're improving, we're improving. Yes, we're improving!" Yes, as we continue to hit the false checkpoint Lift that bring us back to exactly who we were before.

## Destiny of Damnation: Karmic Cul-de-Sac

31. The karmic cul-de-sac is a formula for failure. The karmic cul-de-sac is a destiny of damnation. The karmic cul-de-sac keeps you bound like a hound that keeps you stuck on the ground and no lifting is available from that place. That's why we meet men who maybe we haven't spent time with for five, seven, ten years. They have the same fucking problems they had ten years ago. How is it possible that they've not grown?

32. That's because every time shit gets spicy at the trigger, there is no Shift. There is only a false Lift of returning to what was. Trigger, false Lift, trigger, false Lift, trigger, false Lift, trigger, until one of two things occurs. A man ultimately ends up sedating and numbing out to the reality of no expansion, but the reality of damnation that he's living or two, he will choose to Shift.

33. The more loops you take around the cul-de-sac on the topic, the more painful it is to lift from that place. The more loops you take around this place, the more ingrained the patterns become, the more difficult it becomes because the speed at which you are moving makes it difficult to make the turn on that Shift. Belief systems become rooted deep into the game, defined only as triggers of remorse.

34. My wife and I had fought for so many fucking years on the same topics. She would just look in my direction and I would be triggered, cascading into a Drift down into the trauma, then false lifting myself back up, delusively convincing myself that things had changed. And yet, looking in the mirror, I knew that nothing had fucking changed.

## Shift to Expand

35. So the work that we are about to dive into allows us to have the opportunity not weekly, not monthly, not quarterly, but daily. *Daily* the ability for you and I to see into the possibilities of Shifting. To Shift so that we can Lift. To Shift so that we can fulfill the purpose of our lives. To

Shift from the fuckups. The fuckups are the fire, they are the gift of desire, found inside the gift of the Drift.

36. I'm going to have you consider that you were put here on this ball, this school called earth with one fundamental purpose, and that is to expand. That means that you don't ever really fuck it up; you create opportunities for learning.

37. To most men, it's disgusting to watch how I used to live, spending months and months and months spent in a pattern of damnation. Damning myself. Let me clarify now that God wasn't damning me. I was a slave, even though I was saved. Inside of my game, I had no liberation, I had no eyes to see because everything in my life was driven by this past destiny. There was no future sight inside the eyes inside of me. There was nothing pushing me forward to find the next version of my own humanity. I was stuck living in this place, this pattern.

38. This place that didn't work.

39. No one had ever told me to go search for the learning. No one had ever told me to run full speed into the triggers. Nobody had ever told me or taught me or trained me or educated me to understand that the fuckups were where the fire was. That my desire could actually lead me from growth to find the triggers before they found me. I was never told that I could identify these triggers, that I could hunt them down, that I could custom-create my life to actually find the triggers and from them deliberately leverage them to Lift me: Lift me through learning to a new path, at a new place, at a new possibility, and a new place of expansion that exists up here at the Peak.

## The Points of the Peak and the Pit

40. I want you to look at these two varying points, from this Peak to the Pit. The Peak to the Pit, the place that I originally started, the current path, the current path, triggered by the event, the person, the situation or the circumstance, cascading me down into the ground and then false lifting. Or, rewinding, rewinding, rewinding, down into the Drift, Shift to the learning until a new path is established.

41. Now this gap itself leaves a man who he was and a man who he has become as two very different individuals. This is why you're here. Imagine making these kinds of Shifts *every day*. Men who step in to live the Warrior's

Way step into what we call the Warrior Time-Warp. It's a collapsing of time and a disappearing of the miraculous that allows a man like you and me to grow at speeds that blow the reality of most of humanity.

42. We expand in who we are in business, in our bodies, in our spirituality, in our marriages, and with our children. Brother, there is no place in your life that you have ever grown faster than you'll grow here. But in order to get there, in order to master this Game, in order to take your life on in a way that you've never been able to before, you're going to have to understand the tools necessary, that as you find yourself cascading from the trigger, cascading into the stories, engulfed by the feelings inside the fury of the fuckups, that inside that place, that you have the tools to allow you to freeze, to Shift, to Lift, and to gain the Light and insight that comes at the top of the next Peak.

43. Do this daily and in a month you become unfamiliar, even to yourself. Do this daily and in two months, you become unfamiliar even to your spouse. Do this daily and within 90 days you become unfamiliar even to your children. Do this daily for a year and people who knew you a year ago won't even know who you have become and everything you are searching for, inside of Body, Being, Balance and Business is found outside of the current patterns and new Peaks that can only be found as you are willing to leap into the Void and do the fucking work in the Dark, to learn how to turn on the Light in your darkest nights.

44. Brother, welcome to the journey. It's going to change everything forever. These four tools, of the drift and shift that sit at the core of the Core Four game, are the tools of literal awakening, activation and acceleration, of living the warrior's way to having it all.

## Chapter 11:
## POINTS TO PONDER FROM THE GENERAL'S TENT:

- **POINT #1: The Trigger.** This is the moment that life collides with you in ways that maybe you were not expecting. It is this collision that actually allows you to begin the journey of expansion. If misunderstood, then the Triggers around you daily are simply seen as a Problem and not the window of Possibility that they truly can be.

- **POINT #2: The Darkness:** The Night is not something that should cause you fright. It is in the Darkness that you and I will begin to discover our new light. There is no hiding from the night unless you attempt to cover your eyes and pretend that it does not exist. The Darkness is a Gift at the entrance of the Drift and when we see this we shift but in order to do this we will have to release the rage that keeps us blind in the night.

- **POINT #3: The Drift & Shift:** Understanding how we entered the DRIFT is crucial to our expansion and growth and there is little that will change a man more than the ability to understand what caused his behaviors. Most are afraid to actually know the truth of this fact let alone dive deep into the middle of it and then while they uncover the gift that is hidden inside that Drift. When a man grasps the power of the SHIFT everything around him changes and power returns to the KING.

- **POINT #4: The Lift & Light:** Light and sight. This is the journey of a man every single day living the Warrior's Way. There is no freedom in the fear that holds him tight unless he is willing to attack that fear, examine it and then lift himself from the Pit of despair. To lift one's self requires one to learn and when one learns the game, begins to change. Light is the gift that is found at the end of that journey.

# WARRIOR WITNESS:

### T.R., Arkansas USA:
*"The REAL RAW RELEVANT TRUTH about our RESULTS>>> the status quo is yesterday. Today there are lessons. The choice to listen is made every day. The choice to do the fucking work and take the exit off the shit cycle is made every day. And every day a new Peak in this game with no finish line. Piping hot fresh black-blooded Boom!"*

### D.G. Los Angeles, California USA,
*"Yeah the last few years I think I've hit that circle of death pretty hard. Life is so short and no one should be wasting it going in a circle but it's so easy to be stuck in it. Putting in the work on this and making that a part of daily life is going to be hard at first for me but it seems very worth it."*

## B.H.,Odessa, Texas USA:

*"Revelation: This is broken down so you can see the exact results from our actions and points out for any negative things we might do to get to the Pit there are multiple points were we can listen to our inner light. We all seek to go back after mistakes are made when we should concentrate on how to turn those mistakes into life building progress.*

*Reaction: Follow the path and do the work, the Warrior Code works if we follow it, get on the path and stay on it."*

# THE STACK
## Chapter 12: THE DARK

The first tool to deal with The Drift is about confronting what triggers the Rage within oneself.

SECTION THREE
# THE STACK

CHAPTER TWELVE
# THE DARK

## (RELEASE THE RAGE)

"Niemand ist mehr Sklave, als der sich für frei hält, ohne es zu sein."

"None are more hopelessly enslaved than those who falsely believe they are free."

**- Johann Wolfgang von Goethe**
[German writer and statesman (1749-1832), excerpt from Elective Affinities]

---

## First Weapon in the Arsenal

1. This is the initial stage. The initial understanding of the first document or first tool, the first weapon in your arsenal to be able to deal with the Drift. The Drift is only fearful and the dark is only scary because of the stories that exist about the dark. I live in Orange County, California and the ocean itself is an interesting game.

2. If you're not familiar with the ocean, then, the ocean itself becomes scary. Underneath that water becomes a mystery and inside that mystery, it becomes all of the manifestations of your greatest nightmares and your greatest fears.

## Turning On the Light Inside the Night

3. My young daughter is still scared of the dark inside our own house. Dark in the closet door, dark under the bed, dark in the back of the house. Scared and nervous. My pit bull on the other hand, not scared of the dark. You

open the door in the middle of the night, that dog will run straight out the back door and chase down anybody.

4. For him, the night is a different experience. He actually loves it because that's when all the rats come out and he hunts the shit out until midnight. Night and darkness changes as a topic of conversation when we have the power to turn on the Light inside the night. Our very first document we will reference there and the very first pool in the arsenal is what's known as Release the Rage. There are moments and there are times in which it will become impossible for you to do the work and so you will Drift because your feelings have become so ridiculously enraged that you cannot think straight. There is no ability to investigate your stories. There is no ability to investigate the trigger.

5. There is no ability to Shift. There is no ability to Lift. There is no ability to learn. What you are left with is a homicidal maniac which you have become inside your own mind. The heart is raging with fury and inside that place, we have got to do one simple thing as we put on the fucking brakes.

## Brake Before Hitting Bottom

6. We have to stop you before you hit the bottom. Before your life starts on fire in the Pit. We are going to try to stop you down this path, in this Drift as quickly as we possibly can. Now, the sooner the man recognizes that he's in this place of this insatiable rage, the sooner we can stop the descent. As soon as he's there, in this place of anger and frustration, we now have a tool to assist with putting on the brakes. It doesn't mean we're going to learn anything.

7. All we're trying to do is to create space.

8. The mind becomes clouded in, shutting down. The emotions are attacking. The heart is closing up. Your capacity to see has disappeared and death has become your game. Darkness has become your cap door and inside of that place, the dark is not only *not* going to allow you to see the Light but it will not allow you have any sight until you have burned shit to the complete ground and you sit at the bottom of the Pit, broken.

# External and Internal Hurricanes

9. Now, there are two kinds of versions of you. There are men that naturally are loud and that would be me. Hard to believe. I naturally am extremely loud. My emotions are on my sleeves. My emotions are on the outside. I am easy to look at because when I get pissed, everybody fucking knows. Now, that happened in all locations *outside* of my home but the person that it never happened with was my wife. For some reason, I wouldn't let it out. I would go from an external hurricane to an internal hurricane. I would keep it all bottled up inside. Some of you naturally when you go about your day today are what we call internal hurricanes.

10. When it comes to the darkness, whatever you feel, nobody could tell from the outside. You're like a poker player, who's got a poker face. It never changes place. You're like, really? Dude, you're doing good and everybody from the outside assumes that you are fine and yet, underneath the surface, the rage keeps building and building and building and building.

11. Guys like me, you don't have to worry about me rolling up onto a gas station, or a school or university and pulling some of the insane bullshit you see around the world these days with an assault rifle and just start fucking shooting people. Do you know who does that? Internal hurricanes. Individuals who suppress feelings, suppress stories and deal with triggers over and over and over again until the Karmic Cul-De-Sac of life becomes so disproportionately in captive to their reality that they cannot see a way out. So, these internal hurricanes begin to do stupid shit. *Stupid* shit.

12. We look at tragedies in the news and wonder how any of it makes any sense, but inside the Karmic Cul-De-Sac, it made sense for this internal hurricane of a person. It made sense, no matter how destructive it becomes to everyone else.

13. Regardless of whether you're an internal hurricane or an external hurricane, Release the Rage is a weapon. It allows for you to put the brakes on by getting all of the feelings in you and outside of you down on to paper.

# Learning to Question the Drift's Trigger

14. We do this by asking some very simple questions. We come to the trigger inside of the Drift and Shift and we ask ourselves this question: "In

this moment, what or who has triggered me to Drift, feel angry, frustrated, pissed off, hurt, upset, or disappointed and why?"

15. I'm just starting in the Drift and Shift Model, but the sooner I realize that through regular application of this tool, I'm going to recognize and discover patterns, which will help me shorten my stay in the Drift section and be able to Lift myself out from what triggers the Rage even faster. I will discover the patterns and patterns and bam. I hit the trigger. The trigger then gives me the stories and the feelings. We are drifting.

16. First question goes into play using the Steve and the Stinky Office example, will be broken down step by step, with a blank document of this Release the Rage document located at the end of this chapter.

17. In this moment, here, it becomes a statement that guides you into that Game, and as you get better at it, you can take the training wheels up. You can take the bumpers out of your bowling alley and you could throw that ball straight down the lane, or you can ride your bike without training wheels. In the beginning though, we're going to start with training wheels because there is no pride nor ego in this at all. It's like, listen: I need some help. I need some guidance.

18. We start off with this statement:

Question #1: In this moment, what or who triggered you to Drift, feeling angry, frustrated, pissed off, hurt, upset, or disappointed and why?

**Answer:** *In this moment, _____ (we will put the name of the person in) has triggered me to feel _____ (put the feeling description in) because _____ (the why, or action by the trigger).*

19. Why was I triggered? Here, it becomes the reason. Here were my answers down below:

## Steve and the Stinky Office Example

**Questions #1: In this moment, what or who triggered you to Drift, feeling angry, frustrated, pissed off, hurt, upset, or disappointed and why?**

**Answer:** *In this moment, Steve (the landlord of my office unit in Dana Point) and the smell of the office has triggered me to feel fucking furious because I have addressed this fucking 10+ times* *and the shitty smell continues to pour into my fucking office every single morning when I show up. I bought this fucking place as a sanctuary, not a cesspool.*

20. I like that. A sanctuary, not a cesspool.

21. All we're doing is putting on the brakes in Question #1. This particular situation was actually created the day we recorded this into a training video when I came in the studio to record them. My office studio smelled like shit again. It literally stunk and smelled like shit. I was triggered. I had all these great things I was going to share with you about my wife, my kids and I was like, "Fuck it." We're going to use the thing that's right in front of me, which is that the fucking office is triggering the shit out of me.

22. You would think, "Hey! Garrett lives the Warrior's Way. He's like the founder of *Wake Up Warrior*. He should have all this shit figured out."

23. Oh, no. What I've got figured out is: I get fucking triggered like a mother fucker about a lot of shit all of the time. Instead of letting it control me, however, I grab it by the fucking balls and then I bring it close to me and I say, "All right. I'm going to handle this shit right now."

## Begin by Asking Questions

24. Bam. Off I go, and I do that by asking questions. My goal here is not to be spiritual. My goal here is not to be right. My goal here is to get what I'm feeling on the inside, on the outside. Some of you might feel all stiff and formal, like, "Hmm. I'm very uncomfortable with, Steven. He's not making me feel good." No. This is not a time for you to be pressy pussy with a stick up your ass. It's time for you to fucking go all in on the document. When you use this tool, the goal is to get all your feelings *out*, which means, you're going to type them up in a way that allows you get them out. These tools help you get them out of you.

25. If we don't get them out of you, we can't examine it. If we can't examine it, we can't Shift. If we can't Shift, we can't Lift. If we can't Lift, we don't learn. If we don't learn, we say stuck in the Karmic Cul-De-Sac and we end up doing stupid shit.

26. Question number one starts off very simply. Question #2 continues:

Question #2: In this moment, if you could scream to this individual, what would you say?

**Answer:** (Write out whatever it is that you would scream, completely uncensored and with no holding back)

27. We bring into our mind the person or the situation that triggered us and write it down as we would scream it. Because everybody wants to scream to or at somebody. It's bullshit. Even all of my super organized, collected people, you know, the internal hurricanes that never want to scream that are all super under control. Fuck you. Inside, guess what you're doing? You want to scream to people all the time. You're sitting there being all like calm, cool and collected, when what you really want to do is just grab the old lady at the gas station, and you'd be like, "Bitch! Shut up!"

28. Or you just want to freak the fuck out on your kids and be like, "God dammit! Go to bed!" Whatever it is you want to do, like, we want to yell at people. For those who don't want to yell, it's because you suppress as a mother fucker and that's why you're here.

29. This game is about getting you relaxed, which means, we're going to do this and release our frustrations out in this document. Sometimes, it's going to be screaming at your wife during this. You'd be like, "Bitch! Dammit Woman!" You're probably thinking, "What? Seriously? Did you just say that?" Yeah. I said that about my wife.

30. Or maybe we want to unleash about our kids. The goal here is to imagine a person in front of you and answering this question, being able to scream that out as if they were here:

## Steve and the Stinky Office Example (Continued)

**Question #2: In this moment, if you could scream at this individual, what would you say?**

**Answer:** *STEVE, YOU MOTHER FUCKER! Fix my fucking office smell! You stupid mother fucker. I'm so sick and tired of this shit. Fucking pussy. Fix my shit or give me my money back, you big sack of horse shit. FUCK YOU ASSHOLE!*

31. These are fun, breaking it down, now that I'm not in the moment anymore. As you've noticed in mine, I like to put a lot of mother fuckers. Some of you may not like that. You're going to be like "mother effers." You know what? You're the ones that need to say, "fuck you" to get the rage out so you can move on. Just so you know, use it. This is the time that you trigger your words. State stuff that gets you emotionally fired up.

32. Sharing this actual document with you now, I'm on the other side of it, right? It's actually quite laughable, but that's when you'll know that the shit is working. Trust me. When I first wrote this all down, I was *not* happy. There was nothing funny about it. I was furiously typing what was happening here.

33. This for me was my real feeling as I answered the third question inside Release the Rage:

Question #3: In this moment, if you could force an individual to think, say, feel or do anything, what would it be?

**Answer:** *I would force _____(name of the person) to _____(write down the action).*

34. Now, you might say, "What is this 'force' thing all about?" Just like screaming at people: Inherently, there's a piece inside of us that wants to force people to do shit. Don't lie to yourself. You *want* to force your employees, your wife, your kids, your neighbor, your mother-in-law to shut the fuck up. Whatever it is. Like, there's a piece inside of you when you're triggered, in which you want to be able to control everyone and everything around you. It's not like you don't want to scream at people all of the time. It's not like you want to get angry and stay angry. You're fired up, so you don't want to force people to do things inside this particular tool.

35. In Release the Rage, it's about getting it all out. Let's come back to Steve and let's see what I wished I could force him to do in my mind:

## Steve and the Stinky Office Example (Continued)

### Question #3: In this moment, if you could force an individual to think, say, feel or do anything, what would it be?

**Answer:** *I would force him to accept the fact that he has fucked up over and over on this issue, and that he's losing trust with me as a client because of empty promises to fix the problem.*

36. Again, using the training wheels here on this: What is the action you demanded of them? What are you going to require them to do? What is the action set inside of this that you would force them to do with this thing?

37. We continue to put the brakes on as we move down into the fourth question:

Question #4: In this moment with no filter nor constraints, what do you truly think about this individual?

**Answer:** _____ *(Name of the person) is* _____ *(Make a list).*

38. Now, here's the fun part. We are bullshitters. We even bullshit inside of our bullshitting. It's like the sickening process of disconnection.

## Owning Your Rage by Expressing It

39. The way that we get out our Rage is we own it. We take the power away from it by expressing it. In this case, we express this Rage in a safe location using the tool known as Release the Rage, done in document form and not with the person face to face. At least not yet. I come out and I use this tool with no constraints, taking the name of the person of my trigger which is Steve.

40. Then, I use the one-word descriptions or more to describe him:

## Steve and the Stinky Office Example (Continued)

**Question #4: In this moment with no filter nor constraints, what do you truly think about this individual?**

**Answer:** *Steve is a piece of shit. Steve is worthless. Steve is fucking hopeless as a property manager. Steve is a fucking dick head. Steve has crossed the line for the last time. Steve is a cock sucker.*

41. You might be asking, "Holy shit! What did this guy do?!"

42. Well, literally, he did nothing. I was just pissed off and fired up this morning. When I walked in the office and it smelled as soon as I opened the door, I got triggered. Immediately. A story began and feelings rose up but I was so wrapped up that I couldn't even do the work we needed to do today in production shooting Warrior videos until I was able to resolve the issue.

43. I had to say, "Fuck it. We're just going to take the shit I'm already pissed off about. Forget the stuff I was planning on sharing. We're just going to share this shit because it's real for me right now."

44. This list is about getting out any names that come to mind when this person comes to mind. You should get to a point once you've exhausted the naming of this person where you're like, "Well, I think I got all of my feelings out clearly about this guy and the situation."

45. Now, the funnier part is this: Does Steve have a clue that any of this is going on about him? No.

## It's Not You, It's Me

46. I could just as easily use these tools on my wife, someone else's kids (or my own), friends, with their family, with our business partners, and so on. Across the board, no one is off limits inside a Release the Rage because at the end of the day, Release the Rage is not about them. They were simply the person in the game of the trigger that caused you to experience the Drift.

47: Which then leads us to the next question:

Question #5: In this moment, what is it that you don't ever want to experience in the future with this individual?

**Answer**: *I don't ever want to experience* _____ *(list what it is you don't ever want to experience).*

48. Now, we're going to start looking at future experiences and saying, "Listen. This is the bullshit I'm dealing with Steve right now. As I travel down the journey over here, I don't ever want to experience this shit in the future with this person or these individuals inside the trigger."

49. Let's come back and see what I said with Steve:

## Steve and the Stinky Office Example (Continued)

**Question #5: In this moment, what is it that you don't ever want to experience in the future with this individual?**

**Answer:** *I don't ever want to walk into my office and smell the same bullshit I am smelling. I don't ever want to get another email that says he's fixing shit and then nothing fucking changes. Fuck you, mother fucker!*

50. Again, when you fill random feelings around it, don't let them sit inside. This is not a time to filter. Some of you are going to be hilarious, especially the first few times you do your Warrior Stack, because you're not even going to be able to say what you truly feel. You might put OMG instead of saying "Oh, my God." Or you'll put like F*... instead of saying fuck. People all of the time would write down "F-word." Listen. If you are so triggered by that word, triggered by the darkness that you see around these words, you have no fucking chance to actually have it all. Part of the gift inside of the Drift, inside of your life is to be able to own that you are in a dark place.

## Dealing with the Darkness

51. The only way you're going to put the dark brakes on is to deal with the darkness that's inside of you. That means, you're going to use every fiery word that you could ever imagine even if you would never say it to another person's face. You're going to release all of that shit and get it out. Get it *all* out. Get it on the table. Because here is the hard part. Here's the sad part. You know what most men do?

52. Most men are nice to everybody in the marketplace. They get triggered but they suppress the Rage. Then, they go home and you know what happens at home? Instead of doing this kind of fucking work, they just unleash on their wife. They unleash on their children. They unleash on those inopportune times at the office and they blast people that matter.

## Mastering YOU with Peace Beyond the Rage

53. Part of this game with the Release the Rage is learning to master you: Who you are and how you operate.

54. These questions lead up to our final question of the Release the Rage:

Question #6: In this moment, if you had to put all your feelings into one singular trigger statement, what would it be?

**Answer:** _____(Name of the trigger person) should/shouldn't _____(description of advice we demand from this individual).

55. There's a guide inside of this training wheel that will help you in the beginning. We'll use the name of the individual who is in the trigger and we will simply add the word should or shouldn't:

56. In this case, my statement became:

## Steve and the Stinky Office Example (Conclusion)

**Question #6: In this moment, if you had to put all your feelings into one singular trigger statement, what would it be?**

**Answer:** *Steve should fix the smell immediately and stop bullshitting me with this fucked up solution.*

57. Now, if you've done this part correctly, the Release the Rage weapon will leave you feeling the Peace beyond the Rage. What it does inside the Drift Model is it allows us to get all of that fire out, so that instead of drifting all the way down, we stop right here. The better you get at Releasing the Rage, the faster you stop. The faster you stop. The faster you stop.

58. The distance between the Drift and Lift is significantly less painful than from sinking down into the Pit before doing anything about it. The gap and the distance required to travel and the amount of effort and work it takes to hit the bottom and then pull yourself back out is ridiculously longer and more intense than just hitting these first two and then shifting.

59. Your Shift must come by stopping. The Release the Rage creates the space by putting on the fucking brakes in the Drift. Once we're there, we can move on to other tools, our other weapons that allows the Shift to Lift and to ultimately find the Light inside the Night. What I want you to do now is practice your first time unleashing your shit about something or somebody inside of the Release the Rage weapon.

## Chapter 12:
## POINTS TO PONDER FROM THE GENERAL'S TENT:

- **POINT #1: Identify the Trigger:** You must pick a target and sometimes that target is you. Every single feeling you have inside has been triggered by someone or encouraged by someone. Sometimes it is a situation and not a specific person, but many people and sometimes the target of your trigger is just you. In Stage One you must identify and name the target or else the clarity you seek as you dive into the night will not be found.

- **POINT #2: Release the Fury:** You must Release the Rage within. WHY? Because the Rage within you is holding a gift for you that you cannot see until you clear the clouds and you give it time to grow and to become and allow you to see. There is a Pocket of Peace that cannot be found by avoiding the Pain of the Rage you feel but can only be accessed if you dive deep into the darkness and allow the FURY to come out.

- **POINT #3: Clarify the Fire:** Once the initial phase of the fire has been released, you will be able to start clarifying many of the thoughts and feelings that you're now able to see that you couldn't before. This will allow you to consider how you feel about the person or situation as well as what you don't ever want to experience again now that you have had this current experience that triggered this release.

- **POINT #4: Summarize the Rage:** Simplify the Rage down to a simple statement, Story or judgment. Imagine you are limited to just one statement that you can place on a note card that summarizes the thoughts you're having after having smashed the shit out of the Release the Rage Form.

# WARRIOR WITNESS:

### L.P., Laguna Niguel, California USA:

*"Without releasing the rage, your anger will be misguided. Family and friends who have done nothing will feel the adverse effects of your anger. Your kids who have done absolutely nothing but be good boys and girls could be subjected to misdirected rage and your wife will be subjected to nonsensical anger, because YOU ARE PISSED OFF about something. That's not right. Usually being angry or full of rage does no good, and it really does nothing when you take it out on your loved ones for no reason."*

## C.H., Buckeye, Arizona USA:

*"I keep my emotions inside. All of my emotions. Being able to rage like that, using this document, I can't even describe how much I felt during that. I was able to put my thoughts in paper and out loud for the first time. This shit works! It was never ok before to say what I had in my head."*

## C.B., Tacoma, Washington USA:

*"Fucking hell, once I typed out the Rage, I went through the rest of the stack. I felt all the withheld rage inside me releasing and it created a void of the only word I can come up with, which is emptiness currently.*

*Then as I finished the stack, helpful emotions came flooding in.*

*Purely amazing what this has done for me so quickly.*

*I can't wait for more!"*

## C.M., Rigby, Idaho USA:

*"Fuck, I can find the Rage and I can find the triggers that put me in the Rage, but talking about it and allowing myself to feel that Rage, and knowing that it is okay for me to let it all out. This process is fucking outstanding and very helpful. I have found that after I complete this document, I think about it all day and work through my feeling and begin to move forward with my life and not carry around all of that hate over a simple fucking trigger in my life."*

## D.G., Los Angeles, California USA:

*"This one is super easy and straightforward, just dumping out the feelings on paper. I'm surprised how much better it makes you feel. I love this part of the process. Garrett motivating and inspiring us to be our own therapists, and giving us the tools to do it is one of the most innovative things I've heard of in a long time."*

# THE DARK
# RELEASE THE RAGE

**1. In this moment, what/who has triggered you to drift, feel angry, frustrated, pissed off, hurt, upset or disappointed and why?**

*In this moment ___[name]_____ has triggered me to feel ___[feeling]_____ because ____[why, the action by trigger]_____.*

**2. In this moment, if you could scream at this individual(s) what would you say?**

*In this Moment I would scream ____[description]_____ .*

**3. In this moment, if you could force this Individual(s) to think, say, feel or do anything what would it be?**

*I would Force them to _____[action you demand]_____.*

**4. In this moment, with no filter nor constraints what do you truly think about this Individual(s)? (Make a list)**

*_____[Name]_____ is _____[one word description]_____.*

**5. In this moment, what is it that you don't ever want to experience in the future with this individual(s)?**

*I don't ever want to _____[description]_____.*

**6. In this moment, if you had to put all your feelings into one singular trigger statement what would it be?**

*___[Name]_____ should/shouldn't_____[description of request, counsel or advice]_____.*

# THE STACK

## Chapter 13: THE DRIFT

Once the brakes are put on inside of Release the Rage, Power Focus
becomes the next game inside of The Drift.

# SECTION THREE
# THE STACK

## CHAPTER THIRTEEN
# THE DRIFT

### (POWER FOCUS, PART ONE)

"Thoughts will change and shift just like the wind and the water when you're on the boat;
thoughts are no different than anything else."

**-Jeff Bridges**
(American Actor, singer and Humanitarian
founder of the End Hunger Network)

---

## Applying the Brakes

1. Once you've put on the brakes inside of Release the Rage, Power Focus becomes the next game inside of The Drift. Release the Rage encouraged us to deal with the darkness, the drifted self and the Shift inside that Drift which comes after we've been able to put the brakes on.

2. Now, here's the reality. Sometimes, you're going to *need* to put the brakes on and sometimes you'll be able to put the brakes on without using Release the Rage. This current tool, the current weapon we're going to dive into now, which is Power Focus, could be done independently of Release the Rage or it could be stacked as part of the process of Release the Rage.

3. In the examples I'm going to share with you in this chapter you will see the Warrior Stack version of using Power Focus in congruence with Release the Rage. In other words, I'm going to take content like we were using inside of the other form in Release the Rage, and I'm going to show

you how to roll directly into the Power Focus document now that I've put the brakes on The Drift.

4. We've got some space now. We're not descending anymore into the trauma. We've stopped. Now, we're beginning the game of inquiry. We've got to deal with some more questions. We've got to ask ourselves some questions about where we find ourselves in the Dark. It's like driving like a maniac off a cliff and then halfway down you stop mentally and kind of assess what's going on, asking "Okay, where exactly, where have I gone?" Unfortunately, in a real life scenario we would already be plummeting down, unable to stop the pull of gravity before landing in the Pit. Fortunately for us all, we can mentally stop halfway down from the cliff of insanity and course correct.

## Creator of Your Situations

5. It's very easy in this place to feel weak in the night. It's easy to feel weak in the darkness. It's easy to feel like a victim inside of your circumstance. We want to be able to put the brakes on, but once we're there, establish order that you are the creator of the meaning of your situations. That inside The Drift, once I've stopped the game, I must create space in order to Shift.

6. Let's come back to our form here and let's go in to our questions of our Drift and Shift Model:

Question #1: What is the situation that triggers you?

**Answer:** The situation that triggered me was _____ (description and details). This triggered me because _____ (state why it triggered you).

7. Now, again, I could enter this question from a totally unrelated topic than Steve and the Stinky Office that was the source of our Release the Rage document. I'm going to be using Steve and the Stinky Office here and we're going to keep stacking that conversation. I could enter into this conversation with anything that had occurred where I had been triggered and use that event in a situation where I'm feeling a little bit of fire, but I'm not so out of control that I need to put the brakes on, so that I have the ability to then enter the conversation.

8. Regardless of how you got there, the first question that we're going to use in inquiry inside the Power Focus is:

# Steve and the Stinky Office Example

## Question #1: What is the situation that triggered you?

**Answer**: *I walk into my office again this time and the smell that has gotten worse over and over was back. The situation triggered me because I've had this conversation with Steve over and over, fucking over. I've paid great money for this office and should not have to walk in and have the same shit going on every single fucking day.*

9. As I type this shit up, I'm very much on fire when I'm typing it so I'm not trying to spell check. Don't try to spell check your shit or make sure that it grammatically flows. Nobody is going to look at this but you, and the focus needs to be on getting the feelings out more than on how they are being conveyed. Our goal inside of this is to describe WHAT the situation is. WHAT is the trigger? WHAT is the situation that has occurred?

# Getting Clear On the Cause

10. Within our Drift and Shift model, we're trying to get clear on what's going on up here. Again, what was the trigger? I'm drifting, I'm drifting, but I was able to stop here without doing Release the Rage, or I did Release the Rage and now I'm stopped. Now, I'm saying, "Okay."

11. Once we asked what happened, we go into our second question:

Question #2: What is the story created by that trigger that you are telling yourself and others?

**Answer:** The story that I tell is _____ (describe the story that rises when this trigger occurs).

12. It's important to address this story. See, the trigger happens and the story has begun. We've got to investigate the fucking story and we've got to investigate the feelings. We've got to figure out what in the fuck is going on right here. What is happening with you right here? Again, we put the brakes on. Now, we stop. We're saying, okay, how did we get here? Okay, what's going on?

13. Next, what is the story that I'm telling myself or others inside of Steve? Let's check out what the story was I was telling.

14. The story that I was telling was the following:

## Steve and the Stinky Office Example (Continued)

**Question #2: What is the story created by that trigger that you are telling yourself and others?**

**Answer:** *Steve doesn't give a shit about me and the issues with the office. This story truly has me wanting to fucking kick his ass and burn his fucking building to the ground, which is comical when you think about it because that wouldn't actually like accomplish shit for me.*

15. Nonetheless, it was a real feeling, so I wrote it down. With our little training wheels on, we go back and realize what the story we're telling ourselves is, and we want a specific, short one to two sentence statement. This isn't time for me to ramble on and on; I did that in Release the Rage. I'm going to get narrowed down now in Power Focus. What's really going on? What is the trigger judgment story? What is the judgment? What is the story?

16. What is the statement running in my mind?

*Steve doesn't give a shit about me and issues with the office.*

## Story Quality for Quality of Life

17. It's a pretty good story. The quality of your life and the quality of my life comes down to the quality of our stories: The story of who we believe ourselves to be. The story of who we believe others to be. The story we believe about ourselves and relationship with them. Our stories govern everything about our reality. Once we're stopped in the Drift, we've got to investigate the stories that we're not telling that are supporting the situation we have found ourselves in.

18. Those stories, though they are being told, may not be the most efficient stories to get us out of the Drift. However, they are stories that we will tell here inside the Drift. Even if we've hit the brakes, they will perpetuate us

back down to the Pit and then similar stories will raise us back up on a false plain, only to repeat the Karmic Cul-de-sac for decades. We've got to investigate the story. But not just one story; we're going to start with the first story. Now we are getting down to the core issue. What is the original story?

## What If Your Story Wasn't True?

19. Here, I told myself a story: *Steve doesn't give a shit about me and the issues with the office.* Next question inside the Power Focus is to ask a show stopper.

20. This simple statement right here has the power to change everything: What if it's not true?

Question #3: Is this story true?

**Answer:** Yes or No.

21. Is that story true? What's the story that I was telling? The story that I was telling was Steve doesn't give a shit about me and the issues with the office. The next question in the process of inquiry is simply asking me, is that story true? It's a good story. Is it true?

22. Now, 9 out of 10 times you're going to be fired up coming in to the Power Focus tools and guess what your first answer is going to be? Bam! Yes, it's true. The question to this question itself is answered very simply with a simple check yes or no. Is that story true? In this case, my answer was yes. We're going to hit some more morning tracks here. We're going to give ourselves a second opportunity. I'm going to come back with another question, very similar to the first question.

23. Only this one is going to say: Are you a 100% sure? Like hold on, hold on, Bro. Hold on. Okay, listen. You're fired up. I know you're telling a good story right now. I know you're pissed. Is it true? And they're like, "Yes, you bitch fucking asses."

Okay, cool. Pass.

24. Time out for a bit.

25. I'm not saying it's not true. I'm not saying you can't believe it's true. I'm not saying you're not going to continue to believe it's true. I *am* going to say that that story is not going to give you what you want, but here's

what I'm going to ask you again. I'm going to ask you to back it up real quick. Take a deep breath.

26. Are you sure?

Question #4: Are you 100% sure that that story is true?

**Answer:** Yes or No.

27. Because you're sitting over here inside the Drift, and the quality of your stories are going to either cause you to Shift and Lift to the Light at the next peak or they are going to cause you to continue to descend into the Pit. Are you sure? Are you 100% sure the story is true? Is it true? Are you sure?

28. Now, regardless of your answer, yes or no on either question, we continue on, but we give ourselves another question. By asking the secondary question, it forces the mind to second guess itself for just a moment. It creates just a bit of space.

29. Let's continue with our example of Steve and the Stinky Office:

## Steve and the Stinky Office Example (Continued)

### Question #3 Is this story true?

*Steve doesn't give a shit about me and issues with the office.*

**Answer:** *Yes.*

### Questions #4: Are you 100% sure that this story is true?

**Answer:** *No.*

## Investigating Our Feelings

30. We then go in again to investigate our feelings. If we come back over to our Drift and Shift model, we remember that our trigger links up to the stories that we're telling and those stories tell the feelings inside of us. We've hit the Drift. We hit the brakes. We're starting to investigate. We're identifying what the trigger was, what was going on, what the story was that I'm telling right now that's coming off of that trigger. Is it true? Can I know it's true for sure?

31. Now, this is where we get to stop for just a second, and I realize that you are not likely comfortable talking about your feelings. Neither was I. I realize that you are also probably not clear about what you feel most of the time. I understand that also. That's part of doing this work. Every single day investigating. Every single day inside of the Core 4, using the Power Focus tool as one of the mechanisms for scoring. Release the Rage is a bonus tool, but the Power Focus tool is a daily discipline for the highest level players inside of this Brotherhood.

## Managing the Drift

32. We use Power Focus on a daily basis to train the mind, to manage the Drift. The Drift is on, we hit the brakes, then open the space of inquiry by asking better questions. We open the space by coming to identify more and more every day how we feel.

33. Let's take a look at how I felt about Steve:

## Steve and the Stinky Office Example (Continued)

### Question #5: What feelings come up for you when you believe this story to be true?

*Steve doesn't give a shit about me and issues with the office.*

**Answer:** *I feel rage. I feel anger. I feel frustration. I feel disappointment. I feel fire. I feel upset.*

34. Again, the training wheel item up here is I feel and then the blank will be there; a description of the feeling.

## Opening a Little More Space

35. Now, once I've investigated those feelings, we're beginning to open that space up a little bit more. The next thing we're going to take a look at is:

Question #6: What specific thoughts or desired actions arise from those feelings?

**Answer:** I want to _____(Description of the action). Make a list.

36. The piece that we have and dictated here is the fact that underneath these feelings are the actions. These actions that we have been discussing

over and over again are either driving us upward towards the next peak or are accelerating us back around the Karmic Cul-de-sac and around the story that the problems aren't being solved as we keep looping this bitch.

37. What do we have to do? We have to investigate what our desired actions are. We come over to the question, which asks us what specific thoughts or desired actions arise from those feelings. These feelings are linked up to some shit you think you should do. The trigger, the story, the feelings and some shit you think you should do.

38. Let's continue to take a look over on this question with Steve:

## Steve and the Stinky Office Example (Continued)

### Question #6: What specific thoughts or desired actions arise from those feelings?

**Answer:** *I'm going to send him an e-mail and request withdraw from the office. I'm going to head to his office and scream at him. I want to legally end my contract. I want to punch him. I want to sue him. I want to fucking scream at him. I want to confront him.*

39. Now, again, there are some of you who are going to be like, "Dude, seriously, I am pretty certain that you're a fucking lunatic." Guess what? You would be right. Guess what else you would be right about? The fact that you and every other human being that walks the planet is crazy. You are a lunatic until you are willing to find the Light in the Night and the only way to find the Light in the Night is on your daily Core 4 to do the fucking work we call Power Focus.

## Tracking the Light Inside the Night

40. Power Focus allows you to track the light inside the night. Power Focus allows you to get all of these feelings and thoughts out. We are looking to get out the thoughts and the desired actions that flow from you. Sometimes, they're not going to appear that "positive." They're not going to be all warm and fuzzy. They're not going to be all up on a little vision board you might display at your local church house. These are going to be things you might only say to yourself. These are going to be some shit you're going to pour into the work every single day as you hit your Core 4.

41. Every single day that you do this, you come to understand better the triggers and the actions driven by the feelings, driven by the stories and driven by the triggers that own your ass right now.

## Master Yourself First

42. You want to be more powerful in business? You want to be more powerful in your marriage? You want to be more powerful as a father? You want to be more powerful as a man? You're going to have to learn to master yourself. Self-mastery comes about with identification of the feelings, the stories, the triggers and the actions, the desires and thoughts that run rampant inside of you, but never, never, ever have you and I been trained to look at them. If we did, it was like, once a year.

43. Inevitably, you know when they look at their feelings, you know when most men do a Power Focus assessment of some type at the very fucking bottom. All the way down here most men wait until he hits the rock bottom and then he's like, "Oh shit, now I think I'll do something now that my back is against the wall. I'm between a rock and a hard place, and now I'm going to be all inspired."

44. Or you could just do the fucking work called the Warrior's Way. Every single day, as part of your Core 4. You could do the work *every single day.*

45. Somedays, you might have to put the brakes on and so you do Release the Rage, and then you run yourself straight up and open in the space, finding a new possibility inside of Power Focus. Power Focus continues down this game.

46. We start to ask ourselves another question:

Question #7: If you step back from the story for a second, what do you want in this moment for you, for them, for you both?

**Answer:** I want _____ (description of want) for me.

I want _____ (description of the want) for him/her.

I want _____ (description of the want) for us.

47. I want you to imagine that we're moving along, we're moving along, we're telling the story. We're believing it, we're believing it, then, we go,

whoa! We may step back from the story and I stand up here and I say, wait a second, wait a second, wait a second, okay.

## Learning to Ask Better Questions

48. I'm telling some stories right now, but the only way out of the cul-de-sac, the only way out of the Drift, the only way I can Shift and the only way I can Lift is to get clear about what I want and ask myself a better question. I sit there and I say, okay, okay, what do I want? What do I want in this situation? This takes some work.

49. What do I want? When you know what you want, you're not a victim to what goes on in the Drift. Instead, you begin to focus on the solution on how to get out instead of remaining, looping over and over again. Do you want this? Is that what you want? Do you want to go back to and only repeat the Karmic loop of Drifting and False Lifts? Is that what you want? What you truly want exists over in the Lift, but it's not just what you want for you. We're in the middle of investigating these stories and then we start to ask ourselves better questions.

50. What do I want for me? Someone else is usually involved in this conversation with you. What do you want for them? If I'm in a war with my wife, what do I want with myself? What do I want right now? What do I want for her? More importantly, what do I want for us? Inside of this example with Steve in the stinky office, what do I want for me? What do I want for Steve? What do I want for us? I've got to deal with him. I lease this office from him. We need to be in relationship, but what do I want for myself? What do I want for him? What do I want for us?

## Spinning the Game Around

51. The "what do I want?" question begins to spin this entire game because it starts to set us up to see our stories getting us what we want. Do our stories help us get what we want in this moment? Do they help us get what we want tomorrow? Do the stories today get us to the destiny we desire tomorrow?

52. We ask this question and we step back from this for a moment. I ask myself that same question with Steve:

## Steve and the Stinky Office Example (Continued)

**Question #7:** If you step back from the story for a second, what do you want in this moment for you, for them, for you both?

**Answer:** *For me, I want an office that I walk into that's clean and smells clean to me. For him, I want not to have to contact Steve and for Steve to never have to communicate with me about problems because they're fucking handled. What do I want for us? I want both of us to be able to just communicate one time per year and smile and say hello and then to never have any other communication because there are no problems. Here's your money, I say to him. Here's your property he says to me. The end. That's it.*

## Know What Others Want As Well

53. If you don't investigate the stories and then get clear about what you want, there's no power to pull you out. The power to pull you out of the Drift is found in asking, "What do I want?" It's found in this experience of saying, okay, well, you know what, this is what I want right here.

54. What I want exists out here and that is going to lead me to what I want over here and you can't get to where you want without being in a relationship with other people. You can't get what you want if you're married and your wife is not on board, which means you're going to have to give a shit about what other people want, too. The greatest teachers in training of all time have taught this. If you want to get more of what you want, help other people get what *they* want.

55. Sometimes, you may not even be clear about what you want, let alone what anyone else wants keep you limited. Power Focus itself begins to open that up. It says no, no, no. We're not only *not* going to be victims in the Drift, We're going to investigate the Drift and inside of that we're also going to make sure that the stories that we're telling are getting us what we want.

56. Once we've investigated that, we ask another important question:

Question #8: Will the current story give you what you want?

**Answer:** Yes or No.

57. We have a story that we're telling; the original story. Will it give me what I want? Does it direct me to the destiny of what I'm searching for?

58. I come back over here to the situation with Steve, and I answer this question again:

## Steve and the Stinky Office Example (Continued)

### Question #8: Will the current story give you what you want?

*Steve doesn't give a shit about me and issues with the office.*

### Answer: *No.*

59. The answer for me was no. The story was that Steve doesn't give a shit about me and the issues with the office. That's not even fucking true. I was pissed off. I was fired up and I believed it, but the truth is, that story, even if it were true and even if Steve didn't give a shit about me and about the office, the answer is no: It's not going to give me what I want. I continue down this path and we continue to ask these questions. The questions that proceed now fall into what I call Walk the Block.

## Shifting the Drift

60. Power Focus is divided into two phases: Phase #1 we call the Drift. Phase #2 we call the Shift. Being able to lock both these down allow us to Shift the Drift. We go from the Drift phase, Phase #1, to the Shift phase, Phase #2. Inside of that, we uncover the keys we need to ultimately lift ourselves out of the Drift and towards the next peak. If you haven't practiced the first half of the Power Focus experience we call the Drift, I encourage you to do that now using the example found at the end of this chapter before moving onto the next chapter: Power Focus, Phase #2.


## Chapter 13:
## POINTS TO PONDER FROM THE GENERAL'S TENT

- **POINT #1: Paint the Picture:** At this point you are already heavily into the Drift but you have been able to put the brakes on. Now it is time to paint a picture of what you currently see around you and inside of you. I like to call this the anchor point where you are going to stake an anchor into the Drift Wall so that you can stop falling and give yourself a chance to tell a different story.

- **POINT #2: Clarify the Story:** As you have painted the picture, clarified the trigger and repainted the picture for how you got to where you are it is now time to identify the story that you immediately began telling yourself after you were triggered. This story is not true and it is not false, nor is it good or bad. In this stage, you are simply wanting to identify the story that is driving the feelings you are having and actions you are either wanting to take or have taken.

- **POINT #3: Identify Feelings:** Feelings. Feelings. Feelings. Feelings. They're everywhere and they are impossible for you to manage or leverage if you are unaware or afraid to investigate them at any real level. Your feelings are your fire and if you are unable to understand them, then it will become highly likely that these flames will burn your reality to the ground even if that is not what you desire.

- **POINT #4: What do you want?** This is one of the simplest and yet hardest questions to answer in life. You see, in every single moment, even in the middle of a Drift, there are desires that are guiding your actions. To you and most of the men you know, the ability to be clear about what you want in every situation is complicated and often impossible, but after you have Created Space through the DRIFT, you are able to know exactly what it is that you want.

# WARRIOR WITNESS:

## C.M., Rigby, Idaho USA:

*"The 'show stopper' for me is asking if the story that I am telling myself is true or not. Holy shit! I want to believe that it is true, but after that deep breath, I honestly can know state that it IS or it IS NOT true. What really sets me free from this hate is that I can step back and look at my feelings, realizing that I can find that I am not always right on my first assumption. This action by going through the FULL WARRIOR STACK of tools helps me come to a stronger story of truth as I see it and as I have set the RAGE aside and exposed the real truth! FUCK this is powerful! This is the best freedom I have ever felt!"*

## M.D., Parkland, California USA:

*"Shifting from the dark and deciding or looking at the truth and the different sides of the story, then asking myself what I want and how can I help them get*

*what they want is the kicker and may not be what feel goods in some of my problems, so in the past I would avoid this and not change. This is a powerful tool."*

————————————

## R.B., Boerne, Texas USA:

*"So fucking simple but I have stumbled with this for years. The stories that I am telling myself control me. Change the story and change my life!"*

————————————

# THE DRIFT
# POWER FOCUS, PART 1

**1. What is the Situation that Triggered You?**

*The Situation that triggered me was _____[description & details of what happened & why it triggered you]_____.*

**2. What is the Story, created by that Trigger that you are telling yourself (and others)?**

*The Story I'm telling is _____[specific, short 1-2 sentence statement]_____.*

**3. Is that Story True?**

*[ ] Yes*

*[ ] No*

**4. Are You 100% Sure that Story It's True?**

*[ ] Yes*

*[ ] No*

**5. What feelings come up for you when you believe this Story to be True? (Make a list)**

*I feel _____[description of feeling]_____.*

**6. What specific thoughts or desired actions arise as from those feelings? (Make a list)**

*I want to _____[description of action]_____.*

**7. If you step back from this story for a second, what do you want in this moment For You, For them, For you both?**

*I want _____[description of want]_____ for me.*

*I want _____[description of want]_____ for them.*

*I want _____[description of want]_____ for us.*

## 8. Will the current story give you what you want?

*Insert original story here.*

*[ ] Yes*

*[ ] No*

## 9. What might be possible for you in this situation if the Current Story was False?

*I would be free to [description of possibility]_____ .*

# THE STACK

## Chapter 14: THE SHIFT

The second half of Power Focus gives us an opportunity to "Walk the Block" in order to see triggers and issues multiple ways from different perspectives.

# SECTION THREE
# THE STACK

## CHAPTER FOURTEEN
# THE SHIFT

### (POWER FOCUS, PART TWO)

"And, when you want something, all the universe conspires in helping you to achieve it."

**- Paulo Coelho**
(excerpt from The Alchemist)

---

## Putting the Brakes On the Drift
## by Walking the Block

1. Now it's time for the second half of Power Focus. You will get the most out of reading and applying this next tool if you've done the first half: Power Focus Part 1. Now I'm going to dive into the Shift. The Shift is the point of this training. In this training, we're going to discuss what happens once we've put the brakes on in the Drift. We've opened up the space. We've then identified through inquiry the current stories, the feelings, and the desired actions that we are telling ourselves at the current moment of the Shift. The simple inquisition of this is beginning to open up possibilities.

2. We are going to "Walk the Block." It's a phrase that we use inside of Warrior Week constantly in the trainings with our men who come to Warrior Headquarters in Laguna Beach, California. We say, "Off you go with a buddy. Let's walk the block." They literally walk around Laguna Beach and physically walk and talk out this document, which I'll describe here visually for you as the reader using a house to represent the concept of a block.

3. All four of these sides, if we looked at it like a house, the front of the house, the back of the house, and both the sides of the house, these areas around the house give us the opportunity to be able to discover other possible stories, not just be settled on the fact that, well, here is the original story that I told and that must be true. It's crazy how the initial thought that you have, often times, inside of that Drift is not going to get you to Lift. The initial thought that you have will actually perpetuate the Drift down into the Pit.

4. When I enter into the conversation of my original storytelling, my original story is the front of the block. Changing the story around to have it be about me instead is the left side of the house. This side of the house is the only story I have access to at this time.

## Finding New Possibilities

5. We're going to give ourselves a chance here and inside of the Shift, we're going to literally rotate, like a Rubik's cube, turning the stories and finding some new possibilities. This Walk around the Block is part two of our Power Focus continued. It's a phase inside Power Focus known as the Shift. Now, the Shift is going to ask us again this original story.

6. We start off inside of the work, saying, "Well, what's the original story?"

Question #1: What is the original story?

**Answer:** Write out the original statement in 1-2 sentences.

7. Now, let's go to our example of "Steve and the Stinky Office:"

## <u>Steve and the Stinky Office Example</u>

### Question #1a: What is the original story?

**Answer:**  *Steve doesn't give a shit about me and the issues with the office.*

8. The next question that we will ask inside of the original is:

Question #1b: What evidence do you have to prove this story true?

**Answer:** The story could be true because _____. (write down the evidence stating this story could be true)

9. Not what evidence do you have to prove this story false. All the stories you tell are true. To who? To you.

10. We're going to ask ourselves simply, "When you walk up to the front of this block. Here you are. Here's story number one. What evidence do you have that supports this version of the story, the original version? What evidence do you have to support that as true?"

11. Let's take a look at what I wrote here with Steve. I came in and I said:

## Steve and the Stinky Office Example Continued:

### Question #1b: What evidence do you have to prove this story true?

**Answer:** *Well, again, we're back to the training wheels process. Here is why this version could be true: the response out of things can be slow. I've brought up the smell issue for two months now. It wasn't until I lost my shit last week that they sent anyone here to actually look at the office smell issue.*

12. Here's the crazy part. That story, "Steve doesn't give a shit about me and issues with the office," actually has some legs it could run on. Those legs sit right here on the original version. If this version of the story gives me what I want, then I will keep this side of the story. This side will give me what I want. Maybe. At least we've got some evidence that says it might be true. We've got to keep walking the block though.

13. Let's continue down, then, to our next scenario. This is where things get spicy. We move over to the left side of the block, which is the other side of the house, and we say, "Okay. What is it that's going on over here?"

14. Well, I'm going to turn and I'm going to change the story. Since you are the creator of the story, you have the ability to change the version of the story and the version of the story that we're going to make is the "me" version. What is the "me" version of the story from the left side of the block? We're going to rotate it. "Me" means I'm going to put myself in replacement of Steve in the conversation. Instead of the story being about Steve, we're going to make the story about Garrett.

## All About Me

15. I'm going to replace him or whoever the individual or individuals were in that story. I'm going to replace me in that equation. The "me" version which is the left side of the block.

Question #2a: What is the "me" version of the story?

**Answer:** The "Me" version of the story is _____. (turn the story on yourself)

Question #2b: What evidence do you have to prove this is true?

**Answer:** Here is why this version could be true (List the reasons why this version could be true).

16. I'm now on the left side of the house, or turned down the block to the left, whichever visual you prefer, and face a completely different sight.

17. Therefore, I have a whole new perspective. Let's continue with the Stinky Office example.

## Steve and the Stinky Office Example Continued:

### Question #2a: What is the "me" version of the story?

**Answer:** *Garrett doesn't give a shit about Steve and issues he is facing with the office.*

18. Now, if you look at my behavior, standing over here from this point of reference, that's a very different story. Story #1: Steve doesn't give a shit about me and my issues with the office. Version: original. Version me: Garrett doesn't give a shit about Steve or his issues with the office.

19. These are two very different stories. One gives a trajectory this way. Another one gives the trajectory this way. This story over here is going to give me a result. This story over here will give me a result and both paint a totally different reality. Steve doesn't give a shit about me and my issues with the office. Garrett doesn't give a shit about Steve or Steve's issue with the office. Is there any truth to this? Well, there's always truth because I'm telling the fucking stories, and there's always truth to your stories, too. Let's see if we can get some specific evidence though.

20. Come over to the evidence side:

Question #2b: What evidence do you have to prove this is true?

Answer: *If I look at my feelings about it, I truly don't give a shit about Steve. Truly. I also don't give a shit about any issues he is facing with the office.*

21. This is true. Flat out. It was a fact because I was doing the work on it and I was being completely honest with myself about the fact that I don't care about him.

22. There could be a whole shitload of issues going on with the office, but guess how much I care? I don't. I don't care. I don't care about any of the excuses or stories. I don't care. I don't really know Steve. I don't know him personally. I don't dislike him. I don't necessarily like him. I don't really feel either way with him. That's kind of a weird deal to be standing in a situation where I have that feeling about Steve, and yet I'm saying that Steve has that same feeling about me.

## Turning Down More Blocks

23. Okay, now we still have two more sides around the block. We've got to go to them. We've started opening up the space. Here we are over here in the Drift. When we start opening up the space, there's more options now. We haven't started to Lift yet. We're still in the process of the Shift. We're trying to find out what is the most valuable story that would get us to the destination of where we want to go. What story will ultimately take us there? Let's continue to look.

24. I continue to roll the next question. We're going to turn the story to the back side of the block:

Question #3a: What is the opposite version?

**Answer:** The opposite version of the story is _____(turn the original story around).

Question #3b: What evidence do you have to prove this is true?

**Answer:** Here is why this version could be true (give reasons this could be true).

25. What is the opposite version? Here was the original version: *Steve doesn't give a shit about me or my issues with the office.*

The "me" version: *Garrett doesn't give a shit about Steve or his issues with the office.*

26. And now the opposite side, then, has me look back at my original story and has me say the opposite.

27. The opposite version inside of this conversation with Steve as my example was the following:

## Steve and the Stinky Office Example Continued:

**Question #3a: What is the opposite version?**

**Answer:** *Steve* does *give a shit about me and the issues with the office and is doing what he can to solve the problem.*

28. I'm going to take the complete energy about the original story and I'm going to turn it completely around. If we were walking around the four corners of my house, we would now be facing the backyard, or the opposite side of the block if we were using the Walk the Block visual. I'd walk down the street, turn to the left, walk down the end of that street, turn again, and now I'm on the opposite side of the block that I started on, literally standing here saying, "Steve doesn't give a shit about me or my issues with the office" when I was walking down the first side of the block, but now that you're facing directly back, I'm looking again and state "Steve *does* give a shit about me and the issues with the office and is doing what he can to solve the problem."

29. Now, my mind is already left in this place, then, saying, "Well, which one of these are true?" Well, we've got to get some evidence for the third one first and then let's see what changes: Evidence.

30. That becomes our next question:

Question #3b: What evidence do you have to prove this is true?

Answer: *Well, Steve did send his plumbing team last week out to work on things the day I sent the email to him and they got the smell fixed, at least with the shit smell coming from the gym below me, because the plumbing was broke.*

31. Well, son of a bitch. Dammit. My story is starting to lose some of the legs that it had grown. Now, I'm starting to question what the fuck's going on. I'm like, "Wait a second. What one of these is true?"

32. Steve doesn't give a shit about me and doesn't care about my issues with the office. And yet, Garrett doesn't give a shit about Steve or Steve's issue with the office either. Now I'm also realizing that Steve *does* give a shit about me and the issues with the office and he's doing all he can to solve the problem.

33. I have just created for myself an opening.

## Opening the Space of Possibilities

34. Stretching and pulling myself, opening up the space of possibility for me to see something that I couldn't see before. Inside of that space of possibility, I'm walking the block from original to me to the opposite.

35. I've got these three sides of this block covered; I've covered a ton of distance and the crazy part is, I have a lot of evidence to support that any of these three could be true, even though my original trigger right off the bat is that Steve doesn't give a shit about me or the issues I faced with the office. Garrett, the "me" version, doesn't give a shit about Steve or his issues with the office, and the opposite, Steve *does* give a shit about the issues with the office as he's trying to do all that he can to solve the problems.

36. Now that we've got these three sides covered, we're going to come back to and take a look at the final side of the block. The right side of the block. We have the original. We have the left side of the block. We have the opposite side of the block. We have the right side of the block, which brings me back this direction.

37. The right side of the block is now asking me:

Question #4a: What is the desired version?

**Answer:** The desired version is _____ (create the story you truly want)

Question #4b: What evidence do you have to prove this is true?

**Answer:** Here is why this version could be true (give reasons this could be true).

38. What does it desire? What does this mean?

39. Okay. I've gotten clear about what I want while on this side of the block and I've gotten clear about what I don't want over on this other side of the block. What I don't want, which is in the cul-de-sac off from the block that I'm walking down right now, still triggers feelings, driving all of these desires for particular actions, some of which will cascade me into the cul-de-sac and some that will Lift me to the new peak and the new path. Inside of this, then, I've got to ask myself the final question, "Well, what is the desired story?" I can avoid the cul-de-sac that's heading nowhere. Here's where the ultimate freedom comes.

## Bringing Ultimate Freedom

40. The desired story could be any of the three I've already told or it could be a new story. It could be a new story. Like there is crazy amount of freedom inside of that reality, that your life and my life is driven by the stories that we tell, and the stories that we tell the most, we believe. Inside of the Drift, you and I have the power to create the true desired story that would give us what we wanted. Inside of the Drift, we went to the opposite of the original: *Steve doesn't give a shit about me or my issues with the office* with the "me" version first: *Garrett doesn't give a shit about Steve or his issues with the office.* We then finished the opposite walk with the statement: *Steve does give a shit about me and my issues with the office and is doing the best he can to solve the problems.*

41. The desired version now says, "Huh, what is the version of the story that I actually want?"

42. My original is my left side of the house. My "me" version is my backyard. My opposite version was my other side of the house. Straight ahead of me is what I want, or the front part of my house. If I master this skill, 9 out of 10 times the stories I've told and the original, "me," and the opposite are simply support to create the desired story that will get me the quickest and most efficiently to the destination of my desire to what I want. Let's take a look at what mine was with Steve.

43. I came to that question with Steve. We've been dealing with a stinky office and I came to it again, shifting the original version to the desired version of the story in order to create the story I truly want:

## Steve and the Stinky Office Example Continued:

### Question #4a: What is the desired version?

**Answer:** *Garrett and Steve can fix this problem in time for the event this week.*

44. Now I have an event that's happening inside of this room. I need the office to not be stinky. If the office is stinky, it makes it difficult. If it's difficult, they can't get shit done. I need to make sure this shit gets done, but this story: *Garrett and Steve can fix this problem in time for the event this week*, well, this is the most empowering of all of them.

## Returning the King to His Throne

45. We've come all the way back around the block, we're now facing the front of the house and Garrett and Steve can fix these problems in time for the event this week. Now, standing in this position, I return to the throne as King in control of my stories, in control of my game, in access of the story that will actually move me into action, to do shit, to solve my own problems and to stop being a big fucking victim to my stories.

46. Nine out of ten times, you will choose the desired outcome over the others, but you could choose the others also. Let's take a look, then, at how this played out.

47. We have to find some evidence to support that because that becomes a question with this one, just like it's been with all the others:

## Steve and the Stinky Office Example Continued:

### Question #4b: What evidence do you have to prove this is true?

**Answer:** *Well, there is what Steve can do and there is what I can do. If I sit around like a big fucking pussy about everything and just bitch and moan about it, nothing is going to change it. If I want change, I can make sure he understands my needs, but at the same time, I can take things into my own hands and order an air purifying machine and essential oils diffuser for the office, regardless of what he decides. I'm not a fucking victim to Steve or the fucking smell.*

48. Hmm ... Now that's a very different game. Original: *Steve doesn't give a shit about me or my issues with the office.* "Me" version: *Garrett do*esn't give a shit about Steve or his issues with the office. Opposite version: *Steve does give a shit about me and my issues with the office and is doing the best he can to help me solve the problems.* Desired version: *sitting in the throne, looking forward to what I want.* Of all these stories, what's the desired one that I could tell that would ultimately get me to my destiny the fastest?

49. This leads us to the final question and answer in The Shift, as we summarize our second part of the Power Focus after walking around the entire block:

Question #5a: After Walking the Block, which version of the Story are you choosing and why?

**Answer:** I am choosing _____(version of story) because _____(reason why).

Question #5b: What are you committed to doing about it in the next 48 hours?

**Answer:** I am committed to _____ (fill in with the action that you will take).

50. What did I realize?

*Garrett and Steve can solve these problems with the smell in this office easily in time for the event this week.*

## Looking Forward with a Hopeful Eye

51. That is empowering. That is transformative. That is empowering inside of the fact that it returns the keys and the gift of the Shift back to me. Inside of this place, my Shift has moved to where? When I Shift into the King's throne, when I shift into the fucking King's throne and I sit, empowered by having reviewed the first three stories, I could look forward with an eye of hope in control and power. I leave the land of death in the Drift and I rise to Life with the sight that says, "I am the master of my fate. I am the captain of my soul."

52. My Game itself is up to me and I'm going to change the fucking story. Inside that story, I'm going to Lift myself to get what I want, not to be right. We come back around.

53. Some serious questions start to get asked inside this power of focus. The question is this: after walking the block, which version of the story are you choosing and why? You can always choose the original. You can choose it. You can choose the "me" version. You can choose the opposite version. You can choose the desired version. Any of these four are up to you, and the one that most closely will get you what you want, which 9 out of 10 times will be your desired outcome, the desired story that you tell after reviewing and shifting.

## Choosing Your Story

54. Once you choose that story, you'll choose it and you'll select it and why:

## Steve and the Stinky Office Example Concluded:

### Question #5a: After Walking the Block, which version of the Story are you choosing and why?

**Answer:** *Garrett and Steve can fix this problem in time for the event this week. Why do I choose this one? Because it's the only one that fucking gets shit done. There's no reason at all to even entertain talking about anything else. This is the one that will get it done. Everything else will be a nightmare. Everything else will put me back waiting, hoping, pleading that something will get done. This one allows me to stay on Steve to get shit done, but also allows me and empowers me to find the path to my own answers, to get shit done on my terms and my way.*

55. See, I can sit over here all day long and say, "Well, inside of the Drift, here's what I want and here's the story that's going to get me there," but the problem is between these two, there's the learning, which came through the gain you experienced with Power Focus, but then there's also the follow up question, "Okay, what are you going to do to get your ass there?"

56. What is the work that you're going to do to make that happen? We come back over to the question with what I did with Steve and we come down to that and I say, "Well, I'm committed to____."

57. Again, training wheels to support you inside of this:

Question #5b: What are you committed to doing about it in the next 48 hours?

Answer: *I am committed to ordering the air purifier today, getting the oil diffusers here in the office tomorrow, staying on Steve to fix the issue, while, at the same time, fixing what I can in the next 48 hours.*

## Avoiding Victim Exhaustion

58. There is nothing more exhausting in life than feeling like a victim, feeling helpless, or painting the world to be villains out to get you. This is the problem with the Drift. Inside of that gift called the Drift is a realization and an awakening that must occur inside the Shift. We just used Release the Rage to hit the brakes. Once we hit the brakes, we hit into Power Focus. Power Focus is our second weapon. Two phases: Phase #1 The Drift, which is analyzing how we got from here to there. How did we get there? Triggers, stories, feelings, and desired action.

59. Then, we go into the second part, which is Phase #2: The Shift, where we begin to Walk the Block. We walk around our house and we say, "Okay. Left side: Original.  Backyard: 'Me.' Right side: Opposite. Front of the house: Desired. Of these, what gives me what I want?"

## Sitting On the King's Throne

60. Inside of that, I take a seat in the King's throne, and off I go with action. Power Focus is done every single day. It is part of your power inside of living the Warrior's Way. It is Core 4 at the core. Learning to Shift in the Drift is mandatory. Green smoothies are great, but if you don't learn how to do this work, it won't fucking matter.

61. This is the cornerstone of everything that we do here at Warrior: the daily disciplines of executing Power Focus. It is how you will find the Light inside the Night. How to find the gifts inside your Drifts. What I want you to do now is complete that Power Focus document that you started and finish the second half.

62. This time, walking your block, and finding your seat in the King's throne will ultimately lead you towards what you ultimately want, not a sellout

counterfeit that ends you back in the Karmic Cul-de-sac, disappointed after only a couple of weeks, or even a couple of months later, realizing that Shift never changed, and that the more things change in your life, the more they stay the same.

63. You Drift. We Shift. We Lift and we learn how to manage the Drift.

## Chapter 14:
## POINTS TO PONDER FROM THE GENERAL'S TENT:

- **POINT #1: Original Story:** Your entire life is driven by the quality of your stories and in this stage of the Shift you are going to begin by taking your understanding of the original story that led you into the Drift in the first place. It is going to be a time for you to stabilize and also understand YOU and the gift that this original story was.

- **POINT #2: Me Story:** The second story you will create is the one that is 100% about you. Regardless of who the original story was about, you are now going to put yourself into the frame and use YOU as the one you are telling the story about. If this is YOU already in the original story, then you will literally use your own NAME in the story and you will move to 3rd person speaking about yourself.

- **POINT #3: Opposite Story:** The complete opposite story of the original. You will take a stand and investigate the possible truths found in the opposite version of the story that you have been telling yourself. You can do this in a bunch of different ways but ultimately you're going to flip the script and test the exact opposite statement that you found in the original version.

- **POINT #4: Desired Story:** What do you truly want? In stage one of Power Focus you reminded yourself of what you actually wanted in this situation for you, them and us. This will act as the True North that will guide you back to your King's Throne and allow you to create the ultimate story for the situation that has the highest probability of giving you what you want.

# WARRIOR WITNESS:

## M.O., Parkland, California USA:

"I have been one-sided in my problem solving, stuck in emotions and unable to define what I want out of situations. This is where I open the door and begin to see and define and take a stand and stop lying and look at the truth regardless of the pain.

This is where I open the door for the truth more, no matter how painful and narrow in what I want from this situation and consider what I want for the other person."

_____

## C.H., Buckeye, Arizona USA:

"I have the power to choose which story I tell and which story I live. I have the power now instead of being a victim!

Taking the time to lay it all out on paper makes the process easier."

_____

# THE SHIFT
# (WALK THE BLOCK)
# POWER FOCUS PART 2

**FRONT SIDE OF THE BLOCK**
**1a. What is the Original Story?**

*The "Original" Version of the Story is _____[simple description/ statement]_____ .*

**1b. What Evidence do you have to prove this Story True?**

*Here is why this version could be true _____[reasons it could be true]_____.*

**LEFT SIDE OF THE BLOCK**
**2a. What is the ME Version?**

*The "Me" Version of the story is ____[turn the story on yourself]____ _____.*

**2b. What Evidence do you have to prove this Story True?**

*Here is why this version could be true ____[reasons it could be true]_____.*

**BACK SIDE OF THE BLOCK**
**3a. What is the Opposite Version?**

*The "Opposite" Version of the Story is ___[turn the Original Story around]_____.*

**3b. What Evidence do you have to prove this Story True?**

*Here is why this version could be true ____[reasons it could be true]_____.*

**RIGHT SIDE OF THE BLOCK**
**4a. What is the Desired Version?**

*The "Desired" Version of the Story is \_\_\_[create the story you truly want]_____.*

## 4b. What Evidence do you have to prove this Story True?

*Here is why this version could be true \_\_\_\_[reasons it could be true]_____.*

## SUMMARY
## 5a. After Walking the Block, which version of the Story are you choosing and why?

*I am choosing \_\_\_\_[version of story]_____ because \_\_\_\_\_[reason why]\_\_\_\_\_.*

## 5b. What are you committed to doing within the next 48 hours?

*I am committed to _____[action you will take]_____.*

# THE STACK

## Chapter 15: THE LIFT

This next tool in the arsenal helps bring us to The Lift. Production Focus becomes the process of taking all of that power from the Release the Rage and Power Focus documents and transforms it into production.

SECTION THREE
# THE STACK

## CHAPTER FIFTEEN
# THE LIFT

### (PRODUCTION FOCUS)

"Become a possibilitarian. No matter how dark things seem to be or actually are, raise your sights and see the possibilities...always see them...for they're always there."

**- Norman Vincent Peale**
[American minister (1898-1993) and progenitor of
"positive thinking"]

---

## Adding Another Tool to the Arsenal

1. Welcome to Production Focus. Inside of this chapter we're going to continue the conversation that we began inside the Drift, Shift, and Lift model, but we're going to add another tool to your arsenal. We started with the Release the Rage tool, which was about hitting the brakes, and stopping inside the Drift. The second tool, once we're inside that stopping place, is needed to open the space. We've got to anchor into the triggers, the stories, the feelings, and the actions that we ultimately desire to take which led us into the Drift in the first place. We walked around the King's throne, and we sat down in the seat looking out at what we desired, and now we're here.

2. Now we've got to start the Lift. The Lift process is about taking all of that power and then transforming it into production. As we hit this Drift position, we open up the space using the tools of Release the Rage and Power Focus, but ultimately we would get clear sitting up here at this place that we wanted to go; this is what we were desiring, the Light at the

end of the gift. There was something, sitting from the King's throne, that we could see over here. That gave us a direction but it didn't actually take us further than just the Shift. The Shift put our eyes toward the Light instead of having us look at the Pit or create the false Lift. It allowed us to examine these stories, the feelings and actions, but then to create a new set of stories, feelings, and actions that would lead us towards the Light in a more powerful and productive way.

## Learning to Lift for the Light

3. But the light itself can never be obtained unless we can lift ourselves up to that new peak. So enters the third weapon, the third tool in the arsenal, the game itself, that allows us to take all of this learning about the stories, and to transmute it into a practical system for learning from life. The fastest path of expansion is to learn from life. The only way that you can lift yourself from this point in the Drift, or back in the pattern of your status quo, before you began the Drift, the only way to grow, is to learn. The only way to learn, to get up to this peak, to access that Light, is to dive deep into this Drift and to extract the lessons.

4. In some ways you become your own guru, your own thought leader, your own beacon, to literally become the source of your own lessons. That's right, every single day, being able to dive into, with the conversation with the Voice, through the work inside Core 4, living the Warrior's Way, to learn from your life.

5. I think what you're going to find through this process is that your life itself is far more interesting than you ever imagined. The Universe and God are delivering up lessons for you every single day, but most of your life you have been avoiding them by covering your eyes inside the darkness of night, saying "I'm terrified of this dark. I don't want to look for the light inside of this night." Yet through these tools, through Release of Rage, through Power Focus, and now into Production Focus, we're going to begin to find the learning.

6. Let's start here then with the Lift, and we're going to come back to another series of questions. The Lift, or Production Focus, again, can be used individually. It can be done by itself, or it can be done in a stacked sequence, and it would follow immediately after the Power Focus workshop

experience. As I go through that mini-workshop with myself, now I can step forward into Production Focus.

## What Happened?

7. We're going to start with the simple question of the description of:

Question #1: What Happened?

**Answer:** Describe the facts of what happened.

8. What is it that happened? We're going to start in this one with questions, just like we've done with the rest of the tools. Every single one of these give us the questions, that allow us to get the answers, help us tell the stories, and ultimately lead us to what we want.

9. This becomes a factual-based conversation. It is a description of the occurring of what was going on. Here is what happened, which occurred from what initially triggered us in the first place when we were doing Release the Rage. Even though we've already gone through it a bit to Release the Rage, when we hit the brakes, we've gone through a little bit more in Power Focus when we created the space. Inside the Lift, we'll still reference back to that trigger. Or, if we're doing this document by itself, or using this tool by itself, we may just dive into any experience and go straight back to the trigger of the event and just describe, with no emotion, the facts of what happened.

10. Let's go back to Steve and the Stinky Office, and let's have a little look-see at the description I was using inside of what happened. It was basic, it was simple, and it was:

## Steve and the Stinky Office Example

### Question #1: What Happened?

**Answer:** *I walked into the office and it smelled again.*

11. Now notice, the statement is simple, it's concise, it's to the point, and it simply describes the facts of what happened. Here I was, I walked in the office, and it smelled, again.

12. We then move from the what happened question into the next question. That question is:

Question #2: Why Is That Positive?

**Answer:** What happened was positive because _____(describe the reason it was positive).

13. Why is that positive? I want you to see again the situation of content and context. If I come into Question #1: What Happened and I put "Here's what happened. I walked into the office and the office was smelly." This is what happened. It has no meaning associated to it at all. There's no story in what happened; these are the facts. I opened the door, I walked in, the office smelled. The end, game over. It is all content.

14. This content receives its meaning from the context of what I put as a frame around the content. Any time I place a frame of meaning around anything, any amount of content or any facts, I now invoke feelings. The facts of what happened, and the feelings come in the story around what happened. The context of that content is the outside frame, as if we were dealing with a picture, framing it up with the context, which then allows us to focus on the content.

## Reframing the Picture that We See

15. This frame, or reframing, comes down and allows us to take things that, maybe inherently, we would assume were bad. Walking into the office, as you can tell from the previous work already done about Steve and the Stinky Office, well, guess what? It's not been a real positive thing, at least when it's appeared. We're going to change, regardless of what the event was, and what our natural inclination is to say this thing which should not have happened, and we're going to step in and say, "Listen, here's what happened. Context: here is why that thing was positive."

16. Let's come back and see Steven and the stinky office, and look back at the example that I used. We came down. Why is that positive?

## Steve and the Stinky Office Example Continued

### Question #2: Why Is That Positive?

**Answer:** *Walking into a stinky office was positive because it showed me how big of a pussy I can be sometimes with shit. I make the biggest fucking deal about the stupidest shit sometimes. The government could freeze all my assets and I would be less stressed than I get about stupid shit like the smell of my office.*

17. Or Eggos. I'm going to say Eggos. One time I was running an event for Warrior Week, and instead of bringing us out beautiful waffles for breakfast for the guys, they delivered us up frozen Eggos. Shitty Eggos. At this nice place, we're running our event at Warrior Ranch, and we got Eggos. I lost my mind. Literally, for hours throughout that day, I would keep bringing up the Eggos.

18. Same thing inside of this. Why was it positive? Because it showed me how big of a pussy I can be sometimes with small shit. I make the biggest fucking deal about the stupidest shit sometimes. Inside of this, then, all I'm doing is painting a funny story. This story itself is also linked up to, in this case because I'm stacking it, it's linked up to all the work I've already done in stopping the Drift, inside of Release the Rage, inside of opening the space with Power Focus, and now I'm moving into the Shift and the Lift with Production Focus. I've got a lot of context around that idea, it's not just being pulled out of nowhere.

19. Once I've got the "Why it's positive," we come back to the next question:

Question #3: What is the Lesson Learned?

**Answer:** I learned that _____ (describe the lesson learned in 1-2 sentences).

## Picture This

20. What is the lesson that I've learned? If you imagine inside of this picture then, the facts of what you found and the feelings of the story that you've created and the new context around it, imagine that there is one picture, with you on the picture. You're on the old Instagram and we're going to make a post of you, and you're going to look all wise, and you're going to be like you're deep in thought, contemplating the ways of the Universe. Looking all wise, like you're the most interesting man in the world! And below you is a meme with words or a quote. People are quoting you and

they're putting up pictures of you. Or it's just simply not even a picture of you. It's a document, and on that document there is a lesson for life.

21. What we're going to do is, we're going to create a one-sentence lesson that comes out of the content with the context. Here's what happened, here's why that was positive, here's the lesson that I learned. Here's the lesson from life for me that I'm extracting from that particular experience.

22. Let me give you an example; let's come back over here to Steve and the stinky office. Lesson learned. What I bitch about is never the issue. It is the trigger of the real issue underneath.

23. Again, what happened? I walked into the office, and it smelled. Why was that positive? It exposed me for how I let little shit like the stinky office throw me off my game. It shows me how, when I focus on the wrong shit, I don't get what I want. Inside this is why it's positive. The lesson I learned, or the lesson for life, is what? Here it is:

## Steve and the Stinky Office Example Continued

### Question #3: What is the Lesson Learned?

**Answer:** *What I bitch about is never the issue; it is the trigger of the real issue underneath.*

24. Once I've extracted this lesson, learning begins to occur. This is the breaking off point. We start leaving the land of dealing with the trigger, and we start leading ourselves into the land of learning. If we come back over to the Drift-Shift-Lift-Light model, we must remember that as I Shift, I'm still in the Drift. But as I begin to learn, I begin to transition from the Drift, and my Shift leads me to the Lift.

## Accessing the Lift

25. Our learning becomes the access point to lifting. But we're not just going to learn one lesson. One lesson from the experience we had is not enough. We're going to take that lesson, and inside that Lift we're going to apply it to one, two, three, four key areas of life, which are the Core 4. We're going to take the lesson, regardless of what the trigger is, and we're going to apply that inside the Game, to the Body, Being, Balance, and Business.

Literally taking the manure that was the situation and spreading across all areas of our life so that all areas of our life can grow.

26. The limitation is not just that people don't learn. Most men don't learn from their experience, but the worst piece is that if they do learn, they don't know how to apply it in all areas. They have a great amazing learning experience inside their marriage, but then they go to work, and the office the next day, and the learning they just had inside of their marriage doesn't translate into the learning in their business. Or they have an amazing experience in their business, but they can't see the correlation between their business and what goes on with their children. They have an amazing experience with their children but can't see the correlation between what goes on with their kids and what's going on with their spirituality. They have an amazing revelation in connection with themselves, with God, in the morning, but then inside that place, they can't figure out how to take that back to their marriage.

## Applying Production Focus to the Core 4

27. We're going to take the learning from life inside of this Production Focus document, we're going to take that lesson, and we're going to apply it to the Core 4, starting with Body, Being, Balance, and Business, and this is going to raise us up, lift us up to the new peak, to get ready for, ultimately, the Revelation that sits for us at the top. Now look at all this work. All of this work we've done here along this place is simply creating the momentum and velocity in the Drift, Shift, and the Lift, to get us to the Light.

28. Let's just keep diving into this then:

Questions #4-7: How Does This Lesson Apply to the Core 4?

**Answer:** This lesson applies to my Body _____(state how it applies to the Body). This lesson applies to my Being _____(state how it applies to Being. Repeat "This lesson applied to my _____" with Balance and Business as well.

29. First, we start with the Body. What I bitch about is never the issue, it is the trigger of the real issue underneath. There's my lesson. Now I've got to apply it to my Body. Let's see how we related this inside the experience with Steve and the Stinky Office:

## Steve and the Stinky Office Example Continued

Lesson Learned: *What I bitch about is never the issue, it is the trigger of the real issue.*

### Question #4: How does this lesson apply to my Body?

**Answer:** *When I complain about the food schedule or lack thereof in my house with my family, I do this a ton, it is never about the food choice of healthy options for the kids or me or my wife, but it's always about something more. I get pissed about the shitty snacks in the house because, in the end, the stress of raising children is real, and I will get pissed at Cheetos while still fucking being on my cellphone. Here's the fun part. I become a victim to the lack of food in the house, and being upset about the fact that my five-year-old's eating Cheetos, while ignoring my daughter and being on my cell phone. Thinking that the gateway to my greatest parenting breakthrough is to make sure she has organic chips, instead of worrying about getting off my goddamn cell phone and connecting with my child.*

30. Yet again, Steve and the Stinky Office dilemma has been expressed inside my Body also, in the area of worrying about the wrong shit. Allowing things like Cheetos to get in the way of growth inside my Body, and doing the same thing with my children.

31. Let's continue this down then. We go from Body, which then leads us into Being. Let's look at what we had to say here in Being.

## Steve and the Stinky Office Example Continued

Lesson Learned: *What I bitch about is never the issue, it is the trigger of the real issue.*

### Question #5: How does this lesson apply to my Being?

**Answer:** *What I bitch about is never the issue, it is the trigger of the real issue. I collide with my family all the time about God, and who God is, and what God means. I will argue with my dad over stupid belief systems, about what happens after we die, when the real issue is, I'm scared of how to approach, sometimes, these* *kinds of conversations with my dad that are painful. Instead, I just unleash on some bullshit that means nothing, instead of dealing with the shit beneath the trigger.*

32. Stinky Office, and getting distracted. The lesson that I learned from Steven and the Stinky Office has taught me that what I bitch about is never the issue, it is the trigger of the real issue. I can bitch about Cheetos, but the real issue is I'm ignoring my kids. I can bitch about the belief system my father has about God, or I can deal with the real issue, which is a total disconnection that's existed for decades with me and my father. Easier to argue, easier to bitch about Cheetos, than it is to look at the trigger underneath. Easier to get pissed off at Steve about the office smell than it is to fucking handle the issue. Follow me?

33. All right, let's head forward then and continue through our Core 4. Balance is going to take us a little bit further, so let's see what I had to say about Steve and the Stinky Office:

## Steve and the Stinky Office Example Continued

Lesson Learned: *What I bitch about is never the issue, it is the trigger of the real issue.*

### Question #6: How does this lesson apply to my Balance?

Answer: *My marriage. Wow, don't get me started here. My wife and I get angry at each other all the time for shit that doesn't even matter. We argue about bedtimes with the kids. We argue about money. We argue about sex. When, in the end, what we're really saying is, "I love you and want to connect with you. We have a ton of shit going on, but we are both stressed out about it and it makes it difficult to connect." We just want to connect. So, instead of connecting, we will argue about shit that we blame for not being connected, instead of just being connected.*

34. Let me get this straight. I come into the office and I argue and get angry at Steve because of the smell of the office. Get distracted from the point of actually getting the shit I want this week to be ready for the event. I then take that same lesson that I learned over here, from all this work, the content of the experience in the stinky office, the context of why it was positive, because it exposed that I deal and bitch with small shit that gets

in the way of actually getting big shit done. That lesson itself is translated over here as I take that lesson, I package it up, I translate it to my Body.

35. Well, who would've known. Same things I'm bitching about at the office, I'm also bitching about at home when it comes to food, and it's hiding the reality of disconnection with my kids. I come and take that to Being. Same situation: Wow, look, I've got a stinky office situation. Inside the relationship with my father, too, and in the conversations of God and spirituality. Instead of actually handling those issues, I deal with the stinky office topic and become a victim.

36. I move up to Balance, and it's the same situation. Instead of just acknowledging, "We haven't spent much time together babe, we've been both hustling so damn hard in our businesses, we really just want to connect right now," we'll argue and fight about all the things that we think are in the way of actually allowing us to connect, instead of just connecting.

37. I've taken my third step up here. Now I've got to take my fourth. My fourth step will allow me to knock on the door of the revelation and the insight and the Light inside of the final worksheet tool. Let's keep going then. Balance moves us into Business.

38. Business, inside the Steve conversation, looked like this:

## Steve and the Stinky Office Example Continued

Lesson Learned: *What I bitch about is never the issue, it is the trigger of the real issue.*

**Question #7: How does this lesson apply to my Business?**

**Answer:** *I can focus on all the wrong numbers in Business. Every time I get pissed about how much we spend on journals or software, the internet, it's never why I'm pissed. I'm pissed because I feel out of control and have lost my focus. Instead of just focusing on creation, I end up focusing on contraction. Contraction is not expansion and never will be. I get angry at shit that doesn't matter because underneath it, I feel scared and worried, or stressed.*

## Anchored Down with False Lifts

39. What starts to happen for you inside of these kind of tools, and inside of this particular tool, is you begin to leverage life. The reason inside of Warrior that men don't grow is because one area is anchoring down the rest. It's either your Body that's anchoring you down, and you're having all this success inside your business, but our body is anchoring you to the ground. Or, you're having all of this success in your Body, but your Business is anchoring you to the ground. Or, you're having all this success in your Body *and* your Business, but your marriage and your family and your kids and your spirituality are anchoring you down.

40. Our goal is to learn how to Lift, Lift, *Lift* our entire life up to this next level, or this next peak. It's not to go along in the pattern, get triggered, let the story kill the action, Drift, and then Lift our Business only. Because, if we Lift our business only to this next peak, I can promise you that if your family, and your children (Balance), your spirituality (Being), and your Body have been left down here in the Drift, it will only be a matter of time before this game itself is exposed as simply a false lift. You cannot rise to that level of Light without taking all of YOU with you. You, all of you: Body, Being, Balance, *and* Business, your Core 4, must raise itself to that place.

41. As we culminate inside this then, and we move into the summary with this particular exercise, we summarize with one simple question:

Question #8: What is the ONE REVELATION you are leaving this Production Focus with?

**Answer:** My biggest revelation is _____(describe what the revelation is and why).

42. We then follow that up with the final question of the Production Focus document:

Question #9: What are you committed to doing about it in the next 48 hours?

**Answer:** I am committed to _____(action you will take).

43. Here's what happened. I walked into the office and it smelled. Here's why it was positive: it exposed how much I deal with, and focus on little

shit and get distracted. What was the lesson that I learned? Well, we've gone through the lesson over and over again. What I bitch about is never the issue, but is the *trigger* of the real issue. We took that lesson, we applied that to Body, we applied that to being, we applied that to balance, we applied that to business, and now we've got to say, of all the shit that I've just discussed inside myself, what is the one thing? What's the one thing, right here, that I'm left with, the one revelation?

44. Let's come over to the document with Steve:

## Steve and the Stinky Office Example Concluded

Lesson Learned: *What I bitch about is never the issue, it is the trigger of the real issue.*

### Question #8: What is the ONE REVELATION you are leaving this Production Focus with?

**Answer:** *I must eliminate the small bullshit stories that are burning up my bandwidth.*

45. This is the one thing I was left with: I must eliminate the small bullshit stories that are burning up my bandwidth.

46. This one insight, or this one revelation, will lead me to a place, then, of being able to have the final conversation, which is this question:

Question #9: What am I committed to doing about it in the next 48 hours?

Answer: *I'm going to fix the problem in the office, with or without Steve, in the next 48 hours. Regardless. Steve might show up; he might not show up. Either way it doesn't matter, I'm fixing this shit.*

47. The "doing" allows me to level up my game. It allows me to level up my game, right here. This one thing brings solidification to a new platform on which I am existing. This platform itself grows legs, and can hold me up here on this one insight. The insight will stay up there only if I do something about it. If I don't move anywhere, don't commit to doing any action with this revelation, and at the end of the day all I've done is a document that's allowed me to experience mental masturbation, I've not actually done any work because I haven't changed anything, and quickly I will regress right back down the path.

16

48. So, we come back over to this, and we say what are we committed to doing about it in the next 48 hours? My commitment today, as I'm in the office, is to make sure that it doesn't smell. We fixed it. With or without, I was going to fix it. With or without Steve's help, I'm not a victim. With or without his help, I'm going to move forward.

49. This brings us in conclusion, then, to the Production Focused document. This arsenal can be used independently. It can be used in stuff that, maybe in content, would naturally be positive. It can be used in things that were not positive at all. It can be used in situations that were distracting and-or painful.

## Independent Arsenal Use: Production Focus
## Woman in the Sand Example

50. The day that I put this chapter together, I was out on the beach for a walk early that morning and I came upon a woman who was lying in the sand. Her face was purple, and in my mind when I saw her there, I thought she was dead. She was an 18-year-old girl, her shirt was pulled high up on her body, her shoes were gone, she was covered with sand. There was sand in her eyes, her eyes were shut. There was sand in her ears, sand in her hair, there was sand all over her body. She was lying there. I walked up on her on the beach, and I reached down to move her body to shake her and see if she would respond, but she didn't respond. I reached down and put my fingers on her pulse to try to find her pulse, and at first I couldn't find a pulse, so I thought for sure she was dead. I then flipped her over to see if she was breathing, and then called 911.

51. Inside of this game, I'm going to give you a Production Focus that happened with this to show that this tool in the Warrior Stack can be done separately from the rest of the Stack.

52. What

Question #1: What happened?

Answer: *What happened in this is that, what, I went for a walk on the beach this morning, I found a woman who I thought was dead in the sand.*

53. Why

Question #2: Why was this positive?

54. Well the story continues.

Answer: *As I called 911 they asked me some questions about her. "Is she breathing?" I said, "She's breathing." They said, "Count her breaths," and we started counting her breaths, and the 911 operator was guiding the location to send the paramedics and to send the fire department down to the beach where I was at. We went through a series of questions and then he came to the serious question. He said, "Do you know CPR?" I said, "I don't know CPR."*

*In that moment, it's the first time in a long time I felt exposed as a responder to problems. For a second there was this guilt and this shame that came into me, not knowing CPR. It was positive because it exposed a weakness in me in a place that I thought was strong. A place where I'm a responder who was the first one into the fight, but I exposed myself as weak.*

55. Lesson Learned

Question #3: What is the lesson that I learned from this?

Answer: *The lesson that I learned is that life itself will present opportunities, and those opportunities can only be acted upon if you are trained. Preparation equals training. Training allows you to be prepared. That will be the lesson that I end on: Training allows for you to be prepared.*

Lesson Learned: *Training allows for you to be prepared.*

56. Let's take this and let's apply it, first, to Body.

57. Apply: Body

Question #4: How does this lesson apply to my Body?

Answer: *Physically speaking, it's my physical training that allows me to respond when people get hurt, and I can lift them up on my shoulders. Training allows me to pick my children up. Training allows me to catch my daughter as she's falling off of this embankment onto the ground of rocks. Training allows me to lift the groceries. Training allows me to be prepared to help out when I need to help out. When things are falling down, I can pick them up. When things need to be moved, I can move them. Training my physical body empowers me to be prepared.*

## 58. Being

Question #5: How does this training prepare me when it comes to my spirituality (Being)?

Answer: *My daily meditation becomes my Game, that allows me to be trained, so that I'm prepared. I'm not prepared and then I'm trained. I train and so I'm prepared. Unlike the situation that existed with this woman on the beach. I was not trained, and so I wasn't prepared. No matter how much positive mental attitude I had, I was still not going to be prepared in that moment. There were other things that I could do, but that just wasn't one of them. Spiritually speaking, I can't hope to be connected and have space if I'm unwilling to do the training necessary to be prepared.*

## 59. Balance

Question #6: How does this training prepare me when it comes to my Balance?

Answer: *Marriage. Third checkpoint. Listen, who told me that you and I, that we just supposedly should know how to be husbands? Yet, we assume this shit, we assume that we should just know how to be married. We don't know how to be married. But, we can train to be married. We can train to be Kings to our Queen; we can train to be husbands that matter.*

*Think about that with parenting children. I have three: 17, 9, and 5. Who told me, as a parent? Yet everybody told me growing up, "You'll just figure this out." Why am I not studying it? What kind of training have I put myself through to be the highest level of father that I can be? My training precedes my preparation. When my kids are having emotional meltdowns, and I want to lose my fucking mind over it, in those moments my preparation will be preceded by my level of training. Oftentimes with my kids I'm exposed, just like this woman on the beach exposed me to my lack of training, hence my fear inside of not being prepared.*

## 60. Business

Question #7: How does this lesson apply to Business?

Answer: *Marketing. Marketing. Marketing every day, marketing every week, marketing every month. You can never market too much. Advertising and marketing for your business is a must. Training yourself to wake up in the morning and say, "How am I going to get more leads?" Training yourself to wake up in the morning and say, "How am I going to get more money today for our business? How are we going to sell more shit? How are we going to market more, and how are we going to sell more?" It sounds crazy, but these should be two of the biggest questions you ask every single morning in business. Yet for most entrepreneurs, this is far from the training they have. Training precedes preparation. Being prepared to make moves economically in your business began with a willingness to train yourself to be disciplined in your marketing and your sales.*

## 61. Summary

Question #8: What is the one revelation that I'm getting from the experience on the beach?

Answer: *The one insight I'm left with that would bring the stabilization here to this table is really simple: I must be prepared.*

## 62. Forty-eight-Hour Commitment

Question #9: What am I committed to doing about it in the next 48 hours?

Answer: *I already investigated it, found a class, and I'm going to go through a three-month course to become EMT certified here in Orange County, California.*

63. By the time this book gets published and you are reading it, it will have already happened. I will never find myself in a situation again like that unprepared. The thing that is so crazy to most people, they would have a story to tell. What happened in my world? I did the Production Focus, and I changed my reality. The same thing goes for the silly game of a stinky office, and Steve.

64. Enough reading about *what* Production Focus is. Guess what time it is?! It's time for you to dive into this exact worksheet, this tool, this weapon, and use it, now.

## Chapter 15:
## POINTS TO PONDER FROM THE GENERAL'S TENT

- **POINT #1: WHAT:** The First phase of the game is getting clear about what has happened. After hitting the first two rounds of the Stack, you have created enough distance in the Game to allow yourself to grow and to become absolutely clear about what actually happened that triggered you.

- **POINT #2: WHY:** The Power of controlling the frame is incredible. You are a meaning-making machine and the only possible way that you can create the life you desire is to learn to control the frame around reality. Your story is about what happened regardless of what it was, and why that thing is positive to you.

- **POINT #3: LESSON:** The learning of life is more valuable than you can even imagine. Your ability to head into the Drift, do the work and extract the learning is crucial. During this phase, you will simplify everything you have done down to one simple statement of principle that would describe what you are all about.

- **POINT #4: APPLY:** Now it's time to apply the learning of life to the reality of your experience in the Core 4. Most men fail because they learn one lesson in one area and then don't learn the lesson on the other side. This inability to transfer the learning from one domain to another keeps a man stuck in one-dimensional living. Learning to apply every lesson to all areas of life is crucial. Oftentimes, you create breakthroughs in business which will never come from a lesson learned in business.

## WARRIOR WITNESS:

### K.T., Spanish Fork, Utah USA:
*"I'm beginning to see that my ability to feel everything within my emotions is becoming a sense of power within myself."*

---

### C.M., Rigby, Idaho USA:
*"Feelings now have power and a power that I have been hiding away, not looking at the knowledge that can be unlocked after I drift and shift. I can learn what the true matter is and raise myself to a higher level."*

---

### C.H., Arizona USA:
*"I allowed someone to have control over my emotions and feelings. The story I told reflected that. I now realize that I have complete power over all aspects of my life, no one else does. I control how much I put in and how much I get out of life."*

---

# THE LIFT
# PRODUCTION FOCUS EXAMPLE

## WHAT
1. What happened?

*[Describe the facts of what happened]*

## WHY
2. Why is that positive?

*What happened was positive because _____[Describe the reason it was positive].*

## APPLY
3. How does this lesson apply to the Core 4 Domains?

*I learned that ___[Describe the Lesson Learned in 1-2 sentences]___*

## BODY
4. How does this lesson apply to my Body?

*This lesson applies to my Body because _____[Describe the Application].*

## BEING
5. How does this lesson apply to my Being?

*This lesson applies to my Being because _____[Describe the Application].*

## BALANCE
6. How does this lesson apply to my Balance?

*This lesson applies to my Balance because_____[Describe the Application].*

## BUSINESS
7. How does this lesson apply to my Business?

*This lesson applies to my Business because _____[Describe the Application].*

## SUMMARY
8. What is the ONE REVELATION you are leaving this Production Focus with?

*My Biggest Revelation is _____[Describe the What and Why].*

9. What are you committed to doing about it in the next 48 hours?

*I am committed to _____[Action you will take].*

# THE STACK

## Chapter 16: THE LIGHT

The fourth weapon inside of the Drift, Shift, Lift and Light arsenal is where we gain the ultimate sight inside the night of where we have been in the Drift.

# SECTION THREE
# THE STACK

## CHAPTER SIXTEEN
## THE LIGHT

(REVELATION ROAD MAP)

"When you think all is forsaken

Listen to me now (all is not forsaken)

You need never feel broken again

Sometimes Darkness can show you
The Light."

**-David Draiman**
(lead singer of Disturbed, excerpt from lyrics of the hit song "The Light" from the band's
Illuminated album)

---

### Gaining the Ultimate Sight Inside the Night

1. So, we have now gotten to the Light. Our fourth weapon inside the game of the Drift, Shift, Lift and Light. This is where we gain the ultimate Sight inside the Night of where we have been in the Drift. If we look back through where we hit the trigger, the trigger tells a story, gets some feelings, and then some action that I desire to take. I stopped the Drift by doing a Release the Rage.

2. Inside of that Drift, I anchored some space by doing a Power Focus. From the Power Focus, I eliminated the night, created the King's Throne by declaring what it is that I desire and want. From that place, in the Shift

of the Power Focus, I went into Production Focus. I began to lift Body, Being, Balance and Business. Now, I am elevated up on this pedestal, ready to receive the ultimate guided and executable revelation.

3. See, there's revelation that we get that's like, "Ahhhhhh, that felt nice." Plenty of people get that kind of revelation. And then there are people who are like, "Ok, that felt nice, but what am I going to do now with this thing that felt so nice?"

## Looking for the Light

4. It feels good to feel nice, but I'd like to actually create something different in my life. The new pattern that we are searching for up here cannot exist. The old pattern existed over with the Drift, Shift, and Lift. Now, we have got to look for the Light, because the Light will give us a sight to the new pattern.

5. The difference between the pattern of "Ahh, this feels nice" to "This feels nice, so what am I going to do about it?" is expansion. This gap that is created is shortened to get us Lifted from the Drift and Shift Karmic Cul-de-sac where the Pit and False Lifts reside, due to expansion pulling us to the Light. The sooner we recognize our trigger patterns, the shorter the distance we need to figuratively travel to achieve the Light of Revelation.

6. It's the difference between who I was and who I became. Brother, you cannot shorten this gap unless you fully access the executable Light, which we call the Revelation Road Map.

## Clarifying the Work

7. The next thing we are going to discuss then is, "What am I going to do by clarifying all of the work that I've done?" Now, like all of the other documents in the Warrior Stack, I could use Revelation Road Map as an individual tool in my study inside Core 4 with Business.

8. You've seen me demonstrate this by asking the first question:

Question #1: What is the revelation, insight or distinction that you are getting in whatever environment you are in?

**Answer:** The Revelation that I am getting is _____ (Describe the "What"/Facts).

9. I could use Revelation Road Map sitting at church, listening to a sermon or somebody discuss some great concepts about God with me and I could use the Revelation Road Map format. I could do it in any environment. I could do it on date night. I could do it watching TV. I could do it watching a webinar, a seminar, or even from a book that I am reading. I can use this format anywhere, but the specific example that I am going to give you today is coming in a stacked format. It's coming here with the Steve and the Stinky Office example.

10. So let's go into the first question inside of the Revelation Road Map:

## Steve and the Stinky Office Example

### Question #1: What is the revelation, insight or distinction that you are getting in whatever environment you are in?

**Answer:** *The Revelation that I am getting is my focus and my stories matter. I am a victim to my stories when I choose to be.*

11. The Cheetohs® for snacks instead of something healthy. Being concerned about having a real talk with my dad. Yelling at my wife about the shit that is getting in the way of our connection instead of actually connecting. Right? Focusing all of my time and energy on bullshit that doesn't matter and focusing on the wrong numbers in Business, like production costs such as trying to save money on the internet bill.

12. In this, then, I am going to continue with the revelation: I am a victim to my stories when I choose to be. So, I have identified what the revelation is, but this hasn't done much for me. Yet. All that it's done is open up the possibilities of something cool happening. It hasn't actually created anything, yet. So, we are going to take that revelation and we are going to dive into our next question with it. We are going to say:

Question #2: What is your reaction to this revelation? How do you feel? What do you think? What do you have a desire to do?

**Answer:** When I ponder on the revelation, I feel _____ (describe your list of feelings). I think _____ (share your thoughts) and have a desire to _____ (describe the possible actions).

13. Holy shit. Wait a second. Might the revelation be a new form of trigger?! Let us see, shall we? Trigger, story, feeling, action. Hold on a second. What is your reaction to the revelation? How do you feel? What do you think? What do you have a desire to do? Now, inside of this, your reaction is a creation of another story. This new story is going to compel you down the path to doing something, taking a different action, and moving down this new pattern.

14. So, let's refer back to Steve and the Stinky Office example and see what came about after asking this second question:

## Steve and the Stinky Office Example Continued

**Question #2: What is your reaction to this revelation? How do you feel? What do you think? What do you have a desire to do?**

**Answer:** *When I ponder the revelation, I feel free and hopeful. I think about all that there is in my life where simple distractions through ridiculous triggers are costing me everything. Everything in the sense of costing me time, energy, and money. My desire is to begin eliminating the small ones, one time per week. When I see the pattern, I expose it, share it with others, and change it.*

15. Now, this game of reaction and revelation comes in and I write out my initial reaction to it. This opens up the space inside of revelation, but we haven't done anything yet. Again, I'm still sitting up here in this place. I am contemplating on my little platform. I haven't gone forward yet. I haven't done anything yet. I am contemplating on my platform. Now comes the next phase.

16. As I move forward onto the Revelation Road Map, I now get to the third stage of this document tool:

Question #3: What do you see as the next step actions to take to make this revelation real? What are you willing to do?

**Answer:** I am committed to doing the following _____ (Make a list).

# Procreating Revelation

17. There's revelation and there is creation. Sometimes people confuse these. Revelation sparks the possibility of creation, but without creation, revelation becomes mental masturbation. It feels nice. But in the end, all you are doing is fucking yourself. Who are we kidding? Inside of that game then, Revelation links up to Creation as Procreation. It's you and the revelation, procreating to manifest and create a new possibility inside of whatever area you decide within your Body, Being, Balance and Business.

18. So, this third piece inside of the Road Map is saying, "OK, what is the action that we are going to build upon to make this happen? It is during this stage that we force the mind to become more practical.

19. We come back to the stinky office and Steve:

## Steve and the Stinky Office Example Continued

**Question #3: What do you see as the next step actions to take to make this revelation real? What are you willing to do?**

**Answer:** *I am committed to spending thirty minutes during the General's Tent every week reviewing the small bullshit triggers of the week. I am also creating a new story and commitment every week to eliminate one of them.*

*Now, I could have at least 20 of them to identify every week, but I am going to focus and identify on one. I give a specific thing I am going to do. I have a specific time frame around when or what I am going to do it by. I give a time game of when I am going to do it. I am going to go over it for 30 minutes. I am going to go to the General's Tent review of my week, and I am going to spend 30 minutes and go through all of the triggers. I am going to pick one. And then, inside of that one, I am going to eliminate it that week with a small execution plan.*

20. External expansion is starting to solidify itself. We moved forward. We said, "Here's the revelation. Here's my reaction. Here's the Road Map to now do something about this insight."

## Meeting with Resistance

21. But, keep in mind that inside of that, we also have to identify the dangers that can get in the way, because no matter what we do, our Revelation will be met with resistance. Your Revelation has Resistance. That Resistance is meant to make that process of Revelation into Creation a game of Work. That game of Work ultimately transcends and transforms the Revelation into something of actual Creation. It will manifest and stay. Permanently. The change in your business will stay. The change in your marriage will stay because we stabilized ourselves at the top. That means we are going to have to face some Resistance.

22. If you go straight into Creation after Revelation, and you are not met with any Resistance, then I guarantee that the shit you are creating doesn't matter, or you are doing it wrong. You are doing it in a way that is not actually going to stay for the long haul. So, let's come back and take a little look, then, at the Road Block idea of what we have asked here:

Question #4: What dangers do you see as possibly getting in the way of executing on the committed actions and Road Map?

**Answer:** I can see the following possible danger(s) _____ (Make a list).

23. Let's come over to Steve and the Stinky Office example. Here was mine:

## Steve and the Stinky Office Example Continued

### Question #4: What dangers do you see as possibly getting in the way of executing on the committed actions and Road Map?

**Answer:** *I don't do the work to find these triggers every single week. I don't actually do the General's Tent. That I am a pussy and I don't actually change them.*

24. All of these are pretty good obstacles; pretty good dangers. And I said inside, on the Road Map, that I am going to work on this inside of the General's Tent. I said that the possibility is that, well, I am not going to find time to do it every week and that I am going to find an excuse to not do it in the General's Tent. Even though I am in the Tent, I won't do it. I will skip the 30 minutes. And that I am also a pussy and I don't actually

change them. Even if I do this work, maybe going in that next week I am not going to do any work on that small trigger.

## Dealing with the Road Blocks

25. This Road Block, Question #4, is acknowledging where you may falter on the path to the new pattern, retreat back into the False Lift, and end up on the slope back into the Karmic Cul-de-sac instead.

26. This is possible.

27. I could come clear up through the Lift and start settling into The Light, only to end up cascading myself back down the Game, and end up right back into the Drift and Shift loop all over again.

28. So, how do we maintain this state of expansion in The Light? We look at the last piece of the Revelation Road Map:

Question #5: How will you overcome the Road Block in order to execute on the Road Map?

**Answer:** I will deploy the following strategy: _____ (describe).

29. This is when we now dive into the response, which is the counterpoint. It's the counterattack to the Road Block that could get in the way. Let's see how I concluded Steve and the Stinky Office example with this final question:

## Steve and the Stinky Office Example Concluded

### Question #5: How will you overcome the Road Block in order to execute on the Road Map?

Answer: *During the General's Tent on Sunday, I will dedicate the first half of the General's Tent to reviewing and declaring the small triggers. I will choose one to work on. I will put it on a note card and review it every day in the car when I drive. One a week, for a month, 356 a year. Holy shit. That is revolution. Imagine getting rid of 356 bullshit stories a year that are wasting hundreds of productive hours. THE END. BOOOOM!*

# Warrior Stack Capstone

30. Now, every single day inside of my life, there is a Revelation Road Map being created. Many of them I type up. Some of them I speak into existence in the form of audio. Some of them I shoot into videos on my cell phone. Your life is filled with revelation all over the place, but the greatest form of revelation that we have found inside of doing the work comes from your daily discipline of Core 4. It also comes from the willingness to stack all of the work from Release the Rage to Power Focus to Production Focus, and make a permanent shift in Revelation Road Map. It puts the capstone here on the entire conversation of all of the work you have done, and focuses all of that energy into one executable game that pushes you forward.

## Chapter 16:
## POINTS TO PONDER FROM THE GENERAL'S TENT

- **POINT #1: REVELATION:** The Voice during this Stack is guiding you to see things you have never seen before, and often times during a stack, you will have multiple massive insights that you were not planning on having. By the time you get to the Revelation Road Map, it is time to simplify all of that learning down to the most significant and impactful revelation of all of them.

- **POINT #2: REACTION:** Your reaction to Revelation is important to study and be made aware of in how it makes you think, feel, and the actions that you notice arise as a desire from that Revelation. These reactions are automated and they happened when specific insight happens to a man like you and me. Our target in this phase is to access the clarity of our reaction of the Revelation.

- **POINT #3: ROAD MAP:** What is the plan that I am choosing to take on to actually DO SOMETHING with what I have been given in this stack? It is one thing to get Revelation; it is another to actually take what you have learned and transfer that into practical Production. Results from your own personal Revelation matter, and without them, then, Revelation doesn't really matter. Change MUST occur for expansion to be found, and this requires action.

- **POINT #4: ROAD BLOCK & RESULT:** What will get in the way and how will you know you have accomplished the target of the Roadmap? No matter what it is that you are trying to accomplish, there is an aspect of you that is hell bent on destroying you and resisting whatever commitments that you are making to yourself. You must also be able to clearly measure the result that will show up when you have accomplished the Roadmap. It must be measurable. It must be doable. It must be attainable.

## WARRIOR WITNESS:

### B.H., Odessa, Texas USA:

*"Taking the true issue and then making the necessary changes that come from it was the revelation that I received from this tool. I like taking the situation and turning it into a positive at the end of the process."*

---

### C.M., Rigby, Idaho USA:

*"The revelation that I had was in making that Change in the end when we see THE LIGHT, then setting that Change into motion and fixing it into place and making it a new path, all the while working to raise yourself higher to the next path and Light! FUCKING AWESOME!"*

---

# THE LIGHT
# REVELATION ROAD MAP

## REVELATION
1. What is the revelation, insight or distinction you are getting?

*The Revelation I am getting is _____[Describe the what: FACTS].*

## REACTION
2. What is your reaction to this revelation? How do you feel? What do you think? What do you have a desire to do?

*When I ponder on the revelation, I feel _____[describe your list of feelings]. I think _____[share your thoughts] and have a desire to _____[describe the possible actions].*

## ROAD MAP
3. What do you see as the Next Step Actions to take to make this Revelation real? What are you willing to go do?

*I am committed to doing the following: _____ [make a list].*

## ROAD BLOCK
4. What dangers might you see possibly getting in the way of executing on the committed actions and Road Map?

*I can see the following Possible Danger(s):* _____*[describe the obstacles that could get in the way].*

## RESPONSE

5. How will you overcome the Road Block in order to execute on the Road Map?

*I will deploy the following strategy:* _____ *[describe the strategy].*

# THE CORE
## Chapter 17: OVERVIEW

The Core is the action we begin as we live the Code daily in Body, Being, Balance and Business. It is the reality of the Real, Raw, Relevant Results from The Code.

# SECTION THREE
# THE CORE

## CHAPTER SEVENTEEN
# OVERVIEW

"Struggling and suffering are the essence of a life worth living. If you're not pushing yourself beyond the comfort zone, if you're not demanding more from yourself - expanding and learning as you go - you're choosing a numb existence. You're denying yourself an extraordinary trip."

**-Dean Karnazes**
(excerpt from Ultramarathon Man:
Confessions of an All-Night Runner)

---

1. The Core. What does this mean, the Core? The Core itself is a conversation that we're going to build upon after everything we've covered in the Code. The Core becomes the next step, the next gradual action as we begin to move into the practical formation of results inside of this conversation of the Code.

## Framed by the Code

2. The Code was the frame, so the Core becomes the first beginning of color, a semblance of some type of a result inside of our life. Living by the Code doesn't mean anything if we can't stand for the Core. The Core itself is the *reality* of the Real, Raw, Relevant Results that we were searching for. Only now, the results that we're talking about are not just the results in one or two areas, but the results in four areas at the same time. These areas culminate, becoming a coalescing and unified statement known as The Core: Body, Being, Balance and Business.

3. Now, how did I even discover this idea? That having it all was a concept of taking these four dimensions of life broken into these two sub-compartmentalized experiences inside each one of these dimensions of life? And then bringing about the possibility of having it all defined here?

## Discovery from a Life Not Working

4. Well, it happened different than you might think. It wasn't that I woke up one day and thought, "You know what? I should have it all. It would make a lot of sense if my Body, Being, Balance and Business were all on the same page."

5. This had never entered my reality at all. Like most great discoveries, it came because of a life that wasn't working. It came because of a Game that was not playing out the way I desired it. It came because of a world, and a life, and an experience of that life that was not functioning at a level that I would say was even enjoyable.

6. I found myself more often than not stuck in this one and two-dimensional game of living. From the time I was young, I had been taught as a man that my soul purpose in life was to make the money. I was to go hunt and figure out how to produce a living for my children and family. How do I "be a man" and go about making the dash? Society said that I needed to get the dollars into the bank account so I could provide for my family, put my children through college, and then at some point, way off down the road, I could spend time with my family. That was how I could support them.

7. Then I thought, okay, when my Body is fit, I tend to be a little better at Business. Having been an athlete throughout high school, college and professionally, I had also done a whole array of experiences and events in all kinds of different sports and industries. This entire game made sense for Body and Business. So I was getting these two, but they were the only two I was getting. They were measurable.

8. I assumed that somehow marriage and my spiritual purpose would just fall into play, but what I didn't get was that they weren't as easily measured. They rose and fell based upon my ability to fill up and align these other Core areas in my life.

9. I found myself as a business consultant sitting down over and over again with different businessmen, and we would begin the conversation of

trying to break down what was going on inside the business. I particularly remember a consulting contract we had with a steel company. I sat down with the CEO and owner, and we started having this conversation about what was going on inside the business and why his teams weren't supporting him. We discussed why his managers weren't running it and why this company itself, which once had been a billion-dollar annual revenue business, was declining in value and success.

10. I looked at this guy who was overweight, divorced for the second time, highly addicted to alcohol and tobacco, disconnected from any semblance of purpose with God and said, "Your business has become nothing more than a reflection of your life. See, your business cannot rise any higher than you are willing to become in today's marketplace. You, my friend, have a life that is not working. You're overweight, you're addicted, you're divorced, and your relationship with your children is not heading the way you want it to. Your spiritual purpose is disconnected and disjointed. The only thing you have going for you is your Business, and even that is declining."

11. Like all things comically circulating in the universe called life, when you do not live in harmony, the universe will collapse the areas down to meet the lowest level of capacity in all four of these Core areas. You will become nothing more than a mere reflection of who you are currently being, anchored down by the weight of your disconnect within your Body, Being, Balance and Business.

## Stressed About Getting Distracted

12. There are two conversations that wrap around all businessmen: guilt and sedation. We get distracted by guilt. And then we get distracted by the sedation factor of stress. That stress and sedation mechanism inside all of us has some really weird shit, which has us push hard as we move forward to produce fast, big-ass results.

13. We move really hard and we continue to go, but at the cost of what? At the cost of everything else! We don't look at our families and the relationship with our wife and our children as fuel to get to the Game. We oftentimes look at them as obstacles in the way to produce inside of Business.

14. We don't look at our body as this mechanism that when weaponized, gives us the power and capacity to build a bigger business. We look at it as

something that is just in the way. We don't look at purpose in our divine calling with God as connected to a true purpose within the other areas of our life. And yet, this divine connection empowers our ability to produce lasting results in our bank account and business.

15. Yes, maybe date nights (or lack thereof) with one's wife has an impact in marketing. The time that we spend with our children has an impact on our sales conversions within Business. This made me also realize that the amount of energy that I invest in meditation and spiritual study actually has an impact on my ability to lead, guide and inspire my teams to greatness inside my organization. Therefore, maybe the amount of time I spent at the gym working out and training, as well as the kinds of foods I ate, actually had an impact on my ability to understand software and techniques and strategies inside of sequencing and systems within my business.

16. I discovered this Core 4 conversation, *not* because I was trying to be a holy guy whose sole mission from the start was to make the world a better place. It was my desire to make money and build a business that will last: A business that was driven by purpose. But, I also didn't want to have the rest of my life fall apart along the way in the pursuit of this.

## Discovering A Journey Within While Running

17. Little did I realize the universe was preparing me to take a discovery journey inside of me, uncovering this four dimensionality inside my life that I was not simply a one or two- dimensional douche bag. Instead, I was a man who could have it all. I was called to see this from a different angle.

18. So as the money disappeared like the tide that was swept out, I got to see the reality of my marriage, and it wasn't working. I got to see the reality of my children: I was not working as a father. I got to look at the reality of my spirituality: I was confused, in chaos, wound up and didn't know what I believed. All I knew was that the current reality of my life was *not* working. I got confused even in the conversation of my Body so during those years I became an [27]ultra-runner. I was running every single day. At one point I ran for 32 straight days, a marathon a day before I went to work that morning. Not a marathon combined; a marathon *every single*

---

[27] An ultra-runner is a term defined as anyone running an excessive amount of miles in one setting, whether it is in a race (ultramarathon) or individually, which requires a lot of stamina.

*morning.* I went from 205 pounds down to 172 pounds. At 6'2," I looked like I was anorexic because I was losing so much weight for my body mass.

19. Amidst all of this running though, I was finding the truth. I was learning to live the Code as I was discovering the elemental connections between how our lives integrate, move and flow within one another. If I want big results in my Body, there's an actual impact and process that I can work on by taking results from my Being, Balance and Business which I can also push towards my Body.

## Core Reverse Engineering

20. If I wanted results inside my spiritual purpose (my path with God and the universe inside my Being), there was an actual way to reverse engineer towards my spiritual purpose through my Body and Balance. I discovered that if I wanted to strengthen the outcome within my marriage and my children, then I could take my results inside of Body, Being and Business, harness all of that and reverse engineer those results right back into Balance. If I wanted results with my Business I could do the same: take my marriage and relationship with my kids along with my calling with God, or my spiritual purpose within my Being, and  unify it all up through. This conversation of my fitness and food which has consumed my life within my Body I could also direct to Business.

21. But I'm not going to stand here and pretend like I had some "holier than thou" conversation going on. I was trying to find a way to rebuild myself, and I knew I needed to hunt. I knew I needed to make money. I had to rebuild the Empire that I had lost. I had to rebuild my financial world. I had to produce stability for my life. But what I didn't understand was there was a faster path to doing it.

## Business = Power + Production

22. As we discuss this Core 4 conversation, I want to make sure that you understand this formula: Business itself is a function of Power and Production. These two things come together over and over and over again. My power is my capacity, channeled into production, which then becomes the direction of my results in direct alignment to the amount of capacity or the power that I do or do not have.

23. Most of this we learn as we go around and start leveling up the balance in our businesses. We study marketing, start our sales, systems, and study technology. We study all of these things and we dump our lives into becoming the best businessman we could possibly be. However, we do this at the cost of what? Assuming that one Core area, Business, is more important than another. I'm going to have you consider that the same intensity and strategy that works on my marketing plans in turn works inside my spirituality as well as in parenting.

## Interweaving Core 4 Connections

24. When was the last time you studied how to be a father like you studied your last marketing campaign? When was the last time you studied seduction of your wife the same way you studied seduction of a new prospect to buy the next product, service or experience you're offering? When was the last time that you entertained the reality, intensity and the importance of sequencing inside your spiritual purpose and how you dealt with God, creating space in your life with the same intensity that you studied your taxes, and your accounting inside your business? When was the last time you took on your body and your fitness with the same intensity, managing it with scrutiny just like you would the ads spent in a marketing campaign?

25. For the first time in my life, I started to see these connections. I started to see that I had been playing half-assed in the way that I had approached my life. I was an undeliberated reactor to the way things went on with my Body, Being, and Balance, but in Business, I was much more specific. What I didn't see was my Business could only climb as high as where the rest of my Core 4 was at. In other words, I found that if I could take my Body, Being, and Balance and bring them to a higher level, this in turn would create a domino effect for my Business to rise as well.

## The Fast Way to Level Up Your Bank Account

26. I'm going to submit to you a possibility that the fastest way to level up your bank account and your business as a businessman is to manage the areas of your life known as Body, Being, and Balance. Your Body and its lack or increase of capacity affects your production. Your Being affects your production. Your Balance affects your production. So as we enter into this conversation within the book, I break down into each one of these Core 4 areas and we begin to measure the Game.

## Reverse-Engineering Production Strategy

27. We will search for a way to win every single day. As we dive into the Core 4 conversation, understand that we are talking about a reverse engineered production strategy: a way to get paid, get laid, and a way to make life work while having it all. It's possible, but we are going to have to open your mind up. So here in this particular section we call the Core, we are going to dive deep into each one of these four areas, and break them down into their two sub-areas. We are going to make sure that you fully understand what we are talking about inside the Core 4. Not only that, but how do we actually win, in each one of these areas, every single day?

### Chapter 17:
### POINTS TO PONDER FROM THE GENERAL'S TENT

- **POINT #1:** The Core becomes the next step, the next gradual action as we begin to move into the practical formation of results inside of this conversation of the Code.

- **POINT #2:** When you do not live in harmony, the universe will collapse the areas down to meet the lowest level of capacity in four of these. You will become nothing more than a mere reflection of who you are currently being.

- **POINT #3:** With reverse-engineered production, the various parts of the Core 4 (Body, Being, Balance and Business) overlap and interweave to enhance or take away from the other, depending on how it's utilized.

- **POINT #4:** The fastest way to level up your bank account and your business as a businessman is to manage the areas of your life known as the Core 4 in this Brotherhood.

# WARRIOR WITNESS:

### A.S., USA:
*"The past two months I have been studying and applying the Core 4 daily, and based upon this principle, I have been exercising two times a week and doing yoga but the green smoothies have been a hug milestone for me because I've never liked greens.*

*I never thought that I would be using meditation. The Release the Rage documents have helped me know where to be.*

*In Balance I'm establishing a better relationship with my parents.*

*In terms of my business, I've started to set some goals and achieve those goals in the next 90 Days. Core 4 has allowed me to do things that I've wanted to do for YEARS with a Brotherhood that's like-minded."*

## B.F., Tennessee, USA:

*"Everyone that I interact with have commented on how they have seen a change since the past 6 weeks that I joined. I wish that I had this when I was 16 to give me something to establish the rest of my life on. I don't know how I've been able to achieve success without the Code and the Core before, but it's just now that I'm going through all of this bullshit in my life.*

*My wife, absolute goddess, and a sexy little queen, to this point after 10 years in marriage our sex life has been good, but during that time of the month, I would turn to porn which would then take another week to reconnect because of that. When it was that time of the week this time around, the sexual energy is so much better now, where I could have counted on one hand how many blow jobs I received from her in the past 10 years, but last night, I received the best blow job of my life telling her how much she turned me on after putting my hard penis in her hand and being honest with her."*

## Z.G. Arizona, USA:

*"Since I joined and signed up about 30 days ago my Core 4 Overview has been:*

*Body: the easiest to jump back into, but I had a very fucked up mindset, that once I stopped getting paid or receiving a scholarship for working out, a simple change in the mindset from why should I work out without that to doing it for ME, making an effort every day to sweat. I hate it on the days traveling when I can't hit the gym. With food, I did it in the past so it was easier for me, yet it also required a change in the mindset that I needed to do it for me and others are noticing a difference.*

*Being: I feel lost. As a Catholic, going to church I'm there, but not present and feel like I can't relate to the people in my parish. I've been praying, writing shit down and it's been my way to meditate. I need to learn how to meditate and focus, to have that desire to bring God back into my life.*

*Balance: It's been a 180 change. My wife sat me down before Warrior with papers for separation and what we're doing with the kids. I've started complimenting my wife and told her how beautiful she is, writing her text messages. The affection has started to come back, but the sexual relationship is still not there because she's felt disgusted by me. I've been in a sexless marriage without any passion for the past two years. Now I'm getting nude photos from her and it's getting to that level that I feel In love with my wife again. I'm committed and realize that I have the most AMAZING woman in my life that is so supportive; she just didn't have the king in her life that brought that out in her. With my kids, I've stopped watching TV when I get home from work and so I'm there for them, even if I'm tired. I suck it up and spend time with them. I'm making the effort those days that I'm in town and not traveling to take my daughter to school and put her in bed. I'm committed to not only being a father but that spiritual leader by showing her how women should be treated. Now I'm sick when I can't spend time with my family, and I long to be with them again. I'm so blessed to have them in my life; I'm realizing how absent I've been.*

---

*Business: It's been sucky. The businesses that I built and made millions with are now dead. I've ended all of those relationships with my business partners that go back a few years. I'm currently in a position as a contractor in a surgical environment and I'm working for a different man, whom I hate, and I'm not in control of my own life while I make sure that bills are paid and we're financially stable at home, but now I'm ready to start going out to get a position in the corporate world, and now I'm one of 3 candidates and up for some big interviews, which would oversee multiple states and put me at 300-400K / year again.*

*I love the support of the Brotherhood in Warrior."*

---

### T.M., Georgia, USA:

*"What stands out for me most is the gamification of priority in my life. By making it easy to do and easy to measure it allows me to focus on what's important first thing in the morning, before I get caught up in my day. And through the Warrior Process of reporting each day, it adds a layer of accountability that helps to establish a routine, which is the biggest stumbling block when adopting new habits. I am hopeful that my second (and future) time through these lessons will help me to adopt these without the excuses that currently plague my execution of it."*

---

## M.M., Alberta, Canada:

*"I am excited about the pragmatic practicality of The Core, and leveling up my game. I've been doing much of The Core long before I knew about Warrior, but without the consistency, the simple scoring, and the tracked metrics. I'm looking forward to re-earning & exposing where I was falling short so that I can finally generate the results I want."*

## A.W., Florida, USA:

*"The real revelation for me came in the understanding that I do not need to try to hit home runs in every area of my life. It's more important for me to be consistent over the long haul. And by doing this I will have long lasting results that are actually easier to produce versus always elephant hunting and wishing and hoping for the best."*

## A.L., Idaho, USA:

*"Yep. I'm that guy that did not have the athletic background. At least until my late 20s when I boxed. Greatest shape of my life! I have learned a ton about how my body works since then. This whole lesson helped galvanize my resolve to not only return to fighting, but to remember that my body truly is a weapon and that allowing myself to be lazy and lie about the most important starting place for any change, will only end in more disappointment and failure in every other area. I am amazed at how stupid simple the methods and principles of the Warrior's Way are."*

## J.W., New Mexico, USA:

*"The amplifying power of consistent, small accomplishments every day! Swinging for a home run, or grasping desperately at straws becomes an unfocused waste of time and energy and usually nothing gets accomplished. The beauty here is the simplicity, which makes it seem actually achievable, IF one is truly committed to just doing the work."*

## T.H., Atlanta, Georgia, USA:

*"Hell yes. I feel as if I just graduated boot camp and AIT and I am on my way to Ranger school once again.. The fact that this is something you do over and over again, everyday until it is second nature to you is what I have been missing.. The CORE is what I have been searching for all this time. I am so fucking*

245

*ready to commit and make sure to do this everyday that I added sticky notes to my mirror to remind me every morning. I am ready...So fucking ready..."*

---

## T.H., Florida, USA:

*"The Core 4 overview reminded me of a US Navy Commander's commencement speech on the life lessons he had learned. One of his "lessons" was, "If you want to change the world, start off by making your bed." If you commit yourself to making your bed everyday you will accomplish your first task each day and will encourage continual accomplishment (Results) and attention to detail in your life. Simple singles, everyday! Core 4 is about purposeful actions and a commitment to results."*

---

# THE CORE

## Chapter 18: BODY (FITNESS)

There is nothing that you can do inside of this life without taking your Body with you. Your Body is the only thing that will go with you through the entire Game.

# SECTION FOUR
# THE CORE

## CHAPTER EIGHTEEN
# BODY (FITNESS)

*"To keep the body in good health is a duty... otherwise we shall not be able to keep our mind strong and clear."*

### -Buddha

---

1. Your Body is the only thing that will go with you through the entire Game of life. The only thing, literally. There is nothing that you can do inside of this life without taking your Body with you. Your Body is part of everything; it's part of what you do in your Being, part of what you do in Balance and what you do in your Business. Your Body is the key domino that begins the conversation.

## Encouragement in Athletic Participation

2. Being raised the way I was raised, interestingly enough, my parents were not really into fitness. My mom and dad were not athletes and didn't play sports much, though my dad played a little soccer in high school and college. My parents genuinely were not athletic but they did encourage us to participate in athletics.

3. I had an inclination inside of me to train, compete, play and be a part of sports from the time I was young. From soccer, clear through to my career in college and professional football. I participated in [28]Ironman, CrossFit,

---

[28] IronMan, CrossFit, and Ultramarathons require specific training techniques in order to participate, all of which require a higher level of dedication in order to perform to one's fullest.

ultra-marathons, fighting, paddle boarding and everything else that was active. To do all of these amazing activities, I participated with my Body.

4. My Body is my gateway to power. I meet people day-to-day who were not athletes growing up and maybe that's you. Maybe you weren't competitive in sports, maybe this was never part of your situation, or part of your life. This means that the message of Body becomes ten times more powerful for you, because you've never been given the opportunity to taste what I tasted as a professional athlete.

5. Going from college football at Boise State in Idaho to becoming a professional football player in the arena leagues in Canada, I began to experience this gain inside of me. There were decades of weight lifting. I continued to put hour after hour, year after year into Ironman triathlons until the World Championships in 2007. There were years and years of ultra-marathons, running 100-150 mile races. All of the 10,000+ hours of fitness over the last few decades led me to finding some of the most deep and profound truths about me through my Body.

## A Weapon or an Obstacle

6. If you can discipline your Body, the theory stands that you could discipline your mind. Inside of this game of production and having it all, your Body is either a weapon to be used to produce or it becomes an obstacle; an anchor to compress your production, to openly sedate and kill your opportunity to produce results in your life.

7. You've got to decide where you stand when it comes to your body. There are people who look at Body as simply an obstacle, and then there are people that look at their body as a gateway. So, is your body an obstacle or a gateway?

8. Consider that you can change that at any time that you choose. The Body conversation really comes down to two things:

1.   Fitness: "How do I refine the weapon known as my body?"
2.   Fuel: "How do I feed it?"

## Held Hostage as a Slave to Your Body

9. When you wake up in the morning, your body either gives you confidence or it doesn't. You wake up in the morning and you either [29]go to war with your body or you don't. Most individuals and most businessmen roll out of bed and default into their day held hostage. They become slaves to their Body's cravings and addictions, led around like a bull with a nose-ring. Their body becomes the master, instead of the servant.

10. Every single morning that you wake up, you are faced with a decision:

"Am I going to lead today or will I be led by my body?"

"Will my body become my servant or will it become my obstacle?"

11. As easy as it seems to keep that coffee routine in the morning to roll off the day, it will control you. If you start pulling this off in your teens and in your twenties, as a man continues to rise, he realizes that the energy that he experiences on a day-to-day basis is everything. You either have energy or you don't, and it's all generated first inside your Body.

## Fitness: Training Your Body

12. Think about your last seven days and the way that you've worked out or you haven't. How would we know that you actually gave a shit about your body? What does your current fitness routine look like? How have you trained and what does your body look like today?

13. If you stand in front of the mirror, strip all your clothes off and stand butt ass naked as if you just stepped right out of the shower, are you impressed by what you see? Do you think that body turns your wife on? Is it inspiring to your children? What is the message that your body tells your babies?

14. Some men forget about their bodies until they get the notification from the doctor, "you have diabetes," or "you have cancer." They forget about it as they become lazy, sitting on the sideline of life watching their children play soccer with me because they're too tired. They sit in the chairs with

---

[29] Warrior has a phrase, "Core 4 before you hit the door to help you win the war" (See WD "Core 4…") which means that by getting the daily points in before one even goes off to work, he's much better off for a productive day.

the other fat ass fathers and they don't do a goddamn thing to participate in their children's lives.

15. This was my dad; he got horribly out of shape. I love my father to death but he didn't get this concept of taking care of the Body. He wasn't taught this and so my dad traveled five or six days out of the week hustling and grinding his ass in Business. My dad was selling shit  as hard as he could to provide for our family, doing the one thing that he thought he was supposed to do: make money. This singular focus made him 75 pounds overweight, fighting the diabetic diagnosis he was given years ago ever since.

16. My dad wasn't always this way. It was just something that happened day after day, week after week and month after month.

17. I had a friend of mine a few years ago who was like, "Dude, I don't even know how I got 70 pounds overweight, I don't know how this happened."

18. "Well, it's really easy Bro. When I first met you, you just started putting like three to five pounds on every single year and now it's been ten to twelve years. There's your sixty or seventy pounds right there."

19. Your Body does not destroy itself overnight, but I can tell you right now, don't be surprised by the lack of power and energy that you have based upon the fitness that you don't have. Fitness is not just something powerful businessmen use as a release; it's something they choose, because they see the power, confidence, clarity, courage and creativity that comes from mastering yourself through fitness.

20. So what kind of fitness should you participate in? There's so many programs out there and so many different modalities; it's not about changing up the routine in regards to fitness, but more on changing the way you *think* about it. You wake up every single morning and wage war with your body so that you can attain mastery until it becomes the servant.

## Making Your Body the Servant

21. We can provide fitness to our Body in a couple of different ways:

1. Lift something heavy at least once a week.
2. Pick up something moderately heavy a whole bunch of times.

3.  Endurance work: Running long distances, cycling, rowing and swimming. We should be doing long walks, things that give us the ability to just stretch the mind, body, ligaments and foundation of who we are physically.

4.  Sprinting

5.  Have Fun: Do a hobby throughout the week or weather permitting, whether it's golf, swimming, biking, skateboarding, tennis, surfing, etc...

22. Our body was born to move fast, burst into speeds, move here and move there. Not letting it do what it's meant to do, it shuts down. Then we wonder why our sex drive and creativity is down, our frustration is at an all-time high and our stress levels are dominating us.

23. It's because the body has not been put into an active state that would support us in the pursuits that we're chasing. One of the greatest ways to stay consistent with fitness is to do things you enjoy. Develop hobbies. Whether it's golf, tennis, fighting, skateboarding, lifting weights, or surfing, have some fun-based hobbies that you genuinely enjoy. This connects and moves the body in a self-motivated way. Every single week, we're weaponizing the body and we're activating the mind by treating the body like a tool. A tool of production; a tool that allows us to see.

24. Let me give you some examples. My wife can totally tell when I haven't worked out, and 100% of the time she's on point. My kids know when I haven't worked out, they can look me in the eyes and tell that I don't look like the same human being. Inside of my organizations, when my teams are all in, I can tell which ones have worked out and which ones haven't because their eyes look different. Their eyes don't look the same as when they workout.

25. There are plenty of physiological functions that occur inside our body when we actually work out, but I'm not going to focus on that. Just know that our body turns on our mind and it shows in our eyes when we have and haven't worked out.

26. Here inside of Warrior and the Core 4, every single morning we're going to get half a point for this conversation of going to war with our body. We are showing our body that it is the servant, not the master. That when we wake up, no matter how many eye boogers we have and how tired we are, that we are going to deliberately create a strategy to engage.

## An Accelerator to The Way

27. The Body is not in the way; it's an accelerator *to* the way. Every single morning I'm going to get half a point for my body. It's really simple: either I worked out or I did not. Does this mean that every single day I have to train really hard? No, some days I'm going to just stretch out and do yoga. Or I may go get a massage and chiropractic work. It all counts as half a point.

28. Inside the Armory we'll dive deeper into how we actually go about scoring the Body and some of the different examples for how to play this out. For now, just understand that every single morning you are at war and the weapon is either pointed at you or at the door. Your Body inside of fitness becomes the first gain. The flip side to this is the fuel that we put inside our Ferrari body.

### Chapter 18:
### POINTS TO PONDER FROM THE GENERAL'S TENT

- **POINT #1:** Your Body is part of the rest of Core 4 as well. It takes you everywhere you need to go as the key domino that begins the conversation.

- **POINT #2:** Is your body an obstacle or a gateway? By disciplining your body, you can in fact discipline your mind. The Body does not destroy itself overnight, therefore it doesn't heal immediately in one night or day as well. Your body turns on your mind and it shows in your eyes when you have and haven't worked out.

- **POINT #3:** Don't be surprised by the lack of power and energy that you have based upon the fitness that you don't have.

- **POINT #4:** Here inside of Warrior and the Core 4, every single morning we're going to get half a point for this conversation of going to war with our Body; that it is the servant, not the master.

## WARRIOR WITNESS:

### M.A., Washington, USA:
*"I am in OK shape, so I'm not overweight and obese, getting out a couple of times and run as well as head out to the gym but I'm not consistent.*

*I've always been able to do "stuff" but I feel like I'm able to push myself more. When I did marathons in the past, I feel like I'm not pushing myself now like I did then, so I'm not attacking my body like then.*

*Getting off doing 100 burpees a day have been hard, especially first thing in the morning, but I feel really good when I do.*

*I go up and down with Fuel. I'm pretty good, bringing a decent lunch to work, but when I start to get hungry, I start to eat crap. Instead of 1-2 slices of pizza, I eat the whole thing. Seeing food as fuel is a new concept to me. From 1-10, I'm probably about a 3."*

## K.O., USA:

*"Body was probably one of the biggest things that attracted me to Warrior. I'm eating much cleaner with green smoothies and feeling hard bits under my squishy bits. I worked out for the sake of working out, but this concept of weaponizing the body is pushing me from being OK to giving me FIRE for where I want to be. Super excited to be on this path."*

## Z.G. Arizona, USA:

*"The biggest shift in Body was in my mindset. I never looked at my body as a weapon. I never considered that being fit would make me a better husband, father and businessman. I don't need to get paid to work out or because I'm competing; I need to work out and stay fit so I can be a weapon and machine as the world keeps up with me.*

*While on a business trip in Vegas, instead of partying and drinking, I got up early, drank a green smoothie and worked out, then killed it with work. Not eating like a pig and paying attention to my body by eating multiple times a day with clean food, I've seen great results that I'm proud of. I'm a 6 out of 10, but I want to be shredded again and be at my fighting weight again from when I competed."*

## T.M., Georgia, USA:

*"It's funny how much better I feel after I have a good workout. It's also funny how a hot yoga class can put me into bed by 8:30pm. LOL. I like the idea of using the gamification to prioritize workouts in the morning before your world get's away from you. How the structure is laid out in simple terms like lift heavy*

*shit once a week (Do push-ups of my fat ass count for that one???). My goal now is to manage the rest of my life around this notion of the importance of C4. (Not staying up to late, making sure I have what I need when I travel, etc.). I like it!"*

## M.M. Alberta, Canada:

*"In spite of the fact I do a lot of athletic activities, I struggle to connect myself to the mindset & identity of an athlete - craving the feeling of my body pushed beyond it's limit. The thought "I'm not an athlete" is story that does not serve me. Today I pushed through a workout filled with negative self stories & fatigue. I discovered that's what it means to 'find power.' Power is not an emotional high, but the willingness to push through against emotions & fatigue."*

## M.S., Virginia, USA:

*"Complex workout programs, unrealistic eating regimens, inconsistency and short sighted goals have kept me a slave to my fitness throughout my life. Or, the opposite extreme of doing absolutely nothing with my body. I didn't DO. New targets: sweat everyday, be better today than I was yesterday. Simple . . . powerful. Love the idea of mixing up the activities so I won't plateau or become bored with the same routine each day. Lift something heavy a couple of days a week. Go long a couple of days a week. Go light, a lot of times, a couple of days a week. I'm not focused on getting abs, getting shredded, or putting on size - although these results are a likely consequence of following the warrior way. The focus is to weaponize my body to prepare for war on a daily basis."*

# THE CORE
## Chapter 19: BODY (FUEL)

There are a thousand ways you could fuel your body, but what Warrior focuses on is a simple way to gainify your fuel based upon addition, not subtraction.

# SECTION FOUR
# THE CORE

## CHAPTER NINETEEN
# BODY (FUEL)

*"Let your food be your medicine, and your medicine be your food."*

### -Hippocrates

---

1. The way you eat and how you fuel your body can easily get overcomplicated. There are a thousand different ways to fuel your Ferrari we call Body, and they all work differently. What we have found here inside of Warrior is a simple way to gainify our fuel, based upon addition, not subtraction.

### Drink Your Greens: Advice from the Green Smoothie Goddess

2. We've simplified optimal fuel intake for Body over years of testing to one simple gain: green smoothies. A few years back I was sitting on a production crew producing some videos online for a woman by the name of Liz Phalp, known as the Green Smoothie Goddess.

3. I heard hours of this conversation around green smoothies and I was like, "What does she mean? What is this green smoothie conversation all about?" I would listen and she kept saying, "If there was only one thing that you did, just drink a green smoothie every single day, your entire physiological metabolic grades would completely change in your body."[30]

---

[30] Liz Phalp's entire training protocol was not about some complex diet or fitness routine. It was simply this: work out every day and drink a green smoothie.

4. After hours of indoctrination and spending so much time in editing and post-editing as we built her videos online, we started to consider the possibility that she might be right. I took her advice on how to properly make green smoothies as I took spinach and kale, froze it in the freezer just like she had told me where it was brittle like chips, and crammed it into my newly purchased $500 Vitamix[31] blender. I spent five-hundred dollars on a *kitchen* tool so I could blend frozen lettuce. I was like, "What am I buying this blender for? This is ridiculous!"

5. I took that buyer's remorse and pounded the spinach and kale down into the bottom. I took some fruit. I took some bananas, strawberries, blueberries, avocado and I put it all in there. Then I filled it up with water and blended that shit up, drinking the whole thing. For the first few weeks I was like, "This is the worst idea ever, I don't want to add this to my diet. My intestines hurt like hell, I can't believe how much my intestines are hurting."[32]

6. There's a much smoother way to transition green smoothies into your routine, but I went extreme with this like I do with everything else in my life; and my Body followed suit. I was pooping like crazy so I thought my body was falling apart on me during this mega detox phase. I was like, "There is no way this makes any sense."

7. Liz said, "Just stay with it for another couple of weeks and see what happens." So I did. And for nearly six years I've continued to stick with it. Because of this, the craziest phenomena occurred: I've become more lean, more shredded and more internally on fire than at any point in my entire life with my body. While my fitness built up my desire to weaponize my confidence with my physicality, consuming a green smoothie every single

---

[31] Not all blenders are created equal; higher end blenders such as Vitamix and Blendtec are the most efficient and high-powered blenders out on the market right now. More is shared within the book's tutorials.

[32] I was going through massive intestinal pain as my body learned to integrate all of these greens that it had not had. It was getting more greens in one day with a green smoothie that it had had over the last 5 years in the beginning. This onslaught of nutrients cleaning out my internal organs in a very short amount of time can lead to a buildup in alkaloids, but evens out as the body gets use to the minerals added to the body through the nutrient-density of leafy greens, eventually making the body turn to craving minerals and nutrients rather than the toxins that had built up over the years of not getting enough essential nutrients.

day (which happens to be worth half a point for the Core 4) is also driving me in a certain kind of way.

## Interpretation of Food

8. You've got to understand; the way you think about food is going to determine your interpretation about food. There are trainers all over the world who actually train on this concept.[33]

9. So, I decided that I'm going to become masterful in this conversation of nutrition. I started by asking my trainer friends for recommendations, buying all of these books, only to discover that everybody argued with everybody, like organized religions or politics. Everyone had their own interpretation on what the proper way to consume food was, in which I discovered that there are some insane food routines and beliefs.

10. In a lot of cultures, food is a vital cultural identity providing a social atmosphere of communicating and connecting with other people. I'm not trying to take anything away from that: Food has simply always been fuel to me.

## Fuel Your Body, Or Die

11. A simple fact of life is that we all need these basics: food, water, and nutrients. There are a lot of different ways to go about fueling our body, from looking at food as fuel as I do, to the enemy as someone like my wife that struggled with anorexia did, or a social experience for foodies. However you view food, if you don't fill up your tank consistently then you are in trouble.

12. Within Warrior, you are going to have to create a different mindset around food, the same way you are going to have to create a different mindset around your Body. Eating is fuel and sometimes it's fun, but eating is not for fun all the time. We are not supposed to constantly build our social lives around eating, eating, and more eating. If that's all you've got going on for yourself, you don't have much going on.

---

[33] *Foodtrainers* is one of a few programs that customizes a lifestyle change through looking at a person's eating habits, likening it to pieces of a puzzle. See more in Appendix Resources: Green Smoothies and book tutorials.

13. The flip side of this is a society of people who've become so addicted to the mindset that in order to find the right fitness and food program it's accomplished by subtraction. This creates an internal prison of thinking about food all of the time, from eating disorders to weight loss yo-yoing.

14. Subtracting doesn't work; it creates a feeling of want. How is it possible that in a society of people who have so much information about nutrition, we have become the fattest people we have ever been globally? Particularly here in the United States. I'm going to have you consider it's because we are out of our minds with our focus on food by subtracting calories instead of adding nutrients, leaving a feeling of want as we binge our way to a whole slew of physical issues.

## Eat Like a Grazing Animal

15. The access to power inside the Body is to shift the way you look at food, which is as fuel[34], not as a fun time. We've made food an idol; we worship food intake as the source for enjoyment. You can have a good time, but generally speaking, you need to eat for fuel. It's about looking at yourself as a grazing animal, not as a big ass buffet guy.

16. Your body needs to be fueled more, not less. This is how messed up our psychology is. We have been trained to believe that in order to lose weight, we need to eat less, less times a day. No. If you look at the most elite, fit individuals who look at food as fuel, they are eating many, many times a day. They are not gorging themselves on massive plates of food; they are eating small amounts consistently and continually, constantly keeping the fire stoked as they burn throughout the day a life that is on fire.

## Adding, Not Subtracting Fuel to the Ferrari

17. We have another analogy here at Warrior for how we add fuel by asking the daily question, "Did you fuel your Ferrari?" I'll explain that question in a moment, but I'm not here to tell you that there is one specific program that is right or wrong. What I'm telling you is that you've got to start thinking differently about the *way* you are fueling. If you have big expectations for

---

[34] This requires shifting the mentality that food is not what brings the fun within a setting to what the real source of enjoyment is; the people you surround yourself with.

production today, how in the hell are you going to meet those expectations if you don't fuel your Ferrari?

18. You have an amazing Ferrari of a body: you do the work in fitness to turn your body into the sexy machine before you, so make sure you fuel it correctly. This isn't an overnight change to receive immediate results; it's a daily shift, gradually implementing more. You can spend the next three to four years changing your eating routines just as you would drive your way up to a Ferrari. How do we do that? Here at Warrior, we encourage one specific game, and again it is a game of addition, not subtraction.

## Back to the Green Smoothies: Getting Out a Really Good Shit

19. Our game here is the sustainability through addition. After the crazy ass detox I put my body through as I was implementing daily green smoothies into my life, I was shitting better, which is like, *crazy*. You sit and you think as a young person, "Dude, taking a shit, why is that a big deal? Why does that matter?" Then all of a sudden you start to get older and you are like, "You know what? I get it now. Taking a shit actually does matter."

20. It feels good to take a really good shit. It feels good to have my intestines cleaned out. Some guys even say that taking a shit is orgasmic, and who wouldn't want more experiences like that?!

21. At 40 years old, I'm more lean and fit than I've ever been. My mind is clearer than it has ever been, and I feel *whole* at my soul level inside this weapon I call Body. It's because I'm doing one simple activity when it comes to my nutrition every single day: drinking a green smoothie. Game over. The end. Drink a green smoothie.

22."Yes, Garrett, but what about my diet, and what about my routines?" We've got thousands of different ways you can deal with that too, but inside of Warrior we simplify by getting to the source of the issue, finding that empty intestines that are purged of the literal crap blocking them up allows a man to feel more clean and legit to deal with the metaphorical crap in his life. That's it.

23. There is no magic around it and you can do all the studying you want on green smoothies. There's thousands of different references and recipes,

but I'm having you buy into one simple concept here: the game of addition changes your life when it comes to food. Stop worrying about all the food that you don't want to eat, and start worrying about the things that you are putting in. Begin doing that by adding a daily green smoothie.

24. Did you fuel the Ferrari? Did you have a green smoothie? If the answer is Yes: give yourself ½ point in Body. If you answer No: Don't give yourself ½ point. It's that simple. Create a daily addiction of implementing green smoothies, which will eventually shift from a pattern that you score to something you cannot live without[35]. Now, if I skip my daily routine of a green smoothie, I notice a significant difference inside my own body.

## A Bloated Vacation

25. This happened to me right after I started down the green smoothie-a-day path a few years ago. We went on a trip and I didn't have access to consuming green smoothies for like a week, after doing them daily for about a year.

26. A friend of mine saw something was off with me and he's like, "Dude, what's going on?"

27. "I'm not feeling good, Dude. I feel all bloated and weird."

28. I called up my Green Smoothie Goddess, and asked, "Liz, what's going on?" I told her what I told my friend.

29. "That's how you used to operate all the time."

"What do you mean?"

30. "How you feel right now; you are not bloated. That's called fecal matter impacting itself in your intestines. You've literally been walking around on a daily basis with massive amounts of toxins in your body that have not had a chance to get cleaned out."

## Did You Fuel the Ferrari?

31. Green smoothies purge out the toxins every single day. This helps us think clearer at a cellular level, feeling more whole and full. It's why we

---

[35] Look at the end of the chapter in Warrior Witness for examples by other members of the Brotherhood inside of Warrior about the impact green smoothies have had in their lives.

are more fit and lean; our body is metabolizing shit faster and everything within our body is working better. Every single morning, if we are fueling our Ferrari of a body with a green smoothie, we are cleaning out the most important system under the hood which keeps everything functioning: the digestive tract of the intestines. Having a clean colon and intestines that are fully functioning actually affects how you feel. And when you feel better, you play better. When you play better, your profitability and results are extremely high.

32. Inside of this Brotherhood, we are going to track every single day one simple additional principle, one new addiction added to our life, which is: "Did I drink a green smoothie? If I did, I get half a point." That brings us to a conclusion here with this section on the Body and the sub-category, the Fuel.

## Chapter 19
## POINTS TO PONDER FROM THE GENERAL'S TENT

- **POINT #1:** : There are many aspects of adding fuel to the Body through food, but inside Warrior we simplified it down over years of testing to one simple gain: green smoothies daily. Do this, and the entire physiological metabolic grades will completely change in your body.

- **POINT #2:** The way you think about food is going to determine your interpretation about food. Eating consistently throughout the day with more of a mentality of seeing food as fuel rather than fun allows you to remain in control of your food intake, instead of letting it control you.

- **POINT #3:** : Turning a green smoothie into an addiction rather than simply a habit or routine, your body will expect it and purge out the toxins every single day.

- **POINT #4:** : Did you fuel your Ferrari? Did you use premium or watered down gasoline that's going to help you move in the short term, yet lead to a lot of internal issues soon? The same goes for our bodies; our own personal Ferraris.

# WARRIOR WITNESS:

### R.C. Illinois, USA:

*"Thinking about body and fuel, I used to look at eating as a social issue and enjoyed it as a foodie. I never ate enough that I was entirely overweight, but I definitely never saw it as fuel.*

*The smoothie helps to get my body and mind in order for the day. I was missing it the last few days on the road; nothing really beats the green smoothies made at home, so I look forward to getting back in that routine."*

———————————

### M.A., Washington, USA:

*I've been doing a green smoothie for about 30 days now, every single day, and I love them. I love the energy and what it's done for me, so it's all good there. My wife has been tripping out over Warrior though, she's a little freaked out seeing me google recipes for green smoothies and going to the grocery store for greens. I was able to find the Naked brand juices that makes green smoothies while traveling and I even had a hotel that I was staying at make me green smoothies. They tasted horrible, but I was appreciative that they did it and I got my greens in for the day. Now I'm off to go about the rest of my day right after I finish the green smoothie that's in my hand."*

———————————

### C.S., USA:

*"This is my 3rd day drinking a green smoothie and you know what? I don't love them, but if I can get ½ point for doing that, it's easy and I'll do it without complaining. I'm sure there's a way to making them tasty because right now they're not, but if I can get ½ point for drinking one before 8? Done."*

———————————

# THE CORE

## Chapter 20: BEING (MEDITATION)

In Core 4, Meditation matters and is far more significant that you
might ever imagine. It is meant to expand you.

SECTION FOUR
# THE CORE

CHAPTER TWENTY
# BEING (MEDITATION)

*"Meditation makes the entire nervous system go into a field of coherence."*

## -Dr. Deepak Chopra
[Author, Public Speaker and New Age Leader in Alternative Medicine]

---

1. What is meditation? Why do we meditate? Is meditation the same as prayer? Is prayer the same as meditation? Is meditation something spiritual? Is meditation something scientific? Does meditation matter at all? Inside of Warrior we know that meditation *does* matter and it's far more significant than one might ever have imagined.

## Meditation is for Everyone

2. Around 2005-2006, I was introduced to meditation as I was studying under a few mentors[36] like Dr. Wayne Dyer.[37] These guys were talking about this idea of meditation and that I needed to do it, but I didn't really get what they meant because every time I heard "meditation," all that kept coming to mind was that it's not something you do if you're Christian.

3. So, I wasn't really jiving with it because I had never been raised with the term meditation. I was raised in Western culture where meditation was not something popular; we prayed and pondered. It took a shift in perspective to realize that they were more similar with each other than I realized.

---

[36] Steve Denunzio was one of those meditation mentors.
[37] Appendix Bibliography: Dyer, Wayne and Additional Resources: Meditation

4. With this shift, I also realized that you don't have to be a religious or a non-religious person to have meditation. As it was introduced to me, meditation was this concept of being able to create space. Like, that's it; it was meant to create space. So in 2005 and 2006, I started to study the [38]Power of Intention by Dr. Wayne Dyer, reading his book *Getting in the Gap*.

## Mind the Gap

5. What is the Gap? Dr. Dyer breaks down this concept that in between all of our thoughts we experience on a day-to-day basis, there is a space in between the thoughts known as the Gap, in which we're looking and searching for the Power inside. So, how do we get this? How do we get to this internal Power?

6. Now, I'm not going to take you down some philosophical path; we operate with simple principles in Warrior. The practicality behind the Gap comes down to this: meditation creates space, but the only way that you *create space* is to *eliminate stress*.

7. And so, stress and space go hand in hand. As businessmen who are trying to pursue the path of having it all, it is vital to have tools in managing a marriage, children, family, clients, prospects, employees, payroll, taxes, and all the rest of it that comes up in our day-to-day experience.

8. Part of the reason why we fail is because of stress, which collapses space. The space we're talking about is this Gap that Dr. Wayne Dyer laid out to me back in the day. So, I started down the path of meditation like a lot of people do when they begin. And I'm not going to lie, it feels like this weird experience because it's so new.

## Learning to Think About Nothing

9. I learned the concept of [39]Japa Breath Meditation, in which I was supposed to think about nothing but breathing in and out. "I can do that," I thought. Here we go: 3, 2, 1... And this weird shit would happen right in the middle of this "nothing:" I was bombarded with thoughts, ideas, and concepts.

---

[38] Dyer, Wayne. Appendix Bibliography and Additional Resources: Meditation
[39] See Additional Resources: Meditation in the Appendix

10. What was wrong with me?! I can't do this thing called meditation because I cannot go to this place called Nothing that Dr. Wayne Dyer mentioned and Eckhart Tolle was talking about in *The Power of Now*.[40] I just needed to come to the Power of Now, *right* now. It was this super ethereal idea but practically speaking, I felt like an idiot.

11. So, I got a hold again of Dr. Dyer's book, *Getting in the Gap* on guided meditation. I figured that I found my problem; I can't calm down enough inside of meditation, so I'm going to have somebody guide me with it. I put on my headphones and Dr. Dyer would have me 'toning' with the following: "Gaaaah..." which would go on and on.

12. One day I was sitting and meditating out on my deck, finally feeling like I was getting it. I really wasn't, but I *did* start to feel like Someone was watching me. I thought,

"There is Someone watching me and I'm pretty sure it's God."

13. I was convinced it was some Divine Being; some god that had come down from the heavens with trumpets blowing and angels flying. But what if I opened up my eyes and I end up dying, ascending to heaven with all of these trumpeting angels?! So, then I got scared to even open my eyes by then because I'm not sure what I'm going to see. I do one more Japa breath, "Gahh..." (I became very good at this as you can tell: "gahh," I could do it forever).

14. I finally opened my eyes and what do I see? My wife eating a bowl of cereal, making fun of me the entire time while I was going "Gahhh." Talk about feeling like an absolute ass. I decided right then and there I was never going to meditate in front of her ever again. So, I would do Japa breath quietly in a closet, which was in the guest room with the door closed, down in the basement, hoping that no one would see me meditating.

15. I was meditating because I was told that there was some kind of Power there and I was like, "If I can find some power in this 'gahh' thing that I'm doing here, well then, I'm going to go find it."

---

[40] Appendix Bibliography: Tolle, Eckhart.

16. This led me down a path of every single modality of meditation you could imagine.[41] I went into the land of fantasy, gypsies, and hippies until I came to the practical science of my meditation journey.

## The Practical Science of Meditation

17. To sum up, what I ended up with simply in one conversation with meditation is this: Meditation is about creating space. It's not about God, but it could be. It's not about science, religion, or spirituality, yet it could be about all of them as well. Meditation is about giving a man limitless space.

18. With space you have clarity, with clarity you have confidence. With confidence you have courage, and with courage you have the ability to create more. Your space dictates what you see. When you are overwhelmed with stress, you can't see. I went on a spiritual journey for mediation, but the truth was, it wasn't necessarily a spiritual pursuit.

19. It was far more practical than I ever imagined. If meditation becomes spiritual for you, that's great. If you grow closer to God, that's great. If you feel closer to your Purpose, *that's* great. But I'm going to have you look at meditation as something far more different than this. Meditation is the opposite of what most men do when they feel stressed, which is: they sedate.

## Sedation vs Meditation

20. We have meditation and we have sedation. Before I had meditation, my sedation tool was that I would work out. The more stressed I was, the harder the workout. These were my training for the Ironman and running ultra-marathons years. My workouts became my sedation.

21. What's another way to sedate? Sex. We can easily become consumed with the sedation of masturbation and pornography. Everything becomes about releasing through sex when using this as a form of sedation. We become driven to release the stress so we're like "Dude, I have got to have sex. I've got to have an orgasm." It's three o'clock in the middle of the day and we're totally stressed, so in our mind we think, "I should go online to a porn site right now."

---

[41] See the meditation guides and tutorials within this book where we go into more depth with various types of meditation exercises.

22. Stressed out people do stupid shit, and stressed out guys make poor decisions. They create all kinds of problems and chaos and become victims in their own minds to their stories.

23. We investigate this inside the Code, which states, "Well, it might be true but the problem is that a lot of the thoughts that you're having are very stressful. A lot of the world that you're living in and the speed at which you operate is very stressful, yet it doesn't mean you're doing anything wrong. It just means that you're growing." In order to expand, you're going to have to experience stress.

24. Meditation allows for the release and the expansion of stress. Now, you can have sex or do a workout to get rid of stress. Or, you can work more, drink more, pop more pills or take a couple of good hits of weed to get rid of stress, but guess what my friend? The problem is still there when you come back down from the temporary feeling of relaxation that sedation brings with all of those behaviors.

25. We do all of these things because our minds are stressed. We're like, "Dude, I'm stressed out. I need to get rid of this stress. It's not healthy, I don't like what I'm feeling; I need to get rid of it."

26. But we've never been taught to go to meditation so we go to the tools of sedation. Working out, sex, drugs, alcohol, career, social media, gaming, watching a whole fucking series on Netflix for the 12th time. It's all the same if you're immersing yourself in something as a way to avoid something else. The sedation masks the stress. Now, all of those things are great; I've got no problem with any of them (well, accept maybe the TV binging). You want to smoke some weed? Fine. But I'm going to have you consider that there's another option to sedation.

## Masking Stress or Expanding Capacity?

27. Sedation may release stress, but you don't grow because it's temporary. Meditation, on the other hand, causes a shift in who you're being and actually expands who you are; the more you meditate the more capacity you begin to obtain. With more capacity you're able to deal with stress differently; more effectively.

28. Space is about capacity and capacity is about space. Our nervous system and our minds have been trained to deal with a certain amount of stress so that we can expand that capacity inside of who we are through meditation.

29. Meditation makes us bigger, so when we feel stressed out and go meditate, we not only deal with the stress but we also grow. Or we sedate, stating that, "I'm feeling stressed out so I'm going to have three cocktails right now." Not a problem, I get it. You're going to have three cocktails, that's fine, but understand when you come back down from those cocktails you will not be expanded in your capacity at all. You'll have reaped the benefits of the release of stress but you won't be any more powerful.

## Is Your Mind Serving or Mastering Over You?

30. Sometimes our stress gets so heavy that we feel like we don't have another option, so I'm going to have you consider the reason why in the following idea below.

31. Our stress becomes an overwhelming burden because we don't have the daily discipline for releasing. On top of that, we're not working out, right? We're not handling our Body which causes more stress. We wake up and drag our way into the day when we haven't harnessed the power of the mind by putting it into a servant position. Our mind is not serving us; it's mastering over us.

32. Inside of all this studying and pursuing meditation, it naturally started leading me towards Buddhism and Hinduism. This was after being raised with Western religion (Christianity from my Catholic mother and Mormon father and Judaism from my Jewish aunt), my family was like "He's lost his goddamn mind. He's studying Buddhism AND Hinduism."

33. Look, I get it, I get that it's part of our nature to be cautious about shit that doesn't make sense to us or that we were/weren't raised with, but the shit I was looking for was not being taught in the places I was raised to look. I came to find out later down the road it was all being taught at different levels—I just couldn't hear it. It was all on me; it didn't have anything to do with the religion. It didn't have anything to do with the people.

34. It had to with me. My capacity was deaf. Have you ever done this with people? Like, you talk about a topic that you know really well but they can't hear you? You're watching them, they're hearing you with their ears

but their eyes are glazed over, so you know they can't get it. As I'm studying these Eastern books, I'm reading through this idea that Buddha speaks about called, "The Observer Chooser."

## The Observer Chooser

35. I was like, what does being this Observer Chooser even mean? He went on to discuss insights that as an individual, as a man, you must gain mastery over your mind. Or in other words, you've got to take yourself to a place where you can release pain and pleasure in order to access Ultimate Power. I was like, "Wait a second, okay. Letting go of pain I totally get, but letting go of *pleasure* though? Come on my friend. Come *on*."

36. Now this brings us right back up to guys being led by a stimulus response. They're so stressed out that when something unanticipated happens, they immediately react. There is no space in between stimulus and response. Just reaction.

37. When you're able to get inside that space instead of forcing a reaction to occur, what is found is a deeper agency. Your ability to make decisions is clearer, not because it's spiritual or because God wants you to, but because it allows you to gain clarity. None or all of that could be true, but all I'm having you consider is this: you will have more power when you have more capacity.

## The Capacity to Have More Power

38. Right now your central nervous system can only deal with so much stress, and it is the limiter to your growth. Every time you feel stressed out, your resulting mechanism is to go to a different conversation of sedation. Our society is filled with men who sedate all day long trying to deal with all of this overwhelming stress and the space inside of our mind.

39. Meditation allows us to activate the "trigger response" section in our central nervous system. It gives us the opportunity to see something we couldn't see before or "getting in the gap" as Dr. Wayne Dyer called it. You don't necessarily need to be all 'gaahh' to pull this stuff up but you could. When you're assenting through mantra-based meditation, this allows you inside your own mind to begin to shift the space, to expand the capacity

of "I'm stressed out; I'm going to drink" to "I'm stressed out; I'm going to meditate."

40. When I come out of meditation, I'm sharp as hell, but if I turn to the cocktails I'm going to be dull as hell. This latter choice will also require recovery time, rather than coming out of meditation, where I'm weaponized, ready to go. Meditation takes us from a place of being a Reactor to a Creator.

## Being Present in Influence and Persuasion

41. I am present with the people I interact with because my capacity is large enough that I don't get triggered by all the stress around me. As they're sharing, I'm connecting with them and learning. I'm growing, feeling, and expanding on what they're saying. Now the crazy part about influence and persuasion is the more present we are in the conversation, the more the other person believes that we give a shit. The more that somebody believes that we give a shit, the more influence we have with that person.

42. Meditation is a practical tool that creates space, releases stress and expands who we are. If I meditate, I become greater than what I was yesterday.

## Breaking the Trigger and Response

43. We see the impact daily meditation has because we don't get triggered, responding differently in our environments. We break the social agreement of the trigger and the response. I sit in business meetings and conferences where people say, "I just want to tell you thank you for being so present. You look like you actually heard me, which is so rare today."

44. The most insane impact I saw came from my relationship with my wife. I used alcohol for a long time as a suppression and sedation mechanism: I wouldn't fight with my wife, but I wasn't getting anywhere because we also weren't connecting. It's not possible when you're sedated.

## A Consistent Mechanism for Expanding Capacity

45. Connection under the influence of alcohol isn't an actual connection because it's fantasy based. When you come out of it, guess what? You're two sober human beings that don't know how to connect in reality. Meditation is the only consistent mechanism for expanding capacity inside a loyal

man's mind, heart and nervous system, even though it's difficult in the beginning because we're training our brain to think differently. Meditation is not something you *have* to do; it becomes something you *must* do. It becomes who you are.

46. I meditate consistently between 2-3 times a day for 20 minutes at a time: I typically meditate in the morning, afternoon, and at night. Some days I get in only one meditation and rarely do I miss it, but some days I don't get any meditation, so on those days I don't get my half a point.

## Taking A Stand for the Creative Power of Meditation

47. The only way to be able to have it all is to take a stand for yourself inside of the creative power of meditation. It's not something that we do because we're trying to be spiritual, become closer to God, or more scientific. It's not something we do for any other reason than to create space for all of the benefits that could be (whether you're closer to God or not) more connected to the Universe, feeling more on purpose.

48. Meditation is meant to do one thing; expand you. The only wrong meditation is no meditation, and daily meditation is expansion within the Core 4.

### Chapter 20:
### POINTS TO PONDER FROM THE GENERAL'S TENT

- **POINT #1:** Meditation is far more significant than you might have ever imagined, no matter what your religious background.

- **POINT #2:** Meditation is a practical way that creates space, releases stress and expands who we are. If we meditate, we become greater than we were yesterday.

- **POINT #3:** By becoming the Observer Chooser, you must as a man, as an individual, gain mastery over your mind. Which is, you've got to take yourself to a place where you can release pain and pleasure in order to access Ultimate Power.

- **POINT #4:** Meditation is the only consistent mechanism for expanding capacity inside a loyal man's mind, heart and nervous system, even though it's difficult in the beginning because we're training our brain to think differently. Meditation is not something you have to do; it becomes something you must do. It becomes who you are.

# WARRIOR WITNESS:

## A.S., USA:

*"This was an interesting one for me. I never really did meditation or even thought about it. Honestly, I could never clear my mind because there was always so much going on in my life, my wife's life and with kids.*

*Incorporating it with my daily prayer has been a great tool to utilize it more to help me focus and concentrate more on the positive with my Creator. As I've incorporated more and more of the Warrior doctrine, I'm noticing myself needing to get up a lot earlier. I find myself turning to meditation instead of sedating with alcohol like I used to. I end up waking up foggy and dull, but then how can I take care of patients in the hospital in that state? I've found myself in situations so saturated with stress that I will snap and take everyone down around me.*

*This will help me handle my anger more as I'm seeing all of the Warrior doctrine fascinating."*

## A.C., California, USA:

*"I've been practicing meditation for about 6 years now, so it's a non-negotiable part of the day. The first time I meditated it was for about 2 minutes, which was about 1:50 of me thinking about everything else and NOT meditation. Slowly over time it's created something in my life that's hard to even put into words. It's space and clarity that helps me breathe. I was told by someone to start with a candle, staring at the flame until your mind goes clear. I do it in the morning when the house is quiet."*

## Z.G, Arizona, USA:

*"If I'm using the Code, I admit that I suck at meditation. I was raised in an environment that mediation didn't exist at all, yet we were all operating at a million miles an hour. Now I can see the space that it brings, and I need it because I'm fucking nuts and my ADD mind takes me on paths that are far and foreign that I do not need to be.*

*My way in the past was sedating by watching TV, drinking or working out but none of them really helped. Meditation = growth, focus and power. Focus is a huge one for me so that I'm making my mind serve me instead of mastering over me. I easily get triggered, but now I'm seeing that NOT meditating is costing me money, sex (the lack thereof with my wife) and relationships. I can go from a reactor to creator of my kingdom. The only wrong meditation is NO meditation."*

## M.K., Oregon, USA:

*"Gosh this is hard for me... I enjoy taking the time to sit and be still, to stop the constant noise that's in my head and around me. But then I fall asleep. Every. Fricking. Time. Why I have difficulty taking the time, especially when I'm not at my office, but at home on the weekends or when I am out of my office all day. I have to make something consistent, but it's been difficult. When I do, though, the relief from my stress... the refocus of my time and energy... it's so good."*

## M.M. California, USA:

*"I think this is the single best thing I've gotten thus far from Warrior. The days I meditate I'm far more relaxed and capable of dealing with stress which impacts my ability to deal with conflicts with my queen. I'm working harder at consistently meditating and tuning out and letting my mind slow and yet it has been hard but it gets easier the more I practice.*

*What I liked from this episode was the idea to getting sharper when use meditation to deal with stress rather than using alcohol to sedate and that is something I've fallen into for my whole life."*

## J.M., Seattle Washington:

*"I need meditation in my life. I'm just learning how to do it. I feel once a day is not enough. I'm going to do it twice a day. I need to create space to release my stress. I have used endurance exercise social media, beer, etc to find this release. I want to break the cycle of trigger and response. Especially with my wife and daughter. I'm committed to doing meditation to expand."*

## I.H., Washington, USA:

*"Meditation and visualization for me have been invited part of my life since college. As a college athlete specifically gymnastics I was fortunate enough to*

receive training on meditation as a methodology to calm my mind and focus on the upcoming competition routine. This has served me extremely well in surgery as well-I will frequently take a few minutes to meditate, settle my mind, and then visualize the steps of the next operation. It has also been extremely useful in preparing for missions and receiving casualties. It helps to settle my mind, lower my heart rate, and allows me to be the calm leader in the trauma bay, operating room, or in a field hospital. Where I think I need the greatest work in applying my meditative practice is in my balance with my family. Being mindful, present with complete honesty= expansion and balance."

## T.R., Arkansas, USA:

"I have meditated on and off over the years. I identify closest to Buddhism in regards to spirituality. So at times I have been very active meditating. For whatever the reason, I would eventually stop the practise. A lot of fucking good that does. What I can say is that while meditating, I was clearer and more able to handle stresses. It can be hard at first to feel as though "something" is "happening". I am curious to see what the Warrior Ascension practice is like and am ready to increase my capacity. Time to do the work."

## J.E., Auburn, Illinois:

"Learning to develop a daily discipline to handle daily stress in other ways than suppressing with alcohol, etc. is what I have been missing. Now it makes sense that I can only expand my ability to deal with stress by expanding my capacity through meditation. I like to commune with nature when I am doing outdoor activities. My favorite activities are kayaking with golfing as a close second. These activities are the closest I have come to regular meditation. I am looking forward to learning how to meditate and finding ways to make it part of my routine."

## A.A., Alabama, USA:

"Learning how to not be a reactionary person and be a creation person this is something that I need to do I have never thought of meditation as expanding capacity for all areas of my life I have only known sedation that's the habit I created so I'm looking forward to learning more about this and do it in my daily routine stress has been a big factor in my life cause me not to sleep and worry it's exciting to find a way to deal with it other than being angry and taking it out on others."

# THE CORE

## Chapter 21: BEING (REVELATION)

We all have a Custom Voice inside of us that if we listen to it, the words we say and write become doctrine and beliefs. The entire world of scripture has been built by positive focuses of picking events, deciding they were divine in nature, giving them lessons and then applying those lessons to our lives.

## SECTION FOUR
# THE CORE

## CHAPTER TWENTY-ONE
# BEING (REVELATION)

"There is a voice inside of you
That whispers all day long,
'I feel this is right for me,
I know that this is wrong.'
No teacher, preacher, parent, friend
Or wise man can decide
What's right for you--just listen to
The voice that speaks inside."

**-Shel Silverstein, "The Voice"**
[American children's poet and author, (1930-1999)]

---

1. As we learned from the last chapter, the first part of Being is Meditation which then opens us up for Revelation. Isn't that weird?! Meditation precedes Revelation. I want to meditate and expand my capacity. Once I've commanded my capacity, I can prepare myself to hear the Voice. The reason why you're even reading this book is because I listen to the Voice.

## Listening to The Voice

2. There was an aspect inside of me, a Voice speaking to me, communicating internally but I had never been present enough to distill away all of the noise inside my mind until I practiced meditation. Only then was I able to actually hear my internal voice that was connecting me to Source, God, and a Higher Purpose: my Sole Soul Purpose. I couldn't hear my Voice because I didn't meditate, so my mind was filled with all of this chaos. I would disavow, disconnect and push away this Voice that was guiding a life that you and I

both have: A Custom Voice inside of us. A connection to God, a connection to the universe that's saying, "Listen Brother, here is the path you get to take. You get to go this way. Consider these things, read this book, ask these questions, write this down."

3. Most of us have never been clear enough in our own mind to even give credit to the Voice because it emits all of this other chaos. Meditation strips that away, opening us up for Revelation. Now, being raised in a pretty religious environment with many different belief systems, here's what I can tell you: Everybody at a certain level worships the words inside of books. Doesn't matter if it was the [42]Bible or the [43]Book of Mormon: these were the two books being pushed around for me. Great books and I love them. They're fantastic. If they work for you, great. If they don't work for you, that's great too. Whether we go to Christian scripture or to the [44]Bhagavad Gita, the [45]Dhammapada, the [46]Torah, [47]Qur'an or to the [48]Tao Te Ching, if it provides an environment for revelation, stick with it. Regardless of all the books I've studied now, the thing that has always interested me about scripture was how modern humanity would cling to the words of dead people while at the same time devalue the current Voice inside themselves.

## Quieting The Chaos of The Mind To Discover The Rising Voice Inside

4. I was a poster boy for not listening to the Voice within. Once I started taking meditation seriously, however, space started filling in my world more and more. The Chaos of my Mind started quieting down and I started to notice there was this Voice that was rising. Words started coming to me with insights about my marriage and children. I had customized content that seemed to be downloaded like blocks of data into my mind with a rise of emotions from my soul that went straight into my heart.

---

[42] See Additional Resources: Western Religion Texts in the Appendix

[43] ibid

[44] 700 verse scripture in Sanskrit as part of the Hindu epic Mahabharata. See Additional Resources: Eastern Religion Texts in the Appendix for more

[45] ibid, Buddha's Path of Wisdom

[46] Jewish religious text, also known as Pentateuch which consists of what Christians call the Old Testament, or 5 Books of Moses originally written in Hebrew

[47] The central religious text of Islam composed in Arabic, which Muslims believe to be a revelation from God to the prophet Muhammad

[48] Written by Lao Tzu, classic Chinese text. It is referred to as the Laozi and is also known as Daodejing, Dao De Jing, or Daodejing. See also Eastern Religious Text in the Additional Resources of the Appendix

5. I started hearing these things. I starting feeling and getting these impressions about doing and not doing certain things[49]. The entire Warrior Movement was launched because I listened to a Voice inside of me that told me in 2012, turn on your camera, yell in front of it, invite five guys to join this Movement you've created for yourself and have them begin this conversation. It wasn't as clear then. The Voice just said, "Go!" just like the Voice said "box this shit up and send it around the world." I have created my own set of doctrine based off of listening to the Voice within.

6. While learning from the scriptures, almost everyone I have ever met was talking about how awesome everyone was 2,000 years ago. They totally were. Creating my own personal scriptures isn't to replace what was given to us as humankind, but to make modern application from my own divine insights within those teachings.

## Don't Devalue Your Voice

7. We devalue our Voice because we cannot hear it. That was a direct personal revelation I had one day. Another insight I had was: "They deny the voice because they will not act on it." All of a sudden I started to see the *humanity* in the words of the people who had written down in books that had become scripture to us today. I said, "Man, these are just guys. These are guys who are trying to figure out life. They were just trying to figure out how to live."

8. All of the scriptural texts I just mentioned were about men that were just trying to figure out how to live by writing it down, from [50]Buddha to [51]Krishna to [52]Lao Tzu and [53]Paul. Same goes for [54]*The Power of Now* by Eckhart Tolle or [55]*The Power of Intention* by Dr. Wayne Dyer. All are writings by men who were searching for the understanding of life through listening to the Voice inside of them. We called their journals scripture. We called

---

[49] The Voice gave me a prompting so I pulled out my journal (aka my War Map) and I started writing: "They devalue their voice because they cannot hear it." This is one example of many experiences I've had while listening to the Voice.
[50] Dhammapada
[51] Bhagavad Gita
[52] Tao TeChing
[53] Holy Bible, New Testament
[54] Tolle, Eckhart. See full citation in Appendix Bibliography
[55] Dyer, Wayne.See full citation in Appendix Bibliography

their revelations Divine. While at the same time, looking inside our own lives and saying, "well, I'm a diabolical sinner" or "I'm an idiot. There's no way I can trust myself." My level of distrust in my Voice was so intense, I stupidly thought I wasn't worthy of personal revelation.

## Walking Away to Find The Voice

9. I had become addicted to the following belief: my voice doesn't matter. I had to rely on the faith of others before I had faith in myself. Maybe you do as well, and I'm here to tell you, that's okay. For now. Once you unlock the Power of the Warrior's Way and live your Core 4 every single day, you hold yourself responsible as the King that you are.

10. For me, I discovered this King after hitting rock bottom in 2009 when my epic implosion occurred. Every day I would have to sedate and suppress this Voice that was asking me to consider other possibilities until I finally listened: and walked away from all organized religion.

11. Now, I have no problem with organized religion. Mormonism, Catholicism, Judaism, Born Again Christian, Southern Baptists, Muslim, don't care. That's fine. That is not the point of what I'm saying. I left religion because I couldn't hear my own Voice. I couldn't bring value to the Voice that was inside of me. I could not commune with God and the universe because I was addicted to devaluing my own Voice in replacement of the Voice of people who have died thousands of years ago.

## Your Voice Must Matter

12. Maybe you're in a place where you can actually hear the Voice inside the churches you're in and that's great. Some of you may have never gone to a church, so maybe it's time for you to start. Maybe you need a bit of that organization to just start sparking some of that listening for your Voice. You're all going to be in different places, but the one thing I can tell you is this: regardless of where you go, what you do, how you play or what it's called, there's one massive shift that must occur for you inside of this experience of having it all. Your Voice must matter to *you*.

13. The moment that you realize that your own Voice matters, God will pour down Revelation into your life, customized for your Core 4. You'll

discover that the most important will be living scripture inside of the words you write down, which we call the Black Bible.

14. One of the last times that I was participating inside of any organized religion was in a Mormon church house. I was given an opportunity to share a talk; a presentation.[56] I stood up at the pulpit to share with the people a message, holding up a book of scriptures and I did something that was slightly radical inside of that environment. I asked, "How many of you feel like God is in these words?"

15. Everybody just kind of sat there and then I did what was thought unfathomable amongst Mormons. I took this book of scripture and I threw it in the chapel of this church house. It was like it happened in slow motion: If this was a movie, we would've had multiple camera angles on the book slowly flying through the air then cutting to people's shocked faces until it landed with a thud on the ground, then the camera would speed back up to real-time and pandemonium would break out. But this wasn't a movie. No one knew what to do. **I** was even amazed that I did it. I'm like, "I'm doing this?! Okay. Whoom. Oh shit. I did this."

16. Then I stood there and I looked at the shocked people inside the room and asked them a simple question: "How many of you want to hurt me because of what I just did?" They were too shocked to raise their hands, plus there isn't a lot of speaker/audience interaction in the chapel of the Mormon Church. Besides, raising their hands would have convicted them.

17. I then went on, "Isn't it interesting that because of pulp and paper with the black printed words, we worship a book that most of us don't even study?"

18. "Even worse than that, we would rather hurt another human being because of a book."

## Looking Inside Your Own Personal Book

19. Are we too scared to actually take a look inside the book that God's calling us to write? I don't know what your religious belief system is. I don't know

---

[56] In the Church of Jesus Christ of Latter-day Saints (Mormon Church), people don't interact with the chapel speaker, who is asked by the local ecclesiastical leader to prepare a speech on a specific topic, varying from 10-20 minutes long. No formal training is expected.

where you've come from or what your path looks like. My encouragement here as I'm talking through this topic is **not** to have you leave your church. That's not my target or my goal. For me, I had to. I couldn't hear myself anymore. I couldn't hear God in me. I could not hear the Voice inside of me at all.

20. I could not see my identity beyond the label of being Catholic or Mormon or Jewish. I couldn't see Me nor could I hear the Voice of my Divinity. I couldn't hear God talking to me. Once I stepped outside of that environment of structured religion, I started to see this amazing thing happen. I started to see that I could be inspired by these words all around me. I could read scripture from a lot of religious belief systems and great books from extraordinary people without getting caught up in stories and limited beliefs that in order to believe one religious thing, one must cast aside and condone everything else. I was free to Listen.

21. I could simply live life, and inside of that I had this amazing experience in which life started to teach *me*. Life started to make sense to me. I started to uncover that God's lessons for my life were all around me, all the time. My own personal journey didn't require me to go to a church house or read a certain book. When I was willing to listen to the Voice, I found the education, expansion and revelation I was searching for.

## Search, Ponder and Pray

22. I could pray and ask questions. Inside of that pondering within my meditation, if I was ready with my War Map, in essence a journal with personal revelation which we now refer to as the Black Bible mentioned earlier, I could write down my answers. Every single time I would physically write those answers onto paper, those words mattered in my life. But they may not matter to you. Revelation is a customized curriculum for you and me.

23. Listening to the Voice has saved my life. It's changed my marriage, leveled up my family, changed my bank accounts, and my body; it has liberated me to build my kingdom. The same Voice that I speak of is a Voice inside of you that is waiting, pleading, *begging* for you to listen. Without clearing the space within it using meditation, you'll never be able to hear it speak directly to you. Maybe you don't trust yourself because you trust the words of dead people over the words of your own living scripture. I get it.

I'm sure it was very difficult for them too at the time. Difficult to believe that the universe can speak these kinds of truth into their life.

24. I've learned to believe in my own Voice which gives me instruction on how to operate my life. Sometimes I get it and sometimes I mess it up hard core.

## Journaling the Journey

25. Sometimes listening to the Voice comes through repurposing and rekindling earlier experiences in our life. From a very early age my mom ingrained in my mind the importance of journaling. I had these big boxes of journals from when I was a kid; each would have about two pages written in them. I would start and stop, start and stop. Journaling just didn't work for me at that time.

26. Back in 2009, after I began experiencing my own personal revelation and remembering the instruction from my Mom on how to rely on books to be the only way to teach spirituality, journaling started to work for me. I began writing down the guidance that God was giving me about my life; the insights and actions that I needed to take. I began to recognize the perspective shifts in what I was seeing and also the things I needed to do, so I would break out scriptures and I would read them with the intent of searching for my own personal revelation rather than worshipping the words on those papers. Once I received Revelation, I stopped studying and would immediately dive into the scripture that mattered: my living scripture. MY book of Revelation from God, customized for my life of having it all, which is not your life but solely mine.

## Individualized Personal Revelation: Your Daily War Map

27. The Revelation I get is not going to be the same Revelation you get. I would draw pictures and models and formulas that were coming to me, contemplating ideas and concepts. I would look over business, religious and self-help books and I just write shit down. My daily memoirs began to become the roadmap to my own liberation. They were helping me feel my way through life with clarity.

28. I'm going to have you consider that your daily living scripture is your Black Bible to living. It's your guidance system to creating everything you

have ever searched for and more; it's sitting right in front of you as a divine blueprint to creating life on your own terms.

29. It requires you to listen. If you won't listen to your own Voice (your own Revelation), if you want to continue to put everyone else on a pedestal and put yourself in the shit hole, guess what? It's never going to work. You have to understand that your personal revelation is no more and no less significant than any of the words that have been written down in any book, at any time in the history of this world. This is a bold stand that I don't take lightly.

## Did You Listen to The Voice Today?

30. The only way for you to get the guidance that you need is to listen to the Voice. Did you listen? We'll know whether you did or not because we can look into your Black Bible and see it documented. Every single day, after we meditate, we're going to search for revelation using the Production Focus, which is part of The Lift section of our model. We're going to write that shit down and we're going to begin to build our living scripture for our lives.

## The Lift

31. The Lift becomes the framework that supports us in writing down our Revelations into a document known as Production Focus. Every single day we do it. Every single day we look into the Divine, the Game of our Lives, and we find the lessons. We pick the events that have been hand selected and delivered to teach us. This is no different if you look through any scripture: journeys of what happened because of events that they took action on from the Voice. They shared a lesson, commandment or doctrine from that event and then they made it applicable to all of our lives.

32. The entire world of scripture has been built by production focuses of picking events, deciding they were divine in nature, giving them lessons and then applying those lessons to our lives. This is how we get our half point each day as well, bringing us to a conclusion here for the section of Revelation. Here in Warrior, get used to being asked,

# Did you listen to the Voice today?

## Chapter 21:
## POINTS TO PONDER FROM THE GENERAL'S TENT

- **POINT #1:** Meditation precedes Revelation. Meditating expands our capacity, and once in command of it, we can prepare to hear the Voice.

- **POINT #2:** When we listen to the Voice inside of us and then write down the thoughts that come from it, we are creating our own modern scripture as we follow the promptings of the Voice, God, Higher Purpose, whatever your religious background calls it. Creating our own scriptures isn't to replace what was given to us but to make modern application with our own divine insights within those teachings, thus making it customizable doctrine for us to follow as Kings of our realm.

- **POINT #3:** The moment that you realize that your own Voice matters, God will pour down Revelation into your life, customized for your Core 4. You'll discover that the most important doctrine will be living scripture inside of the words you write down through journaling.

- **POINT #4:** Your daily living scripture is your War Map to living. It's your guidance system to creating everything you have ever searched for and more. You have to understand that your personal revelation is no more and no less significant than any of the words that have been written down in any book, any time in the history of this world.

# WARRIOR WITNESS:

## M.A., Washington, USA:

*"My quick take on Memoirs and with meditation, I want to learn the Positive Focus and am excited to listen to the Voice more; it's actually what brought me to Warrior. There was very much an emotional point in my life that got me to that point of listening to that Voice, talking to Sam, and here I am at Warrior. The Positive and Power Focus in my life is something I look forward to incorporating into my life."*

## J.F., South Carolina, USA:

*"I feel a lot like Garrett described and how he felt when he got into this; very much out of my comfort zone and a bit wacky. However, going through it, I'm excited about the context in which it's framed here in Warrior; I understand the benefit and see the vision in how this can help me to find that space and clarity. I've had that moment, but I've never really understood it. I'm ready to access it on-demand and walk this gateway in which my head is clear and I'm focused. That consistent ability allows me to access that when I want to."*

---

## A.S., USA:

*"Honestly, memoirs was interesting for me because I never really journaled before and feelings were never really something that I grew up talking about. Journaling was not my thing. Positive Focus and Power Focus as well as the amount of meditation have fathered for me the concept of journaling. I do it more and more and am still working on making it a daily thing. It's not easy for me to talk about my feelings, but it's a great way to look at what makes me tick."*

---

## J.M., Western Cape, South Africa:

*"I find that a combination of exercise first, meditation after gives me space to be able to write stuff down. I think I can hear the Voice clearer then and although it's all very random I feel it's almost a expression into reality of getting these things out of my head and onto paper.*

*This has never been a strong point for me and have tried journaling in the past but I think having some kind of routine and clarity opens up space to clear even more out onto paper. Now to keep it consistent."*

---

## J.R., San Diego, California, USA:

*"Amazing how, as a Christian, I have felt and experience that God only uses scripture to speak to us BUT IN FACT, the scripture teaches us that the Holy Spirit is that daily Voice and it lives inside of us! I haven't been quiet enough to hear."*

---

## M.K., Oregon, USA:

*I'll tell you what - the idea that God is revealing stuff to me today, that is worthy to be recorded: that's fantastic insight. I know that the guys in the Bible were just like me, I don't know why I consider their revelation so much superior to my own. The reality is that I can listen to that 'still small voice' just like they did, record what I'm being told, and compare that to their revelation to make sure that I'm on the right path. The hardest part about all of that is making sure I'm listening to the 'right' voice, because I definitely have a voice that tells me to do what's totally contrary to what's good. I love this practice, it's really opened up my view on 'journaling'. "*

———————————

# THE CORE

## Chapter 22: BALANCE (PARTNER/POSTERITY)

Here in Warrior we look at 'Balance' as a description of our relationships, and in this chapter we focus on the subcategory of your queen and posterity (parents, siblings, children, and close friends).

SECTION FOUR
# THE CORE

CHAPTER TWENTY-TWO
# BALANCE
# (PARTNER/POSTERITY)

*"Being deeply loved by someone gives you strength, while loving someone deeply gives you courage."*

**–Lao Tzu**
(Ancient Chinese Philosopher and writer, died 531 BCE)

---

1. Balance. We are not talking about balance in the sense of balancing like a teeter-totter with equal distribution on both sides. Balance is our description of relationships, so in this chapter we'll be looking at the subcategory of partner: your Queen (wife or girlfriend) and posterity: children, parents and siblings. Did you ever consider having a deeply close, connected family? Every single day we are going to get half a point for taking an action with our partner and the selected other family member who would fit into that family and posterity quadrant.

## A Perplexing Balance

2. Let me discuss how this began though. I never could figure out how to actually win the Game with my wife. What ended up happening was that I was constantly in a game of wondering where my Balance was inside that relationship and considering if I was able to make a withdrawal. Just as my debit card was no longer working because I had no money in my account,

the same thing was happening within my marriage when, in 2009, my wife was ready to be done with me.[57]

3. This conversation of Balance perplexed me. My marriage perplexed me. I did not know how to go all in. I always felt like my marriage was in bankruptcy, constantly on the fringe and about to be foreclosed on due to my own attitudes and behaviors about how a marriage was supposed to work (which wasn't much). I was supposed to make the money and that's it; I thought the rest of the responsibility was on her. I was completely oblivious to the fact that she had needs. I thought that if I made the money, then sex would just happen and we would be good. But when I stopped making the money, my marriage was exposed for what it was: a wife who was very unhappy with a man who had been unconscious for years. I was oblivious to this. I had no idea how frustrated my wife was with me.

4. I had no clue how to make my marriage good, let alone great. This is ultimately what caused me to cheat…It looked easier for me to just have a relationship with somebody else that I was not married to than it did to actually work on a relationship with my wife. I was a bullshit artist; a great big liar not living up to The Code. I couldn't even tell myself the truth, let alone anybody else. All I knew was that my marriage was failing, and I had no clue how to fix it.

## Making Massive Deposits into the Love Bank

5. Marriage is hard. The most fulfilling experiences always are. Some couples are able to achieve a good marriage, but it's meant to be great. I am going to have you consider that "good" is the new horseshit. Our entire society has become "good" and what do we have? A bunch of assholes. Good is not why we were put here. Are you telling me you are committing to being in a relationship with a woman, having children and then spend the rest of life in a "good" relationship? Here at Warrior we demand greatness and will not stop until it is achieved by going all in. No more of this half-ass behavior.

6. So, how did I do this when my wife and I decided to go all in on our marriage? I was committed to figuring out a methodology for making strategic deposits in my wife's life. Such that I can have a balance in that

---

[57] I cheated on her, which was both horrible and extremely liberating as it reminded me what I really needed in my life, which was Danielle, leading us both down a journey to going all in.

account so that I can put her into karmic debt. That way, if I come with an ATM card and I want to make a withdrawal occasionally, I am able to. I may be thinking, "Dude, I need some cash today." Maybe I don't need cash again for like five days and then I make another withdrawal. Inside that game in our relationships, we've got to be ahead of our withdrawals by making massive deposits. But also know that these massive deposits are never countered with massive withdrawals.

7. This approach helped me to see the connection in my Core 4 which thrives on consistency. I deposit $100 in the bank and every single day my deal is to make a deposit, but I was curious, how do I swing singles with my wife and make deposits that matter? Or with my children? How do I do it in a way that is not conditional upon their response, that doesn't require them doing anything back?

8. I initially had it all planned out to spend 5 focused minutes of committed quality time with each person when I got home. I was totally pumped to put this theory into play. So, I sat down next to my wife, all fired up and looked at her intensely, like I was trying to extract the answer from her soul, then asked, "How was your day?!"

9. "What's wrong with you?" pretty much sums it up. Yeah, it failed. And probably scared the shit out of her trying to figure out what I was on to act so intense.

10. I came from left field and she had no idea what was going on, let alone ready to give me any kind of response that would lead to a fulfilling connection. Eventually, I got to this place where I realized I had to be able to do something, have a framework that I could follow and a way that I could make deposits that would work. And that's when I looked down at my cell phone after receiving a text. "What if I just text her?" I thought. Hmm.

11. But what am I going to say? None of that "Why aren't you talking to me?" winky-face XOXO emoticon shit. I sat there and then the Voice inside me asked, "Why don't you tell her why you love her?" Really?! Tell her *why* I love her? I don't want to talk to her at all. I don't even know what is going on with her! She's crazy.

12. That was what I was thinking, but also inside my mind the Voice suggested, "Just tell her you appreciate her." So I did. Then the next day I got up and grabbed my phone out again: Well, what am I going to send

my wife now? What am I going to send my mom today, another person that I wanted to reconnect with? Like, what am I going to say to them from my cell phone? Neither one of them responded to the one I sent the day before. All the Voice said was, "Tell your mother why you honor her." I was like "Well, okay."

13. Then the Voice said, "Tell your wife why you appreciate her as the mother of your children." So I did. Then the next day I didn't get any response and this went on. I sent my mom texts every single day for three and a half months. My mom's got some determination after the falling out we had had when I was still being one-dimensional. Guess how many of those text messages she responded to? One. The last one.

14. I sent my wife text messages for almost four weeks and guess how many she responded to? Zero. I learned some things during this process, the first one was this: Every morning I would wake up and I would use one of three words: Honor, Appreciation, Love.

## Honor, Appreciation and Love

15. These words are significant because they are part of the meditation mantras used which can be found in the Warrior Armory on top of being used inside of the communication with our partner and/or posterity/parents.

## HONOR

16. What does it mean to honor someone? Put them up in an equal place, giving them respect for who they are.

## APPRECIATION

17. Appreciation means to add value to. I never honored my wife and my mother on how she had shown up and endured the game with me. I didn't appreciate things that my wife or mother had said in the past or things they had done. There was no appreciation expressed for who they were. For the *gifts* of who they are in every aspect. The gifts of who they have been in my life. Without my mom, I wouldn't be alive. Without my wife I wouldn't have my children. Without my wife I am not the man I am today; I don't become the man I am today without the mirror of my queen. There is no way, and yet how often was I expressing this appreciation? Never.

# LOVE

18. Love means you give a shit. And yet love was a conditional conversation for me. In my marriage, it was if she was having sex with me she loves me, if she was not having sex with me she probably didn't love me. In my relationship with my mom it was: if you are listening to me talk about the pain of my life then that means you love me. If you are not listening to me talk about the pains in my life then you don't love me. It was conditional.

19. Every morning I woke up, and every morning I would select from one of these three areas and I would choose a message that I would type up into my notes. I would save them, then copy and paste it to be sent via text to my mom and to my wife. I would write about things I remembered from the past and the feelings of honor, appreciation, and love would naturally come, giving me guidance and inspiration.

## Awaken and Remember

20. This process of Daily Deposits will start to cause a man to awaken and remember the good, the beauty and the power in the uniqueness of why he chose his queen and the people in his life. We get so wrapped up in our day-to-day experience that we don't even think for a second about what it would mean to the people around us to actually hear us care. How about your children? If they don't have cell phones, sticky notes on bedroom doors do wonders. They have backpacks when they go to school which are great for putting 3x5 note cards with messages on them.

21. I deliberately took on the strategy that I am going to make deposits with no expectation of return response. Whoever I wanted to work on a relationship with for that week or month, I focused on that person. For a long time, it was just my wife. Then it was my mom. Then there were times I would lessen the deposits with my wife because things became fantastic so I started working on other relationships that needed work, like with a brother or sister. Every single day I strategically messaged whatever individual needed the deposit and every time I sent that message in the morning of honor, appreciation and love, I gave myself half a point.

## Simple Success Swinging Single Deposits

22. Now, let's look at this from a technical way. When we make daily deposits it's the same concept as Simple Success Swinging Singles. Every day I get up and I send a text. I usually won't really notice a difference the first day, but I still do it the next day and the next. By the time I hit a few weeks of these Swinging Single Daily Deposits, I see a difference. Trust me, they're reading them and will recognize your sincerity.

23. "Well, Gar, should I do it face to face?"

"No, because then you expect that person to have a conversation with you."

24."Well, Gar, should I text them and have them text me back?"

"No, that's not the point. The point in putting it as an on-demand format is that it allows the person that you are sending the message to to go back and reread, re-watch, or re-listen to it."

25. Yes, you heard me say "watch and listen." What initially started out as texts, expanded to voice notes and speaking little messages. This created a whole new dynamic. I would wake up in the morning and have fun with this. I didn't just stick to one relationship even though there was one I was specifically scoring. There were some mornings I would send a voice note to 12 different people. Takes less than 60 seconds to write or speak a note, and then I would text that voice note to them.

26. They would go something like this: "Hey man, I was just thinking about you this morning and I wanted to tell you how much I honor you for who you are as a human being in my life and I appreciate that time when we went through [this, this and this] together. I want you to know that I love you and that I'm here for you. I know that we don't talk a lot and we don't communicate a lot, but you were on my heart this morning. I just want to let you know I care about you. Thank you for being who you are. I hope you have a fantastic day."

27. Sometimes I like to put some smart ass comments at the end. Right?! I am a smart ass kind of guy so sometimes I throw some smart ass stuff at the end or do some funny inside joke. Depending on the person or the relationship, sometimes they are very serious. And sometimes they are

individuals who I want to build a relationship with inside of my strategic network and business.

## Be a Bucket Filler, Not a Dipper

28. As I was consistently making these deposits, I started to see these two things happening every single day when I hit my Core 4: my network and the people around me began to anticipate these messages from me. It was filling them up.

29. My daughters have this book called *The Bucket Fillers*.[58] I was first introduced to it when my little Ruby was four years old, in which there's this whole story about how there are bucket dippers and bucket fillers. Our life either gets filled up as we contribute to filling others' buckets, **or** it empties as someone dips from our bucket with hurtful words or actions. This simple children's book has life lessons applicable to all ages.

30. It's so simple and also 100% in your control: Message every day. We have Warrior after Warrior inside this Movement who, just like me, turned their entire marriages around with the daily Honor, Appreciation and Love texts that happen every single day.

## Weekly Strategies for Greatness

31. There are other strategies outside of this for weekly actions and activities from surprise date nights with your kids to dropping flowers off to your queen. For Core 4, choose one simple action every single day, which is a deliberate message that is sent to one person who you have selected from either your partner, your posterity in your children or your parents. If you feel like you are on point with those, still send them, then as a bonus send more, even though you are just going to track one.

32. My encouragement is to stick with one person for a week and then maybe switch. Send a message to them every day. Don't switch the person every single day; stick with one person every single day for a week at least. Something profound will happen inside of you just as much as the deposits will change in them, like my daughter's story of the bucket dippers and takers.

---

[58] McCloud, Carol, Katherine Martin, and David Messing. *Fill a Bucket: A Guide to Daily Happiness for Young Children.* Northville, MI: Ferne, 2009. Print.

33. When you begin to take from your own life and give to others, you become more full. That fullness and wholeness affects your confidence, clarity, courage and your capacity to create. What I noticed most profoundly inside my marriage and my relationship with my children is that my guilt went away.

## Replacing Guilt and Shame with Fullness and Wholeness

34. One of the biggest reasons why I struggled at work, on road trips and in business was because I was constantly feeling shame and guilt about how much time I was gone or how I wasn't spending equal time in both areas. I came to realize my kids and my wife weren't looking for equal time; they were just looking for significant deposits.

35. It's the simpleness of the notes on my kids' doors with sticky notes or writing on their mirrors and text messages to my wife or my mom and siblings every single day that changed everything.

36. So, did you invest today? When you send the text, video, audio or message to your specific individual regardless of their response, you are going to get half a point for Balance.

## Chapter 22:
## POINTS TO PONDER FROM THE GENERAL'S TENT

- **POINT #1:** Every single day we are going to get half a point for taking an action with our partner or with the selected other person who would fit into that family and posterity quadrant. Sending text messages or sticky notes on doors also work great.

- **POINT #2:** In order to have a great marriage, it not only takes time and commitment, it requires shifting from the mindset that a "good" marriage is good enough. We demand greatness in Warrior, so you need to make daily deposits into your wife's love bank by sending notes or texts about how you love, honor and/or appreciate her.

- **POINT #3:** When you begin to take from your own life and give to others, you become more full. That fullness and wholeness affects your confidence, clarity, courage and your capacity to actually create as it comes full circle.

- **POINT #4:** Did you invest today? The investment is not in your bank account directly though; the investment is in the relationships that matter to you.

# WARRIOR WITNESS:

### D.T., Nevada, USA:

*"I've spoken to you guys about how connected I am to my wife, but here I am at this thing and yet I'm still in this state of mind that I wish I was single: when I get home the kids are crazy and my hot wife I feel like is looking hot for everyone else BUT me and gets right into the sweats at home.*

*The Balance is gone and then all of these things that I've had great momentum gets tossed out because she's done by the end of the day so I just say, "Fuck it. I'm not doing any of the Core 4."*

*On the surface it looks so fucking good; March was the month that I've collectively made more money than I've ever made my entire life, yet here I am sitting tired and empty because I'm not connected. I'm just venting and know that I need to just hit the ½ point and suck it up. I'm going back through the rest of the Core 4, but I've been slacking. One of my things is this fucking perfection thing; if I miss ONE ½ point, I burn the rest to the ground and can't do the rest. I have to take the base hits."*

# THE CORE
## Chapter 23: BALANCE (POWER)

According to Mahatma Gandhi, if you think something needs to change, "Be the change you wish to see in the world." This chapter is all about how you deal with yourself.

SECTION FOUR
# THE CORE

## CHAPTER TWENTY-THREE
# BALANCE (POWER)

"Nearly all men can stand adversity, but if you want to test a man's character, give him power."

### -Abraham Lincoln

---

## Value In Me

1. I remember the very first time I had a conversation about discovering the "value in me." It was back in about 2002 or so. I was sitting in an Abundance workshop listening to the training of financial advisor [59]Les McGuire, and he was bringing up these topics of how I needed to invest in me. That *I* was an asset if I valued myself enough to invest in myself.

2. "Invest in you." I thought this sounded like a really good idea; but how do I do it?

   1.  Study. I have got to study things that challenge the way I think.
   2.  Start changing what I believe is true.

3. Now, the crazy thing about our worldview is that it operates like a projector inside of a movie theater, projecting the image onto the screen. No matter what we do in life, if we get pissed off about what's on the projection, only YOU as an individual can decide if the screen needs to change.

---

[59] http://www.lesmcguire.com See also Appendix Bibliography

## Changing the Projection Screen Image

4. The construction crews could come in, knock the walls down, replace the screen, but the image on the screen will still project the same story. Let's say you get divorced and find a new wife or cheat on the wife you currently have thinking the answer is in a different woman. You know that change needs to occur, so you attempt it with another woman (change the screen) to change the way you want to see the world, then get pissed when the story remains the same.

5. But that's not quite what Gandhi had in mind when he said, [60]"Be the change you wish to see in the world." Which means: if we want to change what is on the projection, we cannot change the *thing* that's being projected upon; we must change the *projection* itself. If I'm watching a lame ass movie, the only way to stop watching it is to change the movie.

6. During my façade years, I was in survival mode. I had no idea how to deal with the darkness inside of me, so instead, I suppressed and then covered it up with a suit, only to get angry at the screen for what I was projecting. As I mentioned earlier in the book, I then got angry at my wife, children, friends, and clients. I got angry at people outside of me thinking that the problem was the screen.

## The Projection Game

7. I played this projection game all over in life, projecting my own bullshit onto other human beings, yet at the same time I had this other gift: my ability and capacity to see possibility in other people's lives that they couldn't see for themselves. This is why I have always been a great coach, whether it's in athletics, as a business owner, leader, or motivator. It's a natural gift to see more in others, but at the same time, I was also a really good destroyer.

8. Never once through that entire system had I ever questioned my own projection. I had lived almost 35 years believing that the problem was the screen and those that were on it.

9. I never considered taking care of me. There it was, this idea inserted years ago by Les McGuire about how I need to invest in myself and see my

---

[60] Appendix Quotes: Mahatma Gandhi

own value. I learned that I cannot see the value in me until I deal with the issues of the stories I created around me.

## Learning to Be the Master of Your Domain

10. You have to be a master of your own domain and shift your mind in order to change the image on the screen. You must be able to change the way you *see* in order to follow Gandhi's teachings to be the change you wish to see in the world; if I don't like the projection, the key to changing the image dwells within me. I am able to change my reality once I give myself permission. I do not need to wait for someone else to change me, or give me permission. I don't need to wait for anyone else to tell me something that would cause me to change; the change I'm searching for is a change that I can manifest and create inside my own life. Only *I* have the power to do this.

11. I was telling a fucking story that was putting me in my own prison cell. Jesus sat there in the Bible and Christian scriptures saying, [61]"the keys to the kingdom of Heaven are found within. If you seek me you shall find me, if you ask you shall receive, if you knock it shall be opened unto you." Period.

## Waging An Internal War

12. It wasn't until I began studying [62]Buddhism and [63]Hinduism that I really started to understand this projection conversation. That the war that I was really waging was not a war of me against anybody else; it was a war *inside* of me. This really started to drive home as I began to study the Bhagavad Gita, the book of scripture that Gandhi's statement began to inspire inside of me as I followed this pursuit to study the books that had inspired him to lead a revolution.

13. I was like, I never led a revolution. I could barely lead myself and I'm doing a pretty poor job of leading my family, yet this skinny little guy[64]

---

[61] Two separate scriptures are quoted here. The first about the kingdom of heaven found within is located in Matthew 16:19 in the New Testament. The full scripture verse located in Appendix Quotes. The other scripture can also be found in the WarriorBook Appendix, which is taken from Luke 11:9.

[62] See Appendix Resources: Revelation/Religious Script, Eastern Religious Text

[63] ibid, The Bhagavad Gita is religious text in Hinduism

[64] Mahatma Gandhi, see Appendix Resources: Revelation/Religious Script, Eastern Religious Text, Bhagavad Gita, Mahatma Gandhi

changed an entire country and way of being for people, so I'm going to study what he did and how he pulled that off.

## Arjuna's Journey from The Bhagavad Gita

14. I started studying the Bhagavad Gita, and found within this book of scripture a story about a warrior named [65]Arjuna. When he was born his father died, making him the rightful heir to the kingdom in India. He was just a baby and too young to rule, so his uncle decided to take over the kingdom while saying, "Listen, I'm going to hold the crown and maintain the kingdom for you until you're of the proper age to take over."

15. Young Arjuna rose up through the ranks as a soldier, becoming bigger, growing line upon line, precept upon precept, getting stronger, and wiser in his years. When the time came for him to reclaim the crown, his uncle said, "Yeah…about that…so, I'm going to remain king. Fuck off."

16. Arjuna had become this total badass warrior; the greatest India had ever known. He was famous for what he could do with his sword and his bow and arrow. Thinking he had no other choice, he knew what he needed to do to usurp his uncle from the throne and claim his kingdom back, which required combat.

17. The god Krishna descended down in disguise as Arjuna's [66]charioteer to watch the battle on the plains of [67]Kurukshetra because this final battle was going to become the greatest battle in India's history, and Krishna wanted to be right in the middle of the action.

18. Arjuna went down to the plain, ready to battle. He got off his chariot with his sword, looked out across the battlefield, and saw the military forces opposite of his army consisting of his uncle, brothers, and cousins, all against

---

[65] Appendix Resources: Revelation/Religious Texts, in which there is the URL for an online article about the significance of Arjuna's journey as a warrior.

[66] The companion guiding the chariot and horses; in this case Arjuna's wing man, which has a symbolic use behind this military position.

[67] In the WarriorBook 1st Edition, it was mistakenly stated that the battle took place inMahabharata, but that is the name of the epic text the battle Arjuna fought took place in. The battle, according to the ancient text, took place in Kurukshetra, an actual place located in what is now the state Haryana of India

him. For the first time in his world, he began to shrink emotionally. He sat down on the chariot and looked up at his charioteer.[68]

19. "I can't do this. These are my brothers. We're going to kill them; all of them. We are more powerful. The military is on my side. We are going to lead this war and we are going to slaughter my family in order to take this back. I can't emotionally deal with this very well. This is too hard for me."

20. Krishna then revealed himself to Arjuna. The rest of the Bhagavad Gita becomes a story of Krishna guiding Arjuna, looking at the darkness and the light inside of him. Arjuna deals with conflicting emotions and oppositions like life and death as well as power and pain. It is this internal struggle that becomes the ultimate war he had to face.[69] Krishna speaks into the mind of Arjuna and Arjuna goes deeper into his thoughts.

21. As I was reading and studying Arjuna's journey, I began searching for internal solutions inside my own life. I was struggling in my marriage and connection with other people. Why? Because I could not be true to *me;* I was lying to myself. I misidentified that the real war that I was fighting against was not due to external causes, but was actually being fought from within. I wanted to change the *screen* when it was actually the *image* projected *onto* the screen that I needed to change.

## What Would Arjuna Do?

22. When I had this epiphany, I realized that I had to hire a coach; someone who could guide me down this path of discovery within myself. One day, I was introduced to a woman by the name of[70]Byron Katie and the masterfully trained conversation inside of her book *Loving What Is* with what she called, "The Work."[71] The first time I sat down with her, my initial experience with this was insane.

---

[68] The god Krishna, a spiritual divine leader. The whole reason Krishna came down was to teach Arjuna that the real battle faced is not the outside battles but rather the battles that occur within.

[69] It's the concept as found in Matthew 8:22 about leading the dead because he already is, when in actuality the war is within ourselves. Charles Eisenstein wrote an article about the war we have within ourselves, with a direct online link located in the WarriorBook Appendix Resources: Revelation/Religious Text.

[70] Appendix Bibliography: Katie, Byron.

[71] Principles and worksheets can be found online @http://thework.com/en

23. She looked at me and we started our session. For the first time, I wasn't meeting with somebody who was trying to tell me that I should or shouldn't do something. She was just having me talk about things, listening and observing.

24. Little did I realize that what she was doing was training me on the practical system for changing the way my mind operated with the judgments and assessments of the world that I was persecuting and giving advice to. I was judging, and wasn't even conscious about it, at least not in the beginning. My entire life was being mirrored back to me, yet I couldn't see it. I couldn't see the forest for the trees.

25. I sat there in my session with her and she asked me a seemingly very simple question after I made one of my statements about my wife.

"Is that true?"

26. "Well, of course it's true. My wife absolutely, should be more spiritual. Have you seen how unspiritual she is? She doesn't pray. She doesn't wanna go to church. She doesn't wanna read scriptures. She doesn't wanna have family experiences together. She's not spiritual. Yeah, you bet your ass that's true."

27. Then she had me quiet down for a second and stated, "I'm going to ask you a second question. Can you know, with 100% certainty, no doubt, that the thought that Danielle should be more spiritual, that that thought is true? Yes or no?"

28. I was about to say yes, until this crazy thing happened: the Voice said, "No." In that moment, my reality was shattered. My worldview was crumbling, and I was finally heading down a path that would lead to my internal freedom. We have since developed this formula into The Drift and Lift model within Warrior.

## Is That True?

29. I imagined it felt a lot like Arjuna, as he sat there looking out on the battle that he was about to wage against his uncle and his brothers and his siblings, when Arjuna said, "They are dead already." The wars that we deal with are wars within ourselves and Arjuna became shattered in his worldview. It also happened to me: In one simple question, "Is that true?" my entire world shifted.

30. "Who do you show up as and how do you behave and act when you believe the thought that Danielle should be more spiritual? How do you treat yourself and how do you treat her?"

31. My truth started pouring out and I was weeping over how I abused her emotionally and verbally, yelling and getting angry at her. I loathed, shamed and guilted myself as I beat myself up for beating her up mentally, yelling at the kids when they would show these same behaviors.

32. Then Katie told me to take a deep breath and asked a fourth question: "Who would you be if that thought didn't exist? Between you and Danielle stands this thought that she should be more spiritual. What would happen if it didn't exist? What might be possible for you? How might you show up in that relationship and how might things change between you if you didn't believe that thought?"

33. Again, the Voice came into my mind and started to show me. Weeping, I shared these concepts with this woman. "Well, we'd be free to be this and this," and for the first time, I went off on all of the possibilities that I had never allowed myself to see before.

## Stories from a Judgment-Making Machine

34. Every single day, you and I tell Stories. These stories are not true and they're not inherently false, but they're still stories that we're telling. The great dilemma is that we believe them to be 100% accurate and true, so we've then acted upon those beliefs.

35. Every single day, all day long, I was a judgment-making machine. I thought I could get rid of this. I thought that being a judgmental asshole and prick was a bad thing. I would constantly beat myself up because I thought I needed to be nonjudgmental according to my spiritual pursuits in Buddhism and Hinduism. I was walking around kind of like this apathetic pussy for awhile, saying, "It's all perfect. It's all okay." When the truth was, I wasn't creating much at all. I was missing the point.

36. God was sending me Revelation every single day in the form of my judgments and my criticisms and my counsel to other people: my wife, children, family, clients, random people on social media or at the gas station...I was constantly being fed with content. And I was fed up with

it. Mirrors all around me were displaying, "Here's what your projection is. Here's what you're seeing. You can't see you, but you can see you in him."

## Get The Beam Out of Your Own Eye

37. Jesus was like, "You take no concern for the beam in your own eye, yet focus all your energy on the mote in your neighbor's."[72] Only then do we realize that the beam we see in our neighbor's eye is nothing more than a reflection of the beam that is within ourselves, reflecting their weakness back to us. The issue is not in them; the issue is in you. If you want to be the change you wish to see in the world, you're going to have to recognize that the reflections you're seeing are not in the *people* you originally thought you were seeing them in; the reflections you're seeing are in you. *You* are responsible for your results.

## Shifting the Drift Every Single Day

38. This simple tool by Byron Katie started to set me free. Every day, I would wake up and I would find something in my life that I was judging; counsel I was giving. I would take what I call the Power Focus Document, go down and judge someone, then take that judgment into my own mind.

39. I realized that in order to stop the Drift in my life and reclaim the power that had always been there, every single day I would need to take the content that God, the Universe, and LIFE was delivering up to me. I needed to start learning from it by turning it around.

40. Every day, my mind shifted a little more. I went from feeling like a victim to being a victor and started feeling more power and control with my life because I could finally see the truth, which was that all of the trauma and drama within my life was my fault.

---

[72] Matthew 7:3, See Appendix Quotes. A mote is a small splinter of wood used in comparison to a large beam of solid wood as an analogy of the hypocrisy behind judging another person for something that is extremely small while living a life with unresolved issues far greater in magnitude for one's personal growth, such as condoning a person for drinking a caffeinated drink when you are an alcoholic.

# Becoming the Dictator of Truth

41. Why do we follow the Drift and Shift model known as Power Focus every single day for ½ point each? When we make this document a daily action, we choose to change our minds in one click. We begin to build a new addiction into our life that says, "I am the dictator of truth in my life and I am learning from life. So thank you Universe for delivering up these opportunities so that I can learn."

42. In summary here with Balance, the second ½ a point is completing a Power Focus Document every single day. Every single day, half a point. When I send that text, half a point. When I complete the Power Focus Document, half a point. Combined this makes one full point for the day in Balance.

## Chapter 23:
## POINTS TO PONDER FROM THE GENERAL'S TENT

- **POINT #1:** Learn to invest in you. When you see that you are just as much of an asset as anyone else or a business project, you will see rapid growth because you're not functioning from a position of scarcity.

- **POINT #2:** We cannot see the value in ourselves until we deal with the issues of the stories we created around us, so if you want to see the world differently, be the change that you want to see. You have to be a master of your own domain and shift your mind.

- **POINT #3:** Just like Arjuna from the Bhagavad Gita, it's not a matter of dealing with external battles but the war within ourselves that will lead to us asking the liberating question, "Is it true?" about the stories that we tend to tell. There is a darkness and a light inside of him: conflicting emotions and oppositions like death and life, power and pain. Ultimately, it is this internal struggle that becomes the ultimate war he had to face.

- **POINT #4:** Working on the Power Focus document helps us shift the stories that we have been internally telling to take control over them, rather than have them control us.

# WARRIOR WITNESS:

### D.T., Nevada, USA:

*"I'm fascinated with this inner unconquerable power concept. Like eat this shit for breakfast feeling. Like you guys, I'm so fucking tired of the reactionary life I'm living.*

*I'm focused, I'm here, I'm pushing. Trying not to let my need for perfection push me into a Drfit and even more so trying not to swing for home runs. Especially on weight and body. I'm not losing 40 lbs in a week. I will tell you this; I've worked out more in the last 4 weeks than I have in the last year. My mind is open and soaking up the content like a sponge. I'm creating time to listen to the content, while I drive, when the girls are asleep, hell, even when I take a shit. I just have to work on the follow through and focus. So much shit is going on. All of my chips are on the table and tomorrow is a new day. Thanks for the pump up Garrett J White."*

---

### B.L., Ohio, USA:

*"It's amazing how coaches seem to know the cycles that their teams go through and see them when they start to creep up even before the players do. I started to see that the Voxer thread was getting a little quiet. I had a hell of a lot happen in the last couple of days. It was a very frustrating day at work, my body is tired and fatigued, but it's almost as if I heard the Warrior message last night, and then heard, "Get the hell out of bed and do the work"*

*I got up and made it an effort to make this a great day."*

---

### B.W., Michigan, USA:

*"I have tried to change the screen my whole life never thinking the projector might be the problem. When you start to think about perceived shortcomings of others in your own light, you get a bit uncomfortable. Very thought provoking and worldview altering."*

---

### I.H., Medina, Washington, USA:

*"This is perhaps the most meaningful lesson for me because it brought so many things together. The most important of which is the daily internal battle but I fight against long-standing wiring from my childhood. The story I have to stop telling myself is that my words and my actions and my being is predicated on*

313

*the opinion and approval of others. In the process of living my life this way I have really lost touch with Who I really am and what I really want."*

## D.W., Idaho, USA:

*"Be the change instead of trying to change the screen. How I am showing up is being reflected to me in what I am seeing in other people and interactions. It's not the others that are creating my judgements/frustrations, rather it's me that is creating the projection. It's such a selfish and arrogant mindset to believe that it's everything outside of me that needs to change to accommodate me and my needs. This section really demonstrates as to why I am where I am at this point in my life. I have not treated myself the way I have wanted to be treated by others, which has led me to treat others how I treat myself. I am worth it to be that change."*

# THE CORE
## Chapter 24: BUSINESS (DISCOVER)

New information changes our perspective, what we see, and affects our worldview. This is why we have to be careful about what kind of information we're putting into our minds. If we study strategically, and take action on what is being studied, we will change the reality of our lives and Business would continue to expand.

SECTION FOUR
# THE CORE

## CHAPTER TWENTY-FOUR
# BUSINESS (DISCOVER)

"The size of your success is measured by the strength of your desire; the size of your dream; and how you handle disappointment along the way."

### - Robert Kiyosaki

---

1. The very first educational investment I ever made in Business happened in a room as I was sitting with a mentor of mine listening to Robert Kiyosaki, the author of *Rich Dad, Poor Dad*. Now, I had ended up at this event because a few years before, my friend had given me the book as a PE teacher and a football coach. I stood on the sideline during our practice warm-up with our team on a Thursday evening, getting prepared for homecoming the next day. Football had been my life; what I played from the time I was a kid, through college, professionally, and then as a coach. It was everything I could eat, breathe, and sleep.

### New Information Changes What We See

2. New information changes our perspective, what we see, and affects our worldview. What does this have to do with playing football and attending a *Rich Dad* seminar? We have to be careful about what kind of information we're putting into our minds. We have to decide if the information that we're hearing is actually taking us in the direction we want to go. As I read *Rich Dad, Poor Dad*, it changed my world.

3. "What the hell? This rich dad thing is awesome! I've had a poor dad. I've never had expectations for being an entrepreneur. I've never had

expectations for having my own business, or for being an investor or for buying real-estate, or making any kind of money that would be significant."

4. I was raised without a lot of money, and remained in that mindset until I got new information. Robert Kiyosaki's book opened up my mind, and took me on a journey that had me leave the PE and coaching world that I was in and move into the mortgage banking and brokering world. That book was the transition.

5. It helped me attend my first mastermind event that cost $10,000 just to attend, which was an astronomically mind-blowing number to me then. Yet, the results from that event helped me become strategic partners with *Rich Dad*, the company's education platform. We ran the largest Cash-Flow game in the entire country at that time, with 300-500 people every single month playing this board game, *Cash-Flow 101*, which was about investing in the way you think. My mortgage broker firms and insurance companies exploded, and my business world began to blow up in ways I had never anticipated.

6. I started to realize and recognize that the information I put in my mind was the gateway to new possibilities; that if I could study strategically, and take action on what I study, I would change the reality of my life and Business would continue to expand.

7. My car became a mobile university as I drove and consumed content. Long before it was easy to jump on webinars and YouTube and social media, where every person in the world on Instagram and Pinterest gave you positive quotes and witty memes, all of this current shit that is going on did not exist for me. I had to go to the store and buy it. Amazon wasn't there to make it happen. You couldn't do this shit that we see as so commonplace now with a quick search on Google the same way. There was nothing that we have now!

8. I went to the bookstore every week, bought content, and every week, my life changed. I became addicted to this idea of consuming information, long before information was readily available to the marketplace. The very first home study course I created cost me $25,000 just to get four CDs recorded. Nowadays I can record my Daily Fuel podcasts on my cell phone, and it has a very minimal price tag to get this content out to the marketplace.

## How to Strategically Study

9. I share this with you because I was committed to this process long before it was easy. With technology as it is today, you have no fucking excuse. None! There's more FREE and amazing content online, all over the place, that can guide you and teach you, yet most people don't have any idea how to strategically study. Part of the game inside of Discover is to discover new insights inside of who you are as a man, and who you are as a businessman: Who you are inside the conversation of hunting the buffalo and making money.

10. Your perspective drives your production, and your production drives your profitability. If I want to change my production, I need to shift what I'm seeing.

11. I'm helping you see the world differently. The moment you can open your mind up to see the world differently, the game begins to change.

## Having Certainty and Confidence

12. I started to look at what the trifecta experience was of business roles:

    1. Marketer
    2. Closer
    3. Leader, Not a Savior

13. I asked myself the question: "In business, who is the most powerful guy in the room?" In 2009 I attended an event in Los Angeles called SANG, a big author networking group. I'm sitting there, watching these guys walk through the room and they're just different. There was not an arrogance but a confidence that seemed to exude from all of them. Some of them were in suits, some were just in jeans and T-shirts, some were in polos and khakis. There was no necessary color scheme or dress apparel or how they behaved, but there was an energy of who they were as the common factor, and that energy was, "I have certainty and confidence in myself."

14. At the time, I was really wavering in myself as all my businesses had imploded. Although I had made the investment to go to Robert Kiyosaki's event, my life already changing as I was buying all this information, I was also stuck and struggling, trying to pull myself out of despair from the implosion of my businesses in 2008. So, I sat in this event and observed.

15. I watched each of these guys get up to speak and share with the group. They had a common conversation, and they knew how to get leads. On any subject, on any topic, at any time, they knew how to make it rain. With the internet, and with the understanding of copywriting and direct response marketing, these individuals could make it rain.

## Making It Rain As A Marketer

16. The life-blood of your business is Leads: if you run out of Leads, your business dies. I don't care what business, industry, product, program you're in or service you sell, if you run out of leads, you fucking die. That is it. You can't hit payroll, you don't have clients, game over.

17. In 2009, towards the end of that year, I created a saying that became a belief. People would ask me, "Who are you and what do you do?" I would say, "I'm a marketer." They'd say, "What?"

"I'm a marketer and I make it rain."

18. The man who controls the rain controls the game. In less than six years, I began to master the conversation of rain-making, which is the understanding of fundamental persuasion and influence.

19. Here in this Brotherhood of Warrior, we say, "I am a marketer." When I look at you and I say, "You are my Brother." I also say, "You are a marketer. Now make it rain."

20. It sounds so simple. But when you get it, the game changes.

## Closing the Deal

21. That is the first part of the trifecta. The second part of the trifecta inside the business conversation of the core forum is: I am a Closer.

22. I had to start operating in the world with a higher level of integrity, with both the way that I dealt with myself and the Game called Business. I had to be comfortable in the conversation of persuasion and closing. I would look in the mirror and say repeatedly: "I'm a Closer. I live in 'yes' and 'no' There is no 'maybe' for me."

23. I recognized that one of the greatest areas of weakness inside of my life as a businessman was that I allowed too much of my business life to function in a world of "maybes."

24. "Maybes" are the death and the destruction of your business. You can be a marketer all day long and bring the leads and bring the rain and control the game, but you will still go bankrupt and die if you do not have a certainty, a clarity, and a confidence to close.

25. I am a Closer. "Yes" or "no." That's it. There is no "maybe." If you come to my house, my children literally do not understand the word "maybe." They don't hear it ever. You can ask my four-year-old, my nine-year-old, or my sixteen-year-old. I'll listen to my four-year-old talking to my eight-year-old, and she says, "Are you going to come outside with me, 'yes' or 'no'?" My four-year-old will come to me and say, "Dad, can I have three popsicles, 'yes' or 'no'?" Everything in my house is "yes or no," because "yes or no" is a function of decisions.

26. You wouldn't have gotten into this conversation, into this audio, if we had not confronted you with the direct "yes or no?" Are you in? There's more training and more study inside this in the Armory, around strategic seduction and helping you understand strategic selling, and how this conversation plays out even deeper inside of business and inside of life.

## I'm A Leader, Not A Savior

27. The third piece in the trifecta is: I'm a Leader, not a Savior. What does this mean? No matter what I do in business, I cannot save anybody. I can't save you. If you're Christian, my name's not Jesus Christ. I'm not offering you salvation. I'm offering you liberation, but that liberation comes through your willingness to leverage this content and this Brotherhood; to do the work. I can lead you through my own examples, I can lead you through motivation, I can lead you through inspiration, but at the end of the day, guess who's going to have to make the decision to do the work? You.

28. My leadership within business didn't look like this in the beginning; I totally saw myself as a savior called forth to redeem those in the business world. The flip side of that salvation mentality I initially had and conversation of doing the work for others, always ends with the same result. The praise turned into persecution and the exaltation turned into

crucifixion. The same people I was trying to save and serve would crucify me. I couldn't figure it out. It happened over and over again, until I realized that leadership itself is sometimes letting people fucking die.

29. Inside this Brotherhood, we won't save you. Ever. We have a mantra here, "If a Brother wants to die, he's going to die." We're not going to save you. You don't need saving. I might punch you in the face a few times though to get you to wake up so you can choose liberation because I see that the Keys inside of you exist. The incarceration that you experience is one that you created in your own way; the only way out is to choose liberation and access to those Keys is doing the work.

## Holding Business Hostage

30. Your business is held hostage because you don't see yourself as a Marketer, Closer or Leader. You are not a real estate agent; you are a *marketer* of real estate services. You are a *closer* of real estate contracts. You are a *leader* in your industry of being a marketing and closing expert in the real estate space. "I'm a realtor" leaves you stuck at the bottom of the totem pole. "I'm a Marketer" puts us at the top. "I'm a Closer" puts us at the top, and abundance comes from a business that comes from a man that has passionately studied and mastered the skill sets of marketing, selling, and leading.

31. With these skill sets, you can tell the world to fuck off if you want to, and you could do whatever you want because you understand how to use the tools correctly. This business trifecta is a crucial power play, inside this Game called Having It All, as we live the Warrior's Way.

 Do you know how to take a message to the marketplace?

-Inside that message, do you have the balls to hold people to a "yes" or "no" commitment?

-Inside that commitment, are you willing to lead, and even when it's not popular, willing to let people die on their swords who expect you to save them? If you build a business of employees and clients who are all looking to you as a savior, it will always end in your own destruction.

32. Your job every day is to study revelation inside the topics of marketing, sales, and leadership. That's it. In that study, you're going to write that shit

down. You're going to discover new perspectives inside of being a Marketer, Closer and Leader in today's modern game of Business.

## Discovering New Perspectives

33. The interesting part is that this business discovery will influence every other area of your life, not just your bank accounts and your business. These same skill sets which are necessary in influencing a prospect to buy are the same skill sets needed to influence a child to increase their grades at school, or your wife to take you back when you've been a fool.

34. We harp on this here, in this Brotherhood, when we tell you that every single day you're going to get half a point for discovering a new insight or breakthrough in the conversation of marketing, sales, and leadership. We take it very seriously.

## "I Am A Marketer. I Am A Closer. I Am A Leader, Not A Savior."

35. Let that statement tattoo itself onto your very DNA. We don't read just to read, we don't listen just to listen, and we don't watch just to watch. We watch, we read, and we listen to get insights, and with those insights we write those revelations down, just like we do inside of Being with Our Drift and Lift model: we write down new insights and things we can do, actions we can take, and ways of seeing inside these rounds of marketing, of selling, and of leading.

## Chapter 24:
## POINTS TO PONDER FROM THE GENERAL'S TENT

- **POINT #1:** New information changes our perspective, what we see, and affects our worldview. This is why we have to be careful about what kind of information we're putting into our minds. If we study strategically, and take action on what is being studied, we will change the reality of our lives and Business will continue to expand.

- **POINT #2:** Your perspective drives your production, and your production drives your profitability. If you want to change your production, you need to shift what you're seeing.

- **POINT #3:** The life-blood of your Business is Leads. If you run out of Leads, your business dies. Marketers understand fundamental persuasion and influence, exemplifying the process that the man who controls the rain controls the game.

- **POINT #4:** Everything is a "yes" or "no" with a Closer. Combine that with being a Leader, not a Savior, and as a Marketer, and you get a trifecta of for Business success every time.

# WARRIOR WITNESS:

## J.N., Texas, USA:

*"I am a victor, not a victim. Time to take this fucking hill. Thanks, Garrett J White."*

---

## J.W., South Carolina, USA:

*"Thanks for the constant kick in the ass. It's something that is keeping me focused in an area that I would be fading away. Having this environment with coaches that allow us to be honest and pushing us in the right direction, it helps us realize the direction we need to go to. It's not very often that you find people that aren't trying to appease you, especially when you pay them a large sum of money.*

*I fell into a mind drift yesterday after going in with what I thought was a good plan and made a couple of tough phone calls, but I felt a little too pleased with myself and apathetic going into the evening. I'm definitely glad to take some new ground in my consistency in pushing forward and taking new ground.*

*I think that the thing that stood out for me was being a leader, not a savior. I was raised around a lot of small businesses, and through that there was a very consistent message in looking for areas to make it more of a ministry, providing "opportunities" for people that needed a hand. But if you're looking to rely on somebody, you can't make somebody something that they're not. It's not their fault not wanting to be what you want them to be.*

*I had this experience with an employee that I had to let go when I should have fired him after a year of nothing working out. I even apologized for letting him go. I'm training to put on myself that if someone needs to be fired, to do it and not apologize for them not being who they're not."*

## T.J., Texas, USA

*"I am a marketer. I make it rain. I am a man that holds the reign and controls the game. I'm a closer that lives for yes and no; there is no maybe. I'm a leader, not a savior. I am a marketer. I am a closer. I am a leader, not a savior."*

---

# INVICTUS

Out of the night that covers me,
Black as the pit from pole to pole,
I thank whatever gods may be
For my unconquerable soul.

In the fell clutch of circumstance
I have not winced nor cried aloud.
Under the bludgeonings of chance
My head is bloody, but unbowed.

Beyond this place of wrath and tears
Looms but the Horror of the shade,
And yet the menace of the years
Finds and shall find me unafraid.

It matters not how strait the gate,
How charged with punishments the
scroll,

## I am the Master of my Fate;
## I am the Captain of my Soul.

-William E. Henley

*Brothers, you are ALL marketers.*
*MAKE IT FUCKING RAIN!*

# THE CORE
## Chapter 25: BUSINESS (DECLARE)

We can have a drive and discovery of knowledge that it takes to start a business, but if we don't declare it, then we won't become as converted to it.When we stand up in front and start to teach, this trend starts to happen; theories start to become beliefs, therefore in the declaration and execution, mastery occurs.

SECTION FOUR
# THE CORE

CHAPTER TWENTY-FIVE
# BUSINESS (DECLARE)

"Next to doing the right thing, the most important thing is to let people know you are
doing the right thing."

### -John D. Rockefeller, Sr
[American oil industry business magnate & philanthropist, considered to be the
wealthiest American of all-time, (1839-1937)]

---

1. There was a phrase I'd hear constantly as a kid in reference to Jesus who
said, "Once you have obtained my word, then you should declare my
word"[73] meaning that once you have liberated yourself then go liberate
your brothers. This was encouraging continual missionary work and a
conversation with other people by going out and broadcasting it. That was
the Mormon side of my upbringing.

2. The Catholic and Jewish side? Not so much, but on the Mormon side
there was definitely a game of "Hey, go share this message." There was
constantly this Game inside of me that when I had an insight, I should go
share it with somebody. There was also this second thing: in the obtaining
of a witness in your life the next game was to declare it to the world. That
somehow your insights and your revelation didn't mean much until you
declared it to somebody else.

---

[73] Doctrine & Covenants 11:21 (LDS scriptures), taken fromhttps://www.lds.org/scriptures/
dc-testament/dc/11.21?lang=eng#20 See also Appendix Quotes

## Declaring Your Drive and Discovery

3. We can have this drive and this discovery of knowledge, but if we don't declare it, then somehow we won't become as converted to it. With this declaration comes potential criticism and persecution, in which we find out very quickly on how much we truly believe in something or not.

4. The Declaration is an individual's conversion mechanism in being able to converse about new doctrine learned. It's taking your Discovery of *this* content and the Declaration of *that* content to other people by teaching it in other forms that ultimately converts your mind into seeing it differently.

## Teach the Theory Then Apply

5. This brings me back to my college degree in Physical Education Pedagogy, otherwise known as PE: the art and science of kick ball, dodge ball and tether ball. The game of being a PE teacher was about understanding my role in two phases: (1) Theory and (2) Apply.

6. First, we would sit in a classroom and study theory: the use of group dynamics, lesson planning, of dealing with young kids as well as the management and movement of energy inside of a gym.

7. My fellow classmates and I would have our books out, studying theory so that we could then teach what was discovered. We would declare it by breaking into groups and standing up in front of the room, in front of our peers, (which is always a lot of pressure), and teaching in our own words the theory behind what the PhD had just taught us in the book.

## Concepts Becoming Concrete Beliefs

8. When I would stand and start to teach, I would always notice this trend; my theories would start to become beliefs in the process of teaching them. I had a concept that then became more concrete as it formed into a belief when I would teach it. There I was, up at the front of the room, and I would find it very exciting to teach, because I knew that in the teaching I was going to become the most clear. Writing shit down was one thing, but it became a belief as I made it my own, presenting it to others.

9. Now you might be saying, "Well now, Garrett, wait. You can't gain mastery of this until you do it." I understand. Let's go back to the

Pedagogy story. The second phase, Apply, consisted of two subparts: Teach and Do. So, every single week, we would have these student teaching experiences. They were a goddamn circus, so of course they were super-fun for me because I tend to thrive in chaos. A lot of the future teachers who were in the program did not thrive. They wanted to be super-orderly and I used to piss everybody off because I would do my lesson plans at the last minute and participate right along with the students. I was always the slacker who was showing up at the end, then I would outperform everybody. Like, *dominate* 60 kindergarten kids.

10. Everybody was on their stars and their circles, and I was getting standing ovations by a whole group of five year olds who thought that I was the greatest shit that had ever happened in their life that day. Until, of course, someone handed out popsicles and then I was quickly forgotten. Damn popsicles.

## Declaring Mastery

11. Nonetheless, in those environments, I could stand up and immediately declare. In the declaration and execution of that, I gained mastery. Week after week, this was our process:

>-Discover
>-Learn Content and Theory
>-Teach
>-Train

12. We would live the theory that we had been teaching, which then brought a more concrete system for our belief. In doing this, I left the land of believing into the land of knowledge.

13. Here at Warrior you might have to teach a concept for six months before you fully grasp it enough so that you can actually implement it inside your Business.

## Creating a Teaching Environment

14. The declaration phase is simply teaching, but this would require an environment to teach in. You also have to have someone to declare to. Back when I was going to college, we would declare to our peers; fellow

future PE teachers. They were all like me, and we were learning, studying and growing together.

15. When we get out into the workforce today, having easy access to like-minded, readily available people who are ready to listen requires that we have to search for them.

16. Modern technology greatly helps with this. We get to share our insights online as much as we choose to. I have two ways of deciding how I want to teach using this format: on-demand or live.

## Persuasive Copy and Direct Response Communication

17. One of the tools that we use are Persuasive Copy, which requires us to get good at communicating messages that compel people to do things, and another tool is Direct Response Communication, which means exactly what it implies.

18. Your communication is going to start to evolve. It's going to go from general sharing and teaching of concepts to declare direct response behavior, which is saying "I communicate in a way that requires people to do something about what I'm saying. I'm going to train my people who consume information from me, which I'm sharing out of my own living scripture which we refer to as the Black Bible on a daily basis. But when I share and declare them, I'm going to do it in a way that has you do something."

19. This is crucial inside of who you are as the Modern Man Communicator. Inside of this we must be able to bridge the gap between simply discovering and declaring content in the *teaching* format, and declaring content in the *results* format.

## Leaders Have the Balls to Give People Commands

20. People look to leaders to be led, and the Brotherhood inside of the Warrior Movement is making Kings of current leaders in society now. If you're going to spend your time teaching content, we might as well start training your mind to start operating and acting like a Leader, not a Savior. Leaders have the balls to give people commands, orders, and instructions. Leaders have people consider different ways of thinking, doing, and

behaving. Inside of marketing, sales and systems—inside of *life*—you're going to have to be able to do this.

21. Clear communication, driven by a direct response when asking questions and sharing information, changes the information from simply a good idea and "Oh, that's nice" to concepts that actually get people to move forward. In Business, this means dollars. In life, this means relationships that matter through family and friendship expansion. Through your example in leadership and values, you're giving your team players opportunities to expand.

22. This isn't a small thing; it's a big thing, yet it's simple. Every single day we're going to Declare what we learned in our Discovery phase. We're going to pick a platform within social media on which to share it consistently.

## Pick Your Social Media Platform

23. I had an epiphany when I started looking at my Facebook page less as a Facebook page, and more as a daily blog. Uploading videos there became another format in which I could share my discoveries and declare them into the marketplace. My podcast in iTunes, "The Daily Fuel," became another platform in which I could share my discoveries with the marketplace through declaration using audio. YouTube and our videos online with Vimeo became another format.

24. It was beautiful, because just like the text messages inside of Balance, I didn't have to wait for anyone else to approve, listen, or come to my house then sit down and have a coffee in order to listen to me talk about it. I could do it without anyone else's initial feedback, simply standing and saying, "Here is the Game and what's going on. Here is what I discovered today, and how this applies to you."

25. Oftentimes, inside this Game of declaring on some of these social media platforms, followers started looking to me as a Voice, a thought leader in the marketplace and in my industry.

## Being Seen as a Thought Leader

26. In order to pull off some of the big ass things you want to do, the people in your life are going to have to see you as a Thought Leader. More than that, you're going to have to gain mastery of the topics that you're studying,

and the only way to do that is to declare it every single day. You might have a blog that you can create, or update one that you already have. You might have an email list you can send content out to, or a group of people that you can text, sending it to one person or to many people. Maybe you'll send out a daily video to your business, or a text message with a thought about what you discovered inside of your study in business and marketing, sales and systems so now you're going to declare and teach it.

27. Look at this through a couple of different lenses: in the Declaration Phase, I'm either sharing with the general marketplace or I'm sharing with my prospects: people who might potentially buy something from me and one of my businesses. I'm sharing with my clients; people who are already buying from me. I'm sharing with my team: individuals who work for me. Or other: anybody else I think is relevant at the time for the content I am sharing.

## Studying and Discovering from The War Map

28. So, every morning as I study; I've got my Black Bible out to journal in. As I'm studying and discovering, I'm writing down my insights and ideas. Then I move to my Declaration Phase, pulling out my cell phone or computer to broadcast and declare what I've learned.

29. Writing down insights and declaring it as a document in Evernote or some kind of online Word doc allows us to easily cut & paste to share with others. The key here is that we must *declare* and *send* it to somebody; it's not enough to just write it down; putting the thoughts into action act as a way of implementing it as a core belief.

30. So we're looking for that dynamic pressure; that tangent inside our reality that's going to allow us to feel the pressure of producing at a high level content that actually matters. Content that people want to do something about, in which they want to come back and consume again. This praise and this pressure from the public is going to force your study to become even more powerful, a better Marketer, Closer and Leader.

## Becoming Content Creating Machines

31. I **know** this works, which is why we love watching men who come into the Black Box Brotherhood for Warrior start off their networks and

social networks, where all of a sudden they become part of the Content Creating Machines. Everyone's like, "Why do you teach everyone to be good at video? At audio? At copying and sharing messages?"

32. I respond back, "Because in a marketplace of people who want to consume content, the men who know how to take a stand and lead by declaring their discoveries to the marketplace become the kings of the land."

33. This isn't a theory for me that *might* possibly work and bring about deeper resolve inside your daily experience. No, this is radical change in how you see yourself. How complex and deep does my training have to be when I share it online? It doesn't. It could, but it doesn't have to be deep to share your declaration. It doesn't have to be long: one sentence, a short video or audio, or notes from a document that you allowed other people to download. It could be somebody in your team that you send a series of messages to. They don't have to be long, they don't have to be short. But every single day you are going to be in a state of declaring what you discovered to the marketplace, to your clients, to your prospects, to your team, to your family, to somebody else, but you're going to share your information, your insights and your revelation with another person.

## Leaving the Land of Believing to REALLY Believing

34. We have to consider then that your conversion is required to leave the land of believing to the land of *really* believing. A concept becomes concrete for you in the process of teaching. Teaching is what stands before your transformation as a Marketer, Closer, and Leader not a Savior. Every day I'm studying marketing, selling and leading these topics to teach to the marketplace so that my declaration converts me to the theories and turns them into realities.

35. Within Key 4, we'll be doing the execution of these topics. But, for now, inside of Core 4, when I get my ½ point for Business under Declare, it simply means that in some format, through text or video or through audio, either on-demand or live, I taught the concepts from my War Map that I uncovered during the Discovery Phase in Business.

## Chapter 25:
## POINTS TO PONDER FROM THE GENERAL'S TENT

- **POINT #1:** We can have a drive and discovery of knowledge that it takes to start a business, but if we don't declare it, then we won't become as converted to it. When we stand up in front and start to teach, this trend starts to happen; theories start to become beliefs, therefore in the declaration and execution, mastery occurs.

- **POINT #2:** Communicating a message to the market place and being a marketer requires you to get really good at Persuasive Copy and Direct Response Communication in order to sell the idea.

- **POINT #3:** It is crucial to become a Modern Man Communicator: you're a Marketer, a Closer, and a Leader not a Savior. Inside of this we must be able to bridge the gaps between simply discovering and declaring content in the teaching format, and declaring content in the results format.

- **POINT #4:** Teaching is what stands before your transformation, which means that your conversion is required to leave the land of believing to the land of really believing. A concept becomes concrete for you in the process of teaching.


# WARRIOR WITNESS:

### C.T, Louisiana, USA:
1. "You've got to simultaneously think at a high level and get your hands dirty, because focusing in between those is not influential or special; it's safe and you'll plateau. (Clearly Warrior gives us a structure to do exactly that with The Game and The Keys).
2. All the best products have broken the way we "used" to live and evolved us as consumers (My personal examples: Uber, Kayak, Amazon, Apple Pay, Warrior).
3. 5 years ago Instagram and Snapchat didn't exist so while creating biz and products strategy it has to account for the change we can't see come so quickly.
4. Become a broader content provider to the market beyond your primary sell (Garrett maximizes this with Daily Fuel)
5. Cash is Oxygen to Biz!
6. Greatest "thing" ever crashes without cash so you have to sell first. (right in line with "I am a Closer")."

## F.Q., Texas, USA:

*"Leaders give orders; this is helping me a lot on closing the deals recently. You have to order your customers to get the results you are looking for. You get the results when you order, not when you ask."*

---

# THE CORE
## Chapter 26: SUMMARY

Inside each one of these Core 4 areas of Body, Being, Balance, and Business we find daily power.

SECTION FOUR
# THE CORE

CHAPTER TWENTY-SIX
# SUMMARY

*"Don't you ever get the feeling that all your life is going by and you're not taking advantage of it? Do you realize you've lived nearly half the time you have to live already?"*

**-Ernest Hemingway**
Excerpt from The Sun Also Rises

---

1. Throughout this section we have discussed the foundational gain that builds upon the Code of Real, Raw, Relevant Results and then we asked, "Well, what are the areas that we're going to produce results in?" Which brings us to the Core 4: Body, Being, Balance and Business.

## "28 or Die"

2. Inside each one of these Core 4 areas we find daily power. Every single day I can score a four before I hit the door, which gives me the possibility of creating 28 total points for my week. 28 points = Power. "28 or die" becomes the mantra inside this Brotherhood. "28 or die."

## BODY: Fitness & Fuel

3. The neatest part about all this is you get to custom-create the game. The frame has been set inside of Body: Fitness and Fuel. We say "Listen. Do a green smoothie, but create the one you want." For Fitness, "Choose something that's going to make you sweat every day" and if you can fuel every day, guess what? Fitness: ½ point + Fuel: ½ point = Body: 1 point. This allows us to take that body and make it a servant to our soul, our purpose, to the bigger, higher gain that we're playing in having it all.

336

## BEING: Meditation & Revelation

4. If we meditate every day and then get revelation, ½ point each inside of Being. Meditation is going to give me the space that I need, where every time I meditate using Warrior Ascension or a style that I find works for me, I'm going to get half a point every single morning.

5. The second piece with this is my Revelations. I'm going to write those revelations down from my discoveries that I get inside of which we're going to use the Drift and Shift Model to make everything relevant.

6. We're going to use the reality of life's doctrine around us to teach, guide, and extract the events and the content for our ability to share the Production Focus, which is laid out with stating here's what happened, why it was positive, the lesson we learned and how it applies to Body, Being, Balance and Business.

## BALANCE: Partner/Posterity & Power

7. There are two areas of conversation here in Balance. We've got the area of conversation with our partner and posterity; children, parents and siblings, and the people that are close to us. We're going to get half a point every single day for communicating a message with the marketplace that matters to these individuals.

8. We're going to text, send video or audio directly to one of these individuals and we're going to pursue them with the relentless intent through the Daily Deposit text of honor, appreciation and love.

9. Then we're going to flip the script as we look inwardly on ourselves by executing on the Power Document in the Shift Phase of our Model as we come to understand what it is to love ourselves deeply and change the projection that we're putting out into the marketplace. This changes what we're seeing inside of who we believe ourselves to be.

10. The Shift's Power Focus inside of Balance says, "You know what? I deserve to change my projection. I deserve to change the way I see myself." When I do this, I see my relationships differently. I give myself ½ point for this, when combined with the ½ point for my loved individuals makes 1 full point.

## BUSINESS: Discover & Declare

11. Inside of Business, we're going to do two things: discover and declare. Every time we discover, we're going to study under the doctrinal trifecta of marketing: I am a Marketer. I am a Closer. I am a Leader, not a Savior.

12. We're going to marry that up to the conversation of Declaration as we share what we're learning. We study every single day in topics of marketing and sales and systems, which we're going to declare and teach to the marketplace. Choosing a public forum and a platform on which we can share this discovery is done using the framework of Production Focus.

13. We teach, guide and lead ourselves to Business Mastery. 1 point for Business = ½ point Discovery + ½ point Declaration. We collapse this entire game down into a formula for Daily Power, Perspective, Purpose and Possibility that didn't exist yesterday. We are then able to See and Create the Games that we truly desire inside our 90-day challenges, 60-day benchmarks, 30-day benchmarks, our weekly targets, and all the games we're building from living the Warrior's Way to having it all.

## Meeting Inside the General's Tent

14. Core 4 sits upon the foundation of the Code as the first actionable, gamified process of saying, "Listen, today I know I won because I got a four. I got half a point for this and half a point for that. For this and for that, totaling all those up together, I got a four and I won. Everything else inside of my life may not be working exactly the way I wanted it to, but I controlled the one thing I could control today, which is I hit a four before I hit the door to prepare me for the game of war."[74]

15. At the end of the week, we rally everything together inside the General's Tent in our mind to be asked, "How did I do this week? How did I do inside my Core 4? How did I do in the conversation of Power across Body, Being, Balance and Business? How did I do this week, living the four-dimensional lifestyle of having all of these things occurring for me every single day? What do my numbers tell me? What do my metrics tell me?" What are the

---

[74] A common phrase within Core 4 to get them all done before a certain time frame, as explained in greater detail in Section 5: Keys. See also WD "Hit the Core Before You Hit The Door...." at the end of this book.

stories the numbers are telling us about how we showed up this past week? Maybe I got a 17 and I'm like, "Shit, I got a 17 instead of a 28. What are the areas that I missed out on?"

16. When we can metrically see where our Core 4 is out of alignment, it explains why we feel so much chaos and internal conflict: we're not hitting the numbers. Or maybe you have the opposite problem. Maybe you're hitting your 28 but you're still not feeling the Power, so we get to go back into the numbers and say "Okay, well, the numbers are saying that I got a 28, but I'm not feeling the Power."

17. Maybe you played too small inside of your commitments that week. Maybe the text messages you were sending inside of Balance weren't powerful or real enough because you weren't living by the Code inside of that. During your discoveries and teachings, you were reading you half-assed declaration, so although you hit your number, you didn't go all in. Admitting "I didn't go all in this week" helps you assess inside the truth of this idea and how you can shift it.

## Entering The Four-Dimensional Plane of Possibility

18. You're going to hear case studies and testimonials and results and examples of men like you who have come before you, who have taken on this Core 4 lifestyle, leaving behind permanently the one and two-dimensional game of living after entering the four-dimensional plane of possibility as a Warrior Man in today's game.

19. It's not going to be easy all the time, Brother, but it's going to be worth it. It's not complex; it's simple. Study this content and doctrine. Learn it and live it as if your life depended on it. Every single day, wake up with one central focus: "What am I in control of today, all the things that I could play, and opportunities I could create?" That's it. Core 4 is the simplest game to accessing powers the modern businessman has ever discovered.

20. Once Core 4 becomes who you are, not just what you see and think about, it is no longer theory but the reality you live in. You will look back at the life you lived before and say, "How the hell did I ever think it was going to work?" Once you step across a threshold of Core 4 living, hitting your 28 or die per week, four before you hit the door is no longer going to become a negotiable conversation. It is life or death. This is why inside

my left forearm on my tattoo sleeve, I have an eyeball and a skull: symbols that "I choose to see and find life or I choose to die." That's all on me.

21. Every single morning my liberation or my incarceration comes down to my decision to hit a four. It never comes down to the fact that I couldn't do it. It always comes down to the fact that I chose not to do it. Some days you're going to have those days and you don't make up for it, you just get up the next morning and say you know what? I'm going to do better today.

22. Today I'm going to hit my four before I hit the door and through the metrics inside of the system for the Brotherhood, you're going to start to see how you can track this, notice trends that happen and come to understand the patterns inside your own life in ways that you have never discovered before. My brothers, welcome to the journey as we conclude this training here inside the Core 4 modules. It will forever change the way that you see yourself, your queen, family, clients, business, your body, God, and your purpose in life, permanently.

## Chapter 26:
## POINTS TO PONDER FROM THE GENERAL'S TENT

- **POINT #1:** Inside each one of these Core 4 areas (Body, Being, Balance and Business) we find daily power. Every single day we can "score four before I hit the door," which gives me the possibility of creating 28 total points for my week. 28 points = Power.

- **POINT #2:** Core 4 sits upon the Foundation of the Code as the first actionable, gamified process which is then gone over inside the General's Tent. Though the process is simple, it's not always easy. The key is to be able to course correct and move forward towards continual expansion.

- **POINT #3:** Once Core 4 becomes who you are, not just what you see and think about, it is no longer theory but the reality you live in.

- **POINT #4:** Every single morning my liberation or my incarceration comes down to my decision to hit a four.

# WARRIOR WITNESS:

## J.B., USA:

*Why am I committed to the Warrior's Way? It's pretty simple.*

*There are three primary reasons:*

1. I believe and am choosing to believe that it serves my purpose and my why. It's a clear fit for accountability, clarity, confidence, and direction that I've been looking for in the last decade all wrapped up in a nice black box. And all I have to do, is to do the fucking work. Frankly, it's just useful. I'm in.

2. The Warrior's Way is an example for my daughters. I am completely present as a father, I need to be an example of what a REAL man looks like from the sedated one and two dimensional douche bag boys that are trying to get their attention and give them attention. I want them to be able to discern the difference and I'm their best option for that. I am their first love; the first love affair that happens with a girl is with her daddy. She begins to see for herself who she is in his eyes, and to me that's fucking important, and the Warrior's Way creates a path and the strength to mirror for her to look back and see her own beauty. That she is worth fighting for. So I choose it. I choose it.

3. I also realize that my girls are going to look to the men in their life whether that man is treating them with love and respect and honor and appreciation based entirely on how I'm treating their mom. If I fuck that up, then they are going to get fucked, because that's what they'll expect.

*The Warrior's Way is that it provides a pathway for me to honor my wife. To make her my Queen and treat her with respect and love and in doing so set the example for my daughters and son to look to to say that's what I should be looking for in a man. That's what I need, so to me, the Warrior's Way makes that very clear. I'm REALLY glad that I overcame my own story and fear to be a part of this with other amazing men.*

*Every single one of us in the Brotherhood have said in our own way that we don't have an example of what it means to be a man, to be a good dad, but Garrett laid out the reasons. Brothers, that's got to stop. And frankly, it speaks to my calling, it speaks to me to be a small part of changing all of that. And the Warrior's Way is the best way to do that.*

*Part of my goal is to end my day without regret. To go to my grave without regret. That's not the case today, but I do believe, that over time, with this Brotherhood, and by doing the fucking work, I can do that. And that's why I'm committed to the Warrior's Way.*

## B.W., Michigan, USA:

*This is gold. Having to declare and teach a subject forces you to be a subject matter expert. Something I would never had thought of. Genius. Love it.*

## T.H., Florida, USA:

*"I just need to stop hiding and feeling like people will judge me if I share ... And just start sharing daily and not care what others think of me. Fuck it... I'm all in to start sharing what I've learned and see where it goes.... I am a Leader NOT a Savior.... Boom!"*

## J.E., Auburn, IL:

*"This is powerful information and I am going to need to study it again and again. I declared to my wife and business colleague tonight explaining that I am going to warrior to learn new business strategies while working on body, being and balance at the same time. I explained through watching Garrett's videos I feel like I know what is about to happen but actually going to Warrior is the ultimate commitment. I can study all I want but this content requires action. Just as in my business I need to create content in order to ask for clients and prospects to take action! Boom!"*

# THE KEYS

## Chapter 27: OVERVIEW

This statement "We create with the Keys" is a phrase you're going to hear constantly within the Brotherhood of the Wake Up Warrior Movement along with this concept of having it all. It requires reverse engineering production,which we'll discuss in further detail within the chapter.

## SECTION FIVE
# THE KEYS

## CHAPTER TWENTY-SEVEN
# OVERVIEW

"The greater danger for most of us lies not in setting our aim too high and falling short;
but in setting our aim too low, and achieving our mark."

### -Michelangelo di Lodovico Buonarroti Simoni

---

## Searching for Crucial Power

1. The power inside the Code and Core gives us this expanded capacity from which we are ultimately able to produce. We weren't screwing around with the reality that being here inside this Movement was about some kind of feel-good experience. Production inside of our lives is crucial.

2. Now don't bullshit yourself. You and I both know this is fact: We find massive significance in self-fulfillment and running businesses that matter to us. Making money and hunting the buffalo daily as an entrepreneur is part of our life blood.

3. It's in our DNA. Without it, we are unemployable in the Game of Life. You can probably relate; it's impossible for me to play in any other sense that even after a moment of peace, my mind is immediately going to begin creating and saying, "How can I solve more problems for more people? How can I create more shit that matters to me? How can I make more money?"

## Making Money That Matters

4. Not for the sake of making money but because money itself becomes the identifier of the results of value that I'm creating in the marketplace. The

more that I produce, the greater impact my businesses can make inside the world regardless of the industry. The more significance that I begin to feel about my influence on the world in making people's lives a better place helps me as a businessman. I'm more than somebody that's just a thought leader who shares some cool shit on social media.

5. As businessmen, we have the ability on a daily basis to create really big shit, but here's the problem: power comes with a flip side. The Dark Side of capacity and power is formed by what we call the Chaos of Abundance.

6. While in an event with Robert Kiyosaki,[75] he told me, "Having a lot of money or creating a lot of success financially is more difficult to manage than having almost no money at all."

7. I didn't really get it until I started to create significant revenue and had to deal with tax strategies and all of these issues with accounting and employment, payroll tax and everything else that I had never anticipated before when it was just little tiny me worrying about how I was going to make my motorcycle payment that month.

## The Problem with Awakened Capacity: Chaos of Abundance

8. Day to day, my experience began to expand and I saw that having more power inherently creates more opportunity, but inside that opportunity was the possibility that I could do anything because I'm the guy in charge. I'm the one who gets to dictate and create my day to be exactly what I want it to be. But here comes the problem: when you live by the Code and stand for the Core, you will awaken a Power and Capacity inside of you that has never been accessed before.

9. On one side, this is beautiful. But on the flip side, this is a problem because we're going to see all of this cool shit that we had never seen before. We're going to think in our mind that we should do them all until we're running around like a fucking chicken with its head cut off or our brain begins to leak out of our ears.

---

[75] Author of *Rich Dad, Poor Dad* and creator of *Cash Flow*. See Appendix Bibliography and Resources: Business Tools

10. Once we can control our own destiny, we have the ability to see through the bullshit, but then we have to be strategic about what we choose to put our energy towards.

11. We're going to have a conversation inside the Keys that I hope will open you up to see that the Chaos of Abundance can be clarified, but it requires thinking a little bit differently. We'll look at how we do Business on a weekly basis with all this increased power and capacity: a marriage and relationship with the kids that's on fire, being on point spiritually, and with a weaponized body, our study with marketing and sales is on fire. We've got to gather all of that energy into one simple focus.

## Aim Small to Grow Big

12. When I asked a friend of mine how he was able to manage the success from the five businesses he ran and the billions of dollars he was making, he said, "You have to aim small to grow big."

13. We need to learn to be present with the current thought or idea so that we are able to refine in that area rather than be mediocre in everything. The Key 4 is a production conversation specifically meant for Business. Men will ask me, "Well Garrett, why don't we do Key 4 in our marriage? Why don't I do 4 Key Actions every single week inside my Being?" Because it's too much chaos.

## Harnessing the Power of Core 4 With 7 Habits

14. Instead, we develop a narrow, centrally-focused Key action within Business. Inside the Key 4 are four Key Actions we're going to take every single week based on the Power from inside the Core 4, which has been tested for years and years.[76]

15. We take all of the power from Core 4 and point it directly at four significant needle-moving, profit-building, lifestyle-creating actions every single week inside our Business.

---

[76] I have tested the idea of idea of taking Key 4 and spreading it across all 4 domains (Body, Being, Balance & Business). It does not work. It will fail because it's too much to keep track of.

16. Another example of creating steadily measured success was laid out over 25 years ago in [77]Stephen R Covey's book called *7 Habits of Highly Effective People*. This book has impacted millions, including my own life in a big way, and is still heavily circulated today.[78]

## Begin with The End in Mind

17. How many weeks do you wake up as a businessman clear about how you're going to win for the week? It's Stephen R Covey's principle: "I'll begin with the end in mind."

18. We need to have a metric based, measurable "yes" or "no." I won or I did not. The same kind of yes or no that we were looking for inside our marriage, body and spirituality. We need to know, "Did I win this week? Yes or no." Did that win push me towards my 90-day Outcome?"

19. Without this framework all laid out, when you get into the Game of the week and hit Friday, you're like, "Where the hell did my week go?" This is why most men have that tendency to steal from their family emotionally, in fitness, and spirituality in order to try and catch up with the deficit that they constantly feel inside Business.

## First Things First

20. There's a second concept from Covey's *7 Habits of Highly Effective People* known as: "first things first," which helps us prioritize with a time matrix. For instance, I could say, "First things first, there are some actions that we need to be taking on a weekly basis for our business that are super important. They are significant needle movers in our business and if we only got these things done, our businesses would move forward and our bank accounts would fill up."

21. When we operate in the checklist game instead of being strategic about our actions, we aren't utilizing our time management. Instead of moving forward like a sniper with a clear target, it's like we're spraying the neighborhood with a drive-by shooting, hoping a random shot makes its mark.

---

[77] Appendix Bibliography: Covey, Stephan R for full citation.
[78] I eventually want to see Warrior in that same category of global impact.

22. We have to start to prioritize the actions inside our day. The time matrix inside *7 Habits* has been divided into 4 areas:

1. Not Important
2. Important
3. Not Urgent
4. Urgent

23. Inside of these four domains in which some of the things we were doing were important, some of them were not important at all. Some of the things were urgent and some of the things were not urgent at all.

## Avoid The Pit of Despair

24. Within Covey's quadrants, the *not important* and *not urgent* dwell in a pit of despair, with this idea of desperation and death. These are activities you should never be fucking doing. Ever. It's a waste of time. This is like oblivion bullshit, wasting time on social media in the middle of the day when you should be the most productive, and then find yourself having to hustle at the end of the day, calling up the wife to say, "I'm going to be late getting home tonight" because you wasted three hours stuck in the void of death and desperation within the online world. Sound a bit dramatic? I would have you consider that society has become a culture of time wasters because of social media platforms; take ONE day and see how often you check into Facebook, post on Instagram, or Twitter. You may be surprised.

## Focus On Your Own Agenda

25. As we focus on prioritizing our priorities, we then come to this other box: *not important but very urgent.* You know what exists there? Everybody else's fucking agendas. I still remember the sign above the desk of my high school's secretary: "Your failure to prepare does not constitute an emergency on my part." A great reminder to teenage kids when they think they're the center of the universe.

26. Entrepreneurs love to stay in this quadrant until they have learned to be a Closer and function in their business with no fucking Maybes; only "Yes" or "No." This is the area that "maybes" like to dwell. This entire quadrant is also a game of desperation and absolute destruction.

27. The minute you have shit going on and you are starting to make anything happen here inside the Brotherhood, this is inevitable. Your businesses are going to grow, your life is going to expand as you become an impact player inside your industry. People are going to look at you different. When this happens, you're going to become very popular.

28. Men, women, business partners and all kinds of strategic alignment people are going to come out of the woodworks pitching, "Oh, hey. I got this deal for you. I got this opportunity for you. Hey, I got this important thing. Call me. Text me. Email me. We got to go to lunch. Hey, we need that coffee." If you're not careful, you will get wrapped up in the game with all this extra capacity that you have and end up burning it all to the ground out of despair during the *not important/not urgent* or *not important/urgent* bullshit that's on everybody else's agenda.

## Narrowing Our Focus As Men

29. This then leaves us with these other two areas in which all results are found: *important and urgent* and *not urgent but important*. If we can have the power to focus our capacity that we're finding inside the Code and the Core, we can focus it down on strategic sniper-based targets every single week. This third category or the very first box at the top left that Covey declared was the stuff that was *important and urgent*; the shit that needs to happen.

30. This is stuff that every week you wake up as a businessman, you're like, "You know what, there's some shit that has to happen: payroll has to go out this Friday. We've got to close on this contract this week." When you wake up on Monday with the end in mind, there are certain things that are important and urgent; they are on time deadlines and shit that *must* happen this week.

31. Now we also have to be careful in this quadrant, because we could face building a business life that's driven by urgency and importance; driven by fires. It is impossible to have it all if you wake up every day and feel like you are constantly reacting to the fires that are being started. If your Key 4 Actions are important and urgent every single week, you'll get burned out from the hustle and grind.

32. Our target is to begin to shift the Game to the power quadrant: *not urgent but important.* This one gets ignored, yet it's the one that Stephen Covey would constantly pound on as a trainer. As a corporate speaker helping businesses' CEOs, he wanted us to understand our greatest impact in our business and life exists in the *not urgent but important.* These are the strategic moves of CEOs.

33. We can only temporarily function living an *urgent and important* life. If you plan on living as a Brother in this Brotherhood, having it all in Body, Being, Balance, and Business, I can tell you with 100% certainty that you will **have** to master your ability as a sniper to shift your focus from goals with this increased chaos of abundance directly into two quadrant targets with a push to have almost everything in your Key 4 move away from *important and urgent* into *important but not urgent.*

34. As we begin to move these daily Key 4 Actions over as *important and urgent,* here's what happens: we still have stuff that's important and urgent but we're not operating in panic mode to get them done. For a lot of entrepreneurs, this is a scary thing. It's scary to live a life that works because we've lived a life that hasn't worked for so long; it's what's familiar, and so we've leveraged the fuel and the fire that we feel when our back is against the wall.

## Stop Procrastinating Expansion

35. I would deliberately wait to do shit because I felt like I had to have a fire lit under me in order to move. It took me a long time to figure out the cost of this. If you want to be powerful inside this Game of having it all, your business must succeed. It must continue to grow, year after year. Having it all is to expand, multiplying businesses being built and making sure money continues to roll in. The coffers inside the kingdom must continue to be overflowing because in that place of abundance, you can make true impact on the world, where you have an opportunity to have a conversation inside a marriage and with your children that you would not have otherwise when driven by scarcity working 80 to 90 hours a week.

36. The Key 4 is not magical. It is simplistic, but the Key 4 requires us to be willing to narrow our focus down to 4 specific actions:

What

Why
When
How

37. Inside this training, I'm going to walk you through each one of these, making sure that we're on point; all of the increased power that we have coming from the Code and Core is not going to waste, and that it's used to push and exceed the boundaries of what's possible inside our Business all at the same time.

## Chapter 27:
## POINTS TO PONDER FROM THE GENERAL'S TENT

- **POINT #1:** There's massive significance in self-fulfillment and running businesses that matter to you. Creating production inside of our lives is a crucial part of achieving the "have it all" lifestyle.

- **POINT #2:** According to Robert Kiyosaki, author of the bestselling book Rich Dad, Poor Dad, "Having a lot of money or creating a lot of success financially is more difficult to manage than having almost no money at all." We will then be dealing with the Chaos of Abundance, because when you live by the Code and you stand for the Core, you will awaken a Power and Capacity inside of you that has never been accessed before.

- **POINT #3:** "You have to aim small to grow big." This requires creating simple, metric based "Yes" or "No" questions and a focus on priorities.

- **POINT #4:** Ask yourself questions in this order for ultimate expansion with the Keys: What? Why? When? And How? which will all be discussed in detail within the rest of this section.

# WARRIOR WITNESS:

## A.C., Long Beach California:
*"The keys are truly the "Key" I've been looking for. I've always performed better under pressure. Maybe that's only because I lack focus...and rely on instinct. I waste so much energy in NOT planning..."*

## M.M. San Jose, California:

*"I've been in urgent but not important and the not important quadrants for too much time. Strategic thinking is important but not urgent and is key. The end."*

---

## J.E., Auburn, Illinois:

*"IMPORTANT & URGENT. I know what my win will be this week! IF on Friday my wife, son and dogs may arrive in Nashville at our new home and we can have a meal around a folding table in our new kitchen this coming weekend it will be my WIN. I found out at 4:45 pm yesterday (Friday) that our closing which is scheduled for 9/2/16 will not likely happen with the current mortgage lender. I am moving mountains this week to make this happen and I will NOT fail. So this may seem like a common and simple problem to many but it is unique to me. Underwriting at given bank can go FUCK themselves! I will go through them and do this closing without them.... That will be my WIN for the week. The ultimate outcome will give us peace of mind and allow us to keep on our schedule for Nov 1, 2016.*

*STRATEGIC IMPORTANCE:*

*Start new business by creating either an audio &/or video blog inside a growth industry and something I actually know & am passionate about! This is my start small to grow big idea. I wish to create abundance beyond our current situation & I know this is possible."*

# THE KEYS

## Chapter 28: WHAT

"What do you want?" It's a simple enough question, but one that starts the whole Game of the Keys. If you don't nail down this question, the Why? When? And How? in the Keys won't matter.

# SECTION FIVE
# THE KEYS

## CHAPTER TWENTY-EIGHT
# WHAT

*"I know where I'm going and I know the truth, and I don't have to be what you want me to be. I'm free to be what I want."*

**-Muhammad Ali**

---

1. Do you know what your driving force is? "What do you want?[79]" is a simple enough question, but the interesting thing that starts happening when people get asked this is that they respond back with what they *don't* want.

## What Do You Want?

2. "Well, here's what I don't want."

"No, no, no. You don't understand. I didn't ask you what you *don't* want. I asked you what you *do* want."

3. When asking this at an event, a trainer continued around the room asking those in attendance this question and then, of course, confronted me. "What do you want?" I gave him some bullshit answer that wasn't really what I wanted because I didn't realize what I wanted at all. Then he pulled my chair to the front of the room and continues, "What do you want?"

---

[79] WD What Do You Want? A few years ago I was in a workshop in an event in which one of the trainers kept asking everyone the same question: "What do you want?" Not in a snide "You talkin' to me?" kind of way, but more in wanting to know what drives them.

4. He's a really badass dude that eventually became one of my business partners. I said something else and he would say, "What do you want?" over and over again. It felt like this was going on forever.

5. Finally, after that arsenal of "What do you want?" was unloaded, at the bottom of this we actually found something that mattered; something that was significant. There was this wanting and longing underneath, a clarity that was found as we stripped away all this complexity as he left me there in front of the room. He left me sitting with this reality that I'd uncovered in myself. My mind was blown as everything suddenly became more simple.

## The Beauty of Simplicity

6. Simplicity is doable; complexity is not. We might ask ourselves, why is it that most men choose to create lives that are so complex? Why do we do this? Why did I do it for so long? It doesn't take work to live in complexity. It also doesn't mean you're a genius to talk about something that sounds complex.

7. Complexity is the conversation of the ignorant and the retarded.[80] It has limitations in what it is able to do.

8. In using the Key 4, we're saying this entire game of clarity amidst the complexity comes down to a **What**: What do you want? What is the Action? What is the Outcome? What is the Game that would tell us that we won?

9. Keep in mind that simple also does not mean easy. As we ask better questions,[81] we start to discover new possibilities. It was in the questions that I began to strip away the complexity and bring it down to the basics of the simplicity of "Here is what I want. This is the outcome that I desire. Here is why that outcome matters. This is when I'm going to pull it off, and here's how I'm going to do it."

---

[80] When we talk about being retarded as a man, the term is not used as a way of physically being; it is a mental state of retardedness, meaning the mind does not work correctly when you live in complexity.
[81] Better questions like "What do you want?"

## The Impact of a Single Domino/Question

10. Asking "What" is the primary domino which sends the rest of the Key 4 into action. Whether you've played Dominos the traditional way or stacked them up as an amazing work of art lining them up in an intricate pattern, by far the funnest part about Dominos is to watch the power that one domino has as it effects another and then another.[82]

11. No matter how simple or complex the domino line may be, the last domino cannot be impacted until we push that first, initial domino. Sometimes the dominos are not lined up correctly, which then interrupts the synchronicity of the action. When this happens, we course correct, reset the line and go again.

12. Nonetheless, that chain reaction of events, the domino effect, isn't possible unless there is clarity about what the first domino is. The power of the creation from dominoes isn't as significant if you start in the middle or towards the end; most of us don't have the opportunity to just insert ourselves in the middle of something. There are primary dominoes used at the beginning which have the most massive power in the chain reaction of how one small step can become the start to a whole movement.

13. So what do dominoes have to do with the Key 4? Your ability to get what you want comes down to your ability to compress, determining this week, which of the dominoes must be pushed. You ask yourself, "What is the one thing that must happen this week inside my business that would push my business forward in my marketing, in my sales, in my systems, in my leadership, in my automation? Whatever the topic, what is the *one thing* that must happen this week in order to hit my 90-Day Outcome, my 60-Day Benchmark, my 30-Day Benchmark, or maybe even my 5-Year Vision? What's the one thing that's got to happen this week to get the ball rolling in the right direction?"

---

[82] A domino can knock over another domino 1 ½ times its size, leading to a chain reaction of knocking down a structure multiple stories tall from pushing a domino as small as a thumbnail. A simple Google or YouTube search will result in thousands of examples. There are multiple videos on the physics of this as well as creative works of art, all because of one small domino getting pushed over.

14. Like the game of dominoes, we have to line our targets up, one step at a time, in order to correctly push from the first small domino into a forward motion that pushes other targets forward until eventually we have worked our way up in size that leads to a big ass finale of completion.[83]

## Life Lessons from Workout Programs

15. I enjoy working out, especially when I follow a specific training protocol. I enjoy fighting, boxing, and riding. I enjoy Ironman and accomplishing a lot of shit with my Body. One thing I love about CrossFit and SealFit, though, is that they build these workouts known as Chippers.[84]

16. There are a series of these events within the workout that must happen in a particular order with a certain rep scheme at a certain amount of weight, moving from item to item, but we can't worry about what the next movement is because we need to stay present with the current one.

17. These workouts also create a different type of Focus inside your mind because when you get into a Chipper workout, you're not worried about the rope because you're focused on the cow bell squats. Just like in all my years in Ironman, I wasn't worried about the run while I was in the swim.

18. What you need to worry about is the movement that's in front of you. We simplify the game down by asking ourselves one simple question: What is the one thing that must happen this week in order to push my business forward as I move towards my 90-Day Outcome?

## Looking At The One Thing, Sitting Inside The General's Tent

19. We're going to sit down every single week in the General's Tent and have a conversation with ourselves, mapping our Outcomes on paper and saying, "Okay. When I look with the end in mind from today through the end of this week, what is the one thing that must happen this week?" I take that and write it down. I do this with all 4 of my Key 4 Outcomes.

---

[83] Go to: "Domino Chain Reaction" https://www.youtube.com/watch?v=MmMbfSZwyPw to that when dominoes increase in size by 1 ½ times; it requires continual growth and expansion to knock down the highest outcomes.

[84] As an example, you could have a deadlift first, then your 2nd movement might be pullups, and your 3rd might be air squats. 4th could be kettlebell swings and 5th a rope climb. See Appendix Resources: Fitness for a linked article which describes Chippers as the hardest workout ever.

20. I was inspired by Gary Keller[85] for this question from his book, *The One Thing*.[86] It pointed me to the game of simplifying, blending with what Stephen Covey[87] was teaching in *Seven Habits* by saying, "Okay, what is the one thing that must happen? If that occurs, what is the one thing that must happen next?" As you go through this line of conversation with yourself, what you're left with is the following reality: 4 What's that have created 4 Outcomes.

## The Sniper: The Difference Between A Target & A Goal

21. Now we're going to come back to each one of these Outcomes and ask, "Okay. Is this outcome an actual target? Or is it a goal?" What's the difference? Well, a goal is something that can't be measured. A goal is this ideal outcome that we try to obtain. Whereas, a target states "This is deliberate. I can 'yes' or 'no' on this one. Yes, it happened. No, it didn't. Yes, it occurred. No, it didn't."

22. Whatever the target is, it has to be measurable. It has to be looked at *as* a target. A sniper does not have a goal in shooting his gun. There's nothing goalistic about it at all. It's all driven by targets: Here is my target, my assignment, the enemy, and I'm going to line in my sights. I'm not worried about anybody or anything else going on in the environment. I'm not worried about anything else that's going on around me. All of these things can be indicators of what's happening, but I am not pulling my gun out and just shooting everyone.

23. People who think through goals give themselves wiggle room. When I start thinking about one thing as a target, it gets a bullseye placed on it. As I line up my sights and fire, I will know if I hit my target when my target falls. If it doesn't fall, I didn't hit it. There's no wiggle room for maybe. There's yes, it happened or no, it didn't happen.

---

[85] Keller Williams Realty

[86] Appendix Bibliography: Keller, Gary. A book that breaks down the process of what successful people have done, which ultimately comes down to a zeroed in focus on one thing that becomes their primary focus of expertise.

[87] Appendix Bibliography: Covey, Stephen R

## Creative Writing Assignments

24. Creativity is sometimes needed to hit the target. I watch this happen constantly with my daughter's writing assignments. She has a writing teacher who is constantly pushing her to write because she's a very good storyteller, she's got tons of creativity as an artist, and is a very good writer. We'll put together these stories and in her mind, they look like one thing. There's a lot of imagery, there's a lot of fun, there's a lot of excitement, but then when it comes to paper oftentimes what she's writing down she gets frustrated, throws the pencil and tears the paper up. The story that she's writing down does not match what's in her head. Bridging this disconnect is what makes great writers: taking the concepts from inside the mind and communicating them in a way on the paper that is simple and clear. The ideas *here* transfer *there*.

25. As entrepreneurs building these Key 4's, we're going to get these concepts. Sitting and talking about something is one thing, but it's not the same as when it's written down or typed up. The second thing we are going to do is talk about it with somebody. We're going to share with someone else (wife, partner, friend, team member, etcetera) what we're doing. We could even record it and listen to ourselves saying it back. Feedback is crucial.

## Think It. Write It. Speak It. Measure It

26. I'm going to write my thoughts down and then I'm going to speak it. Along with this, I'm going to make sure that it is measurable. Well, how will we know it's measurable and specific? Because we check the box that says, yes, it was accomplished or no, it wasn't. If it's not measurable, it's not a target. If it's not a target, it means that we have a goal.

27. Some other questions that we can use the What do I want? model are: Where am I at right now? or What do I want to happen this week? It may not ultimately end up becoming the One Thing, but we can brainstorm this, and sometimes taking the time sitting inside the General's Tent, we are able to journal down our ideas and concepts. Throughout the week I am constantly writing down in my War Map different "What's" that come to me. It doesn't mean that every idea I have inside the Chaos of Abundance is going to be an idea that I'm going to run with; it just means it's an idea that I have, which I may or may not use.

28. Instead of leaving an idea inside my head to then fall into oblivion, what do I do with it? I write that shit down. Why? Because 1- I don't have to try to remember it and 2- some of my ideas are fucking insane, so when I write them down, I can see how idiotic they were and move on or realize they weren't as far-fetched as I initially thought.

## Surrendering to One Belief in Order to Allow Another to Rise

29. Inside of that we're going to see what must be surrendered. Oftentimes inside of Key 4, we're going to have to let go of something. We're going to have to let go of a commitment to something else, a belief system, relationship, or direction in business. We're going to have to let go of something that was committed to three months ago that right now doesn't make any sense to stay in the Game with any longer. As you look at what you want and where you are, you'll see the gap. You could be like, "Shit. I'm going to have to let go of this project. I'm going to have to let go of this idea. I might have to let go of this team member. I might have to let go of this thing. I might have to surrender this."

30. On the flip side, we may look into that same Gap and say, "Okay. Well, you know what? I have to let these things go, but I'm also going to have to personally level up this week to pull it off. I'm not only going to have to just live by the Code and really take a stand for the Core and 'hit my core before I hit the door so I can go to war.' I'm not just going to have to do that. I'm literally going to have to expand my skillsets in this area." I'm going to have to study this week in order to pull that off or get into conversation with my mentor or challenge somebody in my Mastermind to help me or have a conversation with my wife about direction. I'm going to have to expand myself.

31. If you start with a faulty *what* or you're not living by the Code, you fucking lie about what you want, and you lie to yourself about what's most important, then all of a sudden you take something that was in the *not urgent, important* category and replace it with something that was in the *urgent and not important* category. Next thing you know, you're back into this mess of creating bullshit Key 4's that don't fucking change anything except for giving yourself a hand job because you got a 4 that week.

32. The entire Key 4 mechanism is a tracking game that's stating, "There are 4 Outcomes that we're going to get a point for every single week. I'm going

to get a point for each one of these 'What's' that I complete. If I complete all 4 of those, I'm going to get a 4." That 4 means a ton as long as you don't bullshit yourself; you were genuine and accurate on your "What's."

## Getting in A Weekly Change of Key 4

33. Inside of this, you're going to be lining up your actions and looking at where you're trying to go over the next 90 days. Unlike the Core 4, which we're going to continue to hit every single day, our Key 4 becomes more directional in nature regardless of where we're trying to go. Our What's are going to change week to week, while our Core 4 may stay the same over time. We're going to zig some weeks and then some weeks we're going to zag. Some weeks we're going to course correct because the Key 4's we did the week before weren't as powerful, didn't get accomplished, or showed us something that we hadn't anticipated. By completing our Key 4, it may open up this whole new reality and/or problems we didn't anticipate. That's the beautiful thing about Key 4: if we just stay focused on what it is this week, next week there are going to be four different ones.

34. If you sat down and looked at your marketing, sales, systems, leadership, personnel, fulfillment, business, outcomes, and you set your Key 4, you would accomplish 4 significant Key 4 items every single week. That's 4 a week, 16 a month, 32 over 2 months, and 48 in 90 days. 48 Key needles moving *significant urgent* and *not urgent, but very important* actions inside Business.

35. I'll guarantee that if we go back in the last six months of your Business, you haven't accomplished half of what you'll accomplish using this Key 4 metric-based system in 90 days. Most of your life has been about managing bullshit. If you don't nail the What aspect of the Key 4, then the Why, When and How won't matter.

### Chapter 28:
### POINTS TO PONDER FROM THE GENERAL'S TENT

- **POINT #1:** When asked, "What do you want?" once you find something that matters and is significant to you, once you do this, it becomes this driving force and clarity from the complexity that had been created when focusing on what you didn't want.

- **POINT #2:** Just because we have learned how to make something simple, that doesn't necessarily make it easier and therefore not as important. Complexity doesn't bring importance; clarity does. Like the game of dominoes, we have to line our targets up, one step at a time, in order to get from the first small domino to eventually ones that work up in size that leads to a big ass finale of completion. We ask ourselves: "What is the one thing that must happen this week in order to push my business forward towards my 90-day outcomes?"

- **POINT #3:** Look at our Outcomes as targets, rather than goals, just as a sniper zeroes in on his target; he doesn't make it his goal...it's his mission to focus on the target. We'll need creativity to think it, then physically write it down and finally teach it to others to drive the Outcome home in a measurable way.

- **POINT #4:** Inside of Key 4, we're going to have to let go of a commitment to something else, a belief system, relationship, or direction in business. As you look at what you want and where you are, you'll see the gap where something that you were committed to three months ago no longer makes sense. Expansion within our capabilities and skills sets becomes our driving force as we eliminate the other garbage that's getting in our way of having it all.

# THE KEYS

## Chapter 29: WHY

The dynamic of Why becomes a driving action and purpose behind our production here at Warrior. The Why behind the What matters as you go through the Game of the Keys.

# SECTION FIVE
# THE KEYS

## CHAPTER TWENTY-NINE
# WHY

*"There are two great days in a person's life - the day we are born and the day we discover why."*

### -William Barclay
[Scottish Scholar (1907-1978)]

---

1. Why? This is the second question that my trainer began to ask me after grilling away with "What do you want?" that we covered in Chapter 22. Yet again, I wasn't expecting the next onslaught of questions: Why did I care? Why did that matter? Why was that significant? Why was that a must in my life?

2. The dynamic of Why becomes a driving action and purpose behind our production here at Warrior. We throw fire onto the What's, and we say "Here is why." Here is *why* this matters to me. Why I have to have this. Here is why this is significant and a must inside of my life. This is a question I ask most people I come in contact with on a daily basis. I'll ask my daughters, "What do you want? What is the point of this? Why do you want that?"

## Questions to Change People's Lives

3. These two questions have power to change people's lives, because most human beings are not being asked this: getting clear about the challenge it is to answer "Why" until they do something.

4. If your motivation behind making a million dollars in a year is because it would be cool to say "I made one million dollars in one year!" you're probably not going to achieve it.

5. You're not going to have enough fire inside the gap of the actions that are necessary between where you are and where you say you've got to go. You will not have enough fire to pull it off because you don't have a specific Why linked up in your mind to doing it, so when shit gets tough, when the going gets hard, you'll stop. You'll stop doing it. You'll find a reason not to hit that Outcome. Whether that's a 90-Day Outcome, a Key 4 Action happening every single week, or part of your daily Core 4, the Why behind your Game matters.

## Kokoro Intensity

6. One of the places that I experienced the importance of establishing a strong, clear Why was through an event called [88]Kokoro, a program within SealFit which I've mentioned briefly before in this book. All active and former Navy Seals take civilians and young military guys training to go to [89]BUD/S for the Navy Seal program to qualify through [90]Hell Week. They come into this three-day event with civilians blended in: Crazy lunatics like me show up there and say we're going to do this event.

7. For 70 hours straight you work out. You train. You do push-ups, air squats, pull ups, carry logs, sandbags, and men. You go in the water. You get out of the water. You go in the sand. You work as a group. You work individually. You are cold. You are fucking tired. You are fatigued within the first six hours and you have to endure 70 hours of intensity. The cold baths feel like complete, absolute, torture. You ask yourself, "Why the fuck am I here? Why am I doing this?" It's crazy, yet before we even got to Kokoro Camp, the message that came from Mark Divine's team simply said this: "Garrett you better have a why."

---

[88] No sleep for 70 hours with Mark Divine's training protocol known as SealFit. See also Appendix Resources: Fitness

[89] Basic Underwater Demolition/SEAL traininghttp://navyseals.com/buds/

[90] A 5 ½ straight day program designed to test the endurance of the participants before making an expensive investment into a career that they may not want to continue to pursue due to the required intensity needed. Seehttp://navyseals.com/nsw/hell-week-0/ for more information.

8. The What was clear: Finish Kokoro Camp. Go through 70 hours of authentic Navy Seal training with no sleep. This is what I'm going to do. There were 44 people who registered for Kokoro. 44 people paid, registered, and told Mark Divine and his team, "I'm going to show up and I'm going to do Kokoro Camp. Here's what I'm going to do." Day 1: 33 showed up. This means that 11 individuals already lost their commitment between simply paying for the event and traveling. They didn't even make the journey. Why? Because there was no "Why" that was burning hot enough to help them overcome the reasons inside their mind for traveling, attending, and being part of the experience.

9. Day 1: 33 people began the experience. By the time we finished Kokoro Camp, 70 hours later, there were 17 of us. People weren't getting injured; individuals were breaking. The entire time through this event, the trainers continued to say the same thing, "You better fucking find your why. You better find your why." They'd walk up to me, I had WHITE on my shirt;[91] known by my last name only. Sitting in recon pants and boots, every time I would look fatigued, or that I was having a hard time, feeling tired, that I was 50-60 hours in, no sleep, limited food, body shutting down, and/or my mind shutting down, there would be a trainer that would walk up to me, look me in the eyes, and one of the Seals would say, "What is your 'Why,' White?"

10. On the first night, as we hiked over 30 miles with 30 pound packs on our back, I lost sight of my Why. For three hours I lost sight of it. I sat there, climbing/hiking up this mountain. Carrying this stick that's symbolizing our weapon, with this pack on my back,[92] oblivious to anyone else around me, and I completely lost my Why.

11. I lost the fire, and for three hours I attempted to create a reason—a story—to not finish: Oh, my Achilles tendon,[93] I should probably stop. I'm almost 40, I should probably stop. I miss my kids, I should probably stop. What am I trying to prove? I'll probably injure something again. Maybe I'll die. Maybe I'll have a heart attack right here in the middle of the night.

---

[91] I had printed my last name on a white shirt with black spray paint using stencil letters before I got to the camp.

[92] I swear they deliberately, intentionally got shitty bags that cut into the shoulders to make the experience worse. These weren't some nice ass bags from Dick's Sporting Goods. They're some shitty little bags literally filled with sand.

[93] I've had surgery three times on it

That's what's probably going to happen. I'll probably have a heart attack and die and they'd leave me here to rot.

12. Amidst all of this fucking drama, I forgot my Why. I forgot it. At 4:30 in the morning I was freezing, eating an MRE[94]—some horrible fucking pasta—with a shitty spoon, yet it tasted so good, and I sat there feeling defeated. One of the trainers came up to me again and looked me in the face, asking, "White, what is your Why?"

## What Is Your Why?

13. For a second, I thought back to when my marriage was falling apart.[95] Second marriage: All but done. Finished. I had to explain this in the car one day as I dropped my kids off at school. My daughter was trying to understand why mom and dad almost got divorced when they were little, and my eight-year-old at the time, very inquisitive, kept asking "Why?" over and over.

There was that Why question again.

14. Kids don't accept "Because." They need a clear, simple explanation. They don't understand these wars within ourselves that go to battle every single day.[96] The only thing that's going to give you the weapons, the fuel, is that Why.

15. What was my Why in Kokoro? This split-second flashback pulled me forward from sitting in a freezing shit hole eating fucking MRE pasta with a goddamn spoon. I needed to have an answer. That Why was simply a Voice inside of me that said, "I have a message for you in the morning of the second day." I had heard that Why months before I went to Kokoro. It is what pushed me every single morning to wake up and train for two to three hours while everybody else was sleeping, and then in the afternoon to train for another hour or two. I was running in recon boots and pants in the sand. Running into the surf. Coming back out. Doing thousands and

---

[94] Meal, Ready to Eat. Commonly used by military and within the last few years has been used for civilian home food storage.

[95] Code 7:56-59, when my marriage to Danielle was falling apart and heading towards divorce.

[96] Like the internal war Arjuna was going through in the Bhagavad Gita, see Core 23:14-21, 29.

thousands of pushups and Burpees.[97] Preparing myself to get to this camp, so that I could get to this answer that the Voice told me was available for me at the end of two days.

16. I had a Why, but I had forgotten it briefly. You know what happened to the men and women inside this event that didn't have a Why? They quit. The second night there was a woman by the name of Tequo, the only woman to finish the program. A 42-year-old single mom with two children, which was her fucking big ass Why.[98]

17. Tequo said, "I'm going to prove to my children that I can do this. That Mom is powerful and that we can deal with hard things as a family, and that's why I'm here at this camp." Only woman in the Game. Powerful as hell, this woman, but into the second night, we lost seven or eight people. It was very cold. We were tired. We were shivering. In and out of the surf we went. In and out of the ocean we went. In and out of the water, into the sand. Crawling. Military crawls for fucking hours. Carrying logs around as a team all night long, and I had my Why, and I was on fire. I was fucking pumped having crossed that threshold of wanting to give up earlier. I was on fire. I was going to finish. I was like, "Oh, I can taste the finish line. I can taste the finish line. I don't give a shit. You bring anything to me mother fucker, I will eat it up. I'll eat the goddamn face off it," but Tequo wasn't there.

## Help is Needed When Finding the Lost Why

18. Tequo lost her Why like I had the night before. She was sitting over on the side ready to quit. One of the trainers came over to me and said, "Garrett you're losing somebody."

"Who?"

"You're losing a teammate."

"Who?"

---

[97] Burpees are a common exercise within workouts that involves a slight squat down into a pushup, then popping out of it by jumping into the air. It is most effective when done repeatedly in sets of 10-30/day.

[98] Tequo's "Why" was her children after her husband left her and there was no money.

19. "You're going to lose Tequo. Maybe you should go have a talk with her. She wants to leave," so I went over to Tequo.

20. She was shaking and shivering: a 110-pound woman, 42 years old, single mom, sitting over by herself trying to eat an MRE, shaking. She couldn't stop shaking—shivering and shaking—sitting by herself. Tears pouring down her cheeks, I went up to her and asked, "Tequo what's going on?"

"I can't do this anymore. I'm too cold. I'm too tired. I can't do it."

21. "Tequo, why are you here? Why are you here, Tequo?"

"I was here for my kids. I had to prove for my children…"

Tears pouring down her cheeks.

22. "Tequo why are you here?"

"I'm here for my children."

23. "Tequo if you go home, you're going to regret this the rest of your life. Don't go home, Tequo."

"Garrett, I can't do this anymore. I can't do this anymore. I'm too tired."

24. "No you're cold. Come here." So I brought her over to my boat crew, which was our group of six or seven guys. Big ass dudes, all fucking former college and professional football players, Olympic athletes, successful businessmen in their 30s, late 30s, and early 40s who were beasts just like me.

25. We were all a boat crew together. Big guys. All over 200 pounds. We took little tiny Tequo and put her in the middle of us while straddling the log during our short break. She was right up against my chest with a big guy, Ben, in front of her, and he sat back until we made a Tequo sandwich; this is what we did that night to stay warm. There were no fires. There were no fucking blankets. There was a cold ass ocean, shivering bodies, and fatigue; our nervous systems were shutting down, and the only thing that we had was our Why.

26. I sat there for the next hour while Tequo cried, laying her head on Ben's back as the group was sitting and talking to her. I whispered in her ear the whole time. I said, "Your kids need you to push through. Your kids need you to finish. You cannot quit now. You are too close to the finish line.

There is no reason for you to quit now. Do not quit when you are three feet from the goal. Tequo, you've got to go. You got to stay here. You got to get warm. Close your eyes. Breathe. Breathe. Breathe. Do you see your kids? Do you see your children? This is why you're doing what you're doing Tequo. What are their names, Tequo?" She would tell me. She would fade in and out. Falling asleep on Ben's back, and I would wake her up, saying, "Tequo, you've got to stay with me. You've got to stay in the game. You cannot quit. You have got to finish this game Tequo."

27. Twelve hours later as we held these 800 pound logs over our heads, standing in line with our boat crews, with Mark Divine looking on us as a group until he said, "Kokoro Class 37, you are secure," Tequo graduated. She stood in that picture with us. All 17 of us tired as fuck, and yet with one last burst of adrenaline and excitement, she finished. Why did she finish? Because she had a Why. She had a Why that drove her behavior and her action. She had a Why that managed her pain.

## Getting Leverage on Yourself

28. Your purpose on a daily basis, and your purpose every week with each of these actions: They may not have to be as significant as the Why that Tequo was digging out during the Kokoro Camp with us. It may not be that your life is on the line. It may not be that your kids' lives are on the line, but you've got to get leverage on yourself. Without a Why you don't have leverage. Without a Why you don't have the fire. Without a Why, or when the shit gets hard, you will quit.

29. Monday will begin and like New Year's, it's a new beginning to make resolutions. But the reason most of those goals don't work is because they don't have a Why backing them up. They say they're going to do something new this week or this year, but they don't fucking mean it. They don't have fucking leverage on themselves. The only way to have leverage on you is to assure that your 4 Outcomes every single week, your 4 Keys to the kingdom inside your business, are linked up with linear logic. Logic in your mind that says "This action matters and here's my why…."

30. It doesn't take very long, but if you set a What without a Why, do not be surprised when Wednesday comes, and the *not important urgent* shit with the vampire victims begin to show up, wanting to suck your life dry. The quadrant of *important and urgent* in your life also shows up, which is then

managed by fire, and you become the entrepreneurs that ask themselves over and over again, "Why am I doing this? Is this even worth the stress that I'm going through? Why am I even doing this?"

31. If you haven't gotten there, it just means that you haven't been in the Game long enough. When in the pursuit of having it all, I don't know any entrepreneurs on the planet that don't hit those moments and nights where they're like, "What's the fucking point? Why am I fucking doing this?" Inside your What, every single week, you must have a linked up *why*. It is the ability to leverage yourself.

32. You can look for external reasons all day long by other people, but the greatest power as a player inside this game of Key 4, is to figure out how to get leverage on yourself. When you forget, make sure there are people around you who know what you are committed to as they remind you of your Why.

33. When you have forgotten your Why, like Tequo and I did, in the darkest moments of the night when you're like "I don't give a shit, I can't do this," not understanding that if you just accomplish this Key 4, that the fucking domino that you are pushing over this week is the one that you needed to push over, so that you could eventually topple the 16-foot fucking domino, but if you quit this week on that action, if you don't do it, that 16 foot domino is never going to fall. You *must* have a Why behind your What every single week.

## Chapter 29:
## POINTS TO PONDER FROM THE GENERAL'S TENT

- **POINT #1:** The dynamic of Why becomes a driving action and purpose behind our production here at Warrior. You need to have enough fire inside the gap of the actions that are necessary between where you are and where you say you've got to go by knowing your Why.

- **POINT #2:** Throughout Garrett's whole experience in Kokoro, he had to remember, "Why are you here?" which is an essential question to remain on your mind always, especially when doubt creeps in or shit hits the fan. Without a why you don't have leverage.

- **POINT #3:** If you set a What without a Why, do not be surprised when halfway through the week and the not important urgent shit with the victims and vampires begins to show up, wanting to suck your life dry you crumble because you didn't have a strong enough Why pushing you forth.

- **POINT #4:** The greatest power as a player inside this game of Key 4 is to figure out how to get leverage on yourself. When you forget, make sure there are people around you who know what you are committed to remind you of your Why.

# WARRIOR WITNESS:

### J.E., Illinois:
*"The 4 keys! The Why behind your What matters. If you don't know your Why, you will quit when the victims & vampires show up on Wednesday trying to suck the life force out of you! God Damn Garrett nailed it on this one!!!! Linear Logic.... Boom!"*

# THE KEYS
## Chapter 30: WHEN

When is a very simple conversation. It's the constraint which tells us when the action that we say we are going to take will be accomplished. When gives us a specific timeframe to achieve our What.

# SECTION FIVE
# THE KEYS

## CHAPTER THIRTY
# WHEN

*"Once you have mastered time, you will understand how true it is that most people overestimate what they can accomplish in a year – and underestimate what they can achieve in a decade!"*

**-Tony Robbins**
(American Businessman, author and philanthropist)

---

1. We have a What, Why, and now we have a When. This is the time-frame and constraint which tells us the action that we say we are going to take, this outcome we are going to create, the Why and the fire behind it. That it's going to happen at a specific time under a specific constraint of pressure, based upon time, date, and function.

### When is the Deadline?

2. Inside one of my Keys, I might say, "My constraint is that I'm going to launch these new ads on Google for this new marketing." Okay, cool. Why am I going to do that? Because we need to expand our current marketing portfolio, and start attracting leads into our circle from a different direction. So, we are going to launch two new Google ads this week, and spend X amount of dollars in ad revenue. Why is that significant? Because we need to add to our portfolio of how we attract leads.

3. What's a third question that we ask after answering What and Why then? Well, we have to know deadlines: Wednesday at two o'clock I'm going to blow this up. We've got to put some time constraints on this Outcome, giving it a specific day and time for completion.

# 48-Hour Crunch

4. I'm always amazed when my wife and I go on a vacation for four to five days (with the family or just us as a couple) how much I am able to accomplish in the last 48 hours before I leave. There's a clarity of focus that comes into my mind like no other time in my life. The amount of work I am able to accomplish Thursday and Friday before I know I'm going to London or Cancun for a week with my wife for a vacation, is extensively and radically greater than when I have weekends staying at home.

5. There is something about the time constraint and the finality of knowing I don't have a choice. My flight leaves at 10 o'clock on Saturday morning. I must finish this shit by Friday at this time or it will not happen. *It has to be done.* When your mind knows you are holding to the integrity with the date and time, you're truly going to commit to it, and there is no other option: this *will* be done therefore your mind immediately eliminates the bullshit.

6. Let's look back at our Time Matrix. I will take all of the people, behaviors, patterns, and activities that are *not important*, and *not urgent*, and will say, "Fuck you. This information does not matter to me today, so stop bringing that shit to me. I don't care. I have to make sure these Key items are handled before I go on the trip because once I go on the trip, I will be stressed out about them not being done. The team won't be able to manage shit if it's not ready for them to do."

## Urgently Shifting Due to Constraints

7. This is where it gets a little tricky, so you're going to have to follow me here.[99] We said we're trying to get all of our Actions over to the section of *not urgent but important* so we can be more strategic, but the moment that I put a constraint on that action, that *not urgent* item becomes *urgent*.

8. Watch what I'm saying here: The moment I put up a time constraint (date and time) onto an Outcome, it shifts immediately to *urgent*. Why does it become urgent? Because it is now a Game that must occur by a specific time.

## How to Avoid Creating Failure

---

[99] I know that I spent a lot of time here in this particular section telling you that our goal is to get our Key 4 Actions and Outcomes that must occur to be part of our *not urgent but important* quadrant.

9. Don't wait until the deadline has occurred to recognize when something is urgent. We don't want to be making moves out of desperation. You want to create failure for yourself? Go ahead and create a business constantly driven by urgency inside your marketing. You want to know what kind of marketing or selling you do when you're desperate? Shitty. You end up collecting the wrong clients because the only people that are going to listen to you at that point are victims who want to be saved. You're fucked.

10. Guess what kind of employees work for you when you hire in desperation? Employees who don't really get shit done. It's not in your best interest to live in a world in which the marketplace and the conditions around you are dictating what is urgent to you. The moment that we put constraints, we play a Catch-22 game of leverage on ourselves.

11. Everything inside of Core 4 is a game of commitment and consistency through Simple Success Swinging Singles. Inside of Key 4, it's no different.

12. If you give yourself 30 days to pull something off, guess how long you'll take to work on it? 30 days. Unless you are a goddamn unicorn and some kind of lucky charm carrying, gold basket weaving leprechaun, you (like most men) will wait until when? Day 27, and then all of a sudden you will have massive leverage on yourself.

## Failure is Not an Option

13. What would happen if we just started giving ourselves more time constraints? We will rise to produce under the constraints that we were given. How do we know this? You have a history in Business of producing big results when your back is against the wall and shit is urgent, meaning you can do big shit. You pull off what some would call miracles. Miraculous amounts of production in short periods of time because of one simple factor: In your mind, there is no option.

14. There is a flight tomorrow at 10 o'clock. I must have this shit done tonight, because tomorrow I'm getting on that goddamn plane and if it's not done, it's not done. I don't want the ramifications of it not being done in my life, so I'm going to commit to doing it, regardless of what has to happen. I might have to allow a lot of things that are important to just go away for right now and I'm going to focus on these Keys that I know must be done.

15. Time constraints are about leveling up the way you deal with constraints. We don't become Reactors to constraints. We create them. We don't wait for the world to put the time crunch on us; we put it on ourselves. Do you know how different your life becomes when *you* are the one who creates the constraints inside your Game?

16. If you're not the one that creates the constraints, then there is always this sense of feeling out of control in your Business; that you don't control your destiny, constraints and deadlines upon which these things must be done. I get that we're not going to be able to pull this off every single time. Sometimes there's going to be unexpected shit that is going to come at us sideways, preventing us from not always being able to meet deadlines, but our goal is to create a Game and inside that Game we are the deliberate, conscious Creators of the constraints inside these Keys.

17. Think of the Keys as four big pillars, holding up your kingdom. In between the big pillars are a bunch of little pillars. Inside of these four big Keys are those other, smaller things that have to happen, which will occur naturally anyways. These are things you're going to have to manage as a business owner. This is shit that you're not going to be able to avoid. Ever. It's the shit that naturally comes from running businesses, shit that naturally has to happen every single day regardless, but by sitting back and strategically planning these Keys and then putting time constraints on them, we look at our week and schedule, declaring it to be non-negotiable. It *must* be done.

## Do Not Disturb

18. It is a sacred moment in my week to plan my Keys with the time set aside for doing that as non-negotiable. Phone: Turn it off or put it on airplane mode. Leave it in the office. Send calls to voicemail. Lock your fucking door. Purchase a Do Not Disturb sign. Tell everybody to go away. Say, "Do not disrupt me for the next two hours." Don't talk to me during my planning session for my Keys unless I bring you in to talk to me about it so you can work on the Keys with me. I don't entertain any other conversation or Game, because inside those constraints, planning my Keys is the most important thing that happens.

19. This is what constraint does. The constraint puts some urgency on an outcome, which will give you the fire and the feeling like you have a flight tomorrow morning at 10 o'clock and you're going to Cancun with your wife,

which means this shit's got to be done. If you don't put these constraints on it, and if you don't live by the Code, it won't work. See, this is why we build the Code; to link it up to the Core which then links to the Keys: Live by the Code. Stand for the Core. Create with the Keys.

20. If you're a fucking liar, how much do you think you're going to actually accomplish with the Key 4? You won't. If you can't tell the truth, then when you put constraints on yourself, you will not have the power to actually accomplish them because inherently inside your own mind, you know you're a liar that doesn't keep his commitments. It's amazing to me how many men I meet that will let the world put constraints of time on them. Kings like you. Men who have created big, powerful shit and yet will allow pests—ants, fleas, flies—to disrupt the lion. Why do you allow and tolerate this bullshit? I'll tell you why. Because you tolerate this bullshit in yourself.

## Experiencing Time Constraints from Inside Kokoro

21. Inside Kokoro, there were two very powerful experiences I had in which the two small statements below became beliefs:

1. Details matter
2. Time constraints get shit done

22. We got to the camp and during that first hour they had us come out and stand on the Grinder.[100] There's 33 of us and we just stand there, not knowing what's going on. We didn't have our bags. Nothing. For an hour, we're standing there in the hot sun; they were totally just fucking with us. I didn't know what was going to happen yet, so I just stood there and let my mind wander.

23. I tried taking deep breaths, sure that at any moment hell was about to unleash on us. I didn't know what we're going to have to do, what's going to happen, if they're going to start spraying us down with hoses and ring obnoxious alarms, make us carry shit, drop down and do infinite push-ups…I had no idea what chaos was coming. All I knew was that I was standing.

---

[100] A concrete floor.

24. About an hour into this, all the trainers came out, including Mark Divine. They begin to start yelling at everybody about everything. Every detail that was out. If your belt was out of a belt loop, you got beaten down. If your backpack or your pack was not on correctly and the strap was loose, you got beaten down. All of the beat downs were verbal, but they still had a physical impact.

25. Over and over again, all of the details that were out of order inside that group carried on for the first six hours of Kokoro. If I was to drill home one important specific detail, it was that the details matter. *The details matter*. If you can learn to manage the smallest details, like your belt loop being slightly awry, you will have the ability to manage the big shit when it comes. And there was a lot of big shit before those 70 straight hours were up.

26. The second thing that happened inside Kokoro was the time constraints: everything that we did was on a timer. There wasn't anything we did that wasn't on a timer. If we were going to go to the bathroom to take a piss or dump, they would put it on the clock. If we were going to do push-ups, they put it on a clock. Everything we did was on the clock. Everything. If we were going to eat, on the clock. Everything.

27. But they would speed the clock up. No matter how fast we were going, they would increase the constraints of that time. If they said, "You have three minutes" they would then say, "You got 30 seconds" before the first fucking minute was even up. This is long before I was delirious from no sleep. I'm like, "What the hell, dude? How do we only have 30 seconds?"

28. This crazy thing would happen over and over and over again for us. No matter what the constraints were for time that they put on us, as a unit, we almost always rose to match the necessary result within the constraints that were given. Whether it was three minutes, 30 seconds, two hours, six hours, all night, it didn't matter. Whatever the constraint was, they told us we could do it and that we had to have it done within the constraint. Our mind did not have enough time to sit around and bitch and moan about the constraint; we simply conceded to the Game. Here is the constraint, and this is when it must be handled by. 3,2,1, Go!

29. These two powerful lessons of details and time constraints managed the Game of Kokoro, but these same details also manage the everyday Game of Key 4. Place constraints and commit your word to your constraints. Men

learn more about who they are as a liar to themselves by setting commitments to do certain things every single week and then not doing them like anything else. At the end of the day, if you cannot trust your own commitments to yourself, then what chance do you think you have, truly, of having it all?

## Non-Negotiables Back in the General's Tent

30. Key 4 is non-negotiable. Sitting back inside the General's Tent every Sunday, you prepare to go to war for the week, setting up the constraints of the *when* for your Key 4 strategically. Not half-assed; strategic planning is the difference between building empires and knocking over the 16-foot domino five to seven years before anybody anticipated that you could and the possibility of never knocking that domino down. Time constraints are a detail that matters. When will you have it done?

### Chapter 30:
### POINTS TO PONDER FROM THE GENERAL'S TENT

- **POINT #1:** It is absolutely necessary that we put time constraints on our Outcomes, giving it a specific day and time for completion by asking, "When will this action be accomplished by?" This requires that I put everything into high gear before hitting my deadline. The moment I put up a time constraint (date and time) onto an Outcome, it shifts immediately to urgent because it is now a Game that must occur by a specific time.

- **POINT #2:** Don't wait until the deadline has occurred to recognize when something is urgent. Time constraints are about leveling up the way you deal with constraints as a Creator rather than a Reactor. We don't wait for the world to put the time crunch on us; we put it on ourselves.

- **POINT #3:** If you can't tell the truth, then when you put constraints on yourself, you will not have the power to actually accomplish them because inherently inside your own mind, you know you're a liar that doesn't keep his commitments.

- **POINT #4:** Just as Garrett learned in Kokoro, there are two key statements to remember in order to get shit done: 1- Details matter and 2- Time constraints get shit done.

# WARRIOR WITNESS

## C.T., Louisiana:

*"The idea of choosing to shift something that is in the 'Important but Not Urgent' quadrant to 'Important and Urgent' quadrant by adding the completion date is so helpful when thinking about being in control of my own life and on purpose with my business activities. In addition, tactically blocking time and training my peers, staff, and family to respect that intentionality sets me up to succeed. I wouldn't be living by the Code if I didn't say it feels a bit overwhelming when I think about putting into practice today, but I trust the testing that has happened before me by the other Brothers in The Game."*

# THE KEYS

## Chapter 31: HOW

The reason we have How at the end is because the How is where
we tend to defeat ourselves. Guys will go to How way too quickly
otherwise.

# THE KEYS

## CHAPTER THIRTY-ONE
# HOW

"When you bring your full attention to each moment, a day is a complete lifetime of living and learning."

**-Mark Divine**
(excerpt from The Way of the Seal: Think Like an Elite Warrior to Lead and Succeed)

---

1. Now that we know what we want, why we want it and when we plan on getting it done, we come to the final question to ask ourselves when using the Keys: How are you going to do it? How are you going to pull it off? How are you going to make it happen? The crazy part about most business guys that I meet is this: "How" is the question that everybody wants to go to first. The minute they say the What, they want to go to the How. They say, "Well, how are we going to pull that off?" before taking the time to consider the Why and the When.

## How to Defeat Ourselves

2. The reason we have How at the end is because the How is where we tend to defeat ourselves.[101] If you go to "How am I going to pull this off right now?" at the beginning, then you don't have sufficient leverage nor have you given yourself time-constraints to pull it off. We rise to meet the constraints given to us.

3. See, it didn't work that way inside of Kokoro. They didn't tell us, "Hey, listen. Here's what we're going to have you do. When do you guys think

---

[101] Guys will go to How way too quickly otherwise.

you can have it done? How about you tell us?" It didn't work out that way, because we'd have been big fucking pussies about it. "Well, it's going to take me six months."

4. It worked the other way. They said, "Here's when this is going to be done. 3, 2, 1, go." What?! They would actually tell us beforehand. You have five minutes to pull this off. As a boat crew, you have five minutes. Here are the actions you'll be taking, and *then* they would tell us the How.

## Understanding Sufficient Leverage

5. In the beginning, you might ask, "Why put How off until the end?" and then think "That is all backwards." It's not backwards. Inside the military, they understand a thing that a lot of civilians don't: if you do not understand sufficient leverage on a man, the How will always be impossible, insurmountable, and too big. That 16-foot domino? It's too big; too much. I don't know how to do it. See, without sufficient leverage, you don't even have the mindset to even step into a problem and know where the gap between you are today and where you want to be tomorrow resides. You don't know how much intensity to attack or how to solve it. Ultimately, it's about giving yourself permission to go figure out and find the solution.

6. There are countless numbers of Empires that have never been because men paralyzed themselves over not knowing How because they turned to it too soon. They went to How before they were ever super clear about the What. They said, "Well, here's what I think I want to do, but How am I going to pull it off, Garrett?"

7. "Are you kidding me? Are you fucking kidding me?! What's wrong with you? Deal with the shit in front of you first; figure out why you're doing something before you worry about how you're going to get it done."

## Creating A Clear Action Plan Format

8. When we're clear about our What, we've been able to access the Power of the Fire of the Why, which then links up to When. These times constraints based upon the time that was available gives us the dates and times, specifically, for when we're going to have this shit done. Only then do we enter into the conversation of How, because there's a gap between

where I am and this outcome that I need, want, desire and am committed to pulling off this week with an actual action plan.

-What is the one action that I would need to take in order to accomplish this outcome?
-Why is it significant?
-When will I get it done?
-How will I know that it's done?

9. What, Why, When and How, in that order, to figure out the actual action plan with each Key 4 Outcome.

10. So here we are back again with the simplicity of asking the same kinds of questions clearly stated above, only we're going to deep dive into one area within that outcome:

What are the specific actions that I need to take in connection and relation to this one outcome that I'm moving into?

What is the ONE Action I need to take?

What is the ONE thing that must be done in order to pull that off this week?

What else needs to be done when I accomplish that?

11. And all of a sudden, without having to go down some monstrous path of creating from nothing, I now have an Action Plan. I have a sequence of actions that needs to be taken in relationship to the Outcome that we know must happen in order to move the needle forward towards our 90-Day Outcome benchmarks, and push our Business forward, bringing the *non-urgent, but very important* and the *urgent, important* items to the front of our Game, putting constraints on them, and making them happen.

## Pulling from the Closet of Resources

12. Think of each Action as a shelf in a closet titled *Key 4 Outcomes*. On that Action Shelf are boxes filled with files of Resources to access within that Action. As you go to access them, you can easily see the specific Resources needed or maybe what you don't have yet. It could be a skill set you don't have, so you'll need to pull out the file marked with the team member that has that skill set and bring them into the Outcome. Or maybe it's a consultant that needs to be hired or contractor to bring in as part of the

team. Each of these Resources then becomes another section on your Action Shelf as you continue to go through your Key 4 Outcomes.

13. If you keep these shelves organized with the Action Plan format: What, Why, When, How, you will have clearly marked mini Black Boxes within the Black Box portal. The door to your closet of Key 4 Outcomes can be easily opened at any time in your castle created within your Kingdom of having it all.

14. Bam, bam, bam, our list starts to build, this map begins to unfold, and inside the systems within this Brotherhood, we begin to build out this Game every single week. The map begins to unfold as we look simply at the One Thing inside each one of these Outcomes. Where do we store these maps? In our War Room which has a closet of Key 4 Outcomes. Where do we use these maps? In the General's Tent.

## When the Boxes Touch

15. Now, I'm going to take us on a side conversation for a second, because inside of this metaphorical closet there are going to be times where your boxes may touch. Maybe you forget to put How at the bottom of What, Why, When, How. Sometimes the closet may not remain organized after you forget to put the lids back on your Key 4 Outcomes. Maybe you have a stack of files to be put away and you just haven't gotten to them yet. You have team members with multiple skill sets needed to help you accomplish your Outcomes, but you forgot to make copies of their files or misplaced which box you put those Resources in. You're like, "I'm not even sure what I need to do next or who I put in charge of what because I forgot to write it down. Once I've accomplished this I need to fix that, so maybe I should start making copies and putting some files into another box."

## Capital Idea

16. In order to pull off this whole conversation of keeping the How organized, you're going to need capital. I'm not specifically referencing to just financial capital; capital across the board.[102]

---

[102] This concept was first introduced to me by one of my buddies and old business and strategic partner, Garrett B Gunderson. See Additional Resources in regards to Business Tools at the end of this chapter for more.

17. Here are the capitals that exist:

Mental
Social
Financial
X Factor

## Mental Capital: All The Knowledge You Need Is Inside

18. Our mental capital is our knowledge, wisdom, and insights inside of us. It's saying, "Just do it. Here is the knowledge that I come to the table with. I may just need cash in the form of my own capital to complete my Actions and Outcomes. I already know everything I need to know to pull this off, so all I really need to do is get committed, get it on the sheet, and do it. That's all."

Okay, cool. No problem. I have all the knowledge that I need.

19. Or maybe I need to increase my mental capital. Like in my mind, I don't know how to pull off my Outcome with my current cash flow. It might mean that I've got to hire someone to come in and help me, study something, read a book, attend a webinar, or watch a training video. I've got to borrow the mental capital from someone else in order to pull it off.

## Social Capital: Letting Others Know What You Know

20. There are fundamental ways inside social capital when it comes to pulling things off such as "It's who you know, but more importantly, it's who knows you." You can know a shitload of people, but if they don't know you or what skillsets you provide, you're not going to receive the outcome you desire.

21. This happens in business a lot where people try to pull things off in their own business, but they haven't given a shit about others for years, and then all of a sudden, out of nowhere, they show up with this *not important, but urgent* emergency inside the time matrix with me.

21. "Garrett, I'm doing a launch and I need help with this."

22. "Dude, you forgot about me for two years. I'm sorry, but you do not have any capital with me inside this relationship. Like, your urgent issue is not urgent to me. I don't even know you."

23. I'll get people to reach out to me, too, and I don't even know them. They know me, but I don't know who they are, and so they think that somehow, inside of that, I'm going to support them, but I'm not. I don't even know who they are.

24. When I want to get stuff done, it's who knows me. Who do I have credit with? Who have I deposited value to in their life? Who knows me? Your Empires are built based upon who knows you, not based upon who you know. We can know a lot of people, but our goal ultimately comes to creating so much value in the marketplace that a lot of people know who we are. We create bank accounts with full balances, emotionally, inside our social networks.

## Financial Capital: Hunting
## The Deer and Buffalo

25. Financial capital is very simple: it's cash, credit, and/or the ability to create cash. Some of these bigger actions we want to take moving into our 30-day, 60-day, and 90-day benchmarks, are going to need funding, so I have to find cash. Or, we might have it already, therefore we just need to strategically implement it. We might have credit, so we could use that. Or we might have to go hunt the deer to bring home the meat in order to have the revenue we need to then go hunt the buffalo. When we sit back and say, "I want to hunt the buffalo," you're like, "Well, you don't have a big enough gun to hunt the buffalo. You don't live close enough to the buffalo to hunt them. Go get some deer first."

26. So you hunt the deer until you can get to the buffalo. Sometimes, the capital that we're looking for inside the financial quadrant is something we can just create. We can sell some more products from where we are in order to create the revenue necessary (even that week) to pull off the action that we're moving towards.

# X Factor Capital: Your Unique Ability

27. What is your Unique Selling Proposition in the form of You? As a college and professional football player, as an athlete, and also as a businessman, for years I didn't understand my X Factor.[103] I just assumed, well, you know, it was what it was, but it was a reason why I was always the Captain of my team and leader in my businesses. My X Factor, not my Mental, Social or Financial capital, was the reason why I was building and people wanted to partner with me.

28. You have an X Factor inside of you also. This is a unique skill set that sets you apart from others. Your X Factor will allow you to get into these other networks and tap into these other three forms of capital. Part of the process of being able to pull this off is also learning to lean on your own X Factor[104]. To pull off what I'm doing in over 15 to 20 hours is pure X Factor for me. The fact that I can stand, look at a camera, talk into a microphone without a live audience and throw down this doctrine to you is tapping my mental, social, and financial capital, but the true Power Play is my X Factor. It's the ability for me to do on demand in a studio, here at the Warrior HQ, what most people can't do in front of a live audience of 500 with all that energy coming back at them.

29. Ninety-nine out of 100 entrepreneurs cannot pull this shit off, and they definitely can't pull it off in a way that's clear and concise that people want to buy. So, I leverage my X Factor all the time. Recognizing my own X Factor allows me to recognize that we all have an X Factor, a superpower making us unique from everyone else.

30. So what is your X Factor? What is the capital that you're going to leverage inside that quadrant to get your Outcome done? I can pull some things off with my Key 4 that other people cannot, and other people can pull off actions inside their Key 4 that I cannot because it's their unique superpower: their X Factor.

---

[103] My X Factor is my Passion: it's my fire for what I did, showing up in a room that was not comparable to a lot of other people. It is my unique skillset.

[104] Even while putting together this Black Box, there's an X Factor Capital inside of this for me: I recorded all that you are reading by speaking into a microphone without a script, sent the recordings off to transcriptionists, and then had it put into book form.

## How = Action Plan

31. "How" is the step-by-step actions within your Key 4 Box of questions:

What is the one thing/action that must happen in order to hit this Key 4 outcome for the week?

What is the next action that must happen?

What is the one thing that must happen when that one's fulfilled?

What is the one thing that must happen when the first two are done?

32. You go through this list until you've exhausted the actions that need to happen, whether it's 3, 5, or 10. When you need to ask which resource you need to accomplish your Key 4, you go to your closet and pull out your box of materials. Keeping them organized within their own Box inside the Key 4 Outcome closet will lead to success within the Warrior Movement of the Brotherhood of having it all.

33. Are there Resources in the form of Mental, Social, Financial, and your X Factor Capital? Do you have clearly marked relationships to help you or let others know what skill sets you have of your own? Is there anyone you need to pull or enroll in to help with your project?

## Creating A Masterpiece

34. By the time I'm done organizing this closet by answering the questions above, I can take it to the General's Tent where the What, Why, When and How become a fucking masterpiece. I have blueprints for an insane execution inside of my Business every single week, with all of the power that I have found through Core 4, maintaining the Code so that it does not all go to waste. Doing all of this, I don't fall victim to the Chaos of Abundance with all this increased power and burn myself to the ground. I can actually create more shit in a seven-day time period that is significant for my business moving forward than I did in the previous six months.

## Chapter 31:
## POINTS TO PONDER FROM THE GENERAL'S TENT

- **POINT #1:** The reason we have How at the end of the 'What? Why? When? How?' format in the Keys is because the How is where we tend to defeat ourselves. Asking "How?" at the end allows us to have an Action Plan without having to go down some monstrous path of creating from nothing.

- **POINT #2:** We have a sequence of actions that need to be taken in relationship to the Outcome that we know must happen in order to push our Business forward with its 90-Day Outcomes through our four Key targets. Keeping them organized is crucial.

- **POINT #3:** In order to utilize social capital to help you hit your Key 4, "It›s who you know, but more importantly, it›s who knows you." You can know a shitload of people, but if they don›t know you or what skillsets you provide, you're not going to succeed. When I want to get stuff done, it›s who knows me.

- **POINT #4:** Recognize that we all have an X Factor: something we are uniquely good at. Part of being able to pull off you Key 4 is by utilizing your X Factor and utilizing the X Factor in others.

# THE KEYS

## Chapter 32: SUMMARY

At the end of the day, The Keys are literally keys used to access
your kingdom. They are a resource that will fund the lifestyle and
significance to the "have it all" conversation.

SECTION FIVE
# THE KEYS

CHAPTER THIRTY-TWO
# SUMMARY

*"No one is free who has not obtained the empire of himself."*

**-Pythagoras**
[Ancient Greek philosopher and considered to be the first pure mathematician, (circa 570 BCE-490 BCE)]

---

1. We spent the last couple of chapters going through the Key 4 Actions we need to do every single week. We talked through this Game of Power inside the Code and Core, learning how we access power inside each one of us which expands on a daily basis. "I choose to live by the Code in which the truth will set me free." This fucking line actually matters. Inside of that I have a Foundation, upon which I take the Core and every single morning "I hit my 4 before I hit the door so that I can go to war."

## Learning to Deal with The Chaos of Abundance

2. We discussed in this training the Chaos of Abundance which is infinite possibility that will fall upon a man who chooses to live by the Code and stands for the Core. All of a sudden, on a day-to-day or week-to-week basis, there are options that you never had available to you before to produce results that you never even imagined were possible, to solve problems that you weren't good enough to solve a few months or even two weeks ago.

3. This creates a problem, but we also have the solution:the Chaos of Abundance says that I must say "No" 9 times out of 10. There's a lot of shit going on inside this time matrix that Stephen Covey taught us about from *7 Habits of Highly Effective People*; there are a lot of actions that we

could take. Some of those actions end up in the *not important* and *not urgent* category. This is a disastrous place to spend any time, so we say, "Fuck you. See you later."

## Creating Our Keys

4. Then we have this other area: *not important but urgent* where the agendas of the world begin to put their agendas on us. People inside and out of organizations say, "This is what I need done." But here at Warrior we say, "We don't need this done. Your agenda and your urgency does not make it an urgency for me." No, we take a higher road. Because we're not only living by the Code, we're creating with it by standing for the Core.

5. When it comes to creating with our Keys, we can do it from one of two places: *what is important and urgent* and from the areas of *what is important but not urgent.* We said that our goal is to push all of the Actions we set at a weekly basis onto our Key 4 to eventually become part of the *not urgent but very important* category; the area that doesn't need to happen today. We do this so that we can continue to build an empire that is driven upon our desires, not based upon the conditions of the marketplace or what other people say we should be doing, but based upon what we want to be doing.

## What, Why, When, How

6. As we choose from that quadrant, we ask a series of questions in a specific order:

7. What: "What is it? What is the one thing that must happen this week?"

8. Why: We access the fuel around the conversation of this specific thing that we're going to do. We say, "Well, why must this happen? Why must this be something that I do? Why am I getting leverage on myself to pull it off?"

9. When: We take that *why* and we put on time constraints. We take what started, possibly as a *not urgent but very important* action, and we slide it to the left and we create urgency around it by putting time constraints on ourselves to produce the Outcome. We say, "I'm going to do this by this date at this time." That time constraint, along with the fire of the *why*, connected to the clear *what* that I'm doing that is measured up against my 90, 60 and 30-day benchmarks.

10. How: This game itself now has prepared me to answer the final question: "How am I going to pull this off?" Inside of those Key 4 boxes I have created, I select the one thing that I'm doing inside the first Key. I then ask myself the question again, "What's the one Action that I have to take first in order to pull that off?" Then I go down and I build out my Action List and deep dive into what has been placed on the shelves of my Key 4 closet, which are the Resources that I need. Who are the people that I need access to? What are the skill sets and capitals needed to pull it off? My Capitals are: mental, social, financial and my X factor.

## Accessing The Keys to Your Kingdom

11. At the end of the day, The Keys are *literally* the keys to accessing your kingdom. Whether we look at it from any other direction, the reality of this exists. Your life and your ability to have it all comes down to your capacity to maintain and to build a business that matters to you, while at the same time, you sustain a business that provides for you. It is damn near impossible to have it all if you are struggling financially for long periods of time; the stress and the strain is too much. The pressure on the side of relationships is too intense. It will end up destroying your intent and your desire to have it all.

12. The reason this happens for men who join this Brotherhood at this time is because they access all of this increased power inside of the Code which then leads to an increase of Power inside of the Core. But when it comes to the Keys, it doesn't operate with clarity or simplicity; it requires insanity and complexity. Inside the complexity and insanity rises frustration that says, "I must work harder." Yet, inevitably I find myself in the wrong areas of the quadrant building something that doesn't matter to me, nor will it last as I ultimately find myself burned out or bored, which ultimately leads to burning everything to the ground.

## Create Success in Business
## or Everything Will Fall

13. The Keys are significant. The Keys unlock the gateway to the Kingdom. The Keys are a resource that will fund the lifestyle and significance to the "have it all" conversation. Without the success in your business you're not having it all; instead, everything will fall. We bring everything along at

the same time. When it comes to living with the Keys, we operate like a sniper. We spend the time to plan every single week in the General's Tent to make sure that the shit we're doing this week actually matters. I haven't gotten swept up in a Storm of Activity; I've actually whipped myself up into a Focus of Productivity.

## Chapter 32:
## POINTS TO PONDER FROM THE GENERAL'S TENT

- **POINT #1:** When dealing with the Chaos of Abundance, the Code and Core get us from the area of not important but urgent where the agendas of the world are placed on us to what is important and urgent and important but not urgent.

- **POINT #2:** Asking from the format "What? Why? When? How?" from what is important to us gives us a layout within the Keys to be successful with our Business Outcomes.

- **POINT #3:** The Keys are literally a way to access your Kingdom. Your life and your ability to have it all comes down to your capacity to maintain and to build a business that matters to you, while at the same time, you sustain a business that provides for you.

- **POINT #4:** The Keys are a resource that will fund the lifestyle and significance to the "have it all" conversation by using a sniper mentality to zero in on Business targets.

# THE GAME

## Chapter 33: OVERVIEW

The Game of Life is to create Impossible Games that matter to you. In everything that you've learned, all that I've taught, and everything that I've guided you through, none of it actually matters without the Frame of the Game.

# SECTION SIX
# THE GAME

## CHAPTER THIRTY-THREE
# OVERVIEW

"Each player must accept the cards life deals him or her: but once they are in hand, he or she alone must decide how to play the cards in order to win the game."

**-Voltaire**
[French Enlightenment Philosopher,
Historian and Author, 1694-1778]

---

1. We have become a society of individuals who no longer compete, but that doesn't mean that we don't have the drive to win within us; it's just become so heavily sedated we seem to have forgotten. Most individuals today don't wake up with the sense of competition and expansion of becoming great.

## Reclaiming the Drive to Win

2. They don't have an idea of what it is to win anymore, nor do they even have a drive to win. We will never develop a desire to win if we don't know how it feels to be a winner. We look at youth sports today in the United States, and it's become a joke; a celebration of mediocrity where "Participation Awards" are handed out just for showing up in place of medals that rank 1st and 2nd place and so on.

3. We've become a society of people who say, "If you put in your time and effort, you are entitled to a result, and that somehow if you just show up physically, with no clarity, you should get an award; a trophy for living. This shifts the foundation established on lessons learned from competition to one of entitlement: I am here. Now reward me simply for that, without

having to do anything else. Nothing separates me from anyone else, so therefore, I'm entitled to everything."

## Reestablishing Healthy Competition

4. Here inside Warrior, we say, "Fuck entitlement. That's not our strategy." We realize that the Game itself pays to win. Winners walk the Game of Life. The greatest leaders we've ever known played from a Game of Competition.

5. Competition was never the problem; it's healthy to learn to metrically record who you are today versus who you are two months from now. This is important. Everything that operates inside Warrior is built from the Game of The Code, The Core, and The Keys. All of this wraps up into the conversation of the Game.

## Online Gaming: Fantasy Avoidance Sedation

6. Now, Gaming has become very popular, especially online. A lot of people live in the fantasy land of Gaming.[105] It's actually been projected that an average teenager will have played over 10,000 hours of video games before he hits the age of 20.

7. Gaming is no longer something we can avoid, but the crazy part about it is that gamification has become nothing more than Fantasy Avoidance Sedation. While we do physical things out in life, we feel entitled to results, but inside the gaming world there is no entitlement to anything. We must level up in order to win. There was a winner. There was a loser. There are levels that are passed, but like most of what we experience day-to-day, we have begun to worship the fantasy of expansion versus the reality of results. The fantasy of possible results versus the reality of results. For example, pornography creates a barrier to avoid the one woman in our life who could actually deliver the reality of the fantasy that we worship virtually.

## The Reality of Core 4

8. Body, Being, Balance and Business are all games within the Core 4, my friend. The metrics that we use and the way we play the game inside of Warrior is not a game of fantasy. It is a way to measure reality of who you've

---

[105] They game online with World of Warcraft, Candy Crush and Farmville, millions of user spending thousands of hours playing games.

been and who you are to become. Not with an opinion about who you've been or have become, but a practical, pragmatic, and metric-based way of knowing that you have become more, so therefore you can do more, and suck significantly less. Hence, you actually produce a life that is significantly better than what you had before.

9. Otherwise, everything else that we taught here doesn't stand for anything. It's just another random series of tools that you can put in your tool belt as you randomly wander around with no clarity and receive participation medals by saying you hit your Core 4.

10. Who gives a shit if you got a 4 in your Core 4 if we don't know what the Game is you're trying to win? This section is meant to set the frame down and walk you through the step by step process of your role in how and why we play the Game the way we play it.

## Scoring the Game to Win

11. In order to do this, we've got to understand scoring, otherwise the games don't matter. You see this with kids; they're not interested for very long if they can't win. I saw this while playing wall ball with Bailee when she was eight; if we didn't gain a point every time we hit the ball where the first one to a certain number wins, she would soon lose interest and go find something else to do in which she knew she could win or lose. This is a reality in our lives. If you have lost the ability to know how to track the score or what it even is, you will never know how to improve the score for the win or the loss, and your interest in that experience will diminish.

12. If I don't know how to talk about my marriage, how would I ever know how to score it? Am I winning or losing? I don't know. I have no idea if I'm winning, because I don't have any metric put into place to gauge things. The same goes for my spirituality in Being.

13. "Well, I'm feeling like things are better." Fuck how you're feeling; if you can't metrically prove that you've improved, it doesn't matter. Same thing in your marriage and your relationship with your children, or inside your Body and Business. We've got to be able to score, but we've got to keep it simple otherwise it becomes too intense, so we get overwhelmed and give up. We easily see that in board games.

## Self-Governing Simple Scores

14. Our scoring has got to be simple enough that we can govern our own score. If your scoring mechanism at what you're creating in your world is too intense, complicated, confusing, and then administered to you, you will not experience the scoring system inside the Warrior's Way the same. You've got to self-administer and maintain the integrity needed to hold yourself accountable. Very similar to what you might experience in golf. Even at the professional level in golf, guess who keeps track of their score? The golfers. Tiger Woods tracks his own score; literally carries around his own score card. In The US Open, at all of The Masters Tournaments, he's walking around and he's doing what? He's tracking his score. Now, television might be displaying his scores and all these other people might be tracking, but the official score inside The US Open is when Tiger turns in a completed score sheet, and signs that sheet. Self-administered scoring.

## Create Dynamic Fluctuations

15. Your scoring mechanisms and the way that you score have got to be dynamic and have the ability to fluctuate with who you are becoming. The rules, systems for scoring, and ways that games were played when you were 8 are very different than when you are 28. We've got to have some ability to explain by allowing a little bit of flex inside of that as you begin to grow. It's one thing to play games, but it's another to create Impossible Games.

16. Over a decade ago, a mentor of mine was a gentleman who had been a Landmark Form Instructor for over 35 years. The man ran a 100-mile ultra-marathon at 68. 68! Three years prior to the ultra-marathon, he had never run further than two miles in one continuous run his entire life. Did not start running until he was in his 60s, then ran a 100 fucking mile ultra-marathon before he turned 70. People looked at that and asked, "Why do you play this game? Why do you do this?" It's because he had always been playing a Game that he operated from inside his entire life, which was transferred physically to running, and also to me. I was investing $1,000/ call for 45 minutes which gave me invaluable wisdom from his answers.

## "Create Impossible Games that Matter to You"

17. I was so fascinated with his *why* behind choosing to do the ultra-marathon. I'm like, "Dude, you're old. Why do this? What's the game?"

18. "The Game itself, the Game of Life, is to create impossible games that matter to you."

19. He continued describing to me what these impossible games were to create, which have become the way I live my life: An Impossible Game is a game that requires you to become fundamentally something different than you are today, in order to succeed and to win.

20. A Game is simply something you know you can win right now with the current mindsets, skill sets, capacities, resource, and networks of who you are today. There is a distinct difference between a Game we know we can win right now based on who we are without having to change, and the Game that we now call an Impossible Game.

## Become More. Do More. Suck Less

21. It is impossible, because who you are today is not big enough, sufficient enough as a man, to actually accomplish the game that you say you plan to accomplish. You are going to have to become more. You're going to have to do more, and you're going to have to suck less. In other words, succeed at a higher level than you currently are succeeding. Get out of your comfort zone, think outside of the box, whatever phrase you want to say, that anxiety, fear, and excitement around the conversation of an Impossible Game stretches our minds beyond the current constraints of limitation, and takes us to a place of possibility beyond our current reality and threshold.

22. Now, in the world of fitness, the human body experiences this lactic threshold inside of the way the body operates. Inside your body a clock will begin to countdown, and your mind is keeping track of this clock, which may be a few seconds or many hours.[106]

23. The clock begins regardless of how long it's ticking. Once that clock strikes zero, the body will then flush lactic acid into the bloodstream, which

---

[106] Unless you've trained yourself to operate beyond the threshold and ignore the clock.

will enter the muscles to follow our body's shut down protocol before it red lines. The crazy thing about lactic threshold though, is that it can be trained.

## Training the Threshold to Grow

24. I learned how to raise my threshold while training for the Ironman Championships in 2007, which would give me more capacity and power over longer periods of time. My coach had me do something that didn't make any sense to me:

25. "You're going to wear a heart rate monitor whenever you run during your training, and never go above 120 beats. The moment you hit higher than 120, you start walking."

26. Well, my heart rate at the beginning would jump clear up to 144 BPM, and I would have to stop and start walking, waiting for my heart rate to go down. It took me forever to finish 14 miles that first day and into weeks and weeks worth of training. I was basically walking that entire time, fairly slow to keep my beats per minute (BPM) at 120.

27. I was getting ridiculously frustrated with this experience of training my threshold to grow, but kept reminding myself the Simple Success Swinging Singles principle. I knew that something had to change, so I had to slow back down on my training. Over the next two months, my 12-minute mile went down to 10 minutes, then that became 8 minutes, then down to a 7-minute mile, all at 120 BPM. I could create more work at a faster pace with less intensity and pressure on my body because my heart had become trained to become more efficient; my muscles and my mind therefore became more efficient as a product of the result.

## Pushing The Lactic Threshold Beyond the Comfort Zone

28. Inside all of us is this lactic threshold. Now here's the crazy piece: to step past the threshold and become greater than our current capacity, we have to train one percent beyond the lactic threshold mark we are currently at. You have to train outside of your comfort zone as your mind tells you to stop.

29. My marriage, spirituality, and fatherhood was no different. Inside your world there is a current reality of comfort. Once we become vulnerable and cross the threshold that was comfortable in our Core 4, we want to shut down. The only way to get a different result that is radically different than

where we are right now is to create Impossible Games that require us to stretch and become more than who we were before we started.

## Expand Every Quarter

30. Our entire mechanism with the Impossible Game inside of Warrior is that every single quarter within the Brotherhood we stand for one thing, which is: "I will expand every quarter, across Body, Being, Balance, and Business. I will set a deliberate target on these four areas of my Core 4. I will create a deliberately impossible game that will require me to become *more* in my Body, Being, Balance, and Business in order to accomplish playing the Impossible Game.

## Born Again Every 90 Days

31. Every 90 days we are becoming born again into a new reality and version of who we are. The entire Game is metric-based. We can track, measure, build, and grow with it. The measurements that we're making are not about you in relationship to your neighbor or someone you see on TV, me, or your Brother. The measurements are about *you* in relationship to *you*.

32. Before we start the Game, there is the current reality/performance of who we are now, which will be measured against past performance and the gap between that for where we are desiring to go. We will measure these three points:

1. Past Performance and Reality
2. Present Performance and Reality
3. Possible Performance and Future Reality

33. My past becomes the pendulum that supports me in growing: where I am presently could not have been possible without my past performance; giving me learning, wisdom, and the ability to grow. With that learning, we bridge the gap from our current performance or present reality towards possible performance or future reality. We use the past as a governing force for learning to say, "Here are the adjustments and changes I must make in order to move to this future target."

34. In both of these environments, we are tracking and measuring, with accuracy to predict the possibility of where we are going to be tomorrow based upon numbers that actually matter to you and me. With these

numbers in general format, you and I will be able to score our daily, weekly, monthly, and quarterly games that we play on a day-to-day, week to week, month to month, and quarterly basis.

## Meaning of Life

35. This is why when people say, "Garrett what is the meaning of life to you?"

36. I answer: "It's to expand by playing the game."

37. What is the Game? It's the literal Game of Life, and inside this Brotherhood it is the Game of Life across the Core 4, which we take very seriously.

## Chapter 33:
### POINTS TO PONDER FROM THE GENERAL'S TENT

- **POINT #1:** In everything that you've learned, all that I've taught, and everything that I've guided you through, none of it actually matters without the Frame of the Game. We need to produce a life that is significantly better than what you had before.

- **POINT #2:** We have become a society of entitled pricks that need to bring the competitive drive back that is innately in all of us. Tracking a score helps us to metrically see how to improve the score for the win, otherwise your interest in that experience will diminish.

- **POINT #3:** The Game of Life is to create impossible games that matter to you, which requires you to become fundamentally something different than you are today, in order to succeed and to win. Do more. Be more, suck less.

- **POINT #4:** There is the current reality/performance of who we are now, which is measured against past performances and the gap between that and where we are desiring to go.

# WARRIOR WITNESS:

## J.E. Illinois, USA:

*"Garrett said 'Impossible Game is a game that requires you to become FUNDAMENTALLY something different than you are today in order to succeed & win! In order to do this you are going to have to become more, do more and suck less...' That is why I am here. Expansion and Growth through pain in order to succeed. Every day is training day, time for me to get training."*

# THE GAME

## Chapter 34: THE QUARTERLY GAME

This entire chapter is going to start with getting very, very clear about the Targets inside of the Impossible Game.We can't begin the journey of the 90-day game until we're actually clear about what the finish line looks like.

SECTION SIX

# THE GAME

CHAPTER THIRTY-FOUR

# THE QUARTERLY GAME

*"We all need people who will give us feedback.
That's how we improve."*

**-Bill Gates**

---

1. What is the win? Inside of the 90-Day Game, we had a series of small wins. Small skirmishes, battles, if you will, that ultimately would win the war. We have to see, what is the ultimate outcome of the war?

## Targets: The Ultimate War Outcome

2. Most people, when you ask them, "What do you want?" couldn't tell you because they don't know. They're clear about what they don't want, but those are negatively driven outcomes. An Impossible Game is *not* about something that you don't want to happen in your life anymore. We're going to create clear targets, *not* goals.

3. In a meaningful, specific way, we're saying, "There is a target. I am a sniper. I am hunting this bastard, and I am going to get him." We will know when a target has been met within our Core 4 because we've played the Game.

4. Inside the General's Tent, we write our targets down, talk about it with others then receive feedback on any course corrections we need to make or affirmation that we're on point.

## Feedback About Feedback

5. Feedback is an interesting conversation. What is feedback? Feedback is information. Now, you're going to receive a lot of initial feedback inside the Game, and some of it is going to come from yourself. Maybe it's, "Oh God, that's horse shit." Or, after you write it down, you're going to be a little scared, "Ah. That's really intense. That's going to require me to change a lot." It might even be a little nerve wracking to actually be honest and write it down. This is why the foundation of the Impossible Game is living by the Code. If you fucking lie, then guess what? The game that you play is a fantasy.

6. If you tell the truth and live by the Code, you write down what you truly want. A lot of men will lie about this. They'll write it down but after they get internal feedback, they start to tell themselves a story that the task is behemoth and they aren't able to pull it off. They self-sabotage away their greatness.

7. Sometimes we reject the feedback because it's so different from what we initially were thinking. I'm going to have you consider that sometimes it helps to have somebody who's not in the Game with us to provide that different perspective. They don't have the stories of the Game like we have, so sometimes they'll see it a little clearer.

8. That's how I operated with my wife. In the beginning stage of our marriage, I created a massive problem. We'd been married less than 19 months and I was a mortgage banker broker. We were living in Las Vegas at the time and were out on a walk in the park, my wife and I and our dogs.[107] I was having some problems with my teams, so she was giving me some feedback about the business. My wife is a hairstylist. I said something that was likely one of the most ridiculous statements I've ever made to my wife which cost me for a decade due to the massive ripple effect of the words I used. Here's how it went:

9. "What do you know about business? You're a fucking hairstylist. The next time I need your opinion about business, I'll tell you. Until then, shut your goddamn mouth."

---

[107] We didn't have kids at the time.

10. Yeah, for the first two years of marriage my wife would say, "You're a dickhead. And just so you know, fuck off. I'm going to spend your money and I'm going to likely leave you, you dumbass."

11. That was how I dealt with feedback from my wife when it came to my business before my journey to what Warrior is now. Recently, upon editing this book, my wife gave me feedback about my business again. I didn't get riled up while standing there washing dishes. She gave me feedback; I accepted it. I received it. I didn't do anything to it. I didn't reject it, I was just like, "Okay." I just received it. Now, there are some people's feedback that you should reject immediately, which I'll explain in a moment why knowing the difference between the two is so important.

12. Sometimes you'll deflect the feedback. This means that they'll send it to you and you'll go, "Ah, it's about you, it's not about me." You don't receive it. Or you'll distort the feedback, taking it then shifting the message from what it initially was.

13. When it comes to our Outcomes, we're wanting to *receive*, not reject, deflect or distort. We want to receive the feedback, especially by the people we trust: our Brother within Warrior, mentors, accountability partners, wife, etc… These individuals want what's best for you. Here's a little checklist:

### Approved Checklist of Feedback Personnel:
1. My Queen and Children
2. Parents and Siblings
3. People That You Pay for Advice
4. People Who Pay You for Advice

## My Queen and Children

14. If you are my Queen or my children, you have earned the right to have an opinion and to give me feedback, which means I'm not going to reject, distort, or reflect it; I'm simply going to receive it so you could give it to me full force because the Queen's opinion matters.

## Parents and Siblings

15. This second group of people consist of the people who brought you into this world and grew up with you. They have the right to have an opinion. Now, this doesn't mean you have to accept that what they're saying is true

for you, nor is that the case from your wife; it just means they get a free pass to tell you how they're feeling.

## People That You Pay for Advice

16. The individuals inside the Brotherhood fit into this group. It consists of those who are saying, "Hey, here's my coach, my mentor, my accountability partner. I pay these individuals, hence they have the right to give me some feedback about my Outcomes, and where I'm trying to go with my life; the problems I might be facing, and the targets I'm chasing."

## People Who Pay You for Advice

17. Last group consists of the people who pay you. Hence your clients, students, and people that work and pay you to receive a product, service or an experience. They're entitled to an opinion too.

## Circle of Influence

18. So, we have these four groups, but if anyone else wants to give you feedback, yet they're not in any of those groups, tell them to "Fuck off." We get feedback from those who are actually in our circle of influence.

19. Going back to the feedback discussion I was having with my wife while washing dishes, I was receiving it but not really taking anything from it. That is, until I gave her another piece of information. Her feedback radically changed. She understood where I was and we got on the same page. She added a piece that I had not considered which had a very valid point. My 90-day Outcome shifted one degree because of feedback from the queen, which in turn changed the whole overall trajectory.

20. Our targets have got to be written down so that when we get some feedback about them we can document it before we just start running. Sometimes, our own perspective in playing the Impossible Game distorts and/or is beyond our current reality. We are going to need some guidance and some assistance to refine it as we get clearer, focusing it down with the new, valued insight instead of if we were just creating it on our own.

## Framing the Target Positively

21. We're not creating negatively driven Outcomes, so we need to make sure that we frame the target positively. Meaning, we shift from focusing on what *can't* be done as we try to eliminate something, and instead focus on what we *can* do as we focus on adding something. Rather than saying, "I'm going to stop drinking alcohol," we say, "I'm going to add a green smoothie" to our 90-day outcome. We play the Impossible Game by addition, not subtraction.

22. We have tested this over and over again; if you try to create Outcomes driven by negative tensions and negative elimination strategies, your Game will not work. It's not inspiring to eliminate shit, and the concept of subtraction leaves us in want. It's inspiring to create new shit, to obtain new things. The crazy part is, a six pack actually becomes the result of a fitness challenge that I'm working towards vs stating, "Hey, I don't want to be fat anymore." That's very different. The fruit of losing the weight becomes the consequence of the challenge that I'm moving towards that becomes easily measurable.

## Visibly Checking Off the Box

23. Not only must our Target be framed in the positive, but it needs to be able to have a box that says, "Yes, I did it." Or, "No, I did not." This cannot be open for opinion: Yes or No. We don't do Maybe's in Warrior.

24. Make sure your checklist is visible; none of this mental list shit. What I mean by that is, we've got to create it as a visually-enticing Outcome. We've got to be able to paint it in a way that our mind plays into the visionary side of this.

## Make a Deadline

25. It's obvious that we'll need a deadline. If I've gotten the picture in my mind with this clear feedback on it, and I know it's measurable because I can check yes or no, then there has to be a specific deadline, which means I need a date to have the Outcome done.

## Being Realistic About the Impossible

26. There is the "several steps beyond your reality" kind of Impossible, and then there is just "completely impossible" impossibility. If you're a businessman that's worked for the past 10 years to create a revenue for $500,000 a year, but then set a 90-day Target to produce $1 million, that falls in the "completely impossible" category, you dumbass.

27. When we play these games, we're playing them every 90 days with a four-week transition until the next 90-day Outcome, and so on. This means we've got to play just beyond what is rational to our minds, yet still within the reality of saying, "Listen, I could fundamentally get there even though I know I'm going to have to change." It can be so far away that in and of itself there is a sense of impossibility created to us that is suffocating. For example, maybe your wife is sleeping in a different bedroom than you, and you two haven't had sex for nine months. You set a 90-Day Target for your wife and you to be having sex twice a day. At the end of 90 days, you will have had sex 180 times and are sleeping in the same bed.

28. Sounds awesome, but dude, you have not had sex with your wife for six to nine months, and she sleeps in a different bedroom. I appreciate your Impossible Game desires, but there is realistic, and then there is, "What the fuck are you talking about?" We've got to make it an impossible yet achievable gain that we can taste.

29. Maybe if a Brother said, "Well, I'm in a serious relationship, I'm only dating this one woman and in 90 Days I want to get engaged." Okay, cool. Now we can have some conversation here. This is the point of feedback from the Brotherhood, using all of the forms and resources we're going to give you inside the Armory to help you walk through and create specific outcomes for each one of these areas of Body, Being, Balance, and Business.

## BODY 90-Day Outcome

30. Body must have a competitive Outcome; it must be something that you are doing that will stretch you competitively. We have found complete failure in focusing on fat loss and body fat percentage, so we must push to an Outcome that is competitive in nature which allows us to know that we accomplished it with a "Yes" or "No" outcome, using weight loss as a positive consequence of that behavior. We have men who have done Iron Man, fought, signed up

for CrossFit competitions, 15Ks, swimming and surfing competitions. It doesn't really matter, but there has to be some kind of an Outcome that is competition-based in nature that would get you nervous about the work that needs to be done daily to pull that off.

## BEING 90-Day Outcome

31. Where Body is easy to measure, Being becomes tough. How do you set a target that is measurable specifically with Being? It's difficult to track, "Did you become more conscious? Did you become more present? Did you become more purpose driven? Do you feel like your relationship with God is closer?" How do you track any of that?

32. There has to be a way to measure it. We've had guys who have led and launched meditation retreats who have never meditated before. That's scary shit! You're like, "Dude I'm going to put 10 people in the room and teach them how to meditate for two days, but right now I don't even know how to meditate myself; I've only done it twice!" Well, guess what? You're going to have to become a different kind of man to lead a meditation retreat.

33. We've got individuals who have decided to get in or out of certain religions. They're like, "Over the next 90 days I'm going all in with my church, and I'm going to make a decision at the end of 90 days, 'I'm in or I'm out with this church.'" We've got individuals who want to investigate different religious belief systems. They're like, "Listen, I'm going to go investigate this church for 90 days, and at the end of 90 days I'm either in or I'm out. I'm either going to get baptized into this church or I'm not."

## BALANCE 90-Day Outcomes

34. There are two big aspects of Balance: your partner and your children. You're going to create one with your wife and one with your children, so you're running two different Outcomes at the same time. Two different Targets or Impossible Games inside the relationship factor; if it's too dictated upon another person's behavior, then you will fail.[108] This has got to be a challenge in which you are creating an Outcome that is driven by something you can control inside that relationship.

---

[108] The key quest inside Balance Outcomes is that you have got to be able to do something that you can control. Further examples are shown in the rest of the book.

# BUSINESS 90-Day Outcome

35. The Key point in Business really comes down to two target areas:

Money
Lifestyle

36. The money targets are going to be gross revenue, net revenue, and take home revenue over the next 90 days inside the Game.

37. As I move towards these Outcomes, Targets, and Impossible Games, I am also committing to building a kind of lifestyle where I'm not going to work on Friday or before 10:00 on weekdays. Or I'm not working on the weekends at all, or I'm going to hire these two new people, assistants, to support me so that I can hit these goals and at the same time not affect my family life. So, there's lifestyle and there's money.

## Becoming More Than Who We Are Today

38. These Impossible Games are going to require us to become more than who we are today. As we get clear on these targets, which will excite us to go to war, the rest of the Game that we're about to dive into supports us in pulling off the impossible.

### Chapter 34:
### POINTS TO PONDER FROM THE GENERAL'S TENT

- **POINT #1:** What do you want? Why does it matter? When are you going to get it done? How are you going to do it? We will know when a target has been met within our Core 4 because we've played the Game.

- **POINT #2:** The foundation of the Impossible Game is living by the Code, where feedback is an essential play by your Brothers. If you tell the truth and live by the Code, you write down what you truly want.

- **POINT #3:** It's important to learn where your feedback is coming from to help you decide whether or not to accept it or reject it. The key is whether or not the feedback is coming from your approved list of people within your Circle of Influence.

- **POINT #4:** When playing the Impossible Game, there's the "several steps beyond your reality" kind of Impossible, and then there is just "completely impossible" impossibility. Make sure you have some semblance of reality with your Target.

# THE GAME

## Chapter 35: THE MONTHLY BENCHMARKS

The monthly 30 and 60-Day Benchmarks support the Quarterly Gains.
They give a metrically based assessment on where we are and if we
need to course correct to reach our 90-Day Outcome.

# SECTION SIX
# THE GAME

## CHAPTER THIRTY-FIVE
# THE MONTHLY BENCHMARKS

*"Some men give up their designs when they have almost reached the goal; While others, on the contrary, obtain a victory by exerting, at the last moment, more vigorous efforts than ever before."*

**-Herodotus**
Ancient Greek Historian, considered the "Father of History"
(484 BCE-424 BCE)

---

1. My very first Ironman was scary as shit, and I probably did the entire race completely wrong.[109] But, I became addicted and hooked to the race even after the mistakes, participating in many Ironmans after that.[110]

## Life Lessons from Ironman World Championships, 2007

2. As I started to take the competitions more serious, I began to train my ass off and eventually ended up in the Ironman World Championships in 2007. Arriving in Kona, Hawaii my mind had been trained to operate with these games very differently.

3. We got there early in the morning, and I loved it because they stamped the numbers on my arms. I got my pack on, nervous and excited to be participating in something that I had only watched videos of, yet there I was in the middle of it all.

---

[109] It was the longest 13 hours and 59 minutes of my life.
[110] Like the Silverman in Las Vegas, which was considered at the time to be one of the hardest Ironmans in the world because of the ele

4. There's just so much energy at the World Championships; everybody in that water had earned the right to compete at the elite level they were at. We all had to train our asses off to be able to even get in the water, so there's almost this sense of relief that came when I got there because I thought back to the (literally) thousands of hours I'd ridden my bike, swam in a pool when nobody was awake, and ran my ass off through the night when everybody was sleeping, finally coming to a head amongst all of those other athletes. I knew that I had to show up that day to make shit happen.

5. So, I got my goggles and skinsuit[111] on and we went down to the sand, then began swimming out into the warm ocean to tread water out in the middle of the bay waiting for the start. I remember laying on my back, floating and looking up into the sky at these helicopters that were above, and it was so surreal for me because I'm like, "Shit, I have watched this on television, and now I'm in the show."

## Handle The Work in Front of You

6. As I was lying there, my coach's words came back into my mind: "Handle the work in front of you. Move buoy to buoy and benchmark to benchmark, and success will be yours. You've done the work." Good thing these words kept running through my mind, as you'll soon see.

7. Imagine 2,000 people packed in like sardines at the start, treading water[112] about 200 meters off the beach. There was a boat 1.2 miles out into the middle of the ocean that we had to swim out to, which from the beach can barely be seen, but once you're down in the water you can't see that shit at all. All I could see was the guy behind me, the gal to my left, the woman in front, and the dude behind; everything became tunnel vision.

8. The countdown clock began, "10, 9, 8…" until I could hear everybody there yelling, "3, 2, 1, BOOM." Then the cannon went off.

9. If you've ever attended or watched Ironman videos, you can see all these thousands of people sitting there calm, treading water until BOOM all hell breaks loose and suddenly it's like you're in a goddamn blender. White foam goes everywhere as all 2,000 swimmers begin to paddle or stroke with their

---

[111] The water is super warm in Kona so we didn't wetsuits like we would in cold water
[112] All of the movement's under the water

arms and kick with their feet. It's absolute chaos for the first 500 to 1,000 meters of this swim, bumping into people right and left.

10. I was about 100 meters into this swim and these people, this gal, continued to slam me. I was getting pissed, frustrated because I wanted to swim clean but I was in the blender. In my mind I decided, "The next person that cuts me off I'm punching in the back, and I'm going to shove their ass under the water."

## Getting A Karmic Bitch Slap

11. So, wouldn't you know it? The next person to cut me off was a petite 5 foot 3, 100-pound woman. I didn't give a shit; I was like, "I don't care. Dark Warrior's out to run this bitch, so here we go." She started to cut in, I turned my paddle hand into a fist, and BOOM, down into the water she went. Bye, bye. I came with my left arm and I did the same thing to a guy much bigger than me on the other side. BOOM! Down under the water he went. I was like, "You motherfuckers didn't know I used to be a violent dude in the football world! This is not new for me: I will knock all of you out!" I was feeling really good because I've cleared a path for myself. But karma was about to bitch slap me back to China.

12. About six seconds later, I swam up on the feet of a guy in front of me, and I took a heel right into my eye socket and my left goggle. Water started to fill up so during one of my strokes I adjusted without any lasting results, even stopping to take them off and readjusting, only to discover the goggle got cracked.

13. I was 150 to 200 meters into the World Championships of a 2.4-mile swim after training every single day for years to get to that point. There was no option of stopping, nor were there extra goggles lying around in the middle of the ocean, so I was left with the decision to swim or quit, and quitting was not an option. So I swam. With one eye. Just call me One-eyed Willie!

14. I started to panic for the next 50 to 75 meters because I couldn't fucking see. The salt water was causing my eye to swell up, plus the kick of the heel into the eye ... good job, karma. That'll teach me to hit two other people and push them under the water.

## Focus On the Next Buoy

15. I began to move over to the right. My right eye could see, so I was able to view the big ass orange buoys, which were all I was worried about. This became my focus and the only possible way for me to make it through the swim.

16. All I did was follow. I followed the orange buoys. I would sight, look for the buoy, go back in the water, paddle six to eight strokes, sight, look for the buoy, and paddle. I stayed on course with one eye completely sealed shut from saltwater and the big kick to the face I'd taken. All I focused on were those buoys, all the way back to the beach.

17. -2.4 miles later, goggles were off, eyes swollen, and I'm running up the steps barely able to open my left eye from the kick, swollen and compressed in the remaining goggles for roughly the last hour of the swim.

18. During the first 30 miles of the bike portion I couldn't see out of that left eye. Twenty different times during the swim I started panicking about what this swollen eye meant for the run and bike, but then I shifted that focus back to looking for the next buoy, and then the buoy after that. See, inside of Ironman, you can't worry about what's coming up. You have to deal with the work that's in front of you and work towards the next benchmark. The next buoy. The day is long enough, but if you start to mind fuck yourself and worry about how you're going to perform in the entire competition, your mind begins to implode on itself.

## Shit Is Going to Happen

19. The same principle applies for heading into your 90-day Outcomes. There is shit that's going to happen. It is not *if*: it's guaranteed. Some of it's going to be karmic and some of it's just going to be shit that happens as you're heading to your 90-day target. You're going to be left with a decision: quit on your Outcome, or swim.

20. Do the work in front of you, focus on the buoy, and hit your benchmarks. Inside of these quarterly challenges, you are going to have two big benchmarks and buoys: Buoys every single week and every single day.

21. No matter how much we get punched in the face or can't see the next target, we say, "Calm down. Take a deep breath and ask yourself this: What is your next benchmark?"

## 30 & 60-Day Leverage Benchmarks

22. We break the challenge down into two big benchmarks: 30 days and 60 days. Why? Because if you create an Impossible Game that's accurate, a target that matters, and a target that feels realistic but impossible, it is going to require you to change. There is a lot of shit that's going to happen between today and that 90-Day Outcome that's going to move you all over the place. It's not going to be a straight line.

23. If you followed me with a tracker on my swimming course in the 2007 Ironman World Championship, I was all over the place because I lost the peripheral and had to course correct over and over. We do not panic over the course corrections necessary inside of those 90 days. We calm down and we breathe, saying, "Focus on the 90-Day Outcome, but leverage with 30 and 60-Day checkpoints or Benchmarks to give us an indication that we're on the right path."

## The Ability to Course Correct

24. Part of the reason why most people fail inside of any challenge is that there's not enough ability to course correct when aware of problems. If I had no buoys and I had no checkpoints inside that Ironman swim, nor on the bike and run, my mind would have imploded on itself. There was too much chaos going on. I needed to be able to anchor down. We need to be able to look at our 30-day benchmark and say, "Here is the measurable yes or no."

25. "Yes, I'm on target." or "No, I'm not." You need to be able to answer this question in 30 days. Take an assessment, step back and say, "Okay, I just got out of the water, I'm now in transition. I've got to bike. I've got to get out on the highway and ride my ass off, all the way to 68 miles out, then turn back around and come back.

26. That next phase into Ironman is just like my 30-Day Benchmarks, which are my first assessment and second phase of the 90-Day Outcome. It gives me a chance to assess how I've done and where I'm currently at

and how I'm feeling. Am I ahead, on track, or behind on my targets? The 30-Day Benchmark version of Ironman is my first assessment after the swim, which gives me a chance to check my gear, rehydrate, and recommit to the rest of the race.

27. I take an assessment at 60 days in my third phase of the 90-Day Outcome. Like in the Ironman, I run. This is the final leg of the journey. As 90 Days comes rolling in, I'm done with a marathon—26.2 miles—run down the chute, and they yell, "You're an Ironman."

## It's Hitting the Benchmark That Matters

28. The target stays [113]the same every time, but between the time I left the beach to go tread water and the cannon goes off, to the time that I cross that finish line, there was a shitload of up and down circus acts going on. I felt awesome at times, I vomited a little bit during the race, and I didn't feel excited more than a few times. But amidst the whole deal I knew there was no possible way to go down that finishing chute if I didn't first finish the swim.

29. If I didn't finish the bike, there was no finish. I needed to hit the second (30 Day) and third (60 Day) benchmarks prior to that to get to the home stretch. You can do this shit. I don't care how you feel. Where do we need to adjust?

"Well, my legs and my calves are hurting…"

"Awesome, tape that bitch up."

"My knees hurt a little bit."

"Good, let's tape that up too."

30. Inside your challenges it is crucial that you have these checkpoints, where you can sit in the Tent for a minute and ask, "Okay, where am I at? What do I need to adjust? Am I on target, yes or no?" That's the question we've got to be able to answer with our 30-Day, 60-Day and 90-Day Target Benchmarks.

---

[113] Similar to hitting the first 30-Day Benchmark

## Slow Down and Assess

31. A lot of guys would be like, "Well, Garrett, I'm not sure if I'm on track."

32. I know. That's why we set up our 30 and 60-day benchmarks, because you don't know how you're going to feel coming into that transition. That's why we slow down and assess. We say, "Here's what I thought my benchmark should be."

33. You may completely surpass it. You may not go far enough. But your 30 and 60-Day Benchmarks are absolutely mandatory in order for you to stay on point, pull you out of the Game for a moment to reassess if need be, then send you back in so you can coast into the 90-Day Outcome and declare, "I am an Ironman!"

34. Where guys screw this process up is when they say, "I can observe it" instead of writing it all down,[114] from the Targets to the reassessments and course corrects. It's not going to be very effective because that observation itself is based upon a lot of twisted stories inside my own head. So how do we cut away from the half-assed bullshit? We use measurement and metrics to cut to the truth. We're measuring yes or no's with this so we can actually see the truth, not the distortion of our justification for being on or off.

## Checking 'No' Hurts

35. To check no, hurts. Believe me, I know what it feels like to have to admit, "No, I'm not on path. No, I did not hit my benchmark." And then we ask the question, "Why not? What's going on?" You look back and you're like, "Dude, I'm doing all the wrong work." This happens to guys. They're off point. But they don't do it by observation or how they feel, they do it based upon measurements.

36. The other way to try and manage your Game is to do it through judgement. Well, that's the wrong way. Are you on Target, yes or no? What are your numbers telling you? Are you hitting your Core 4? Your Key 4? Are you on point with your metrics? Are you hitting the General's Tent to plan? Are you hitting your numbers?

---

[114] This can be done inside the General's Tent, using the War Map, or simply brainstorming on a sheet of paper; there's many modalities to writing your shit down; just find what works for you and utilize it.

37. We're not judging whether you hit your targets as good or bad. That's the beauty of metrics. Metrics and numbers don't give us a biased opinion about what is. The weight scale doesn't give us a biased opinion; it just tells us the facts.

38. All right my friends. We'll bring a conclusion here to this next component, which is the Monthly Benchmarks of 30 and 60 days. Now we've got to figure out what the hell's happening each week and every day in between these benchmarks.

## Chapter 35:
## POINTS TO PONDER FROM THE GENERAL'S TENT

- **POINT #1:** Do the work in front of you, focus on the buoy, and hit your benchmarks. Shit is going to happen, but if you just keep calm, course correct, and continue to move towards your Outcome, it will be accomplished.

- **POINT #2:** If you create an Impossible Game that's accurate, a target that matters, and a target that feels realistic but impossible, it is all going to require you to change.

- **POINT #3:** Inside your challenges it is crucial that you have these checkpoints where you can ask, "Okay, where am I at? What do I need to adjust? Am I on target, yes or no?" That's the question we've got to be able to answer with our 30-Day, 60-Day and 90-Day Target Benchmarks.

- **POINT #4:** We're not judging whether you hit your targets as good or bad, just the facts. That's the beauty of metrics.

# THE GAME

## Chapter 36: THE WEEKLY TARGETS

In between all of these benchmarks and the end journey for Warrior
to result in our Impossible Games, there is a weekly war to face in
Business. The Weekly War specifically inside of the Challenge is going
to be Business focused only.

SECTION SIX
# THE GAME

CHAPTER THIRTY-SIX
# THE WEEKLY TARGETS

*"The most deadly thing on a battlefield is one well-aimed shot."*

## — Gunnery Sergeant Carlos Hathcock
[USMC Sniper, with a service record of 93 confirmed kills during Vietnam Conflict]

---

1. In between all of these benchmarks and the end journey for Warrior to result in our Impossible Game, there is a weekly war to face in Business. Why leave the rest of the Core 4 out? It's too overwhelming to keep track of 16 Key Outcomes. Simply put, it's too much. Know when to pick your battles, Brother.

## Focused Business

2. Men join Warrior because they are Businessman and have found success there, otherwise they would not have qualified for this Elite program. We are taking that focused strength and giving it a chance to become super. How? With the Key 4. One of the things that just blows my mind is how crucial the initial stages were for a businessman those first five or six years. This created long-ass days, measured by how much time I was spending in the office, on the phone or my laptop. There was a fundamental fucking problem to measuring my start-up success by how many hours I spent doing things. Here's why.

## Two Different Time Systems: Employee and Entrepreneur

3. Dan Sullivan,[115] a strategic coach, taught me two really powerful principles, both of which blew my fucking mind. Here's how it went down: there are two different time systems that the world operates in. There is a time system of the *employee mindset* and there is the time system of the *entrepreneur mindset.*

## Thinking Like An Employee

4. The employee mindset measures everything by two things: time and effort. They feel that because they put in the time, they've given the effort required to feel entitled for some kind of a reward. "Hey, I put in the time, therefore I put in the energy and the effort. I should get paid, have an amazing marriage, rocking body, and my relationship with God should be on fire. My business should be booming because I put in the time watching the webinar and studied the videos about marketing. I've made the effort so my marketing should be fucking smashing it." Yet, the reality was this: that mindset is a driven game of failure as an entrepreneur.

5. The problem resided in *how* I was running my weeks, by time and effort, which I would never have admitted because I didn't even know it was happening. I'd just get to the office. I had my team members, my business partners and three assistants running this chaotic circus every day with me that looked like we were getting a lot of shit done. Everywhere I turned there was a battle to be had, a machete out, slaughtering all over the place, fight over here, over there; every day I had the feeling like I was getting shit done.

6. Here's the sad reality, though. My oldest daughter was just born. I would leave around 6:00 every morning and she was still sleeping (well, after getting up multiple times at night which my wife took on, so she was sleeping as well). I would come home around 9:00 at night and she was still sleeping.

7. I had gotten into a pattern of doing this from when we were first married. We didn't have the kids so it was no big deal. My wife would work, I would work. It's what we did. We would see each other at night, stay up late, and continue to work. This pattern didn't change for me once we had kids.

---

[115] See Appendix Bibliography "Strategic Coach"

The first two or three years of my daughter's life, I couldn't tell you what happened. I had to create these outlandish bullshit stories to justify the guilt that I felt as a father for not being around, not to mention all the time that I wasn't spending with my wife.

## Paying the Price for Success

8. Why was I doing this? Why was I making my family suffer under this story that I believed that I've got to be willing to pay the price for success? Now, before I answer that, know that you *do* have to pay the price for success: some weeks you're going to have to grind 80-100 hours, and you're going to have to travel a lot; I'm not saying that that's not happening to me even today.

9. What the major shift was for me was realizing that I was heading into my weeks to go to war completely unprepared. Maybe I had a 90-Day Outcome in my mind, a target I was moving towards: an impossible gain. Maybe I even had 30-60 Day Benchmarks, but I did not have a weekly War Map to operate off of. What the fuck was supposed to be done this week that when done it would ultimately push me forward? These weren't conversations I was having because I was thinking like an employee.

## Making the Shift to Inside an Entrepreneur's Mind

10. The other belief system that Dan Sullivan began to teach me when I got into Strategic Coaching was this: the entrepreneur mindset does not measure the game based upon time and effort. It says, "Listen. There is one governing factor inside of my world. It's not how much time it took me to do something; sometimes I may need to do shit for the week that requires 100 hours, but then some weeks I may need to only put in one hour."

11. The time it takes me to do something is not the relevant conversation. What is relevant is the result.

12. I was raised in a world of that employee mindset with a family that said, "You can get anything you want, but in order to do that you're going to have to be willing to work your ass off."

13. As an entrepreneur, though, I had to shift it. There are too many Brothers that I meet on a day-to-day basis who operate in their businesses

like employees instead of operating based on results that are *not urgent, but important* when it comes to marketing, sales and systems, leadership and fulfillment processes. Every single week I had to shift the way I thought. Amidst all the infinite possibilities out there I had to ask myself a question: What are the Key items that must happen?

## Putting Key 4 Into Play

14. Key 4 now allows me to walk into the office on a Monday morning not filled with chaos and feeling like I need to put in a lot of time and effort. I know I'm going to work hard; it's what I do. It's just who I am to out-hustle everybody. I'm also at a point in Business that I better be clear about the Games I'm playing every quarter.

15. How do I muscle out the hustle from the workplace when I'm creating time to spend with my family? The reality is that there's a piece in my mind that's always running and rotating, constantly panicked and paranoid that I might not be getting shit done that I need to get done, but that also applies to my Core 4. I make the shift, which we'll go into more detail shortly.

16. There are some battle environments you don't need to get into every week, and some that you do. The only way you'd be able to know this is to come into your week in business clear about your Key 4: what's the One Thing, the first action for that and then the next after that which needs to get accomplished? All of the sudden my weeks become four series of Key 4 that takes me to my first benchmark. Sixteen Key 4's later I'm in my Business Benchmark at 30 days. I take an observation about where I'm at, then go back into the trench. Then in my 60-Day Benchmark, I observe and course correct towards my 90-Day Outcome.

17. Like in the boxing ring, the game's not over until the bell rings. We train to run men through these processes over and over again. When do broken ribs, noses, injury and knockouts happen? When a guy quits two seconds before the bell rings. He moves his hands down and undefended, gets his ass knocked out; not because he couldn't have sustained the blow any other way, but because somehow in his mind he decided it was time to end the game two seconds before the bell rang.

## What We Care About Matters

18. This same concept goes for spectators leaving a sporting event like football before the game actually ends, thinking the outcome is already set, only to miss out on the big fucking turnarounds in the last minute, the kind that require multiple reviews to clarify the epic shit that just occurred. And yet, even their own fans were doubting the team. In your life, sometimes your own family and friends will doubt your validity at times. They're going to fucking doubt you with two minutes left to go. In this Game with Business, you must play under guidelines that say, "When I wake up on Monday morning, I know how I'm going to win: there are 4 Keys that I'm going to hit this week. We're going to frontload them." That means we don't wait until Friday to do all 4 while we deal with the urgent nonsense of the week.

19. We set up the Game so that Monday, Tuesday, Wednesday and Thursday we have stacked all the work necessary to get our Key 4 done by Thursday. That way if we have to buy a vowel or Bonus Day on Friday, Saturday or Sunday, we can.

20. What typically happens with men in this Game is that they push these Outcomes to the end and say, "Well, here's the 4 things that must happen this week, but I'm going to deal with all this urgent stuff that just kind of gets thrown at me. I'm going to react to it and focus on results that are brought to my attention that may or may not matter. I'm going to live in the world with *not important and urgent* and *important and urgent* instead of living in the world of *not urgent, but important*, and say this shit's got to be done. I'm getting this stuff done this week. I don't care what happens."

21. Let's shift that around; what if a football team said, "I don't care if the fans leave the stands with two minutes left in the game; I'm not worried about them. What I'm worried about is getting the ball back."

## The Last Crucial Plays

22. Once we get the ball back, we've got to get a first down, another, and then we'll be within striking distance. If I get freaked out because the fans are leaving the stands, then we aren't going to get the ball back, or if I do get the ball back my mind's not going to be right, which means we are not going to get the first down. If I try to go 80 yards for a touchdown right

out of the gate, we're fucked, so all I'm going to worry about is getting on the field and getting the ball back.

23. Okay, now we got the ball back. All I'm going to worry about is what? Key 1: get the ball back. Key 2: get the first down. Key 3: get another first down. Key 4: strike and fucking win. It's not rocket science, gentlemen. So why don't more guys pull this off? Why won't they get clear about the What, Why, When and How every single week inside their Key 4? Because they're not committed, that's why.

## What You Say You're Going to Do

24. There's this crazy thing about life: you don't get what you want, deserve, or think you're entitled to. You get what you're fucking committed to.

25. How do we measure your commitment? Not by what you say, by what you do. While I was in Kokoro, the 33 of us that started were playing shitty as a team those first few hours of the 70 hour event. We had a pretty shitty first quarter, which was an indicator where the event was going and the trainers knew it, so they started getting all up on us big time. We were just not performing. They would say, "Get down." We were slow as shit to get down. We wouldn't get down, so they would punish us. Then they'd say, "Get up." We wouldn't get up fast.

26. As a group it just wasn't working. As a team we just weren't working together. They would say, "Get this shit and bring it over here." We would do it slow. It sucked. We weren't together. We weren't unified and everyone was feeling sorry for themselves. Finally, things started happening:

"Hey, do you hear us?"

"HOOAH."

27. It was funny, because our actions did not match the intensity and the excitement which we as a group were saying, "HOOAH."

"Are you in?"

"HOOAH."

28. One of the trainers came out, one of the SEALS and he said, "Here inside this Brotherhood, here inside this Game, let us help you understand

something. We don't give a shit about how excited you are with your fucking 'Hooahs' if your actions don't represent. We don't listen to what a man says. We listen to what a man does with his feet."

## What A Man Does with His Feet

29. "Let's try this again. How about we take some of that energy from your fucking 'hooahs' and we actually get your ass moving the way I'm telling you to move. If you spent less time trying to look pretty and actually do the fucking work, we would have no problem here, so let's try it again in 3-2-1, off we go!"

30. And off we went, moving sandbags and doing all kinds of crazy shenanigans inside the camp for the remaining 70 hours straight.

31. We learned quickly that words mean little; actions mean a ton. Inside this Game with your Key 4 you can preach all day long about how you're going to do it, but if you're not committed to actually sitting down and creating this shit every single week inside the General's Tent, you're done.

## Side Note: Date Your Wife

32. Here's a few little side notes for Key 4, two bonuses that don't have to do with Business but have to do with changing your life. Every single week, you're going to take your wife, your queen, on a date. Non-negotiable. You're going to drop the fucking excuses, coordinate the babysitter, the event, and what you're going to do for the date. "Garrett, I don't know how to find a babysitter!" Bullshit. You have these massive targets in your Business, but the story that stands between you and courting your wife is the fact that you cannot find a babysitter?! It's a fucking story. Quit telling it.

33. You want to make more money? Take your wife on a date every week. Non-negotiable. You want to hit your Key 4 better? Take your wife out every week. In the beginning she might resist it, but you better take her on a date every week. This does not include bringing the kids with you. That is not a date; it's a family outing. Family date nights are great and need to be done as well. I'm not talking about that. I'm talking you and the Queen away from the house.

34. If you can't invest in your queen and have a specific time set aside every week from the house, the kids and the Game, guess what? Fuck you with

your 90-Day Outcomes. If you can't do something small like take your queen out every single week on a date, how in the hell do you think you're going to pull that off? Stop bullshitting yourself. Date night every single week and track it. Danielle and I never miss. We go every single week, even when we don't want to because we have too much shit going on; we force it to happen. Why? Because we understand that the Key to Expansion and Production is to make sure that the queen and the king are on the same page.

35. You cannot go to war in business every week and be worried about coming home only to have your queen put a knife in your fucking neck while you're sleeping. Send messages throughout the day: "I love you. I appreciate you. I honor you. Thank you for being who you are. Go get them today." When we do this, the King is at peace in his kingdom.

## Getting Energy from Your Children

36. On that note, you have no idea how much energy you're going to get from your children. I spend date nights with my children, individually, every single week and they love it. It's only a few hours, or maybe one; 30 minutes would work as you're present that whole time. If you've got eight kids, you might have to do 30 minutes. With one child you might do eight hours. I don't know. You figure it out.

37. Leave the house and take a drive in your car; go somewhere that is not at home, and take a date with your child; create something fun for them to experience. It doesn't have to cost you much. I just went skateboarding with my daughter, we rode her scooter and played Wall Ball; it doesn't have to be rocket science crazy. It's super simple. The bonus-bonus side note is to arrange a planned family outing once a week. You can rock the Business world and making non-negotiable date nights are simple, but never doubt their effectiveness in living the Warrior's Way of having it all.

## Spending Essential Quality Time

38. What does this have to do with your Key 4? You're going to need to create a huge capacity to pull off the Key 4 and stay focused, and one of the ways you can find that is by filling yourself up emotionally with your kids and with your wife. You've got to invest and spend quality time with them, using deliberate strategy with it more than you would anything else.

# Chapter 36:
# POINTS TO PONDER FROM THE GENERAL'S TENT

- **POINT #1:** There are two different time systems that the world operates in. There is a time system of the employee mindset and there is the time system of the entrepreneur mindset. The entrepreneur mindset does not measure the game based upon time and effort; it's the result that's relevant.

- **POINT #2:** Be clear about your Key 4 weekly targets. In this Game with Business, you must play under a guideline that says, "When I wake up on Monday morning, I know how I'm going to win: there are 4 Keys that I'm going to hit this week. We're going to frontload them." It takes commitment to get the work done this way so that if we need to allot ourselves more time over the weekend, we can because we put most of our focus at the beginning of the week.

- **POINT #3:** Make weekly date night non-negotiable with your wife. The Key to Expansion and Production is to make sure that the queen and the king are on the same page.

- **POINT #4:** Get individual dates in with each of your children once a week. Make them customized and possibly even do a family outing once a week to ultimate capacity.

# THE GAME

## Chapter 37: DAILY ACTIONS

Core 4 is a daily war, and Daily Actions help prevent us from growing out of power.

# SECTION SIX
# THE GAME

## CHAPTER THIRTY-SEVEN
# DAILY ACTIONS

"To be nobody but yourself in a world which is doing its best, night and day, to make you everybody else means to fight the hardest battle which any human being can fight; and never stop fighting."

### -e. e. cummings
[American Poet that signed his name in lowercase form, 1894-1962]

---

1. Every single week inside our 90-Day Outcomes, 60 and 30-Day Benchmarks, we have Business Outcomes and Date nights for our relationship that we're going to hit weekly. But Core 4 is a daily war, and Daily Actions help prevent us from growing out of power.

## Business Event Analogy

2. When we go to Business Events, there's a tendency for guys to want to use this time as an opportunity to relax, but what does "relax" turn into? Typically, a bunch of guys drinking way too late on the very first night they show up to an event, staying up until 3:00 or 4:00 in the morning.

3. And yet, I'm wrapping up by 10:30 pm: "Well, see you guys later. I got to go to war in the morning with my Core 4."

"Oh, you're a pussy. You should come out!"

"Nope. I already know where this is going to end up."

4. They go out, do their shenanigans and the next morning I wake up and do my Core 4. I gain my power, my capacity stays open, and I'm back on

fire having a good time at 10:30 am while they're sleeping until 1:00 pm. I've hit my Core 4 in the morning which means my power has expanded. By the time they show up in the afternoon, I see them and they have *that look*.

## Don't Get That Look

5. Do you know what I'm talking about? That look particularly from those guys that are not in their 20s anymore; they're in their 40s but partying like they think they're still frat boys. They pretended they were 20 last night, and then they look at me:

"Dude, how are you doing?"

"Oh my God, Dude, you should have heard about it last night. It was awesome," they try to grin, with glazed-over eyes.

"Well, I could tell. I'm looking at how awesome it is right now."

## Choosing Consequences

6. It appears the consequences of your decisions from last night are not exactly paying off like you thought they would, except for the fact that you're living in a fantasy story that was created under intoxication. Congratulations, you dumb fuck. They look at me and I'm like, "Look, Dude. You're faded. Was it really worth it? All day long you've been in survival mode."

7. This phenomenon is how a lot of people take on their challenges and their New Year's Resolutions: they think that they're all in to make the change, yet they're still doing the same shenanigans from before.

8. "Garrett, why do you work out? You're fit."

"You're a dumb fuck. Dude, do you think fitness was like a gift that just came from God?"

9. "Garrett, why do you work so hard? Your business is so amazing. Why do you work so hard?"

"Did you think is just showed up magically that way because some pixie dust got sprinkled around?"

10. "Dude, why do you take your wife out so much? Why do you spend all this time working on your kids and your relationship? Why do you spend so much time studying etc…?"

"Seriously? Listen to how stupid that question is when you're asking it: I'm not saying you're stupid, but you're behaving stupid right now because that's a stupid question.

These are consequences of being willing to do the work every single day."

## Daily Drives with The Core 4

11. These guys and I were at the same page of intensity and excitement, yet they felt like I was missing out by not going out with them. The reality was, the next day, there we were in the rest stop: their car was no longer moving forward. Yeah, while I was sleeping, they were partying it up, having a good time "building some good stories" yet here's a business owner who doesn't take time to be with his family and focus on daily Regeneration of Power through the Core 4 every single day. This is a man who doesn't say, "I'm going to wake up and hit the 4 before I hit the door so I'm prepared to go to war with my Key 4."

12. Whatever you do, don't slow down to a stop. This doesn't necessarily mean you have to go too fast either; it just means you don't get off the freeway. Think Tortoise and the Hare Fable but on the freeway with cars.

13. There were all of these individuals at this event that got on the freeway of life: Lamborghinis throttling down while I was sleeping. They were having a good time. They were killing it. They were going 200 miles an hour down the freeway, screaming and talking about all the stories they were going to have. The next morning, guess what they did? They parked in the rest stop. Now, I was going about 90 miles an hour once I got on the freeway, but here's the thing that's crazy: I slowed down. I didn't use the off-ramp and rest areas; I recovered, slowed down, and went again. See, I could travel 30 miles an hour on a freeway and not require getting off to a rest stop; I simply merged over to the slow lane, and yet I will still dominate people who try to go 200 miles an hour only to burn out, and then end up in a metaphorical rest stop.

## Daily Core 4 Fuel and Power

14. Core 4 is Simple Success Swinging Singles, meaning it's how you use the fuel to give you the power you need to pull this off. It brings your Body, Being, and Balance along the journey with your Key 4 Business targets. If we don't hit Core 4, we will not have the power in this area, the bandwidth, nor the endurance to accomplish any possible gain. Breaking the whole process down: we went from a Game of 90-Day Targets to our current reality through which our 60 and 30-Day Benchmarks guided us with mile markers every single week we got Key 4, and then we said every single day, "We're going to go to war with our Core 4."

15. Core 4 is the fuel; it's the fire that will allow us to get there. How often? Only on the days you want to have power. If you don't want to have a Power Day or increase your capacity, don't do it. If you need capacity and power on a daily basis, you "Hit the Core 4 before you hit the door so you can go to war with your Key 4."

## Morning Fuel

16. Why do we use this phrase? We're setting up the framework for the rest of our day based off of how we started the morning. If you wait until evening to do your Core 4 because "that's when I feel like I operate the best," you'll be spending that time making up for the asshole you were as a slave to your body during the day, sending apologies instead of gratitude texts to your wife and kids, not leveling up at work because you didn't get a green smoothie and workout in that morning.

17. So you try to get a workout in before bed, only to remember that meditation also needed to get done, exhausted and agitated after cramming in some cardio when your body wants to start to relax down for sleep. Now you're on a fucking roll. So, you decide to meditate right before sleep as you lay in bed. You'll be saying, "I hit my 4…" but you can't even get that out because you're already asleep. Fuck you with your 'Core 4 before you snore,' you dumbass; that's not how we play this Game. It does no good for you to be, "Hey, Garrett. I hit my 4 before I snored so I could get slaughtered some more." That is not the mantra we have here. We're not going to give you any points for having a 4 before you snore, so that when you wake up you can get slaughtered in war the next day. There are Zones that we accomplish our Core 4 in:

Zone 1: Before 0800 hours
Zone 2: 0800-1000 hours
Zone 3: 1000-1200 hours
Zone 4: 1200-2400 hours

18. The ideal time we want to hit Zone 1 is before 8:00am. Why? Because that gives us a whole day to go create a lot of shit, not get slipped into the Time and Effort Trap, and focus on results. This is when we do the shit that's *not urgent and important* and deal with *urgent and important*.

19. Zone 2 is between 8:00 and 10:00 in the morning, which is going to get tracked along with Zone 1 every day, assessed every week. I'm tracking not only my Core 4 points, but I'm also tracking when I finished. This tracking mechanism lets me see the difference inside my own life.

20. Zone 3 is going to be between 10:00 and noon. Zone 4 is anything after noon. We found over the last few years we've done this, if you don't get the Core 4 done by noon the effectiveness goes to the floor. Same thing you find with sleep. You can go to sleep at 9:00 or 10:00, sleep a couple of hours before midnight and then wake up earlier, like 3:30, 4:00 in the morning and you actually feel refreshed, excited and pumped. You can go to bed at 1:00 in the morning, sleep the same amount of time, wake up and feel exhausted and fatigued throughout the whole day.

## Effective Body Rhythms

21. Your body rhythms work more effectively when you sleep before midnight versus after: You get bonus credit for how much you're sleeping before midnight. That's why for me it's non-negotiable. I'm like dude, 10:00, 10:30, 11:00 the latest I'm asleep in bed every night so I will then wake up at 3:30, 4:00 in the morning and work on whatever shit I didn't get to the day before in the morning when I'm awake. I want to cash in on as many bonus credit minutes of sleeping before midnight as I can to put towards my lifestyle of having it all.

22. Same thing goes throughout the Core 4 with every action that you complete before noon in Zones 1, 2 or 3. Any of those three zones are going to give you rewards. On the flip side, you're going to get less power as those zones move forward. Zone 4 is the least powerful; where you hit the wall.

23. Now, we're not saying don't accomplish your Core 4 in Zone 4; it's just not going to be as powerful. Better to hit your Core 4 in Zone 4 than not hit it at all.

## Racing to Finish In Zone 1 or 2

24. In the Game, every single day is a race to finish in Zones 1 and 2. What you're going to start to notice inside the metrics and the systems of the Armory as you track this is the connection between when you finish your Core 4 and you're effectiveness in Key 4.

25. You're going to see how your Power allows you to accomplish your 30 and 60-Day Benchmarks more effectively, compressing time because your weeks feel more full and whole getting 10x more done. With results-driven behavior, you can see the patterns of your patience going up as your capacity and ability to lead expand through finishing in Zones 1 or 2.

## Non-Negotiable Daily Actions

26. Inside your Core 4 you're going to be doing a Power Focus Document using the Drift and Shift model, which has training tools and tutorials inside this book. This is non-negotiable. It is part of our point system to put us in power with Balance every single day. Other non-negotiable daily documents are Production Focus and journaling in our Black Bible. Whether we're writing it in our paper journal or using the software, either way we're going to make sure that we're journaling every single day.

3 Non-Negotiable Daily Documents:

1. Power Focus
2. Positive Focus
3. Journaling

27. The fourth thing I'm doing is tracking my metrics with my Core 4. Which is saying, "Hey, Body, Being, Balance and Business: I've got this. Here's my ultimate number for the day. Here's the trackable form. Every single day at the end of the day I'm reporting back on these. I'm looking every single day, quickly updating my metrics inside the system. Here are my numbers."

28. Remember, occasionally there's going to be some days you're just not going to be there. You miss putting the number in, but you'll be able to go back and do that again. Nonetheless, our goal every single day is to make sure that we're tracking what our score was that day so when we wake up the next day we can look and say, "Well, yesterday I got a three. My day didn't go as well as I wanted. Today I'm smashing a four." Or "yesterday I hit a four and I'm going to stay on my streak."

29. If we're on a roll, we want to be able to keep maintaining that. If not, then we can physically see an adjustment from yesterday to where we are today.

## Core 4: Expansion Daily Tool

30. Core 4 is our Daily Tool of Expansion. It provides a daily weaponization of our mind and body so we can go to war with our Key 4 for the week with our two bonuses: date night with the wife and children. Each one of our Key 4's are pushing us towards those benchmarks whether it's our 30, 60 or ultimately 90-Day Outcome.

## Meditation Side Note

31. As a final side note, even though meditation is tracked once inside Core 4 as part of your scoring system, most of the Brothers and I actually track multiple times a day. As we level up our Core 4 Daily Actions, every single day meditation becomes more and more mandatory to keep my capacity open.

32. I'm going to go over with you deep dive training in the Armory of this book on how to actually create your Core 4 every single week. We're also going to explain the essential importance of this inside the General's Tent section in the next and final section of this book. You may eventually get to a point where you're tracking meditation two and three times a day: morning to get lit up, afternoon to keep you maintained and night to clear your space from work as you walk in to be home with your children. This is how you can stay present when hustling with the Chaos of Abundance.

33. Don't overwhelm yourself in the beginning with multiple mediation sessions though; it's not something you have to do. Just know that that is one of the Daily Actions that may occur a little bit beyond what your

normal Core 4 is, which is the Daily Action. It is a very, very simple tool but it is also very, very powerful and absolutely necessary to continue to push forward towards your 30, 60, and 90-Day Impossible Games.

## Chapter 37:
## POINTS TO PONDER FROM THE GENERAL'S TENT

- **POINT #1:** Many successful businessmen can be on the same level intensity and excitement as Warriors within the Black Box Brotherhood, but it's in the Daily Actions that shows where his true commitment lays.

- **POINT #2:** Use the phrase "Hit the Core 4 before you hit the door so you can go to war with your Key 4" on a daily basis, broken down into four Zones for maximum benefits in Zones 1 & 2.

- **POINT #3:** There are three non-negotiable daily documents: Power Focus, Positive Focus, and Journaling that need to be done on top of Core 4, which is our Daily Tool of Expansion. Don't forget your two bonuses: date night with your wife and children.

- **POINT #4:** Meditation is a very simple yet effective tool in providing clarity when facing the Chaos of Abundance that comes with success.

# THE GAME

## Chapter 38: THE GENERAL'S TENT

The General's Tent is this idea that you as the king inside your commanded Body, Being, Balance and Business, need time with your empire, kingdom, castle, queen, and family every single week.

## SECTION SIX
# THE GAME

### CHAPTER THIRTY-EIGHT
# THE GENERAL'S TENT

"The time to take counsel of your fears is before you make an important battle decision. That's the time to listen to every fear you can imagine! When you have collected all the facts and fears and made your decision, turn off all your fears and go ahead!"

**-General George S. Patton**
[US Army General during WWII]

---

1. You as a man need specific time that you must take in order to assess how the war is going. The [116]General's Tent is where the greatest decisions are made: in execution, about skirmishes and battles, as well as where to allocate troops and resources.

### Where the Greatest Decisions Are Made

2. Across the board, in every major war that's ever been won or lost, the decisions that impacted that war were not what was happening in the trench; it was the decisions being handed down to execute on the battlefield by the generals in the tents.

3. So what goes on in the tent? Strategizing, automating, understanding, learning, course correcting, evaluating, expanding and setting your targets and visions. The General's perspective gives you the ability to succeed in the trench warfare you face on a daily basis within the Core 4. In the trench war, you are with Key 4. That gives you the ability to pull yourself out once

---

[116] This is a term that was brought into my experience by a couple of different trainings I've had over the years.

a week from the trenches and into the place of the General's Tent. Without leaving no man's land,[117] there is no true growth.

4. Let's come back to the Ironman stories. I know. You are like, "Dude, he's back on the Ironman kick. How many times are we going to have to listen to another goddamn story about the Ironman?"

Well, you are going to get one more. Shut up and listen.

## Getting Smacked Back onto Course

5. So here goes the story. One Goggle-Willie was the nickname I gave myself. There we were swimming.[118] I struggled those first 500 meters trying to figure out this one-eyed swimming thing. I would start drifting to the left because I lacked peripheral vision. Moving to the left and about every one and a half to two minutes I'd hear this loud smack on the water that quickly became the signal that I needed to turn and course correct, swimming back towards the inside of the swim course.

6. Now you might ask, was this smack like a lightning bolt from heaven? Or a big whale that was jumping out of the water and landing on the surface of the water, identifying that I was off course? No. These were a bunch of guys on paddle boards who were riding around on the outside making sure all the swimmers stayed inside a confined area and didn't get off course. They would smack the water, "Hey Dude. You are off course. Get back on."

## Following in The Wrong Direction

7. Another Ironman experience in another race was on the bike portion. One of the guys inside the lead pack got off the path. He didn't make a turn and we all continued to follow him, so the entire pack rode 20 MILES in the wrong direction. We did it fast though. After hours of group riding, we couldn't drop back on each other and ride like a normal cycling team. After riding hard at 21 miles off we were found, course corrected and turned.[119]

---

[117] This is a WWI term that described the battlefield areas throughout Europe. The opposing sides created a series of trenches to reside in and would go "Over the Top!" to battle, then retreat or move forward, based upon which side had more force. This type of warfare was a relatively new method to be used, and epitomizes the strategies used during the Great War.

[118] Refer back to Chapter 29; You remember why I could only see out of one eye in the 2007 World Championships, don't you? Yeah, the karmic bitch slap.

[119] We were a total of 42 miles off course before getting back into the race.

That was a horrible day. I started out super pumped on the bike but I can't tell you how depressing it is to get 21 miles down the road going the wrong fucking direction because you didn't recognize that you missed the turn.

8. One reason we have the General's Tent is so that we don't get off course. We need to be able to become the surf on the paddle board, smacking the water of our life letting us know we're off course. We need to be the ranger who is out on the course that says, "Hey listen. You missed the turn, but you missed the turn about four hundred meters ago not twenty plus miles. Turn around."

## Measure, Assess and Review

9. Part of the reason why guys do not succeed within the Core 4 is because they don't measure and review often enough. Maybe they are doing the metrics but they are not doing anything to study it. Imagine running your business without accounting; how's that working out for you?

10. And then we get guys who will track everything. Once you track it though, now comes the Game of assessing it and reviewing it inside the General's Tent. We have to be able to look at what's going on frequently so that we can make micro adjustments to the game. What feels like a big deal is when you are 21 miles down the road and somebody says, "Hey Dude. Just so you know, you missed a turn 21 miles ago."

11. The "What the fuck?" wouldn't have even been the same if it had been a mile.

"Hey Dude. You are a mile out. Turn around."

12. This is what happens when guys don't review often; I've watched it happen for years. You don't want to step into the General's Tent and be strategic for life, do you? It is the same thing about being strategic about your Business. So many entrepreneurs working inside their business, they take almost no time to get strategic about working on their business. It's not a new statement; you have heard this before, a thousand times.

## What Goes On Inside the Tent?

13. Ideally, the General's Tent is to be something done on a Sunday. If your week starts on a Monday, we want to do it on Sunday because it is the last possible moment to review everything so we get a full review of the week.

14. If that's not possible, then some guys will do a session in the General's Tent on a Friday, Saturday or early Monday morning and review the previous week. Whenever it is, it's just like weighing yourself on a scale. Whatever day you do it, stay consistent and pick the same day, same time, roughly every single week.

## Gratefully Compressing Time

15. We assess and course correct or maintain, but the General's Tent also allows us to have gratitude. Part of the process that guys struggle with is they grow so fast here. You enter the Warrior Time Warp and life moves so quickly, it becomes difficult to actually appreciate how fast you've grown. Every single week inside the General's Tent, we are going to be grateful. We are going to appreciate our path and what we have gone through in the previous week. We are going to go through the work that we have done and say, "Dude, holy shit. I am moving. Like, I am adjusting. This is beautiful. This is wonderful."

16. We will self-sabotage ourselves if we don't acknowledge everything we've actually done. I promise you, inside this Game, weeks are going to collapse and feel like months. Days are going to feel like weeks. What starts to happen is that you love playing the Game so much because every day is so rich and so full, it becomes difficult to pull back the reins.

17. The second piece with gratitude is that it gives us perspective; without gratitude we lose vision, and without appreciation, we lose aspiration. We have to have these inside our world and the General's Tent to give us a chance to use those two things in a powerful way.

18. Make sure that you hit your Core 4 before you hit the door…of the General's Tent. Some guys think, "You know what? I am doing the General's Tent today. I don't need to hit the 4." Are you fucking kidding me? It's the one day during the week where you are making all your battle decisions. It's probably the day that you shouldn't wake up with a hangover so if you

are going to go out, go out on Friday, make it through Saturday then hit the tent Sunday.

19. Our war is prepared inside the tent. Our strategy and our ability to step out of the Game and to really get strategic for the week comes on the wings of our Core 4. Now, assuming we have done that, we are going to go through three different phases:

Phase 1: Turn in Reports
Phase 2: Make Assessments and Course Correction
Phase 3: Strategize Upcoming Week

## Phase 1: Turn In Reports

20. Phase #1 is where we are going to go through the turned in reports; it's the process to do Core 4. That qualifies us to enter the tent. Once in, our first Game is Return and Report. We need to be accountable for the numbers and accountable for the work that we did or we did not do in the previous week.

21. Again, on each one of these documents, we are going to do deep dive training on this inside the Armory but I want you to grasp the concept here. I have done my Core 4 for the day and those numbers are also going to show up on my metrics that I am returning and reporting on.

22. I pull up my Return and Report document: am I following the framework, format and what I am going to go through? "Okay. How did I do in Core 4 this week? How did I do in Key 4 this week?" I go through them, read all my Positive and Power Focus Documents for the week and release the numbers that I finish. Inside my Core 4, I am going to look at what happened over the last seven days, look at my journal entries, and any of the Key 4's that I executed on and what the Outcomes are from it.

## Phase 2: Assessments and Course Correction

23. Inside this phase and documentation, I am going to again review everything I've done and come up with some clear assessments about how I perform and lessons learned from my Core 4. What were things that worked? That didn't work? What adjustments do I need to make? Inside my Key 4, were there some things that I missed or that I hit but were too easy?

24. I am going to list out all of the lessons I have learned and course corrections like I was coaching myself, standing on the sideline watching my own game saying, "Okay. Here's some things I am seeing. Here's what I would adjust based upon the facts of what you produced for me and the metrics and results from the previous week. I'm going to make these changes this week and I'm going to be clear about them."

25. I make some notes, then once I have done my assessment and my course correction, I have been able to answer for myself, "Am I on track with my next benchmark? With my challenge? What about my current benchmark that I am pursuing?" and most importantly, "Am I on track to hit my Outcome for this challenge, yes or no?"

## Phase 3: Strategize Upcoming Week

26. Third piece then is to get strategic about the next week. This is where I do my planning, coming in and saying, "Okay. Here is what I saw. Here are the lessons I learned. Here is the place I need to adjust. What are my new commitments for this week in Core 4? Body, Being, Balance, Business. Do I need to make some adjustments? If I do, what are they?"

27. I'm putting all of this into the Core 4 New Commitment document. Second piece of this is we are going to go to Key 4. I am saying, "Are there some adjustments I need to make in my Key 4 this week? Okay cool. Here's what I am doing, why I am doing it, when I will get it done and how I am going to pull it off."

28. By the time I leave this third phase inside the General's Tent with my new commitments, I am now solid to enjoy the rest of the day or simply just relax into the fact that I have done the work necessary to prepare me to go to war for that week.

29. Finishing your weekly time in the General's Tent is crucial, whether you do it in the morning, afternoon, or at night. Whatever day you decide, block out the same time, because the General's Tent is non-negotiable.

30. Do not be surprised if you are having problems staying on track with your Core 4, or if you refuse to get in the Tent with yourself. It's a place that takes some getting used to until it becomes your sanctuary to look forward to once a week.

## Preparing to Expand Your Kingdom

31. The General's Tent has become one of the most cherished experiences of my life every single week; it is the only thing that has helped me not lose my mind. Once the war starts on Monday, I've already sat in there thinking strategically about the overall arching outcomes of my day, the upcoming week, over my month or the year. Visualize being up on a throne in your castle and then Monday comes; there is no more strategy going on up in the castle because the war is outside the walls and you're commanding your troops to expand your empire. Which means you leave the castle, the strategy room and you disappear out through the walls of the kingdom with a small band of assassins and you go to war.

## Becoming the Warrior King

32. Inside that war, you don't have time to be worrying about big arching strategies. Worry about the two guys right in front of you who are trying to kill you, or the skirmish you are in right now. Inside of each of us, there is a Warrior and a King. The Warrior is the guy in the trenches doing the fucking work while the King is the guy strategizing for the war so that his Warrior side fights effective fights every single week. This is how he successfully hits the score to win the war.

33. The General's Tent is a counsel for kings. It's a counsel with yourself. It's a game in which you play and operate to get the support that you need to pull off this game. So as a review to all of this, the General's Tent covers four things:

1. Hit Core 4 to get our buy-in and prepare ourselves mentally before we even hit the door of the Tent.
2. Do a return and report as we look over our documents from the past week.
3. Make an assessment and course correction.
4. Move to new targets and new commitments.

34. Brothers, the General's Tent is a non-negotiable activity; the moment you make it negotiable, you are fucked. It is the glue that keeps the Game together. You don't do it: Game Over. You do it, religiously live it, and give yourself no options to not do it, explosive results will be yours as you watch for that inevitable time that 16-foot domino comes crashing down.

## Chapter 38:
## POINTS TO PONDER FROM THE GENERAL'S TENT

- **POINT #1:** Strategizing, automating, understanding, learning, course correcting, evaluating, expanding and setting your targets and visions occur inside the general's tent. This gives you the ability to succeed in the trench warfare you face on a daily basis within the Core 4.

- **POINT #2:** Like the life lessons Garrett shared from his Ironman experiences of getting off course, the General's Tent provides the access to the tools necessary to course correct when needed.

- **POINT #3:** We have to be able to look at what's going on frequently so that we can make micro adjustments to the Game through measurements, assessments and reviews. This allows us to see what we've been able to accomplish, giving us perspective that having it all is attainable.

- **POINT #4:** The General's Tent is non-negotiable, and the only thing that may help you not lose your mind, gluing everything in the Black Box together.

# THE GAME

## Chapter 39: SUMMARY

"I was searching, hungry and wanting more, just like you, Brother, to be part of this Brotherhood inside the Black Box that is now before you. I didn't know how to get it, though, because it didn't exist; I hadn't created it yet. My prayer is that here, inside this Brotherhood with this Game and this Box, you'll find exactly that."

## SECTION SIX
# THE GAME

## CHAPTER THIRTY-NINE
# SUMMARY

"I've missed more than 9000 shots in my career. I've lost almost 300 games. 26 times, I've been trusted to take the game winning shot and missed. I've failed over and over and over again in my life. And that is why I succeed."

### -Michael Jordan

---

1. It took me years to put this formula for the Game together inside my own life. As my world unraveled in 2007 and 2008, the reality of not being able to have it all was squarely upon my shoulders as scarcity and poverty replaced it across the board in my Core 4, even though I didn't know what they even were at the time.

## Accessing the Entry Point

2. I was searching, hungry and wanting more, just like you, Brother, to be part of this Brotherhood inside the Black Box that is now before you. I didn't know how to get it, though, because it didn't exist; I hadn't created it yet. I was confused and searching, not knowing where to go, and so I tried everything, everywhere. The one thing I did know was this: the entry point to having a different answer comes through access.

3. The very first time this happened in the beginning of 2008, I was required to make a decision. I had several pieces of real estate that were falling into short sale positions[120] and I remember sitting there having just met

---

[120] Defaulting on the property (which happened laterthat year in 2008)

a gentleman who was a mentor and coach, someone who could offer me some perspective on life and where I was at in business, but his requirement was steep to me financially at the time. Just like it might have been steep for you to get here into this Game.

4. This is a feeling a lot of men will have as they go into a 90-Day Challenge: they start to feel this massive weight and pressure on them about trying to create the Impossible Game.

5. So I was sitting there in this situation, when an interesting reality rested on my shoulders in early 2008. I had enough money inside my bank accounts to do one of three things at the time:

1.   Hold onto the money and not give it to anybody
2.   Pay the mortgage on all these real estate properties.
3.   Take the money and invest it in this mentor's Mastermind that he was running.

6. I remember sitting there, and I didn't even have the balls to tell my wife, because I already knew that the answer was going to be really simple for her: "Keep the money for us."

7. I was left with this really harsh reality, sitting there with these mortgage statements and bills that had been sent to me by hand. I was in the basement of my beautiful home, badass cars still in the driveway and garage. Custom-tailored suits…I mean, as far as the rest of the world knew, everything was fine, because I was doing a good job of fucking lying, but to me, I knew I was very, very, stuck. Little did I realize how deep down the dark hole to Hell I was about to go over the next couple of years, but in that moment, I was left with a very clear path.

8. I remember holding these statements and looking at the amount on the payment from the bank. It was late at night, dark outside, and I sat there in the unfinished part of my basement where I had this little desk. It later became this kind of sanctuary,[121] where I could lay my grievances—penance that I was paying for fucking life up—so I would work out of this like a little cave, a hovel with concrete walls that weren't finished inside this basement, and I was holding this mortgage statement. The decision was clear: you're not going to change because you don't have the answers, nor do you have the capacity in you to fix this shit right now.

---

[121] This is the origin of where they idea started from for the General's Tent.

9. Looking at the mortgage statement, my mind was like, "If you pay this now, guess what's coming next month? The same bill. Guess what you don't have? You don't have any more fucking answers, and you'll be out of money, and there'll be nobody in your world to give you a perspective that's different than what you currently have."

10. And so you'll buy some temporary side relief, and for a few nights (if you make those payments), you'll feel relief that you paid all your bills, but within a week, your panic will start to rise again, and within two weeks, you'll be into the darkest, deepest place ever, because inside that hole, you'll have no other fucking voice but your own, and that Voice has betrayed you. Not *The Voice* that comes from God, the Voice of the Spirit or the Voice of the Universe speaking through you. No; I'm talking about the voice of your own scarcity, frustration, and chaos.

11. So I remember I took those mortgage bills, called the banks, and I said, "I can't make my payments right now." Of course, they were pissed and fired up, so I just changed my phone number (which of course they found), and then I took down my voice mail, which I didn't have again for, like, six years because I was so paranoid of the financial hole that had been dug. Not that I'm recommending any of these tactics, mind you.

## Making One Last Investment

12. I made an investment in a coach and a mentor at that time which changed everything, because every single week, in my darkest moments, I'd be able to get into a conversation: I had bought access to another perspective and a listening ear, someone who had been to the gates of Hell which was where I was going, but who had hope. Hope that shit could change, my life might be different, and that I could make it through this to turn shit around.

13. I wasn't going to have hope paying my mortgage payment at the time; all I had was a guarantee of the payments showing up the next month, the statement due, and me not being able to pay it, with no new answers to the current problems I was facing. So, I found right out of the gate, there

in 2008, that the biggest thing that a man looks for in accomplishing big outcomes, challenges, voyages and quests, is *Access*.[122]

## Accessing Action Plans

14. Once discovered, this Access led to action plans. See, when I invested in this coach, he gave me different things to think about and different things to do, just like you investing here in the Black Box; you bought *access* to the Black Box and the Brotherhood. But it came with a price, and you were left with a decision: either I make this investment in the Box and within the Brotherhood, or I don't, and if I don't, I'm left with my own Voice, problems, and my own way of solving them. In paraphrasing Albert Einstein, "Man's mind has not the capacity to solve a problem at the level of thinking which it first created it."[123]

15. So we're left, oftentimes, trying to solve shit in a cul-de-sac of karmic chaos that reality is constantly moving around in a circle. We're trying to solve unsolvable problems but fail because we're not big enough; we don't think big enough. We're actually being less, and inside of that, we're doing less.

## Blueprint to Having It All

16. You know, it's one thing for me to *tell* you about having it all, but what you've just uncovered inside is the actual *blueprint* to having it all. We've gone through the Code, the Core, the Keys, and now we've covered the Game. Fundamentally, you have all the tools; you have access to the necessary action plans, and now you get to customize it. In being part of the Brotherhood, you get access to these conversations as a group and with other Warriors.

17. The next thing I realized when putting the framework into what is now Warrior together was that I needed accountability. Plenty of people around the world may know what to do but they don't know how to access the accountability that's required from within to find solutions. It's not complex; accountability is simple, but it requires doing the fucking work.

---

[122] The path that gets you to access a different voice, information, and/or new way of speaking and therefore changing the way you're currently operating.
[123] *Note:* Actual quote is "No problem can be solved by the same consciousness that created it. We need to see the world anew." See Appendix Quotes

## The Simple Game of Warrior

18. The Game of Warrior and having it all is not complex. It's very simple, but knowing what to do and then doing it are two different things. Having leverage on ourselves and the accountability inside our own Voice and our word is why the Code is so important. If you're inherently a fucking liar, then no matter what you tell yourself you're going to do, or how clear the action plan appears to be, you're not going to do it. You *know* this. It's not like I'm giving you some fucking revelation; these words are hitting you with a harsh reality: you're either going to fucking get leverage on yourself or you're not, and if you get leverage on yourself, then you'll do the shit you know you need to do.

19. The Game is so simple, it's ridiculous. Now, getting access to accountability inside yourself is a different story; we need to report to others. This is what I loved about the coach that I hired back in 2008: every week, I had to report back to him about shit I was doing. I had these action plans, I would do them, and then I would have to come back, and I would have to share them. Sometimes at the beginning, we're not accountable enough to ourselves, and so we need a partner; a spouse, friend, mentor, mastermind group, or Brotherhood to support us in this thing that we say we're going to do because we waver.

20. We waver because of the journey to an impossible reality of toppling the 16-foot domino, and there's a lot of shit that can go wrong with that. We don't know; it gets scary, dark, and confusing. Shit doesn't turn out the way we're thinking and sometimes we can't anticipate some of the shit that's going to happen. You can't be ready, truly, for the unknowable, except to have the capacity inside yourself that says, "You know what? I'm going to do what I say I'm going to do because I'm in the Game of Accountability. When I get clear on a plan, I'm going to fucking execute, and I'm not going to wait for weeks or months; I'm going to execute now! I'm going to measure the course correction and enter the General's Tent every single week, where I'm going to make a measurement of where I've come from and where I'm committing to go the next week."

21. This is where accountability becomes huge, both from within yourself and from the outside in.

## Association Through the Brotherhood

22. One of the things that didn't exist inside this relationship with this mentor I had was that there just weren't any other guys like me. There wasn't this Brotherhood of Association; there wasn't anybody else around me that felt what I was going through and I didn't know of a way I could access a group like that. I didn't feel connected to anybody else around me, so I felt horribly alone. Part of why we built the Black Box and why these Games work is because men like you and I get to unify ourselves with a Brotherhood at all kinds of different levels, and participate on a weekly, monthly, quarterly and annual basis inside experiences that allow us to connect with other men who are up to the same thing. Men who live by the Code, stand for the Core, create with the Keys, and play the Game every fucking day. It's a totally different game to have access to that kind of conversation and relationship.

23. This weird thing starts to happen when you have these kinds of associations. Even if you are miles, states, or countries apart, whether you're on the other side of the fucking globe or down the street, when you wake up to war today, or go into the General's Tent, there's a recollection in your mind and you realize you have access to a Brotherhood. You have access to a group of people who are doing what you're doing. They're going into the Tent, and maybe they're having the same Resistance. We face pitfalls and make choices every day, yet there's this Power that rises up inside of us as individuals just knowing that we're not alone; knowing that there's other men like us who are going through what we're going through. We're turning their lives around from having a one and two-dimensional life to ultimately playing the Game, living by the Code, standing for the Core, creating with the Keys, and playing the game every single day.

## Driving Force for Warrior Week

24. These four statements become the driving force behind our Warrior Week experiences: Access, Action Plans, Accountability, and Association. It became the driving force behind the Brotherhood and Black Box. We knew that even if we had access to the action plans, we needed accountability with other men, fellow Warriors, and so the summary I want you to really get is this: you're going to need to get Access, my friend. You're going to need to get access to clear Action Plans, which we've given you. You're

going to have to do the work for it and face accountability. The Black Box consists of people that you trust and people who trust you; who can give you associative advice and feedback inside this Brotherhood.

25. Ultimately, you're going to need association, because as you try to build your kingdom, there's a world full of one and two-dimensional men who will not understand it. They are not going to get it, at least in the beginning. They're not going to give you praise for the initial steps on your journey, nor will they give you valuable feedback and a positive direction for the things you're doing just out of the gate. Like the guy who loses 200 pounds or the man who goes from bankruptcy to becoming a multi-millionaire, people want to praise the end result; they want to see the After picture, not the "everything in between" ones. Ironically, a lot of those people that praise the After pictures are the same ones who spit and piss on the man who was taking the journey in the first few months or years, stating that what he's doing is impossible as he walked into the gates of Hell to find the keys to his own kingdom, making his way back out to reclaiming his own power.

## Keys to Your Kingdom Can Only Be Unlocked By You

26. Brothers, I've given you the Keys to a Game that we know works. What you do with it from this point is on you. You have access to action plans, accountability and association inside this Brotherhood worldwide. Whether you choose to ascend or implode will be up to you.

27. I'll leave you with one final thought as we summarize the Game: No matter how clear you get on these Games, the work you do in the General's Tent is not the war. The war requires you to get to work, which can sometimes be brutally ugly or create very beautiful experiences. The War reminds us that we are not entitled to what we want out of our 90-day Outcome. We do not get the outcomes of the 16-foot domino falling over simply because we started the game. We are not entitled to having it all simply because we bought the Black Box. In order for you to go from good to great and from great to superhuman as a man in today's Game, you will get 100% of what you are ruthlessly, fucking committed to producing.

28. My prayer is that here, inside this Brotherhood with this Game and this Box, you'll find exactly that.

## Chapter 39:
## POINTS TO PONDER FROM THE GENERAL'S TENT

- **POINT #1:** The greatest thing that a man can look for in accomplishing big outcomes, challenges, voyages and quests is Access.

- **POINT #2:** In being part of the Brotherhood, you get access/blueprints to these conversations as a group and with other Warriors that hold you accountable.

- **POINT #3:** The Game of Warrior and having it all is not complex. It's very simple, but knowing what to do and then doing it are two different things.

- **POINT #4:** No matter how clear you get on these Games, the work you do in the General's Tent is not the war. The war requires you to get to work.

# THE SUMMARY

## Chapter 40: THE GAME

The Game is the Doctrine Review. Life is a literal game because we choose to make it that way. This doctrine that has been learned here in the Warrior's Way becomes the foundation of how you choose to play.

# SECTION SEVEN
# THE SUMMARY

## CHAPTER FORTY
# THE GAME

"The good news is that the moment you decide that what you know is more important than what you have been taught to believe, you will have shifted gears in your quest for abundance. Success comes from within, not from without."

### -Ralph Waldo Emerson
[American essayist and poet, leader of the Transcendentalist Movement 1803-1882]

---

1. Brother, we've come a long way so far here inside the Black Box. We have covered a lot of content you've only begun to discover.

## Diving into Doctrinal Concepts

2. I don't know what part of the journey you are in: If this is your first, second, or fifth round through the content and doctrine here of the Warrior's Way, but here in this particular section, as we come to a conclusion inside the Black Box, I want to review some of the concepts. We're going to dive into what I call the doctrinal concepts: the four fundamental mantras that run who we are as men, and Brothers.

## "I Live By The Code."

3. To live by the Code—to live by anything—simply means that this is who I'm being in life. From the very beginning of my development as a personal development trainer, as a person searching to find myself as a businessman, husband, and a father, I was understanding this one simple concept: "Be, do, and have."

4. Across all of the Warrior t-shirts and across a lot of the stands we dig in our marketing we say, "Be more. Do more. Suck less." The beginning stage of living is a function of Being. All results that you and I are searching for come out of a Being-ness. To live by the Code doesn't simply mean that inside your mind you intellectually understand Real: the facts, Raw: the feelings, Relevant: the focus, and Results: the fruit. See, you can intellectually understand this, but to live by the Code means it must become how you see the world. Living something is *becoming* that thing.

5. You know, we look at the conversation of preaching, teaching and sharing the conversation of Warrior, and we say this constantly here inside the Brotherhood, "You have an obligation, stewardship, and a responsibility to take the things that you're experiencing here as true and to engage other men with this conversation, to share with them the fruit that has brought so much joy inside your life. That it has changed the way you see yourself, hence the world that you live in, the queen that you are currently partnered up with, your children, your posterity, and the entire world that you operate in.

6. That sharing, though, is very unnatural if you're coming from a place of not living, but simply contemplating it. To "contemplate" the Code versus "live" the Code requires you to actually practice it on a daily basis. It is the foundational concept in everything that we do here in Warrior: living by the Code.

## "To Stand For The Core."

7. Mantra number two that we stack on top of that is "to stand for the Core." While I live for and by the Code, this itself is a function of who I'm being. It also means that I'm going to get off my ass and take a stand, about doing something with this Core conversation. The Core is not an idea of contemplation or mental masturbation and saying "I'm going to have it all." The Core requires doing.

8. No, no, no. I'm going to take a stand for living this way. Even while those around me may be simply living one and two-dimensional lifestyles, I choose as a Warrior man in today's Game to make a commitment to not only become the Code, but to end that Being-ness to do what is necessary to create the results in my life in the Core. I am *being* the Code, and from

that power, I then take a stand and move forward in producing results inside the Core of Body, Being, Balance, and Business.

## "I Create With The Keys"

9. As I begin to build those results in Body, Being, Balance, and Business and access that power, this third mantra layers up by putting the first two mantras to work. It's time to focus make it productive; this is when we move into the Keys. We say, "I create with the Keys."

10. We live by the Code, stand for the Core and create with the Keys. When I create, I create with focus, power, and intention. I don't randomly walk into the Game of Wandering Generality when it comes to my week in business or creating targets to move forward; when it comes to building an Empire as a businessman, I say, "What? Why? When? and How?"

11. Keys allow me to access Results inside Business, which allows me to fund the Game of having it all. People ask, "Well, Garrett, why do you put so much emphasis on the business end?"

12. "Without bank accounts overflowing, the prosperity and the abundance that comes from the financial wealth that you are building in business becomes increasingly difficult to not slip into scarcity inside of these other areas."

## "Play to Win the Game Every Single Day"

13. The fourth mantra is super simple: "Play to win the Game every single day." Day-to-day life itself truly is a Game. Here inside Warrior with our game of five metrics, systems, tools, and the Brothers around the globe, you are given an opportunity every single day to wake up and say, "I may have lost yesterday. I may have completely fucked it up then, but today is a new day. Today I can choose to play the game and win."

14. Win today. It's one thing to play a game; it's another thing to play to win. I can show up and go through the motions, like at the gym: I can grab a glider, drink a Diet Coke and read a book as I casually exercise. Yes, I'm playing the game, but I'm not playing to win.

15. Playing to win requires a different focus; it says, "I am clear, Garrett, about my Core 4 commitments. I know how I'm going to win today." We

declare, "I'm clear about my Key 4 commitments for the week, and I know how I'm going to win this week, Garrett." It also says, "I know what my 30 and 60-Day Benchmarks are. I know what my 90-Day Target Outcomes are, Garrett. I know where I'm trying to go."

16. When I wake up and play the game to win today, I can actually tell you what winning looks like. I can tell you the story that these numbers signify. When I hit a four inside my Core 4 and Key 4, I hit a total of 28 for the week, plus my 4 for Key 4 and all the sudden I have a 32. Those numbers tell a story about your actions and results. They tell a story about your commitment to move forward as a Warrior in having it all.

## The Game Is Real

17. So the game itself is real. It's real for you; it's real for us. It's real for all the men inside your reality, and all the men who you haven't met yet but will come to the Brotherhood in the future. The Game is real to all of the men inside this Brotherhood who choose to play by the beat of a different drum. Who say, "Yes, my life is a game because I choose to make it that way. This doctrine that I have learned here in the Warrior's way becomes the foundation of how I choose to play."

> Live by the Code.
> Stand for the Core.
> Create with the Keys.
> Play to win the Game every single day.

## Chapter 40:
## POINTS TO PONDER FROM THE GENERAL'S TENT

- **POINT #1:** Living by the Code isn't just about being Real, Raw, and Relevant with a ruthless commitment to Results; living by the Code means it must become how you see the world.

- **POINT #2:** Standing for the Core requires doing by taking a stand and moving forward to produce big ass results in the Core of Body, Being, Balance and Business.

- **POINT #3:** We live by the Code, stand for the Core and create with the Keys. When I create, I create with focus, power, and intention inside Business to fund my "have it all" lifestyle.

- **POINT #4:** "Play to win the Game every single day." This requires a different focus: What, Why, When and then How at the end.

# THE SUMMARY
## Chapter 41: THE ARMORY

The Armory is exactly what it sounds like; it's the place where all the weapons and tools are for you to get a lot of shit done here at Warrior.

SECTION SEVEN
# THE SUMMARY

CHAPTER FORTY-ONE
# THE ARMORY

"Language is the armory of the human mind, and at once contains the trophies of its past and the weapons of its future conquests."

**-Samuel Taylor Coleridge**
[English Poet and Philosopher, co-founder of Romantic Movement, 1772-1834]

---

1. There's been a lot of content, tools, and ability for you to expand who you are up until this point. Throughout this entire Black Box experience I have been referencing the Armory. The Armory is exactly what it sounds like; it's the place where all the weapons and tools are for you to get shit done here at Warrior.

## Tools from The Weapon Box

2. The Armory is a weapon box created for you; a toolbox that allows you to create bigger results across Body, Being, Balance and Business through deep dive training into each one of the Core 4 areas by myself and other trainers brought in both internally and externally to this Brotherhood. The Armory has content, articles, book references and support tools to get you where you want to go.

3. I'm going to help you build the frame around how to think through the Armory before going through the details of what is specifically in there. Ultimately, this is the Content and Process of how Warrior works.

476

## Ordained as Men for A New Way of Living

4. The first thing to understand is theory. Unless you have bought into the theories that we speak of here inside the Warrior Doctrine, nothing else matters. The greatest disagreements in life come from people arguing tactics and tools without having first gotten on the same page with theory.

5. Our theory stands as the following, and that is simply that we have been ordained as men, called to usher in a new way of living, which demands that we as businessmen do not just make money, but that we create a framework to have it all across Body, Being, Balance, and Business.

6. The first phase inside our experience is to have it all, and once we have it all it's to learn how to more effectively and efficiently fund it all and then in the third phase how to leave it all behind for our posterity.

7. In order to do any of that, you're going to find a lot of tools inside the Armory that may not make any sense to you right now because you don't need them yet. You haven't learned the skill sets to use them nor have you reached a certain leg in your journey that would require its use. Don't over-complicate yourself inside the Armory. You will develop the tactics that will then require the right tool, but you'll need to know where to go inside the Armory to find it in the first place. One Brother may see a situation and choose a hammer as he smashes it to pieces, while another decides to attack like a surgeon with a tactical approach.

## Theories, Tactics and Tools

8. Tactics are strategies. Right? They are ways to take principles in our life, then implement and execute them. Tactics and strategies are different for everybody; theory is where we unify while tactics are where we begin to diversify. Whether you're the hammer or scalpel guy, both of these could accomplish the Outcome, but it's about who *you* are and how you operate.

9. For example, you may be an introvert with a quieter approach; you're a circus on the inside, not the outside, so you use a scalpel. If you're an extrovert, your circus is on the outside, so it's likely that you tend to lean towards tactics and strategies that support you using a hammer.

10. When you go into the Armory, understand it is going to support you based upon who you are, so some of the tools are not going to be

as effective for you. If we get confused, we return to Theory, which are principles and then move into tactics. We have theories, tactics, and tools; used in that sequence. Theories on the bottom, tactics or strategies as the next step, those being driven based upon principles, which are nothing more than the strategic action that we're taking in order to implement the theory that we're talking about in real play. The tools, then, are the third piece that we're looking for. Not the first. When I have a problem, I'm not coming in and immediately looking for a tool, because I don't necessarily know exactly what I'm trying to solve.

## Being Worthy to Use the Tools

11. While transitioning from the gym as a PE teacher to the office as a businessman with a desk and then as an entrepreneur, I met a man who was far superior to me in entrepreneurism, business, marketing and sales. I thought myself important as I wore a suit to work and sat down in my basement office, which had a hollow door and was wedged in the corner of the townhouse business condo basement. I did have a window though, so I at least had that going for me. One day this businessman brought me a stack of letters.[124]

"What the hell are these?"

"The Gary Halbert letters."

"Who the fuck is Gary Halbert and why do I have his letters?"

"This guy's the Godfather of direct response marketing."

12. I started reading through some of these letters as I was sitting in my swivel chair, there in my suit feeling all official, not sure what I'm supposed to do next, reading these letters. I got through about two of these letters and I'm like, "This is the most pointless bullshit I've ever seen in my life. Why in the hell would I give a shit about these letters?"

13. I took the letters, folded them up nicely and I put them in one of the Office Depot vertical files I had just purchased. Sliding the drawer shut, I said, "Well, what shall I do now?"

---

[124] These are now available online, in PDF form for FREE. Go to Additional Resources: Business located at the end of this chapter for more information.

## Studying to Recognize Gold and Pearls

14. I share this with you because those were gold. *Gold.* Fifteen years later I look back at that and laugh. "Dude, you had pearls given to you but you were a swine.[125] You had no perspective to actually understand the tactical tool that you had been given."

15. It's not an issue of the fact that the tool was not working, nor even that the tactic was not viable; it's that I wasn't big enough to know how to use it to its full potential because I wasn't operating at the potential required to know how to use the tool.

16. There's going to be some tools, concepts and ideas inside the Armory that you're going to pick up for the first time which are not going to make any sense. And then you're going to come back six months later to the Armory inside the Brotherhood after having executed your ass off across Body, Being, Balance and Business, living with the Code and creating really big ass results inside the Key 4, hitting your targets after your first challenge. You're going to listen to an audio, pick up an article, read something or watch one of our recordings. Then you'll find inside the Armory that content as if it was for the first time because you finally see the pearl before you. You're going to go, "How is this possible?! This couldn't have been there before." Yet it was, but you didn't have the eyes to see.

17. Part of the process is understanding that the Armory is not this one-time visit. The Armory, itself, is a tool that is constantly evolving: we are constantly adding to and taking away—based upon the demands of this Brotherhood—content, resources and tools to support you in hitting your Outcomes inside the challenges from your 90-Day experiences. Don't discredit the Armory just because you went one time and the stuff that you saw was overwhelming or you didn't understand it. Continue to report back to the Armory every single week.

## The Transformational Armory

18. Next piece in this: we go from Theory to Tactics to Tools and that is Transformation. The Armory is also going to be loaded up with supplies and tools that will allow you to experience action. The only way that you

---

[125] In reference to the scripture Matthew 7:6, See Appendix Quotes

get a result is when you leave where you are and go to a new place. That is it. A different result does not happen by staying in the same situation. I did not get a different perspective in the movie theater demanding that the image on the screen change by moving into a different goddamn seat. If I'm sitting in the front, I have to get up and go to the back if I want a different perspective, which also relates sometimes to my marriage. If I'm sitting here today and my marriage looks like this, then I'm going to have to go over here in order for my marriage to improve.

19. You'll also notice inside the Armory that there's going to be content and references to tools that are about getting you into action. Make sure that you're getting off your ass and doing things on a day-to-day basis. These are result based actions (Simple Success Swinging Singles), that will support you in actually taking all the theories, all the tactics and the tools, and actually transforming your life. We are not building the Armory so that you can sit around and mentally jerk yourself off with a bunch of information. This is not the point of the Brotherhood Armory. The Armory was built to get your results at a place to meet you where you are. In order to do that we need more information, tactics and tools, and we need action in order to transform your world from one place to another.

## Transcendent Content

20. The last piece you're going to notice inside the Armory is going to be Transcendent Content. Purpose and spirituality are pertinent to your growth inside Warrior: who you see yourself to be spiritually changes over time. We're going to have influences of content that is specifically about spiritual paths which will be created inside your Black Bible. These are not religious paths; they're *spiritual* paths which question and challenge the two fundamental questions of a Warrior Man which is this: "Who am I?" and "What is the purpose of my life?"

21. It is amazing how much power and permission inside your life is garnered upon your definition of these two concepts. As you evolve and grow, knocking out your first 90-Day Challenge you'll realize, "Holy shit, it worked!" and then when you knock out your next 90-Day Challenge, you further realize that who you are is more than you were before.

## Being More Than You Were Before

22. You are more inside of this Brotherhood than you were before. Hence the idea around "Who am I?" expands with every single transformative action that you take. Like an onion, you begin to peel away the outside layers, uncovering this hidden [126]Pearl of Great Price inside of you at the center. This powerful perspective ultimately leads you to a place in which the true desire for your life is to leave a legacy that matters. This is why we say, "To be a Warrior is to have it all, fund it all, and leave it all."

23. There's a stacking process to this at each level that who I am evolves, expands and becomes more powerful. Who I believe myself to be inside the mirror of my humanity begins to change how I operate, think about life, my wife, business, and bank account. How I operate with my skill sets and mindsets, contribute to society, and what I choose to ultimately do changes, and the Armory provides a means to be ready for these changes.

## Investing in A Spiritual Life

24. That all comes down to what? A willingness to invest in our spiritual life, challenging the status quo about what we consider to be the purpose of life. People look at me and they're like, "Well, Garrett, how did you get where you are?" There's a lot of things I've done, but one of the things that I did for years at a *very* high level was to study spiritual books from all spectrums of belief systems. Every day for hours at a time I would study and read them, contemplating concepts because these altering realities set the background and the foundation for how I saw myself and the purpose I had in life.

25. There was a spiritual sense of calling in what we do here at Warrior for me; if this wasn't true, I can promise you I would have never endured the eight years that it took to ultimately build this Brotherhood to a place with the access you have today. The blood, sweat, and tears, day after day, week after week, month after month, year after year would not have been possible without a deep dive bigger picture of how I saw myself spiritually with this calling that I felt distilled upon me. The mantle and the responsibility were felt long before the Black Box Brotherhood existed.

---

[126] A spiritual term regarding the beautiful interior and what a gift it is to share with others, but it takes time and levels of expansion to get to that point. See Matthew 13:45-46

## Tactical How-Tos

26. In summary, inside the Armory you're going to find content and training on theories in Body, Being, Balance and Business. You're going to find tactics that will support those theories, AKA Tactical How-Tos: specific resources, software tools, books to reads, concepts, workshops you could go to, mentors you could hire, people that could support you in getting those results and then transformation.

27. The final piece is Transcendence, which is helping you understand that you are called as a king to lead a movement, and to help you see the spiritual nature around what it is that you're doing because it *does* matter. The Armory is not merely a place where we store recordings; it is a searchable asset that allows you—based upon who you are being today and the things that you feel you are lacking today—to be able to enter in and search for the truth that the universe needs to deliver up to you today.

28. This doesn't mean that you won't find answers outside of the Brotherhood; of course you'll find answers elsewhere, but our job in creating the Armory is to bring as much as we possibly can into one place to support you in accessing the highest level of power inside yourself so that you can access the highest level of results in having it all.

### Chapter 41:
### POINTS TO PONDER FROM THE GENERAL'S TENT

- **POINT #1:** Think of the Armory as a toolbox that allows you to create bigger results across Body, Being, Balance and Business through deep dive training into each one of the Core 4 areas by myself and other trainers brought in both internally and externally to this Brotherhood. It has content, articles, book references and support tools to get you where you want to go.

- **POINT #2:** Tactics and strategies are different for everybody; theory is where we unify while tactics are where we begin to diversify according to our strengths.

- **POINT #3:** The Armory was built to get you to take action in order to create results at the place to meet you where you are.

- **POINT #4:** In Transcendent Content, purpose and spirituality are pertinent to your growth inside Warrior as who you were before one 90-Day Outcome is entirely different than where you are now.

# THE SUMMARY
## Chapter 42: THE BROTHERHOOD

You're not nearly as different as you would like to play yourself to be,
which is why we have the Brotherhood for Warrior. You are not nearly
as alone as you choose to be.

## SECTION SEVEN
# THE SUMMARY

## CHAPTER FORTY-TWO
# THE BROTHERHOOD

Rise up, warriors, take your stand
at one another's sides,
our feet set wide and rooted
like oaks in the ground.
Then bide your time, biting your lip,
for you were born
from the blood of Heracles,
unbeatable by mortal men,
and the god of gods has never turned his back on you.

**-Tyrtaeus**
["Arete" excerpt, Spartan Poet known for political and military elegies,
latter 7th Century BCE]

---

1. Brother, one of the greatest lies you and I are living today as Warrior men is that we were to do this life alone. Everything inside the resistance of who you and I are as a man tells us a lie, but I'm going to have you consider that that lie is not going to come around once; it's a lie that's going to come around consistently for years and years in your entire lifetime.

## The Big Lie

2. Sometimes, this lie is going to be stronger than other lies, but it's going to have you believe this idea that you're alone and are inherently different. "Well, you know what Garrett, I'm hearing these ideas. I'm seeing these other men, Garrett, but you know what, my story is different. I'm different,

Garrett, and I'm alone in that difference." I'm calling bullshit. You're not different. You're not nearly as different as you think you are.

3. You're not nearly as different as you would like to play yourself to be. You are not nearly as alone as you choose to be. Yet, your sense of feeling alone comes in this one, inherent lie that this manipulative little bullshit story plays inside the recesses of your mind, which says, "I am alone. I am alone in this war. I am alone in this Game. I'm alone in playing the Warrior's Way to have it all." This is why the Brotherhood was built, and the Black Box Brotherhood became something in life after years of testing, proving this doctrine and this experience to be sound.

## Unique Modern Warriors

4. We knew that the key glue to a man's liberation inside the conversation of the Warrior's Way to having it all came down to eliminating this lie. You're not different; you are unique. You are not different though. Your feelings, your pain, your suffering, your aloneness, your fears, all of this shit is normal, but it doesn't feel normal because you've been a liar.

5. Who you are inherently and your pain is not different. Neither is your pleasure; it might be unique or you might be with a different type of woman than you were before. You might be in a different city or country than me, and your uniqueness is yours. Your differences though…there are none. We're men called to live in this modern Game called the Warrior's Way to having it all. Modern businessmen called to lead and to usher in an entire Revolution of a new way of thinking and behaving, and it requires specific guidelines to become a part of it.

## Buying Access

6. Where I live in Orange County, California, there is a series of locations in which one cannot access certain beach clubs, restaurants, hotels, or clubs without access. You have to have a specific card in order to enter into those facilities. The card itself comes at a price; where your home is or what you've bought as far as the membership that gives you access. I carry several of these black cards in my wallet, and stickers on my cars that give me access to places that everyone else doesn't have access to; only those who have purchased it.

7. Very similar to what you're seeing here inside the Black Box is that you bought Access. You paid for the right to play. I can have access all day long, but if I don't utilize the resources inside the accessibility of the thing that I'm choosing to access, well, that's on me. It simply creates the opportunity for you to have a new experience, but will only be utilized if you *choose* to access it.

8. The first thing we knew is that a man needs to have Access to: The Doctrine of Warrior, Action Plans, Accountability, Association, and ultimately Ascension to leave the land of where they were to the place they wanted to be.

## The Doctrine of Warrior

9. Without the Doctrine, the Warrior Movement doesn't exist. Everything that you've been given here inside of this Black Box and WarriorBook has been a guide to the foundational doctrinal ways of seeing the world and the way that we tell you, teach you, train you, and educate you to see yourself inside this new world. Without this worldview, nothing that we speak of will work for you. There is no tactic, tool, or strategy that I can give you that will ultimately liberate you from yourself if the world you see is so small and one dimensional in nature.

10. If you open your mind up through this conversation here inside the Black Box to see a different world, you have a part bigger than you ever imagined was possible; not as a peasant in the shack but as a fucking king on the throne with a crown. When you see yourself as a king, and the reality that the world you're building as a kingdom is to expand into an Empire, the way that you play is different.

11. Part of what you're accessing is a new set of eyes and permission through this Doctrine that says, "You were not built and born into this world of despair, to be weak, or fall. You were put here to Rise above it all. You were put here to liberate and remind yourself as you awaken to the reality that YOU ARE A KING. Inside of this kingdom and inside of this kinship that you experienced was a divine birth right to rise and lead in your families, environment, and the communities around you."

12. You can't do that if the world you see fits in a fucking shot glass. The Game is bigger than that. It's an ocean as far as you can see, but if all you

can focus on is this small little shot glass of possibility, then it doesn't matter what I tell you because all you'll end up seeing is limitation.

13. Access to the Doctrine changes your life. This is why in Christianity, the literal publishing of the Bible after the invention of the Gutenberg Press caused a Revolution inside of the Christian faith.[127] Why? Because for years, (1) the people couldn't read, and (2) control of the words in the books were given to the righteous "leaders" or the priests at that time.

14. The people were controlled without knowledge and information, but once the Bible was printed, people had access for the first time to the Word. They learned to read it, then studied to understand it, so God could communicate to them directly through customized revelation.

15. Prior to that, it was simply the interpretation of the content from one who would stand in front and declare the Doctrine, saying, "This is the doctrine." Then from that place, you'd be left to interpret. Some say the greatest revolution that ever happened in Christianity beyond Jesus Christ was the access the printing press gave mankind, which ultimately liberated the Word and made it available to other people.

16. This global impact didn't just affect Christianity; it affects every single religious belief existing on the planet. Here we are inside the Black Box with an opportunity for you to See the Doctrine; not the way I tell it, but the ability to listen, watch, and read it, having access to how it makes sense to you, and the Voice inside of you giving you the customized version of the Warrior Doctrine that will serve you, your queen and your family for as long as you choose it to.

## Accessing Action Plans

17. I can have access to Doctrine all day long, but even if that information is powerful, we know that information itself has never been enough. Simply having a book of good words doesn't change anyone. It creates an *opportunity* for us to be able to see something different, but inside of that comes the customization of it: the Action Plans.

18. You receive access to Action Plans inside the Armory and inside this entire process with the Black Box Brotherhood membership; live and on

---

[127] See Appendix Additional Resources: Gutenberg Press

demand access to be able to custom create with example after example of what it might look like in your world to have customized action plans.

19. You're never left with the limitation of what was last week; you can adjust, and we can adjust these Action Plans. As part of this Brotherhood, you have the ability to get feedback and opportunities to see how other Warriors are doing by saying, "Hey, listen, I probably wouldn't do it that way. I tried it this way over here, and here is what my result was. You might think about doing it a little bit different."

## Black Box Accountability

20. The Black Box Brotherhood membership allows you to also have access to accountability inside this software, custom creating your accountability system for yourself, reminding us that the way you want them, when and how you want to be reminded in the version that's important for you to be reminded by.

21. See, I can remind you all day long, but when you remind yourself, it's totally different. When I'd put a reminder inside my calendar, and use the Black Box System and the King software to support me in this, what I've created for myself is an opportunity to remind me. Like immediate feedback from taking a video of yourself, then playing that video back a few weeks later to remind you of what you felt. Maybe if you took a video of yourself when you felt fantastic, you could play it for yourself when you're not feeling fantastic.

22. Customizing the Accountability also exists inside our training calls that happen both live, on-demand virtually on line and within this book, supporting you to be able to utilize accountability and camaraderie, creating within the software pods groups, associations, and even groups of men inside your own community to circle and rally around. Localizing the Black Box helps you not wait for someone around the world to hold you accountable as you say, "Hey, you know what, there is no one in my community that's currently living this, and accountability is the best way that I can succeed so I'm going public with it, hosting my own Warrior Mastermind. I'll bring men into my home and say, 'You know what, guys? We're going to learn some new shit. I'm going to teach you the Warrior's Way.'"

## Association with Fellow Warriors

23. Part of what allows us to not feel alone is the Association with other men. You might be a guy who has been used to playing by yourself because you're the leader amongst followers. Most of the men who come to Warrior were men who felt this self-perpetuating aloneness, because any opportunity that you play with other men to create big shit together ends up as a game of distancing yourself and continuing to work alone with the pawns that work for you.

24. Inside this Game of the Brotherhood, we create the opportunity for you to see yourself through your Brothers. This association[128] is choosing to live in a way that is not the norm of society; it is the modern way of living as a Warrior Man, and you have that Association.

25. Without it, it is easy to slip into your own bullshit again. Of what? The same lie that started off this section, which is the lie that you're different; that you are alone.

## Ascension to Having It All

26. Immersing yourself into the Brotherhood through Access to the Doctrine, Action Plans, Accountability, and Association leads to the final point, which is access to Ascension. The first time I heard the term Ascension was inside of Meditation.

27. I was studying with an Ishaya monk, and in this process of studying years with him in meditation, there was this idea of Ishayas' Ascension or the Ascendant. The Ascendant is a word to reference High Power, Source, God, and Ascension, in which we go through a process/journey of doing away with the carnal state in which we live in by ascending into the Divine of who we truly are.[129] Now, regardless of what you believe or how that might sound to you, Ascension itself is simply the concept of rising above the current reality that you're in.

## Snowshoeing Up Mountains

---

[128] In this case, a group of men from around the world who hold the Keys to the Kingdom inside their own lives which comprises the Black Box System Brotherhood.

[129] According to Maslow's Hierarchy of Human Needs, this would be considered the peak of man, reaching self-actualization. See Additional Resources at the end of this chapter: Meditation

28. I loved snow shoeing for years.[130] In the winter when the snow would fall, we'd put on our snow gear and packs, then for the next three to five hours, one to three of my friends and I would hike up to the top of these mountains using our ski poles and snowshoes, and then run straight down the face of them. I'm not going to lie; a couple of times, we thought an avalanche was going to fall on us as we were running, which is probably not the best idea, especially since we didn't have the avalanche beacons inside our backpacks. Again, probably not the best idea.

29. One particular day we were hiking up the side of this mountain early; we'd usually leave around 3:30-4:00 in the morning before the sun came up and this day was no exception. My wife and kids were sleeping. I took a little coffee, put the suit and shoes on, and BOOM, out the door I went. Now, remember that snow requires cold, and at that time in the morning in winter, it's so cold that my nostril hairs would start to freeze a little bit as soon as I breathed in, yet I would also eventually sweat from wearing all my North Face gear, so I'd have to unzip it hiking up these powdery switchback trails, even though it's cold enough to freeze your fucking nose hairs.

30. It took us around three hours to get up to a peak. Once there, we actually crossed the cloud line, so down below all we could see were clouds, as if we were perched on top of them. For about two hours during the hike before this though, we would enter the cloud barrier, where we could see only about 30 feet around us. It was amazing to be inside this cloud: so quiet. So peaceful yet powerful. Where it got epic, however, the piece that always inspired us to continue snowshoeing every single Sunday, was ultimately the crown jewel on the experience when we would get through the cloud cover and hit the summit about 15 minutes later.

31. At the very top of this peak, we would stand up above the clouds, which would look like a blanket that covered the valley. We would stand up on this peak, and eat some food that we had packed up. We would have some water and sit back in the snow.[131] The quiet perspective while up there was so different: no cars, stress, or worry resided on top of those clouds. There was only peace; no immediate concern about or for the people down in the valley.

---

[130] This was during the time of my ultra-marathon years.

[131] The cold didn't really affect us because of the super high-end gear we were in, so it worked out really well.

## We All Have a Peak to Climb

32. We had literally ascended from the base to the peak of the mountain. To do that, we went through the clouds in order to arrive to this powerful peak of stillness. Each one of you inside this journey of Warrior and Brotherhood are going to go through this same kind of climb. You're going to leave what's clear, and then you're going to enter the Void. It's going to be unclear. It's going to be cloudy, barely able to see 30 feet in any direction.

33. You're going to hear from Brothers who are at the peak, and they're going to be yelling down to you, "Just keep going, dude. You only got about another hour and a half. You're going to be just fine, man. Just keep following the trails of the switchback. I know it looks freaky, dude. You're going to be fine. On that one area right over here, just lean close to the wall; you're not going to fall off. I realize that's 100 feet down. You're going to be just fine though; walk around close to the edge. You got at least six feet. It's totally wide enough. It's stable as hell. You're going to be just fine. Just stay to the left going up against the wall, and go."

34. Listening to the Council of Brothers who are at the peak, you're also shouting down to men who aren't even beginning the journey. You're saying, "Dude, it's not so bad. Just come on up here. We're still in the clouds, but dude, you can do this. Come on up."

35. The men standing at the peak look across the valley to another peak, and see another group of men; Brothers in the Brotherhood who have left that peak, descended into the Valley, and climbed up to a new peak that's even higher. Standing from peak to peak, you look across the valley, and all you see are clouds below; the Void between these peaks. It's difficult sometimes to say, "Well, should I go on this journey? Should I leave this peak that I'm going to have to go down into the valley to ascend again to a higher peak?"

Yes.

36. Ascension is what we have access to the most here; it is the ability for you to ascend and transcend the life that you had before in contrast to the life that you're about to have. The Brotherhood is about Access to Doctrine, Action Plans, Accountability, Association, and Ascension, but, at the end of the day, all of that Access means nothing if you don't utilize it.

## Chapter 42:
## POINTS TO PONDER FROM THE GENERAL'S TENT

- **POINT #1:** You're not as different as you think you are; you are unique.

- **POINT #2:** You paid to have access all day long when you joined Warrior, but if you don't utilize the resources and use the tools inside the Black Box, well, that's on you. Accountability allows you to share your customized approach to having it all.

- **POINT #3:** The Black Box gives us access to Ascension within our own potential which we find is limitless, as we rise above the current reality that we're in.

- **POINT #4:** The Brotherhood within Warrior gives you access to fellow ascenders making the climb to have it all, holding each other accountable just as you hold yourself accountable, but no one can make the climb for you.

# THE SUMMARY

## Chapter 43: THE LEAP

The Big Leap consists of the final words of wisdom as you begin the journey into the Void of having it all.Every morning the Divinity of your Darkness is going to rise up and create Resistance inside of you to challenge you to become more, which is possible as long as you choose to daily live the Warrior's Way.

## SECTION SEVEN
# THE SUMMARY

## CHAPTER FORTY-THREE
# THE LEAP

"One small step for man, one giant leap for mankind."

### -Neil Armstrong
[First Apollo 11 pilot to walk on moon, first lunar spaceflight, July 20, 1969]

---

1. The Big Leap. This is kind of like my final farewell to you as you've read through an incredible amount of content. It is the final words of wisdom as you begin the journey into the Void of having it all. In order to do that, I'm going to talk through a couple of concepts and ideas that I have found to be absolutely crucial being successful and living the "have it all" lifestyle, but also in building a life that maintains it.

## Maintaining The "Have It All" Life

2. See, it's one thing to build something, it's a whole other thing to maintain it; all worthwhile things are. A lot of people can make money, but to maintain it is the difficult deal. To get married is one thing, but to build and maintain a marriage that works powerfully is difficult. To build a family that stays functional, not dysfunctional, takes a lot of work. There are a lot of ideas and concepts that I've had to consider and play with over the last 39 years—particularly the last 15 years as an entrepreneur—attempting to figure this Game out.

3. There's a distinction between salvation and liberation, where some people look at what we do here and they're like, "Ah, it's a cult. You know, they're like a religion; they're a church."

4. You can think whatever the hell you want from the outside, but it always brings up this idea of Salvation. There are people who will say, "Well, Garrett, you can't offer up salvation."

5. I'm not offering salvation. I'm not a Savior. Warrior is not a saving environment; inside the Black Box Brotherhood, you will find no salvation here.

## No Salvation in Black Box

6. Now, depending upon your belief system and how you operate, when it comes to this idea of salvation, it's possible inside your world that you may consider yourself to be saved; maybe you do, maybe you don't, either way is irrelevant to me for this particular conversation. Let's put that to the side because I know a lot of people, a lot of men even in the Christian faith, who consider themselves to be saved, but they are slaves on a day-to-day basis.

7. "Yes, I'm saved, but I'm a slave, Garrett. How do I get myself out of this incarcerated state even though I know 'I'm saved'?"

"Well, you've got to start playing a Game of Liberation."

## Game of Liberation

8. Liberation says the following: "you can help a Brother, but you cannot force a Brother to live a life that he was born to live. You can encourage a man to stand up and reclaim his kingdom, but you cannot force this man to ultimately do it. The decision for liberation sits squarely on the man; only he holds the key to the bonds holding him back."

9. No one in your world has incarcerated you. Not your wife, children, or business partners; NO ONE has done anything to you. Your current state of incarceration OR liberation is upon *your* shoulders and rests squarely upon your head.

10. So, what is liberation? Liberation is the ability to break the bonds that hold us bound to this one and two-dimensional life that we're living. It says, "You know what? I refuse to continue to play the game in the way that I'm playing it. I refuse to remain incarcerated inside my own mind and soul. I refuse to continue to live in this incarcerated state in this shack outside the walls of my own kingdom. I am choosing liberation."

## Self-Liberation from Incarceration

11. The Warrior Movement is a scientifically proven system to deliver results in all areas of your life, elevating you to a place of superhuman in a world of mediocre liars dying, going through their lives incarcerated. Warrior liberates and leads a revolution inside your own home, world, and businesses, but this requires you to also not see yourself as someone in need of saving. You are not seen as broken here at Warrior; we see you as someone who is incarcerated, where only *you* hold the keys to your own liberation, if you choose it.

12. We do not pick a man up and take him to a place he cannot go; we reach a hand down and slap a Brother in the face saying, "Yes, you know it is time for you to go. You are not weak, a victim, or entitled. Your life is exactly where it is because you operated on what you knew best at the time, but if you want something different here Brother, we will not pick you up and carry you to your Promised Land. No one can do that for you because we're building up our own kingdoms."

13. It's only a matter of time before you will regress and fail if you were carried up and placed on your throne by others, knowing that you didn't pay the price. There is a certainty that comes from a man who leaves the shack and rises to the throne on his own—with the support of his Brothers cheering him on—knowing that he must do it alone and be the one who hunts the wolf, for no other way is he qualified to lead his people, queen, and family, than if he takes the journey alone and returns a king.

## Not An Overnight Change

14. The second concept is this: You're never going to change your life overnight. It's not going to happen. One of the greatest struggles I had when everything in my banking world imploded from 2007 through 2008 was that I lived in this fantasyland story. I lived like I was going to hit a homerun, and by doing that, all of our problems will be over in six months.

15. Well, that home run mentality lapsed into one year, which then became two, and almost turned into three as I sat and floundered, trying to hit home runs. Meanwhile, nothing was changing in my life. Every single year it was like I was back to the same fucking reality that I was in the year before. See, Warrior was not built to change you overnight, yet there

is a very high probability that over a short period of time, your life will significantly change, and that over a year's time period, put you in a place that you have never imagined possible in your Body, Being, Balance, and Business. It will not happen, however, because you decided to pick up the bat and swing for the fucking fence every single morning when you woke up.

## Stop Stopping

16. When it comes to changing your world and the Game inside your life as you leave the one and two-dimensional world that you came from in order to produce a multi-dimensional/four-dimensional superhuman experience, you move steadily forward by slowing down. You're going to have to play from the Game of Simple Success Swinging Singles, where you need to slow it down and be willing to master the fundamentals by learning how to get on base every single day.

17. There is stability in this, rather than going 100 miles an hour down the freeway until an obstacle is in the road in front of you, forcing you to slam on the brakes. You pull the power brakes, and then throw the wheel left for a power slide only to proceed in rolling your car five times, and then finally when it lands on its tires, you try to start the engine up again, not acknowledging the wreck you just created because you want to go full throttle with an engine that's now broken. What makes a whole lot more sense when coming up on an obstacle while driving at a high speed is to slow down. Put the brakes on, signal, pull off to the side of the freeway if needed or stop. Then, look for traffic, turn, get back on the right freeway, decide where we're trying to go, look at the map and then go.

## Learning To Not Be Sexy

18. Simple Success Swinging Singles in the short term is not sexy; it's not sexy at all. It's not sexy to men to live the "have it all" lifestyle in the beginning because even though you're feeling powerful, people around you are like,

"Where are the results? Show me some results."

19. "Well, they're coming. I'm hitting my scores, I'm winning before I hit the door, I'm hitting my keys every single week. You know what? It's working"

"Well I don't see anything changing."

20. "Just sit and wait; it's going to. Like a thief in the night, you're not even going to see me coming because I'm getting up to bat every single day hitting a single. And then I'm getting up tomorrow, and guess what? I've hit a single. No, I haven't scored yet, but I get up the next day and hit a single; I do this until the bases are loaded. I stand up, no outs, and I score. I get up to bat again Day 5, and I score. Day 6, score, and I get up to bat Day 7, having now scored singles every day which becomes the game that I play and win."

21. That kind of steady consistency, though not sexy like the home run, is what builds Empires. It's what transforms bodies permanently, not just for a few months. Say I made $100,000 in the last quarter after I figured all this shit out, but burned out on my way, so I wind up doing nothing for the next six months. It might have made more sense for you to make $20,000 the first quarter and while you did it, build the foundation behind you to duplicate that $20,000 the next quarter in your next challenge, and add another $20,000 to that, and if you did that over four quarters, guess what happens? You increase your income to $40,000 over that quarter which steadily rolls into $60,000 then $80,000 because you built a foundation that will last. Why? Because the shenanigans and hoopla of a home run weren't there. There was a single, single, single, every single day.

22. You want to stop getting frustrated with having to start over? Quit fucking stopping. Slow down. As my [132]Navy Seal friends told me, "You fall behind, it's a shitload more energy to catch up than it is just to stay up. How about you just stay up instead of trying to catch up after taking breaks?" Fair enough my friend. Fair enough.

## Be The Change, Don't Talk About The Change

23. There's a tendency that I used to have (which I don't so much anymore), where I'd get really excited about change. I'd be like, "Shit's going to change. In my body, with my business, spirituality, and marriage; it's going to change in the life around me." This is what I would tell myself, but the problem was, I needed external validation to support me in that change. So, I told everyone around me how I was going to change. For whatever reason, I couldn't get enough leverage to have enough confidence or certainty to give

---

[132] These were the words my Navy Seal friends used on me when we're training in Kokoro. "Easier to stay up than catch up, Garrett. Quit fucking falling behind."

myself permission to change. I found it a whole lot more effective to just be the change than to talk about being the change.[133]

24. Don't tell your wife you're going to change; just start being the change in her life. Start showing up differently. When she responds with X and you normally defer to Y, use some [134]verbal judo and don't respond the same way you usually do; respond in a higher way.

25. You don't have to tell her, "I'm changing because I'm in the Black Box." Instead, just say "Nah, I'm just being a better husband. That's all."

"Well, Babe, I've been noticing this about you doing this, this, and this."

"That's great that you noticed, Babe."

26. Say that instead of going up to her and pointing out, "Hey, you know what? I've been a total asshole so I'm going to do things different, and I'm going to change."

27. Don't talk about change. Just *be* the change, and you'll surprise attack people with the space and permission to grow inside this Brotherhood and inside our Games. Tell us at Warrior what you're going to do; we want to hear it here because we'll hold you accountable to it. Outside of here, if they're not in the Box,[135] they don't get it.

## Reasons or Results?

28. Part of the great struggle that humanity has today is that we believe that somehow we're entitled to shit, which has begun to fester up as a lack of action. When I operate from the place of, "Listen, I'm not entitled to shit. If I want something different in my life, it will be upon *my* shoulders to create a different outcome. This means I've got to get clear about what I want, where I'm at, and what the work is between these two points; am I ready to do it?"

---

[133] Mahatma Gandhi: "Be the change you wish to see in the world."

[134] See Additional Resources at the end of this chapter on: Business, Verbal Judo

[135] In other words, those not in the Black Box Brotherhood or familiar withthe way how Warrior operates.

29. The results-based conversation becomes a conversation of change and says, "Listen, I'm going to change because I must change, and the only way I'm going to change is if I live in a land of results, not reasons."

30. The problem is, before you got to Black Box, most of your societal pressure came from people who said, "That's okay. It's okay for you to show up with reasons instead of results. It's okay for you to not be your word. It's okay for you to not be committed. It's okay. We understand."

31. The reason why they allowed you to be okay is because they don't want to be exposed for who they aren't being either; if they hold you accountable to the results you said you were going to get, then they too must also become accountable for the results they said they're going to get.

32. Here inside this Brotherhood, we flip the script and we play differently. We say, "No. Your reasons and results are not the same thing."

33. "You are not entitled to what you desire. You are entitled to what you are ruthlessly committed to fucking creating. That is it. If you aren't ruthlessly committed to creating it, do not be surprised when the thing that you said you wanted gets replaced with a reason for why you didn't get it and an excuse in being the victim, blaming another person for being the reason why you didn't get it.

## A Daily Decision to Have It All

34. It's not a one-time, weekly, monthly or quarterly decision to have it all. Having it all is *not* easy. It's simple, but it's *not* easy. Know what else isn't easy? Being a one-dimensional douche bag with a life that's not working at the level that you know it should be working.

35. Before you got here, most of the men that you associated with lived the easy/hard lifestyle, defined as, "I just do the bare minimum of what is mandatory and necessary today. I'm going to avoid the hard conversations within myself."

36. I do today what's hard so that tomorrow is easy. Not easier because life is easier; easier because my capacity has expanded. I hit my Core 4 and Key 4 every day focusing on doing the *urgent and important* and the *not urgent, but important* items.

37. It has to do with the capacity of the man, and so when I say that "it's hard easy," what I mean is that it's easy because your skill sets and your mindsets have expanded, hence the doing of the task has become easier and simpler because you have become more. This path of *easy hard* is a path of *hard* because your skill sets and mindsets do not continue to increase and expand to deal with the demand of the innovation necessary inside the life that you and I are living day-to-day. This creates conflict against our very nature which is to expand.

38. Our society is moving fast, and if we're not focused, we're going to lose ourselves inside that process. Let's back up to this idea then: it's a daily decision to follow the Warrior's Way. Every morning you're going to wake up inside the Divinity of your own Darkness, not necessarily wanting to get up and go workout; you don't want to meditate, etc… In that moment you're going to have to make a decision. By noon you might have to make a decision again to bring out the Dark Warrior. Just settle into that idea.

39. Every morning the Divinity of your Darkness is going to rise up and create Resistance inside of you to challenge you to become more, to choose it again today even though you chose it yesterday, and this is why the phrase "What have you done today?" actually matters. What you did two weeks ago unfortunately does not necessarily equip you to deal with what's going on today. Today, you must specifically choose to live the Warrior's Way.

## Chapter 43:
## POINTS TO PONDER FROM THE GENERAL'S TENT

- **POINT #1:** It's one thing to build something, but a whole other thing to maintain it; all worthwhile things are. A lot of people can make money, but to maintain it is the difficult deal.

- **POINT #2:** Liberation comes when we're willing to take the leap into the unknown. It is the ability to break the bonds that hold us bound to this one and two-dimensional life that we were living before.

- **POINT #3:** You're never going to change your life overnight; having it all is a process, and it takes time to lay that sure foundation. But once set, you will not fall. Steady consistency builds Empires.

- **POINT #4:** Become the change that you want to see, then tell us in the Brotherhood so we can hold you accountable. Once you learn to do today what's hard, tomorrow becomes easy. Simple Success Swinging Singles on a daily basis.

# AFTERWORD

## OPERATION ROSETTA STONE

### By Natalie C Martin

What do you get when you have a history and English teacher turned stay-at-home mom who becomes the only female member of the Wake Up Warrior Team? A lot of historical references and the ability to decipher content.

In January of 2015, I was hired to write the show notes for *Warrior On Fire*, a podcast Garrett launched sharing his insights that encompassed the doctrine of Warrior. These episodes became known as *The Daily Fuel*. As a mother of four young children, I became exposed to a whole new world of thinking. And swearing. I had never heard someone use "fuck" so many times when talking about Christian scriptures in a positive way; yet anyone who knows Garrett will say he is not the typical man![136] He's an anomaly, which is what it takes to shift the current mindset of how the modern man thinks today.

### Experiencing Expansion

It requires a lot of drive to be involved in Warrior, so when Garrett coached me on how to expand my responsibilities,[137] he provided an environment that helped me learn new skill sets to keep up with the constant expansion of the Wake Up Warrior Academy. However, it wasn't until editing of the first edition of *WarriorBook* that I truly experienced what this expansion to be more, do more, and suck less meant. It was exhausting yet liberating to finally give myself permission to expand in what is known as the Warrior Time Warp, as I solely embarked on all of the editing of the first edition of *WarriorBook* within the month of November. I hadn't been told that what I was doing was the job of a whole editorial staff, completing in a few weeks what normally takes months to accomplish in publishing a book from

---

[136] See further information in Introduction "Gift of the Goddess: Operation Rosetta Stone" section

[137] From Daily Fuel editor to editor of the Warrior Week yearbook and coaching call notes, I was able to immerse myself in the importance of what Warrior entails.

start to finish. This [138]paradigm effect worked in my favor to complete the [139]Impossible Game.

All of my life I had been told to stop. Slow down. You don't want to make others feel bad because you're accomplishing things. Don't take any more responsibilities on. When I hit those stories within Warrior, the Master Coach Mentor helped me find permission within myself to become more; and through a series of trials by fire, I have been able to rise up like a phoenix on the 2nd Edition of *WarriorBook* and compile *The Manual* at the same time in order to see clearly what my role is within Warrior.[140]

## The Journey

I'm the feminine counterpart,[141] the librarian, the nurturer of the ambition Warriors have. I had to start small in order to go big, which allowed me

---

[138] Founded by Thomas Kuhn, a paradigm effect is a theory which states that what goes against one's paradigm (their worldview; what they know to be true) will be nearly impossible for them to see. Read more about Thomas Kuhn in the online article "Thomas Kuhn: the Man Who Changed the Way the World Looked at Science":
https://www.theguardian.com/science/2012/aug/19/thomas-kuhn-structure-scientific-revolutions

[139] Becoming more than what I started out as. See Warrior Dictionary: "Impossible Game" for further explanation.

[140] In Joseph Campbell's monomyth, *The Hero with a Thousand Faces* (cited on next page) this is defined as the "goddess figure" or typically a female helper the hero encounters while already on his journey to help provide him aide.

[141] Murdock, Maureen. *The Heroine's Journey.* Boston, MA: Shambhala, 1990. Print. See diagram image on next page of what this entails.

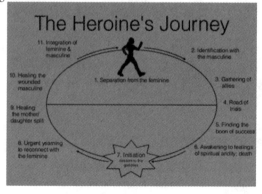

to gain access within myself to tackle the block[142] that Garrett and Jeremy had in putting together *The Manual*. This reference guide looks completely different than what it started out as, but it wasn't until the shift that I refer to as "Operation Rosetta Stone" occurred that Garrett was able to see a new angle and approach for putting *The Manual* together.

Editing is what allowed me to be called to Warrior in the first place,[143] but it is through my research and development that my greatest strengths lay. Within the second edition of *WarriorBook*, you will find cross references and footnotes throughout each chapter. These have been compiled for easy reference within the Topical Guide, while those new to Warrior vernacular or desire further explanation behind a concept can find these in the Warrior Dictionary.

## Gift of the Goddess: Operation Rosetta Stone

This new edition became enhanced[144] while working on *The Manual* at the same time, which is a completely different book than what it started out as. While journaling in my War Map one day, I came up with an analogy likening *The Manual* to the Rosetta Stone; it was just a bunch of hieroglyphics and foreign letters set in stone until someone familiar enough with the language of Warrior knew what to look for. I was able to decipher, or make out the meaning of something not clear—the content. This set the foundation for what Garrett knew he had to do in order to make *The Manual* clear and concise.

---

[142] *The Manual* was a book that was meant to be published within a few months after the first edition of *WarriorBook*, but every time Garrett attempted to put it together, he had a mental block; a writer's block of the mind in seeing the way how the book was supposed to come together.

[143] I am the *Daily Fuel* Editor for Garrett's *Warrior On Fire* daily podcast and have become the developmental editor for Wake Up Warrior.

[144] The 2nd Edition of *WarriorBook* was enhanced with footnotes, cross references, dictionary and topical guide (index) on where to find various topics and themes throughout the book.

In *WarriorBook*, we get the Hero's Journey,[145] a monomyth that Joseph Campbell defines as "the typical adventure of the archetype known as The Hero, the person who goes out and achieves great deeds on behalf of the group, tribe, or civilization."[146]

Just as Arjuna from the Bhagavad Gita fought his internal war, so too did the founder of the Warrior Movement go through his own journey. Garrett so masterfully shows through example how to Live by the Code, Stand for the Code, Create with the Keys in playing the Game of having it all. This pattern of living does not make him a Savior, but a Leader so that we all may embark on our own journeys as heroes.

It required Garrett's mastered ability as a storyteller to put into fruition *WarriorBook* in such a short amount of time, but it was this storytelling that got in the way with *The Manual* because the pictures, or hieroglyphics of the Warrior Movement, were there. Eventually it had its own phoenix experience of rising out of the ashes by starting anew; but the process remained disorganized and scattered until it could be connected with an analogical process that I saw in likening Warrior as a blend of the Spartan and Athenian in a man. The Hero was unable to complete the Return of His Journey until the "Gift of the Goddess" (refer to chart on opposite page) provided the tools the hero needed.

What does this mean? In following the roles refined in *The Man with a Thousand Faces*[147] by Joseph Campbell, there is a goddess figure[148] that gives the Hero tools while on his journey in need of rejuvenation. Inside

145

[146] Unknown. "Hero's Journey." *The Writer's Journey.* Hero's Journey, n.d. Web. 29 Mar. 2016.
[147] Campbell, Joseph. *The Hero with a Thousand Faces.* Princeton, NJ: Princeton UP, 1972. Print.
[148] The YouTube video, "The Hero's Journey: Initiation Phase - Meeting the Goddess in the Monomyth" the goddess figure helps the hero along on his journey and gives him weapons or tools as help when the hero faces adversity. https://youtu.be/c1FLU3zDV8g

of each of us is the mindset to create, but unless we understand what this entails by valuing what our surroundings encompass, that which we create will be for naught.

What was decoded in *The Manual* eventually led to the doctrinal foundation of how to live the Warrior's Way, which had a journey of its own.

## The Wake Up Warrior Phalanx

In Ancient Greece there were many battles fought, and just like any civilization, wars were waged in order to rise to power. The Persian War brought the city states of Greece together to fight and eventually win against the Persian king, Xerxes.[149] It required a unification of differing mindsets in order to achieve success, and one of the ways the Greeks were able to do that was in their military strategy of the phalanx.

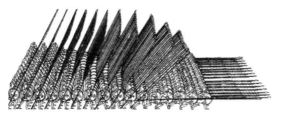

The warriors all relied upon each other to form a weaponized tool of destruction (see image above), as they layered rows of spears that would pierce forward as one, interlocking their shields as protection against the enemy.

## "He Who Rules With A Spear"

Garrett, whose name means "he who rules with a spear," is the leading commander of Warrior; the Brotherhood are the soldiers, whose weapons are the shield (Code) and spear (Core) which must be practiced and used for the daily war modern men face, which is why it's so vital to "Hit the Core 4 before the door" every single day.

With this unification, battles are won, but an internal civil war will ensue if we don't understand and value the different ways of thinking that comes. In

---

[149] The Greco-Persian War in which we are referencing occurred between 492-449 BCE

order to avoid a Peloponnesian War [150]within Warrior, one must understand the Spartan and Athenian mindset within a man's own mind.

## The Spartan & The Athenian

Ancient Greece was set up in city states, or regions that were all ruled under different sets of laws. Land-locked Sparta operated under a monarchy, with a very simple and regimented form of living in which the men and women all lived in separate barracks, wearing simple, coarse clothing and valuing warfare over the arts as a way of preserving their society. Sparta resembles more of the Body and Business aspect of the Core 4 in Warrior.

Athens, on the other hand, was monumental in being the city-state that gave us the origins of democracy, the arts, philosophy, and a higher way of thinking which we define as Expansion. This would entail the Being and the Keys of Business within Warrior.[151] Located right on the sea, an Athenian's greatest strengths were in naval warfare with the trireme (easily maneuvered long boat with a metal ramming tip on the end, powered by synchronized rowing and sails).

It was with this weapon that Greek victory in the Battle of Salamis[152] occurred against Persia despite having a ¼ of the ships (between 310-400 in comparison to over 1200) under command of a Spartan leader[153] working with Athens and other Greek city-states, forcing Xerxes to withdraw.

However, this strength in working together was tumultuous for the Greeks from the beginning, and within one generation, the separate values that Sparta and Athens held most dear became their downfall as Spartans feared the rise that comes from expansive thinking.

---

[150] A civil war between Greek city states that occurred between 431-404 BCE with an eventual Spartan victory after creating an alliance with Persia, whom they had fought 30 years earlier. After this war, the Golden Age of Greek rule within the Ancient World had ended. For a comprehensive description, see: http://www.britannica.com/event/Peloponnesian-War

[151] *Note*: Neither civilization incorporated the teachings of what we know as Balance in creating what we see in modern times that composes a strong family unit: Spartan men would have to abduct his wife from the female barracks in order to copulate, while Athenian women had very few rights and most kept to the confines of the home.

[152] This battle occurred in 480BCE, and so there were still a few decades of warring off and on with Persia before the eventual retreat and Greek victory over the war, but this battle was monumental in demonstrating the unbeatable strength that occurs when Greek city-states worked together. Further exploration can be found at: http://www.ancient.eu/salamis/

[153] Eurybiades

## Avoiding A History Repeat

Why is this relevant? What does all of this have to do with the Black Box System and modern day? History repeats itself unless we learn from the past. Sparta valued the warrior, but those aren't needed in times of peace, so they found a reason to go to war. Athens, on the other hand, allowed hubris (excessive pride) to cloud the longevity of the politics they had taught, devaluing the militaristic approach of living Sparta valued as archaic. Both civilizations had patriarchal rule and though Sparta saw women more of as equals, the role of the female was still completely separate from that of the male. Neither civilization accomplished Balance.

In order to qualify for the Warrior program, a modern man must fit the role as a successful businessman. In other words, a man must qualify under the Athenian way of living. Warrior Week then provides a Spartan-esque environment of breaking down the chiseled statue of a man and exposing the warrior beneath through a regime of military drills in order to instill the importance of unity. The Brotherhood goes through his own Hero's Journey in a compressed time. This week is exhausting, but elevating, just as the victory of the Persian War was for the Greeks. Afterwards, the Warrior goes back to Athens, after experiencing a dose of Sparta, and he begins to war within himself against valuing the simple things in life while in the pursuit of having it all. The Hero's Journey is far from over.

## The Battle Within

Unless he can understand and value the Spartan and Athenian within himself, the Warrior will fall. The standards required for maintaining Wake Up Warrior Academy through the Code and Core will fall away if one does not continue to see value in merging both the warrior and artist within one's self together.

That is the ultimate success of a hero's journey: maintaining the Code and Core as he continues to expand, recognizing that even the smallest details matter. By seeing himself as the king of his own city-state, the Warrior men within this movement make sure to surround himself with others with the same high standards and way of living.

The phalanx that is Warrior will only work as long as the soldiers remain strong. History has shown countless times how true this is. But what will make the hero's journey within Warrior complete in the pursuit of having it all? It requires a strong commitment to Living by the Code and Standing for the Core, EVERY SINGLE DAY.

The tools are provided within, and now you have the responsibility to train with them daily as you embark on your own Hero's Journey.

# WARRIOR DICTIONARY

*Composed by Natalie C Martin*

## A

**Access.** One of the 4 A's used in Warrior Week. The entry point to having a different answer as found in Section 5: The Game. It is the path that gets you to access a different voice, information, and/or new way of speaking and therefore changing the way you're currently operating. Once discovered, this leads to Action Plans. *Game 39: 13 (throughout chapter), Summary 41:28, 42:5-8, 16-20, 26*

**Accountability.** One of the 4 A's used in Warrior Week. We must hold ourselves accountable as we don the crown of being a Warrior King. We are never entitled to anything we haven't worked for, and the best way to know whether or not we have been doing that is through metrically-based outcomes that we use integrity and honesty with in functioning at a higher level in order to achieve four dimensional living within the Warrior's Way of having it all. *Summary 42:822-26, 43:31*

**Action Plan.** One of the 4 A's used in Warrior Week. A system of execution within the Keys after asking What, Why, When which is the How. It breaks down the Outcome into smaller, achievable targets to hit as well as in what order to execute them using Stephen R Covey's Time Matrix.

Within the WarriorBook, it is broken down in a shelving system analogy, in which each plan is within its own box, which is then placed on a shelf marked Key 1, 2, etc… and all organized behind the doors of a closet with the title Key 4 on the outside. *Keys 31:11-14, Game 39:14, 16-19, 24, Summary 40:16, 41:18-19, 42:8, 17-19, 26, 43:28 (lack of)*

**Addition, Not Subtraction.** This principle operates on the mentality that in order to create a positive lifestyle, we need to continually add beneficial things like green smoothies and targets to reach for. We especially apply this to the Body of Core 4. We actually create the opposite effect from what we initially desired when we attempt to eliminate. *Core 19:1, 17-19, Game 34:21*

**Aim Small to Grow Big.** This statement was given to Garrett by a successful billionaire about how to learn to be present with the current thought or idea that we currently have. "Just be with the thought and with the idea.

You have to aim small to grow big and you must be willing to narrow your focus." *Keys 27:12-13 (v 12-17)*

**Approved Feedback Personnel.** This is a list of approved people in our lives that have permission to provide us with information. They are our circle of influence. That doesn't mean that unwanted feedback won't still be attempted to be thrown at us, nor do we have to follow all of the feedback from this circle of influence, but it is vital that we receive it. Knowing who we care to listen to helps us sort through and cast aside the feedback that is sent from an unreliable (and unapproved) source.

Those personnel that are on the Approved Feedback list consist of:

1. My Queen and Children
2. Parents and Siblings
3. People That You Pay for Advice
4. People Who Pay You for Advice

This is an especially important list to remember while in the Quarterly Game, as we will be bombarded with feedback and suggestions. That's just the natural order of human nature as we seek to expand; there will always be someone more masterful or learning behind us. *Game 34:13-20*

**Armory.** The Black Box Armory is a reference area for further links, tools, articles, templates, and files that will help those in the Warrior Brotherhood succeed. It is the content and process of how Warrior works, created as a toolbox to help aide those in the Brotherhood with reference and support tools to get us to where we need to go. *Foundation 4:18-19, Code 10:15, Core 22:15, 24:26, 26:18, Game 34:30, 32, 37:26, 32, Summary Chapter 41: The Armory*

**Ascendant.** Ishaya's Ascension, or The Ascendant is a state of being, according to Ishaya Monks, in reference to High Power, Source, God, the Divine, and so forth. It is a process of living in which we have learned to leave the carnal state of man as we ascend into the Divinity of who we truly are. *Summary 42:27*

**Ascension, Warrior.** This is the ever expanding state that men within the Brotherhood strive for. It is rising above the current reality that we're in, eventually operating on a higher plane than all those around us, feeling the responsibility that comes from this ultimate way of living. There is a whole section that can be found in the Manual that goes into extensive detail on how to ascend within Warrior as the King that you are. *Game 39:26, Summary 42:8, 26-36 (Mountain Ascension 28-35)*

**Association.** One of the 4 A's used in Warrior Week. A group of men from around the world who hold the Keys to the Kingdom inside their own lives. It is through the power of association with like-minded men that comprise the Black Box System Brotherhood that we are able to not only lean on each other but hold ourselves to a high standard by surrounding ourselves with elite individuals. *Summary 42:8, 22-26, 36*

**Authentic Entrepreneur.** The name Garrett J White, the Master Coach Mentor, created for his foundational businesses within the Warrior Movement after having a rebirth in what is now shaped as the Wake Up Warrior Academy. The purpose for the name was to continually remind himself to honor The Code, which is about stopping the lies and telling the truth, especially to one's self. *Code 5:57-67*

**Automation.** This process in business allows us to avoid the Chaos of Abundance by utilizing software that will automatically provide information to consumers. It is structured within the General's Tent as well as monitored during these weekly sessions. *Game 38:3*

# B

**Balance.** One of the Core 4, generally mentioned as the third within the group due to alliteration purposes rather than level of importance. Balance refers to our relationships, which is then further broken down for one's spouse, commonly referred to as the Queen or Goddess, children, parents &/or siblings, and very close friends.

There are suggestions mentioned within the text of the book regarding how to approach each of these sub-areas of the section, but ultimately it comes down to consistent actions done everyday for at least one member of the group (usually the Queen, for ½ point) and may involve others (also for ½ point).

Acknowledging more than one person does not result in limitless points: ½ point for Goddess, ½ point for another family member/close friend. If more actions have been done for the day, it is still equal to 1 complete point. *(Core 4, see also* Husband, How To Be *and* Fatherhood, Parenting *in*

Topical Guide*), Foundation 3:15-17, 4:10-11, 23, Core 17:4, 18, 20, 24, Game 37:26, Summary 40:5*

**Become More, Do More, Suck Significantly Less.** A statement made within Warrior about focusing on continual expansion, or in other words, succeed at a higher level then you currently are succeeding. This is made known through metrics of the Core 4 weekly readings and what the Outcome results have been. If we are not challenging ourselves, we are not becoming more, so it's a reminder that we can't stay sedentary yet still expect growth; as we become more, we end up doing more than we did before, and during all of this we become the Kings we always were, dawning our Crowns as we build our Kingdom. *Game 33:8, 21*

**Begin With the End in Mind.** This statement is one of the principles of Stephen R Covey's *7 Habits of Highly Effective People*. When we operate with a set outcome for a target that we make, we are able to be clear to ourselves as well as others what we want. It's asking, "If I'm going to begin on Monday, what is the end outcome for that week inside my business? How will I know that I won? What is a win for me?" *Keys 27:18*

**Being.** One of the Core 4, generally mentioned as second within the group due to alliteration purposes rather than level of importance. Being refers to our spiritual nature, and looking inwardly to discover our own individual divinity. There is not a specific religion encouraged or discouraged to live the Warrior's Way; just finding one that personally speaks to you and going all in with one's dedication and devotion in living a life of having it all.

Meditation is a key component in achieving one's Core for Being, and a few mantras are shared within the Warrior Program. See also *Meditation* in the Warrior Dictionary. Daily meditation may be as short as 5 minutes or could expand into multiple sessions or an hour+ session. No matter the duration, meditation must be done daily in order to achieve the ½ point within Being. There are many different tools and techniques to quiet one's mind. *Foundation 3:14, 25, 36, 4:9, 23, Code 6:34, Core 17:4, 20, 24, Chapter 22: Balance (Partner/Posterity) & 23: Balance (Power), 24:35, Game 33:12, 34:31-33, Summary 40:4, 41:21, 24*

**Black Box System, Brotherhood.** The Black Box System is the video, audio and text series exclusively within the Wake Up Warrior program that is currently not available to the public. The Warriors have received it in a literal black box that houses all of these tools, shipped around the globe to those in the Black Box Brotherhood. It is an amalgamated system of different business principles, tactics, tools and teachings all broken down into a simple, achievable form that is to be performed on a daily basis.

Do not confuse simple as easy, however. Many of the teachings within The Black Box require a lifetime of dedication and at times vulnerable honesty that is more difficult than one initially would want to admit. Like playing a musical instrument, the more the Black Box principles are put into practice, the greater the mastery, but it requires daily commitment. *Foundation 1:27, 3:3-40, 50, 4:1, 18-19, 52-53, Code 5:26, 8:58, 10:1, 15, Core 21:1, 24:19, 29, 26:22, Keys 31:14, 32, 36, Game 34:16, 36:2, 39:2, 14-16, 22, 24, Summary 40:5, 41:16, 25, See Chapter 41: The Brotherhood, 42:34 (Council of Brothers), 43:12-13, 27, 30-32*

**Body.** One of the Core 4, generally mentioned as first within the group due to alliteration purposes rather than level of importance. It is our physical state of health covering diet, fitness and lifestyle. None of the other Core parts will mean anything if this Core group falls apart. There is ½ point for food (Fuel), and more specifically drinking a green smoothie or ingesting nutrients through greens. The other ½ point usually entail physical fitness, but it is very individualized according to the needs of the day, consisting of anything from getting a massage to performing a series of weights.

Body also becomes part of the mantra-based power words, the fifth mentioned in Chapter 23 of *The Manual*, Section 6: Warrior Ascension. When seen as the gift that it is, this Body itself becomes our weapon, tool, and instrument. It became the vehicle into which life itself could be experienced on a day-to-day basis.

*Foundation 3:13, 38, 4:6-8, 23, Core 17:4, 7, 20, 24, See Chapter 18: Body (Fitness) and Chapter 19: Body (Fuel), Game 34:21-22, 30, 37:21 (rhythm for sleep)*

**Born Again.** This is not a religious term, but rather an experience with the body as a whole, within the Core 4, due to the results from successful Key 4 Outcomes as we play the Game. If we follow the program within Warrior correctly, every 90 days we are becoming born again into a new reality and version of who we are. This is measurable through the metrics and results of the self. *Game 33:31*

**Bridging the Gap.** This is a concept needed within Business to accomplish and make relevant the different targets we set in regards to our Outcomes set. It helps us to see the relevancy behind the work that is being done, and if we see more of a gap than a bridge, we have an opportunity to course correct within the General's Tent, using our War Map, and other various tools meant to help create clear "Yes" or "No" Outcomes. *Keys 28:24, 29, 29:5, 31:5, Game 33:32*

**Business.** One of the Core 4, generally mentioned as fourth within the group due to alliteration purposes rather than level of importance. The two areas of business are *money* and *lifestyle*. In order to fund life, one needs to find a successful career to accomplish that. Instilling integrity and ethics within the workforce helps one sleep better at night and be able to afford family activities, and so this Core group is the key to making everything else happen. See *Keys* for more explanation on applying supreme focus for success within Business. *Foundation 3:26, 29, 37, 4:12, 23, Code 9:19, 31, Core 18:4, 7, 9, 13, 20, 24-25, See Chapter 24: Business (Discover) and Chapter 25: Business (Declare), See Section 4: Keys (Refers to strategic planning inside of Business), Game 34:26, 35-37, 39:3*

**Business Trifecta.** The trifecta of Business that we follow here in Warrior is as a Marketer, Closer, and Leader, Not a Savior. Each of these are broken down in a more extensive form within The WarriorBook, but ultimately when using these three tools together, you become a powerful weapon in the business world as they offer very clear guidelines of where you are at as a businessman. *Core 24:12-35, 25:20, 30, 34*

# C

**Capital.** We have a capital gain in Warrior, but rather than just focusing on the *financial* wealth in the form of money or property, it is also a capital gain in our *mental, social,* and *X factor* which embodies the individual.

Mental: our knowledge, wisdom and insights.

Social: who you know, and who knows you

Financial: cash, credit, &/or the ability to create cash

X Factor: unique selling proposition due to individualized skill sets *Keys 31:16-30, 32:10. Game 36:14*

**Chaos of Abundance.** The Dark Side of mass production, especially at the speed in which the Brotherhood of Warrior operates. It is the flip side to creating really big shit in a very short amount of time. The higher we climb, the greater the fall, especially when operating in compressed time. *Keys 27:5, 11, 28:27, 31:34, 32:2, 37:32, 39:13 (karmic cul-de-sac of chaos)*

**Closer.** This is the second part of the Business Trifecta (Marketer, Closer, Savior Not Leader) that gives us an opportunity to be very clear, especially with our clients, associates, and even family members by not operating in 'maybes.' It is through asking a question, and then receiving a clear "Yes" or "No." *(See also Business Trifecta), Core 24:21-26*

**Code.** This term refers to the statement in Warrior of stop lying with yourself and others with the alliterative phrase Real Raw Relevant Results. Each of those are discussed in more detail, but in sum, Real and Raw refer to being openly honest with yourself and others, but it serves no purpose if there is not a Relevant purpose to the honesty in order to produce Results that will help the person expand. *Foundation 3:32, 4:18, 20-22, 24, 41. See Section 2: The Code, 7:47-48, 8:57-58, 9:36, 10:37, Core 17:19, 20:23, 22:4, 26:17, Keys 31:34, Game 33:5, Summary 40:8*

**Core 4.** This term refers to 4 components that make a whole man, also set to alliteration: Body, Being, Balance and Business. Body refers to our physical state of health, diet and lifestyle choices. Being refers to our spiritual nature. Balance refers to our family life, broken down into specific relationships with wife/significant other, children, extended family members (parents & siblings), and very close friends. And lastly Business refers to our contribution in the marketplace.

The Core is a daily action broken into points, totaling a potential 4 points/day and 28 points by the end of the week. These daily points are then broken down into ½ point increments in order to cover specific non-negotiable actions daily.

The individual is responsible for fulfilling and marking down these points, which are administered based off of an honor system with a simple yes or no the action was completed for that day. Once the day has ended, the individual does NOT go back and change the score. *Foundation 1:56, 3:29, 4:15, 23-26, Code 5:1, 8:40-41, 54, 9:20, 66, 68, Warrior Stack 15:28-40, See Section 4: The Core, 17:20, 24, 21:9, 22:31, 26:18-22, Game 33:5,*

*13, 29, 36, 34:30, 36:1, 37:1, 7-11, 14-15, 22-33, 38:9, 18-30, Summary 40:8-9, 41:2, 43:36*

Core 4 Daily War: *Foundation 4:23, 41, Core 17:4, 22:31, Game 34:38, 31:1*

**Create with the Keys.** The third part of the Warrior phrase: *Live by the Code. Stand for the Core. Create with the Keys.* This is part of an amalgamation of the main Code and Core doctrine and completed with the Keys within Warrior to serve as a ready reminder of how we should operate on a daily basis. When we give ourselves permission to create the kingdom that we have always wanted, we also acknowledge the responsibility that it takes by putting constraints within our Business with deadlines and status quos to be met. *Keys 30:19, 26:5, Game 39:22-23, Summary 40:9-12*

Creation (Creator): *Code 9:55, 10:1, Core 20:40, Keys 30:16, Game 34:20-21*

**Creating Space.** This is in reference to Meditation and quieting the internal chatter that resides in the mind. In other words, it quiets the Chaos of the Mind. Once the tool of meditation helps to pull back layers of clarity in the mind, this opens up the potential and opportunity for Revelation, or modern personal insight which becomes the individual's own personal doctrine and beliefs. *Core 20:17*

**Crucible.** This action has multiple meanings in Warrior, one of which is an expansion from Warrior Week in which those chosen Brothers are put through an even more intensive training of military drills and physical strategies to be incorporated into the marketplace and life.

This term is also applicable for the mental state that a Warrior goes through when making the shift into four dimensional living. Though simple, living the Warrior's Way is not easy, and expansion comes with it a Refiner's Fire that at times can feel more like a death sentence than personal salvation.

# D

**Daily Actions.** These action steps performed on a daily basis prevent us from growing out of power. *Game 37: Daily Actions*

**Daily Deposits: Honor, Appreciation and Love.** This principle is found within Balance (Partner/Posterity) in regards to sending daily messages to the Queen and family members. The most common way it is done is through a text or note with the trifecta Honor, Appreciation & Love. These deposits are meant to fill, not add only to take away just as much or more so that when a withdrawal is made, it is more openly allowed and sometimes freely given.

A fine balance must occur in maintaining sincerity, especially with one's spouse, so that it doesn't become a task to simply be completed for the day, but a continual and measurable act of commitment towards one's Goddess. *(See Text: Honor, Appreciation & Love), Core 22:20 (Daily Deposits), 10-22, 26, 30*

**Daily Fuel.** The name of the podcast episodes Garrett has from his site http://warrioronfire.com. These are how he does his daily Positive Focus documents, developed and mastered in speaking form. *Core 24:8, 25:23*

**Dark Warrior.** We each have a Dark Warrior inside of us, and too often it is seen or viewed as something evil. It can be, but it can also bring out a passion and fire that can only be ignited when faced with darkness. It's acknowledging the mirrored behavior in our own life when we encounter something that we don't like in others, as described in Debbie Ford's *Dark Side of the Light Chasers.* There is a Divinity in the Darkness that this brings out, and sometimes we are faced with something that we don't want to do, yet it is through this challenge to become more; we push ourselves further because of the resistance. *Code 7:26, 49-50, 9:48, 67, Summary 43:38-39*

**Declare/Declaration.** A principle inside of Business that there is a responsibility that comes from learning, and once something is learned, it is then declared and taught in order to further instill the belief in one's life as well as passing the teachings on to encourage continual learning. This principle is covered extensively in Chapter 25: Business (Declare). *Core 25 throughout, 1-5, 27-29, 33*

Declaration of Independence: *Foundation 3:4-6, 10*

**Details Matter.** A concept developed when Garrett attended a Kokoro Sealfit Camp, which is a military term for focusing on the little things. The reason behind precision within the military is as a living example that if we focus on even the smallest of details like polished boots and pristine uniform and living quarters, the big shit will not be a concern because they will be covered as well. *Keys 30:21-25*

**Did You Fuel the Ferrari?** This question is asked in regard to the body, seeing the body as a high end mode of transportation like a Ferrari, and because of that, it needs high end fuel to keep it going. Under the principle of Addition, Not Subtraction, Warrior sees green smoothies as the high end fuel for our Ferrari. *Core 19:17-18, 23, 31, Game 36:12-15, Summary 43:11*

Fire/Fuel: *Foundation 1:29, 2:31, 3:28, 4:20, 23-24, Code 7:23, 63 10:1, 7, Core 17:13, 18:8, 28, See Chapter 19: Body (Fuel), 26:3, 27:11, 32, 35-36 Keys 27:20, 29:5, 11, 14, 17, 29-34, 31:8, 36:12-15 (Fuel the Ferrari)*

**Direct Response Communication.** Exactly as it sounds, this business tool works in establishing open forms of communication, being clear about expectations and clarity within those outcomes. *Core 25:17-18 Distractions, Core 17:12*

**Drift.** This inevitable experience in all of our lives is mentioned in detail within the Warrior Stack. It is a caused by a trigger that occurs within our life which will continue in a karmic loop of repetitive behavior unless the core issue is confronted and resolved, seen more as a gift then a trigger point. When this shift occurs, the Drift is resolved and in its place further expansion within one's self on a higher and deeper level. *Warrior Stack 11 throughout, 13 throughout*

# E

**Empire.** A level within the Warrior program that has become enhanced after "graduating" from the Warrior Week program. In this level, the Brotherhood has already been living by the Code and standing for the Core, enhancing the creation with the Keys to a more honed in level. It is within this level that more in-depth training occurs for such tools as Strategic Seduction and taking the learnings from Wake Up Warrior Academy to the next level by teaching and customizing the principles within one's own specific marketplace. *Keys 30:30, 31:6, 32:5, Game 38:31*

**Employee vs Entrepreneur Mindset.** As businessmen, we operate from two different time mindsets, which are as an *employee* or an *entrepreneur*. And employee operates based off of time and effort, with a salary based pay mindset, meaning that they put in the clocked hours every day, do the work placed before them, and their employer pays them according to the contract made within the business. An entrepreneur, on the other hand, operates more from achieving results, meeting benchmarks rather than pre-set dates put together by the employee. *Game 36:3-17*

**Emotional Constipation.** An analogical state in which we dwell by not releasing our feelings and emotions on a regular basis. *Code 8:24-27, 51-52, 10:31*

**Expansion.** The ultimate reason we are placed on this earth. The concept of Expansion is broken down in great detail within The Manual, but ultimately it has been defined within Warrior that we are constantly expanding and learning from our experiences. If we don't expand and grow, then we remain stuck in scarcity. *Code 5:41-43, 51, Core 20:48, 21:21, Keys 27:1, 28:30, 32:1, Game 33:7, 37:4 (fantasy of), 38:3, 27, 39:15, Summary 41:1, 21, 43:36, 39*

**Extended Adolescence.** A recent definition of millennial men that have missed important milestones required in order to mature and become independent. Men are remaining single and living with their parents longer than ever before, leading to a focus on short-term gains rather than establishing careers for a long-term reward. *Foundation 2:4, 43-47*

# F

**Feminist Movement.** Though there have been a few waves of the Feminist occurring, from suffragists fighting for a woman's right to vote to women tackling the workforce on the home front while the men were off to war during WWII, it is the Feminist Movement of the 60s that created a major shift in gender roles within society.

Women began believing the lie that they were the same as men, so therefore anything a man can do, so too can a woman. They associated equal with the same, and decided that all positions could be filled by a woman eventually. This shift in co-leadership within the home became sole leadership for women running all domestic duties. Within a few generations of men going to work outside of the home and into factories and businesses, the way a family operated completely changed.

And yet, it wasn't enough for women to solely fulfill domestic anymore. They had had a taste of the workforce, and they liked the flavor. Domestication had never been openly acknowledged as a needed contribution within society; it was an expectation that seemed to make sense. Man goes out to hunt the buffalo, and woman stays at home to raise the children and clean up after the kill.

All of that changed during WWII; many men were off in the Pacific and European Theatre fighting a second world war, and with the need for modern machines, more workers than ever were needed in the factories to produce. Women took on masculine roles, and developed a taste for the workforce on a scale that had never been allowed before.

By the time the Feminist Movement morphed with the Civil Rights Movement (also known as Second Wave Feminism), the workplace was somewhere that hard work was openly acknowledged rather than the quiet gratitude for domestic guardianship, and so we currently see more and more women choosing careers over family. Gender roles are overwhelmingly confused and no longer seen as unique.

Within the last few years a new wave of feminism has occurred, bastardizing even further the roles men and women were genetically programmed to do. To be feminine is considered outdated, yet it is in the discovery of femininity that masculinity can be defined. *Foundation 2:32-33, Appendix Resources*

**First Things First.** A principle from Stephen R Covey's book *7 Habits of Highly Effective People* about taking things one step at a time, according to priority of importance. There are always items that we HAVE to get done in the day (Urgent), items that NEED to get accomplished (Important), SHOULD (Not Urgent), and IF POSSIBLE (Not Important). Once we are able to prioritize our time better, we are able to utilize more throughout our day. *Keys 27:21-25*

**Founding Fathers.** The Founding Fathers of the United States of America were bad asses. They believed in a cause and were willing to pay the price in order to society and future generations could have inalienable rights and freedoms unlike any other country had seen before. Signing the Declaration of Independence in 1776 was just one component to Founding America, further strengthened with the Constitutional Convention between 1787-1789. *Foundation 3:4-6, Appendix Resources: America's Founding Fathers*

**Four-Dimensional Living.** This term is used throughout the book in regards to living The Core 4. Instead of operating in one area as a strength, it's creating more dimensions within a man to further make him whole in his Body, Being (spirituality), Balance (relationships) and Business. Instead of spreading oneself too thin by tackling on multiple areas instead of focusing on one specific strength and mastering it, becoming 4 dimensional makes a man uniquely complete in all four areas of his life by finding a customized Game Plan that he commits to living every single day. *Foundation 1:56, 2:3, Code 8:40, 9:66-68 Core 17:3, 17, 26:15, 39:23*

**Framework.** This is the generalized process of setting strategies up in order to have a smooth flow with one's targets. We may not have all of the details in this phase, which is fine because it allows for course correction upon execution. It is usually done inside the General's Tent for our Quarterly Challenges, and Monthly Benchmarks, through looking at our Weekly Targets. *Foundation 4:23, Code 5:1, Core 17:2-3, 21:31, 22:10, 26:12, 27:20 (18-20), Game 33:10, 34:21-22, 37:16, Summary 41:5*

**Fuel.** Within Warrior, we use Fuel in many different ways, from what we put into our body (food and green smoothies) to our inner drive, or the fire within. It is also applicable to the daily podcast found at http://warrioronfire.com in the *Daily Fuel* episodes. *Foundation 1:29, 2:31, 3:28, 4:20, 23-24, Code 7:23, 63 10:1, 7, Core 17:13, 18:8, 28, See Chapter 19: Body (Fuel), 26:3, 27:11, 32, 35-36 Keys 27:20, 29:5, 11, 14, 17, 29-34, 31:8, 36:12-15 (Fuel the Ferrari)*

# G

**Game.** The Game is a metric system referred to within Warrior as a combination of The Code, The Core and The Keys. We "Live by the Code" and "Stand for the Core," while expanding prosperity in the kingdom by "Creating with the Keys" in the Business part of Core 4. In other words, the Game of Warrior is literally a gamified science that takes all the power from The Code, The Core and The Keys, strategically inserting the tools, techniques, tactics and theories into a transformative game within Business creating daily, weekly, monthly and quarterly targets.

This is all part of The Game, and the break down is most applicable in regards to Business due to the complexity; it is not realistic to apply The Keys to all 4 areas of the Core 4. By honing in on Business, we provide the financial expansion to fund the rest of the areas, developing better results because of focusing on One Thing.

The sixth mantra mentioned in Chapter 23 of *The Manual*, Section 6: Warrior Ascension tells us that life itself is a game and when you begin to participate in life as a game, you take it serious but you don't take it *as* seriously. It becomes a competition with one's self for eternal expansion.

*Foundation 4:37-42, 45, 5:1, 52, Code 6:37, 7:4, 42, 9:37, 52, 10:1, 15, Core 17:5-6, 26, 18:1, 22:2, 24:22, 24, Keys 27:3, 28:29, 29:32-33, 30:8, 16, 28, 31:11, 14, 32:1, See Section 6: The Game, 35:33, Summary 40:13, 42:3-5, 12, 24, 43:16, 27*

**Gamification.** It is a natural part of human nature to be competitive and gain motivation in any accomplishment by having a prize at the end. In order to do this, one must play the Game going full in. *Foundation 4:25, Core 26:14, Game 33:7*

**Gateway to Power.** A term used in describing the Body, which is the ONLY thing that will come with us everywhere, no matter what we participate in. It is recognizing the foundational importance of properly maintaining one's health, especially through fitness, that will make targets and outcomes achievable, no matter what part of the Core 4 it is in. *Core 18:4, 19*

**General's Tent.** This is a metaphorical title for a specific room or office in which you are able to plan out your ideas every week, and is non-negotiable in order to play the Game of Warrior. It can be a physical location set aside for this specific purpose or be located within one's own mind and then the set location is superfluous in being a necessity. When the General's Tent is pitched in the mind, laying out strategic strategies and game plans comes together, and when properly organized and stored within their own boxes and closet, these plans can then be executed and lead to prosperous success. The General's Tent covers four things:

1. Hit Core 4 to get our buy-in and prepare ourselves mentally before we even hit the door of the Tent.
2. Do a return and report as we look over our documents from the past week.
3. Make an assessment and course correction.
4. Move to new targets and new commitments.

It is here that we summarize how we did playing the Game of Core 4 the past week, if we hit our Weekly Targets (Yes or No), course correct if needed, and strategize for the upcoming week. Documents are provided in completing this, which can be found with examples in *WarriorBook Manual*. The General's Tent is a counsel for kings and the glue that keeps the Game together. *Core 26:14-17, Keys 28:19 (19-20), 30:18, 30, 31:14,*

*34, 32:13, Game 34:4, 20, 24, 35:30, 36, 36:31, 37:32, See Chapter 38: The General's Tent throughout, 39:8 (origins of), 20, 23, 27*

**Gap.** This term is in reference to the marketing tool sub-category Possibility for Paradise from Strategic Seduction. It is not to be confused with the term "Getting in the Gap" which refers to meditation. The Gap is a business term for where the money is made through the art of influence and persuasion. *Keys 28:29-30. 29:5, 31:5, Game 33:32-33*

**Getting In The Gap.** This term is used by the late Dr. Wayne Dyer which can be found in his book *Getting in the Gap: Making Conscious Contact with God through Meditation* which uses practical application in meditation tools we can use to progressively handle stress without turning to sedation instead. *Book: Appendix Bibliography, Core 20:4, 11, 39*

**Great Depression.** From 1929-1939, America went through a dark economic period which started prior to the stock market crash which is normally described as the beginning of this period in time. Bank runs, Prohibition of alcohol, Dust Bowls and one hard time after another lead many families to become desperate, sending anyone able to in the family off to work in an attempt to make ends meet. Credit was not regularly instituted during this time, and if a bank failed, there was no way the person could get their money back until programs were created to prevent another national collapse in such an extreme.

Not to be confused as a Recession, in which times are temporarily hard or a specific area within the marketplace collapses while others stay afloat. This definition is in reference to the overall decade of downturns in the Western industrialized world.

Yet from this time we learned the true meaning of grit and resiliency, had A New Deal to help men get back on their feet, and a humility required to make changes. *Foundation 2:25*

**Great War, The.** The Great War, War to End All Wars, and World War I are all synonymous to the time period between 1914-1918 in which modern warfare occurred with a global impact. America did not join the war until 1917 after one of her ships were sunk which was providing food and medical supplies to Britain.

There were many towns throughout Europe that lost entire generations of males because of the death toll from a war that many thought would be over within a few months. As the years carried on, modern warfare machines continually progressed, but shell shock syndrome (which we commonly call PTSD or Post Traumatic Stress Disorder) was never really addressed in some of those few veterans that came home after experiencing trench warfare. See *The Great War* in the Appendix Resources section for more. *Foundation 2:21, Game 38:2, See Appendix Resources*

**Green Smoothies.** This is a combination of dark leafy greens blended with various fruits to provide daily nutrients our bodies need as fuel. There is a high nutrient deficiency found in adult businessmen due to high stress situations that don't always allow for the best eating habits. One area inside of the Body metric system for Core 4 is the importance of getting the nutritional benefits from leafy greens through daily green smoothies.

When consuming a green smoothie becomes a non-negotiable part of the day, it provides fuel for the weapon which is our body and helps us meet one ½ point part of Body in our daily Core 4 standings. *Core Chapter 19 Body (Fuel), Game 34:21, 31:16*

**Gutenberg Press.** Johannes Gutenberg revolutionized the way how Western Civilization thought with the invention of moving type in the form of a printing press during the 15th century. Prior to this time everything was painstakingly handwritten, and the majority of the population in Europe was illiterate.

When Gutenberg invented movable type, suddenly access to pages that could be printed on over and over again allowed more to receive it, and though it influenced the way how spiritual text was consumed (prior to that it was orally received by the majority through educated clergymen), the majority of the first books published and distributed to the public were filled with traveling information. This seemingly small act that revolutionized the printing world led to other revolutions throughout the centuries. *Summary 42:13-16*

# H

**Hard Easy.** As we expand, we go through the experience that what was seemingly impossible during the Impossible Game becomes possible. That what was so difficult becomes manageable, but that doesn't mean that it eventually becomes easy in the simplicity of following through on the execution of our expectations. It loses its complexity that adjoined the difficulty, but anything worthwhile is not going to suddenly become too easy, especially if it continues to help us towards expansion. Instead, it becomes "hard easy," meaning that it's "easier" because your skill sets and your mindsets have expanded, hence the doing of the task has become easier and simpler because you have become more. *Summary 43:37*

**Having It All.** The mindset of living a life/lifestyle of having it all is a very customized one. It entails living the Core 4 every day, weaponizing one's body so that whatever he may face, he's ready for it physically, mentally, spiritually, financially, and emotionally. *Foundation 1:54-55, 3:12-17, 26-29, 32, 37-38, 44, 4:1, 57, Code 5:11, 6:28, 9:55, 67, 10:14, 27, Core 17:3, 17, 18:6, 20:14, 21:26, Keys 27:36, 29:32, 30:29, 31:32, 32:13, Game 36:37, 39:16-18, 27, Summary 40:7, 11, 16, 41:5, 22, 28, 42:3-5, 43:1-2 (maintenance), 18, 34*

**"Hit the Core Before You Hit The Door In Order To Prepare for War."** This phrase is in a pneumonic form in order to provide a memorable way of trying to get the Core 4 done on a daily basis before even starting the rest of the day, or going off to work. It prevents procrastination and unreliability on how others see how you perform. *Core 26:14, 22, Keys 28:30, 32:1, Game 37:3, 11, 15, 38:18*

**Honor Appreciation and Love.** These are the three words to send in a text or note form on a daily basis to your Queen and another selected family member (your posterity: children, siblings, parents, etc). Doing this simple action within the Balance quadrant of Core 4 helps create a karmic debt between you and the receiver. Therefore, it is meant to be done without the expectation of having them respond back or reciprocate. If they do, fantastic, but never "honor, appreciate and love" with the expectation that they need to follow suit. *Core 22:12, 14-16, 19 (See also Daily Deposits and Text: Honor Appreciation and Love)*

**Hunt the Buffalo.** A term in regards to Business about providing income. It's the duty as the Provider to go and make money to take care of one's loved ones and progress in life, but it has also become a way of separating a man from his family by having to leave the home in order to provide. With that has brought a shift in the way how a man sees his role in the home that has led to what we call in Warrior as the Systemized Sedation of Man. *Core 24:9, 27:2*

# I

**Impossible Game.** Within the Key 4 we put together an Outcome that can only be accomplished by becoming more than what we started out as. It is a game that requires us to become fundamentally something different then we are today in order to succeed and win. We make it impossible yet achievable through expansion of self. It seems impossible to attain based off of where we start, but as we expand through this relentless push towards more, what initially seemed unattainable activates the Inner Warrior, unleashing more than we thought possible in achieving our targeted outcome. *Game 33:15-21, 29-30, 34:2, 5, 20-21, 26, 28, 37-38, 37:33, 39:4*

**Industrial Revolution.** A period of time in history that occurred during the 18th and 19th centuries. It began in Britain and made its way over to America towards the end of the 19th century.

There are many resources on the subject, but for brevity within The WarriorBook we have focused on the influence this period of time has had in shifting the mentality of society on roles that for centuries had been performed by both parents together, and the divide which occurred and continues to effect society today. *Foundation 2:9-24*

**Information Age.** The Information Age is the very rapid, yet still relatively young period in society in which technological advances have become accessible to everyone, not just the privileged few that could afford the high price tag. What was cutting edge a decade or even a year earlier soon becomes archaic, and the human mind has yet to process how to use technology. Unfortunately, we are seeing a new addiction interacting with devices rather than humans, and even though we have more information available to us than ever before, we have regressed in basic human skills. *Foundation 2:40-42*

**Ironman.** There are multiple analogies Garrett uses throughout the WarriorBook in regards to this triathlon race designed by the World Triathlon Corporation (WTC). In 2007 Garrett participated and completed the Ironman Championships in Kona, Hawaii, which requires qualifying from a series of triathlon Ironman races held throughout the world, either placing in one of the other races or some Ironman 70.3 races. It consists of a 2.4-mile swim, 112-mile bike ride and a marathon (26.2 miles), raced in that order back to back. It is considered to be one of the most difficult one-day sporting events in the world. *Core 18:3, 5, 20:20, Keys 28:15, 17, Game 33:24-27, 34:30, Game Chapter 35 Throughout (2007 Championship), 38:4-8*

**"Is It True?"** This question is from Byron Katie's teachings within her book *Loving What Is* in which we learn to stop lying to ourselves in order to move forward. The empowerment that comes from honest and earnest expansion helps one to live the Warrior's Way. *See also Katie, Byron. Core 23:25-40*

# J

**Japa Breath Meditation.** This is a simple but not necessarily easy way to focus on one's breathing within meditation through chanting a mantra-based, repetitive tone. It allows one to create space within their mind by focusing on a singular thing (breath) and through the increased oxygen that comes from slowly breathing in and out, further clarity occurs as well as the meditative benefit of the vibrational impact from toning. *Core 20:9, 12-14 (experience being watched), Appendix Resources: Meditation*

# K

**Karmic Cul-de-sac.** This is a state described within Warrior in which we are not expanding due to a cyclical pattern of repeating one's Drift over and over again due to triggers. We're not noticeably regressing, but circling around doing the same things over and over again, never growing but remaining where it's comfortable and safe. When this happens, lost opportunities for growth pass us by. Within the images used in Warrior it has been given its own spelling as Karmic Culdisac, but the definition is still the same, regardless of the spelling. *Warrior Stack 11-16 throughout*

**Keys.** The Keys are a broken down, detailed way to expand, specifically focusing in Business. It is a science of numbers. Asking the interrogative words in the same sequence: What? Why? When? How? provides the consistent template for specific outcomes which are broken down into 90, 60, and 30-day increments. See Outcomes, 90 Day; Outcomes, 60 Day; and Outcomes, 30-Day for more. *Foundation 4:28-36, Code 5:1, Core 24:29, See Section 5: Keys, 27:16 (defined), 32:6 (series of questions), Game 33:5, Game 36:2, 14, 16, 23, 37: 24, 30, 38:22-23, Summary 43:36*

# L

**Leader, Not a Savior.** The third part of the Business Trifecta (Marketer, Closer, Leader Not Savior). We are not Saviors for others, but leaders. It easily gets confused in a world of people just wanting to be saved, but no one is going to save you within Warrior. By providing an example as a Warrior King, we are acting as influential leaders within our own family, community, and marketplace. You are required to do the work, not rely on someone else as well as provide a mark of leadership for employees and those that work under you as a reminder that you're going to show them *how* to do something, but not do it for them.

Outsiders to Warrior confuse the program as a salvation program rather than one providing leadership and a way for the individual to liberate *themselves* from a life of scarcity into one of having it all. No one will do the work for you, but that doesn't mean that there won't be examples leading the way towards self-liberation. *(See also Business Trifecta) Foundation 4:55, Core 18:10, Core 24:27-29, 25:20, Summary 43:3-5*

**Leveling Up.** This term is in reference to the finding harmony in Core 4 by recognizing that we are only as good as our weakest Core 4 area. By elevating the amount of time and energy spent in the weaker areas, eventually we will be able to live a life of having it all. *Core 17:23, 26, Keys 30:15, Game 33:7*

**Liberation.** The ability to break the bonds that hold us bound to a one or two-dimensional life. We do not operate in the form of salvation here in Warrior. Rather, we follow the Business Trifecta example as Leaders, not Saviors, within the Brotherhood to help provide tools that the individual can use. This is a Gateway to no longer living incarcerated inside of one's mind and soul. *Core 25:1, Summary 42:4, 43:7-15 (Game of)*

**Lift.** The third tool in the arsenal of the Drift, Shift, Lift and Light model for the Warrior Stack, The Lift is a state in which the karmic cul-de-sac of the Drift and Shift occurs, and being able to create permanent change occurs. The document used to do this is called the Production Focus and occurs as part of incorporating the statement developed from the Drift & Shift (Power Focus, parts 1 & 2) into the Core 4. It is key to incorporate The Lift as a daily action tool to live a life of having it all across all areas of the Core 4. See Section 3: Warrior Stack for further detail, especially Chapter 15: The Lift.

**Light.** The second mantra mentioned in Chapter 23 of *The Manual,* Section 6: Warrior Ascension which entails the energy behind something that comes into our life. Light becomes the fire and fuel that builds our drive in life towards possibility, and is the fourth tool in the Warrior Stack model. The document used in congruence with this is The Revelation Road Map, which, when done in full, leads to permanent change and expansion towards a life of living the Warrior's Way of having it all. See Section 3: Warrior Stack, Chapter 16: The Lift (Revelation Road Map) for more.

**Live By the Code.** The first part of the Warrior phrase: *Live by the Code. Stand for the Core. Create with the Keys.* Simply put, the Real, Raw, Relevant Results become a part of life. This is part of an amalgamation of the main Code and Core doctrine and completed with the Keys within Warrior to serve as a ready reminder of how we should operate on a daily basis. When we LIVE by the Code, that means that we will stop lying to ourselves and those around us, operating with integrity in order to make every experience we go through result in relevancy. *Foundation 1:27, 4:37, Code 10:2, Core 17:26, Keys 27:8, 28:30-31, 30:19, 32:2, Game 34:5, 39:22-23, Summary 40:3-6, 41:16*

# M

**Mantra.** The third of three tools used within Warrior for meditation, the first is known as Shift Move and the second is called Core Breathing. Mantra-Based Meditation entails a statement that allows your mind to focus on a specific series of words that have power. There are four specific mantras suggested and used within Warrior which help with meditation, especially for those using meditation for the first time upon joining the Brotherhood. Select from one of the four or run all four during your meditation, but we have found it to be the most common to work with one or two daily.

The four Mantras provided within Warrior, explained in exclusive Warrior training within the *Wake Up Warrior Academy* is summed up into these 4 Mantras:

Mantra #1: Honor _____ for my light and life.

Mantra #2: Appreciate _____ for my body and the game.

Mantra #3: Star word unconditionally loves and accepts me.

Mantra #4: Om integrity. Om empathy. Om power. Om power. Om empathy. Om integrity.

Mantras allow us to go to a state of focused thinking, as completely clearing the mind within meditation is extremely hard to do because of random thoughts coming in and out, so instead, it helps us to focus on one thing, and the toning which follows with some mantras such as Om leads us to a more peaceful state in which to gain clarity and operate after completing the mantra. Repeated multiple times helps to retain that tonal clarity. The target is to complete a 20-minute session, but in starting out, setting aside 5 minutes sets the stage and can be done at incremental stages throughout the day. *Core 20:39, exclusive* Wake Up Warrior *book* The Manual, *unavailable to public access.*

**The Manual.** This book is a reference guide used in conjunction with the Black Box experience, in this case more specifically with the 2nd edition of *WarriorBook*. It provides tools, examples and worksheets for Warrior men to be able to visualize through examples what these tools of Warrior are all about as well as why we do them, when we do them and how. "It was published under a limited edition in 2016 exclusively for *Wake Up Warrior* and is no longer available after that first print."

**Marketer.** The first part of the Business Trifecta (Marketer, Closer, Leader Not Savior) in becoming a powerful weapon as a businessman. It is through Marketing that you are able to attract clients and business in the first place, so if you are not able to snatch a client up at the beginning with strong marketing strategy, your business will die. It is the foundation of Strategic Seduction. *(See also Business Trifecta), Core 24:16-20*

**Mastermind.** Typically, a Mastermind is a group of likeminded entrepreneurs that are continually expanding and mastering their skills within business. Usually a conference or summit brings these expanding individuals together. Warrior has its own Mastermind group called Syndicate. *Code 5:3, 10:15, Core 24:5, Keys 28:30, Game 36:13 (operating as), 42:22*

**Meaningful Specifics.** This is information that we go into a pursuit of learning with the intention of listening to the relevance our own personal Voice is telling us. We learn while creating an outcome for having answers. Quality information leads to revelation.

**Meditation.** One of the key components with *Being* as part of Core 4, meditation is simply defined as learning to quiet one's mind in order to be present. This can be done chanting, toning or with music, guided within a group, self-hypnosis, aromatherapy, and many other ways that work best when customized according to one's own preferences. It is synonymous with the action of praying & pondering according to Christian (Western) society.

Within Warrior we have three forms that we teach (which is definitely not limited to) which are Japa Breath, Transcendental and Zazen Meditation. The only wrong meditation is no meditation and does not require a specific pose or position in which to do it. Meditation itself gives us access to releasing stress, creating space, expanding capacity, accessing agency and ultimately creating power. We do this through a series of four mantras provided within Warrior, but know that you are not limited to these four.

It is a daily action worth ½ point in The Game, and is measured based off of one's honor system. It does not need to be long nor accomplished in one sitting; it can be spread throughout the day, especially when about to face a situation that will require more focus and clarity. The statement within Warrior is "take your meds," meaning meditation on a daily basis. *Core 20: Being (Meditation), Appendix Resources: Meditation, 22:15, Game 37:17, Summary 42:26-27, 43:38*

**Metrics.** Inside of Warrior, we use metric-based systems in order to provide us with measurable results and outcomes in a very simple "Yes" or "No" the action got done. This helps us to measure and mark where we started and where we are heading, which should be in a continually progressing slope of expansion if following the Warrior's Way. This practical and pragmatic tool helps us to visibly see that we have become more, do more, and suck significantly less. *Foundation 4:40-41, Code 9:19, 26, 38-40, 68, Core 17:7, Keys 27:19, 28:35, Game 33:5, 8, 31-34, 35:34-37, 37:24, 27, 38:21, 24*

**Monthly Benchmarks.** This is part of our 90-Day Outcome, provided as a way to make sure that we are on track to hitting our quarterly target by breaking down smaller targets to be hit along the way. It consists of hitting a 30-Day and 60-Day Benchmark. *Game 34:27, Game Chapter 35: Monthly Benchmarks, 36:9, 37:30, 38:25*

# N

**New Commitment.** A document to be used within the General's Tent when something within the Core 4 and Key 4 that needs to be course corrected and recommitted to. *Game 38:26-28*

**Non-Negotiable.** There are certain items within each of our lives that become non-negotiable, meaning that the option to not meet a commitment or follow through with a plan is not an option. Weekly Date Night is a good example of this: by making Date Night a non-negotiable item to meet within Core 4, you have given yourself a specific priority in which to devote continual courtship with your spouse or significant other, children and/or loved one.

Other non-negotiables are daily journaling in the War Map and filling out the Positive Focus document, and the Power Focus (as needed for the last one). *Keys 30:17-18, 30, Game 36:32, 37:21, 26 (26-29), 38:29, 34*

# O

**Observer Chooser.** A term used by the late Dr. Wayne Dyer about gaining individual mastery over one's mind, releasing pain and pleasure in order to access Ultimate Power. It strips away the distractions and allows us to focus internally on what drives us; our purpose. *Core 20:35-37*

**One-Dimensional Living.** This is what Garrett calls a flat man, or a man living out one or two aspects of his life, whether it's in Body, Being, Balance or Business. This isn't like focusing on one strength and mastering it; when it comes to a man's Core, he needs all four aspects of it in order to be whole, like the legs of a table. If only one is strengthened and maintained, the other legs will lose their integrity as they wear and eventually collapse, destroying the whole function of the table. A man cannot be truly successful in life if he continues to operate solely as a businessman, but has horrible health, a rotten father and husband, and has no integrity. The same goes for a man that may be physically fit and successful in his business, but has failed in multiple marriages and no sense of religion. Living the Warrior's Way doesn't work if all of the Core 4 are not maintained equally, bearing in mind that one area may need a little more care than another at a time, but never for the sake of stopping maintenance entirely on the other areas. *Foundation 2:63, Core 17:6, 17, Game 39:25, Summary 43:10, 16, 34*

**One Thing.** Developed from Gary Keller's book, *The One Thing*, this is looking at a specific target or set of targets in order to reach an Outcome. It can also apply to a specific skill set to be mastered. *Keys 28:20, 31:14, 32:10, Game 36:16, 39:2, Summary 40:8, 42:9, 43:10*

**Outcomes.** A metric-based format for specific Key targets made for the Core 4: Business to be completed within 30 days, 60 Days, or 90 Days.

- Quarterly Game: Our 90-Day Benchmarks in which to make a planned target for in expanding who we are in Business.

- Monthly Benchmarks: Our 60-Day Benchmark is a check in of making sure that we're on track for achieving our 90-Day Outcome. The same goes for our 30-Day Benchmark, which is broken down in the last measurable outcome: weekly targets.

- Weekly Targets: Our 30-Day Benchmark is reached after weekly planning it out within the General's Tent making sure that we are on track, step by step, in grinding our way to the Quarterly Game.

*Keys 27:19, 28:33 (90 Day), 29:30, 30:12 (30 Day), 31:11, 25, 32:9, Game 33:31 (90 Day), See Section 6: Game, 34:16, 18, 21, 37, 37:30, 38:25, Summary 41:8, 17, 42:9*

# P

**Pathway to Power.** This term within Warrior is in reference to the journey the Brotherhood must take to get to his desired outcome. It is usually a difficult one, and almost always requires course correcting and possibly abandoning one direction in order to achieve something even greater in another. It works in conjunction with Valley of Pain, a Refiner's Fire in which that which does not break us only makes us stronger. *Code 9:20-21*

**Persuasive Copy.** This tool in business requires that we learn how to excel in communicating messages that will compel people to do things that will be of benefit within our business. It tends to be used with another business tool, Direct Response Communication. *Core 25:17*

**Play to Win the Game.** This is the 4th mantra in Warrior Doctrine of Living by the Code, Standing for the Core, and Creating with the Keys. When we state that we are playing to win the Game of having it all, it means that we are all in and have a ruthless commitment to relevant results. It is a natural part of human nature to be competitive, and so this principle of playing the Game of Life becomes even more clear as we understand the rules found inside The WarriorBook to win. These rules reside in the fulfilling the Core 4 and Key 4 every single day. *Summary 40:13-16*

**Power Focus.** This is a two-part document, one of four Action Document tools known as the Warrior Stack used with the Warrior Brotherhood, the others Release the Rage based off of Byron Katie's teachings and Production Focus, based off of Dan Sullivan's Strategic Coach program, which can both be located in the Bibliography, and Revelation Road Map.

The experience from The Power Focus is meant to work in conjunction with Byron Katie's Release the Rage, both tools modified to fit Warrior from her book, *Loving What Is*. It is meant to be completed AFTER the Release the Rage document has been completed. When we practice Power Focus, it takes us from a powerless and stuck state (which is not reality) to one with a new option of possibility. It does not necessarily need to be completed on a daily basis. It could, but not required. *Code 10:15, 32, 37, Game 37:26, 38:22*

**Production Focus.** Also known as the "Exponential Positive Focus," this is one of three Action Document tools used with the Warrior Brotherhood from Dan Sullivan's Strategic Coach teachings, the others being Release the Rage and Power Focus, based off of Byron Katie's teachings, which can be located in the Bibliography, and Revelation Road Map.

Production Focus allows Warriors who use it to find relevancy in the breakthroughs and discoveries that will ultimately help shift the way how experiences are seen in life. This is an action document meant to be done daily, but can also be done multiple times in a day as well. The saying "What, Why, Lesson Learned, Apply" helps us remember the layout.

Taken from *WarriorBook, 1st Edition,* Chapter 15: Being (Revelation):

> *Something that we do here at Warrior is a Positive Focus. This can be done by studying something or simply experiencing some event of the day, running through the parameter of What, Why, Lesson Learned, Apply which we go into inside the Armory.*
>
> *We take an event from the day, look at the experience and state: "Here's what happened. This is why it was positive. Here's the lesson that I learned which God has delivered up to the palette of my life, and here's*

*how it applies to the rest of my life across Body, Being, Balance, and Business.*

*Positive focus becomes the framework that supports us in writing down our Revelations. Every single day we do it. Every single day we look into the Divine, the Game of our Lives and we find the lessons. We pick the events that have been hand selected and delivered to us to teach us. This is no different if you look through any scripture: journeys of what happened because of events that they took action on from the Voice. They shared a lesson, commandment or doctrine from that event and then they made it applicable to our lives.*

*The entire world of scripture has been built by positive focuses of picking events, deciding they were divine in nature, giving them lessons and then applying those lessons to our lives. This is how we get our half point each day as well, bringing us to a conclusion here for the section of revelation.*

*Code 10:15, 33-35, 37, Core 21:30-34, 24:35, 25:26, 26:5, Game 37:26, 38:22*

**Progressive Era.** The Progressive Era was a period of widespread social activism and political reform across the United States, from the 1890s to 1920s. Though this helped to enforce stricter, more humane labor laws, the emotional well-being of men was not even considered a thought to be worried about. *Foundation 2:24*

# Q

**Quarterly Game.** This is our 90-Day Outcome, which is metric-based target to hit in Business, broken down into smaller benchmarks to maintain the right path. *Keys 22:33, Game 27:31, See Chapter 34: Quarterly Game, 35:19-21, 36:34, 38:25, 39:4, Summary 41:17, 22*

# R

**Raw.** An alliterative component of The Code which consists of becoming vulnerable in sharing one's truth. To "Get Raw" is to share one's feelings, but it doesn't mean that we allow others to take advantage of us when we are telling the truth, nor does it mean that we vomit out random "truths" that have no purpose in being shared. Sometimes when we share our truth, it makes us vulnerable, but that doesn't mean that we don't gain power from that vulnerability. *Code 5:68-69, See Chapter 7: Raw (Feelings), 10:6-7, Core 17:2*

**Real.** An alliterative component of The Code which consists of being authentic by stop lying and tell the truth. "Be Real" is the facts, a simple act of honesty doesn't mean that it's also easy, especially in regards to honesty with oneself, but it is essential if one wants to live a life of having it all. *Code 5:68-69, See Chapter 6: Real (Facts), 10:3-5, 9, Core 17:2, 18*

**Release the Rage.** This is one of four Action Document tools used with the Warrior Brotherhood known as the Warrior Stack, the others being Production Focus from Dan Sullivan's Strategic Coach program, Power Focus, which consists of two parts, inspired from Byron Katie's teachings known as *The Work*, which can be located in the Bibliography, and Revelation Road Map.

Release the Rage can be used as needed, whether it is multiple times, once a day, or every few weeks, to help clear the pent up feelings that hold us back from expansion and moving forward. Meant to be completed first and then work in conjunction with Power Focus. We have modified these teachings from Byron Katie's book *Loving What Is* to be specific for the Warrior program. *Code 10:15, 31, 34, 36-37, Warrior Stack 12 throughout*

**Relevant.** An alliterative component of The Code to "Stay Relevant" which consists of being relevant with the honest statement made. Any person can be honest, but if it doesn't have any relevancy to the topic at hand, it will not result in expansion. If a statement, even spoken in truth, has no relevancy, then there is no purpose in stating it in the first place. *Code 5:68-69, See Chapter 8: Relevant (Focus), 10:8-11, Core 17:2*

**Results.** An alliterative component of The Code which consists of taking the relevancy behind our truth and seeing the results that come about. This "Ruthless Commitment to Radical Results" leads us to expansion. *Code 5:68-69, See Chapter 9: Results (Fruit), Matthew 7:20 (KJV, NT Holy Bible), 9:24, 32, 10:12-14, Core 17:2, 20, 18:6, Keys 30:13, 32:2, Game 37:18, 38:24, 34, Summary 40:5, 11, 16, 43:18, 29*

**Return & Report.** This is a document completed while inside the General's Tent based off of the measurable data collected over the week. This data is from the Core 4 and Key 4 as well as any documents completed. We ask ourselves if we are following the framework, format and what we are going to do. Looking over the metrics within these statistics, it allows us to make a clear assessment on whether or not we need to course correct or continue forward with the same momentum. *Game 38:22*

**Revelation.** This term refers to the individual, which can be found in Chapter 15 of *WarriorBook* as a subtext of Core 4: Being. It follows Meditation (Chapter 14) and focuses on the Custom Voice that we each have inside of ourselves. *Core 21: Being (Revelation), Core 23:36, 24:32, 35, 25:2, Summary 42:14*

**Revelation Road Map.** This is one of four Action Document tools used with the Warrior Brotherhood known as the Warrior Stack, the others being Release the Rage and Power Focus, which consists of two parts, both inspired from Byron Katie's teachings known as *The Work*, Production Focus from Dan Sullivan's Strategic Coach program, which can be located in the Bibliography.

This is a simple but powerful document that resembles a journal entry written as a result of an insight, epiphany, or that "ah hah!" moment that comes from making a realization which leads us towards expansion. It is directed in such a way to bring about the most relevance from an eternal truth that one has discovered and then how it can be applied to bring about Power. Found in Section 3: Warrior Stack, and explained in greater detail in Chapter 16: The Light (Revelation Road Map).

**Reverse Engineering Production.** Creating a way for Shift to occur from an old, broken way of doing something or state of being into a new one that will make it possible for a "have it all" lifestyle. It is breaking the pattern in one's life and creating a new path. *Core 17: 20-22, 27*

# S

**Sedation, Game of. The Sedation Game.** The Game of Sedation is in reference to the toll that modern men are experiencing after the last 3-4 generations of men have gone from the cottage industry to the assembly line, or in other words, from an agrarian life to an industrial one. We have always had businessmen in the marketplace, but we have seen a dramatic shift in less than 100 years in which more men than ever before have been able to open up their businesses from small-scale to global.

This dramatic expansion comes at a cost, however. Within the last few decades, gender roles seem to have swapped, and the mentality of a man hasn't had time to process all of the changes that have occurred and so he sedates himself. Whether it's with technology, addictions, or victimization, with the increase of businessmen, there naturally comes an increase of sedation tools.

Prostitution has been around for a few millennia, but the ease that man can now access it in the form of pornography makes it an epidemic and the root of many modern day problems as a main tool for sedation. *Foundation 1:6, 2:8, 3:3, 6, 11, Core 17:12, 18:6, 20:19-29, 38, 44, 21:10, Game 33:1, 7*

**Self-Administered Scoring.** The way how we score the Core 4 and play the Game in Warrior is based off your own word. We score ourselves, and therefore we hold a higher accountability in doing so for our actions. Operating with integrity for the Code is essential in living the Warrior's Way. *Game 33:14-15*

**Shift.** The state that is required in order for a man to have the desire to pursue a life of having it all. The process of Strategic Seduction must occur in order to cause a shift from one way of thinking and operating to the way the Brotherhood thinks and operates. This is also an essential part of the Warrior Stack, categorized within the Drift and Shift Model, in which the cyclical pattern of dissension in life (The Drift) can be avoided faster or all together based upon the recognition that one makes that he is falling into a pattern we refer to here in Warrior as the Karmic Cul-de-sac (spelled culdisac in the images) because of the recognition of the trigger that then makes the duration of the Drift shorter and the ascension to the lift made shorter through this mental Shift. *Foundation 1:16-18, 63, Code 5:69, 10:13, Warrior Stack 11-16 throughout, Warrior 14 throughout, Core 15:13, 26, 17:40, Keys 21:33-34 Game 27:3, 28:21, 30:9, 13, 15*

**Simple Success Swinging Singles.** This term is used to remember that it is in one step at a time that we can accomplish greatness. It's not as sexy as a home run, but it's through the consistently of the steady grind that we are able to reach our targets, especially if they're so ambitious they feel more like an impossible dream than a reality. That's where swinging singles everyday gets us back to home base, each and every time. *Core 22:7, 22, 31, Keys 30:11, Game 33:27, 36:23, 37:14*

**Sniper-Based Targets.** This term is in reference to shifting away from the "making goals" mentality to focusing on a "target." The difference between a goal and a target for a sniper is very pronounced; a sniper doesn't have a goal to shoot his gun; he has a target to aim for. A sniper hones in on a specific target which results in a clear "yes" or "no" outcome: Did you shoot the target? Yes or No. Did you reach your Outcome? Through making individual targets, we can answer "Yes" or "No." *Keys 27:30, 28:21-23, 26, 32:13, Game 34:2-3*

**Stand for the Core.** The second part of the Warrior phrase: *Live by the Code. Stand for the Core. Create with the Keys.* This is part of an amalgamation of the main Code and Core doctrine and completed with the Keys within Warrior to serve as a ready reminder of how we should operate on a daily basis. When we STAND for the Core, we maintain honor yet again by meeting the ½ point requirements within the Core 4 (Body, Being, Balance & Business) by measuring whether or not we have hit the Core. *Foundation 1:27, 4:37, Keys 27:8, 28:30, 30:19, 32:2, Game 39:22-23, Summary 40:7-8*

**Stories.** This is a common term referred to within *Wake Up Warrior* in regard to the false beliefs that we believe to be true which hold us back from expansion and growth. They are commonly addressed and referred to whenever dealing with the Drift and Shift Model of cyclical patterns in our lives.

**Strategic Seduction.** This term refers to the relevancy behind marketing strategies to convince clients and team members that the plan you have set out in the General's Tent comes into fruition. It is a tool that can also be used across the Core 4.

There are different points of view within Strategic Seduction to keep in mind:

1. Worldview
2. Self-View
3. Road Map
4. Compel Action
5. Commit to a Yes

In the Road Map, we are delivering the following: *prison, paradise,* and a *framework* for success. It is here that we commit the mindset. Within those views there are 6 stages within Strategic Seduction, each stage defined in greater detail within the Warrior Dictionary:

1. Set the Frame
2. Find the Pain
3. Expand the Pain
4. Release the Pain
5. Desperation to Desire
6. Make the Offer

*Core 24:26*

**Strategic Selling.** A carry-over from Strategic Seduction, it is the process breakdown of how to use this marketing tool by addressing the problem, possibility, path, pitch and commit.

Steps to Strategic Selling:
(Problem, possibility, path, pitch and commit)

1. Communicate a Message
2. Possibility of Paradise
3. Road Map: Paint the Path
4. Call to Action: The Pitch
5. Commit with a Yes

**Strategically Studying.** When we strategize our battle plan within Warrior, we are laying out the framework and foundation for our Kingdom to be built. This process is done within the General's Tent especially, but has also been known to take place after meditation or when epiphanies occur. Writing out in the War Map will help these thoughts shift from an idea to a concept meant to be studies and strategized over, especially within Business. *Core 24:6, 9 (6-11), Keys 27:10, 30, 30:17, 30 (planning), 31:25, Game 36:38, 38:3, 12, 19, 26-28, 31, Summary 41:8-9*

**Systemized Sedation of Men.** This is a term referred to in Chapter 2: The Foundation of *WarriorBook* as the process that it took in history to create the sedated state that a modern man seems to easily dwell in. This man is taught that expressing feelings are bad, so therefore a lobotomized version is better than a maniac that voices his feelings. *Foundation 1:60-65, 2:8, 3:47, Code 6:20, Core 17:12, 18:15*

# T

**Target.** Instead of marking down goals, within the Wake Up Warrior Program we call them Targets because they are a specific outcome rather than a generalized idea that goals are made up of. Targets require clarity and accuracy in action in order to get the job done, just as a sniper has a target to aim for, rather than a goal to shoot someone. By calling our desires outcomes targets, we shift the mentality and know that hard work and training is what is required to reach the desired result. *Code 6:6, 8:23, 43, Keys 27:30, 28:21-23, 26, Game 33:30, 33, 34:16, 18, 21, 37, 36:28, 37:14, 36:3*

**Teeter Totter Effect.** The Teeter-Totter Effect is described within the section on The Code as a simple "right" and "wrong" mentality, but it's also inaccurate. The most efficient way to get out of this mindset is to shift from doing what is right to what is going to lead to freedom. To some this is the same, but not all that is "right" will lead us to liberation. When we free ourselves from the mentality that if Exhibit A is right, then Exhibit B must be wrong. Humanity does not always operate in that mode, and so when we operate under "it is what it is" we are able to pull ourselves off of the ever unbalanced teeter-totter. *Code 5:18-28, 43, 7:46 (44-47)*

**Text: Honor Appreciation and Love.** These are the three words to send in a text or note form on a daily basis to your Queen and another selected family member (your posterity: children, siblings, parents, etc). Doing this simple action within the Balance quadrant of Core 4 helps create a karmic debt between you and the receiver. Therefore, it is meant to be done without the expectation of having them respond back or reciprocate. If they do, fantastic, but never "honor, appreciate and love" with the expectation that they need to follow suit. *Core 22:11-14, 25:24, Game 36:35, 37:16, 26*

**Theories, Tactics and Tools.** Used in that sequential order, these are the 3 T's of how to use the Armory. When we go into the Armory, it is going to support us based upon who we are, so some of the tools will not be effective until the skills sets learned from Theory and Tactics makes them applicable.

- Theories: Principles
- Tactics: Strategies
- Tools: Evolving Support

*Summary 41:8-10*

**Thought Leader.** Becoming a creator of original thought and content in order to be the leader in your business community. You provide through example how you want something to be communicated and shared. *Core 19:26, Keys 27:4*

**Threshold**. When playing the Impossible Game, we will hit a threshold, or spot that requires growth in order to push past otherwise we will red line within that area. Through continual expansion, however, the threshold also shifts, so what was once our threshold barrier a year ago is now stages below where we currently operate. It requires taking a leap into the unknown in order to pursue it, which might be why not very many people are able to increase their threshold; they reach their limit and call it quits. To push past the threshold requires going 1% beyond the current reality, and it can continue to be pushed. *Game 33:21-22 (lactic)*

**Time Matrix.** Developed from Stephen R Covey's *7 Habits of Highly Effective People*, this principle breaks down life's demands into sub-categories based upon importance:

1. Not Important
2. Important
3. Not Urgent
4. Urgent

*Throughout Keys 27:21-24 (breakdown), 28:31, 34, 29:31, 30:6, 31:11, 20, 32:3, Game 34:25, 36:13, 18, Summary 43:36*

**The Tools.** This is the term used to describe the items that make up Warrior, which are: Release the Rage, Power Focus Parts 1 & 2, Production Focus and Revelation Road Map. Within more in-depth training of the *Wake Up Warrior Academy* these tools also include Shift Move, Core Breathing, and Warrior Ascension (also shortened simply to Ascension). Daily use helps a Warrior to expand, but use of each one on a daily basis is not required.

Some, like Power and Production Focus, are done daily, but others like Release the Rage are done as needed. Some tools may be used with others, and some may be used multiple times in a day. Use of these tools is meant to help a Warrior pursue a life of having it all. Breakdown of how to use these can be found in Section 3: Warrior Stack.

**Transcendence.** This is a realization that you are called as a King to lead a movement, and to help you see the spiritual nature around what it is that you're doing because it *does* matter. The tools found in the Armory help make this possible, especially once you know how to utilize them. *Summary 41:27, 42:36*

**Transcendental Meditation.** This mantra-based form of meditation was developed by the late Maharishi Mahesh Yogi as a technique for avoiding distracting thoughts, helping to promote a state of relaxed awareness and enlightenment. It is an excellent form of developing inner peace when having to face unavoidable stress. *Appendix Resources: Meditation.*

**Tunnel Vision.** A state of focusing on something so intensely that one is unable to see anything else surrounding him. Within mantra-based meditation, it is the overall outcome in the Brotherhood is to be able to train you on how to eliminate tunnel vision and stay present when focusing on the One Thing, which is different than tunnel vision because it allows the mind to create *more* space, rather than putting up blinders to everything else when zeroing in on something. One way in which to do this is to reduce your heart rate by focused breathing and mantra repetition. *Game 35:7*

# V

**Valley of Pain.** The Valley of Pain metaphorically speaks of the process we go through within Warrior in order to achieve greatness. It tends to work in conjunction with Pathway to Power, which is hardly ever an easy path to take. It's a Refiner's Fire of one's capabilities, insomuch in that which does not breaks us makes us stronger. In Strategic Seduction this is also experienced the more real we become about ourselves. *Code 9:20-21, 47, 67, Core 17:19*

**Value In Me.** It is vital that we make an investment in ourselves in order to properly fill others up (like the concept of the Bucket Fillers). *Core 23:1, 9*

**Voice.** The Voice is your own personal intuition, Whispering of the Spirit or connecting with the Universe. What or however you want to call it, your personal Voice gives you power to pursue your life's passion, but only if you listen to it. *Foundation 1:36-37, 3:6, 14, 36, Code 7:19, 60, Warrior Stack 15, Core Chapter 21 throughout, 21:11-13, 23:27, 33, 25:25, Keys 29:15, Game 39:10, 14*

**Void.** The space between starting and completing something. In this case, the daily grind that is required to hit our Quarterly Challenges after declaring what it is we want to accomplish yet not knowing the specific steps in getting there. This is why we have monthly benchmarks to help us reassess and course correct if needed until we hit our goal. In Chapter 36 of The WarriorBook, Garrett uses an analogy of climbing a mountain and going through the cloud line before reaching the summit. The Void is the cloud line, in which what we see is a limited perspective. *Code 9:47, Summary 36:32, 35 (28-36 Climbing Mountains, what happens between base and summit), 43:1*

# W

**Wake Up Warrior Movement.** *Wake Up Warrior* is the name of the elite Academy program in which all of this operates from, geared specifically towards male entrepreneurs and businessmen pursuing a life of having it all. It is in reference to becoming "awakened" and remembering the Warrior Kings we have always been. This reawakening provides core leadership skills that can be incorporated into every facet of life, shared with family, work colleagues, and even complete strangers as they see the confidence radiating from a Warrior that is part of the Wake Up Warrior Movement. *Foundation 4:1, (Movement) Code 5:11, Core 19:20, Keys 21:1*

**Walk the Block.** A phrase used during Warrior Week in which the men pair off and "walk the block" which isn't necessarily walking down 4 cubed sides of a street but taking time to look at four versions of the story that is holding a person back from expansion and growth. These 4 "sides" consist of the following symbolic form:

> Front Side of the Block: Original Version
> Left Side of the Block: ME Version
> Back Side of the Block: Opposite Version
> Right Side of the Block: Desired Version

Once these four versions of the same story are looked at and approached in a figurative way, sometimes done through physical action by walking and talking about the story, we can then come to the summary: *After Walking the Block, which version of the story are you choosing and why?* This conclusion will provide us with an open viewpoint and instead of reacting out of uncontrolled emotion, the situation has been approached from an overall point of view. Explained in more detail as part of the Warrior Stack in Section 3, Chapter 14.

**Wandering Generalities.** This term is in reference to the concept that if you do not have a plan (Focus) for your life, then don't worry, someone else will plan it for you. The thought originally came from Zig Ziglar about the importance of avoiding wandering generalities by making meaningful specifics in life. *Code 8:12-13, 15 (11-23), Summary 40:10*

**War Map.** The War Map is another name for your journal. And yet, it is so much more than simply writing your thoughts for the day down for the sake of posterity to know who you were; it is a way to create your own personal doctrine and beliefs; a place for scripture. Physically writing out one's thoughts creates a shift in the mind that allows us to look at situations using a different part of the brain. It is your daily living scripture. *Code 6:32 (32-35), Core 21:13, 22, 25-28, 23:42, 25:18, Keys 31:14, Game 37:26*

**Warrior Ascension.** This is the ever expanding state that men within the Brotherhood strive for. It is operating on a higher plane than all those around us, feeling the responsibility that comes from this ultimate way of living. There is a whole section that can be found in the Manual that goes into extensive detail on how to ascend within Warrior as as the King that you are. *Game 39:26, Summary 42:8, 26-36 (Mountain Ascension 28-35)*

**Warrior King.** The title that all men are able to receive if they're willing to pay the price to get there. Within each man is a divine stewardship over his kingdom. Wake Up Warrior Academy uses tools and programs to bring this individual system out in each man that is willing. *Code 8:40, 53, Core 21:9, Game 38:32, Summary 42:10-11, 43:13*

**Warrior On Fire.** This is site for the daily podcast episodes known as Daily Fuels created by Garrett in which he shares his daily Power Focus thoughts of the day. Each episode is called a Daily Fuel which consists of 3 main points with a brief, two bullet description of the point, a Question of the Day, Challenge of the Day and Quote of the Day. Listeners are encouraged to implement the lesson taught in each brief Fuel as well as share it with others.

**Warrior Stack.** Found in Section Three of the book, this is a description of the daily documents completed within Warrior as a means of processing through blocks that get in the way from living the Warrior's Way of having it all. The Drift and Shift model breaks down the stages that a man goes through, which can get activated through a frustrating event and started once a man falls into the Pit of limited beliefs, the Dark, known as Release the Rage as the first step. The Stack then consists of the Drift, Shift, Lift and Light, broken down into Drift (Power Focus, Part 1), Shift (Power Focus, Part 2), Lift (Production Focus) and Light (Revelation Road Map). When performed on a daily basis, the Power Focus, Parts 1 & 2 and Production Focus bring an elevated way of approaching situations in life that could debilitate others, but because of this Warrior tool, becomes a power instead. Release the Rage and Revelation Road Map are documents that can be done on a more as needed basis, but when told to complete a Warrior Stack, the four documents that must be completed, in order, are: Release the Rage, Power Focus (1 &2), Production Focus and Revelation Road Map.

**Warrior Time Warp.** This is what occurs when living the Warrior's Way in which time has been compressed. Growth within Warrior moves at a rapid pace. It's a collapsing of time in which men in Warrior grow at speeds that blow the reality of the rest of humanity. Expansion is on the fast track, where the difficulty that then ensues is learning to actually appreciate how fast you've grown in such a short amount of time. Reflection and looking over the metrics within the General's Tent allows us time to be grateful for where we were to where we currently are. *Warrior Stack 11*

**Warrior's Way.** This term refers to some of the core doctrinal beliefs within the Wake Up Warrior Academy. It consists of The Code, The Core, and The Keys, which if obtained, will lead to a powerful life of having it all. *Foundation 1:27, 2:3, 3:32-33, 37-38, 4:18, 45, Code 5:2, 6:28, 37, 10:1, 36, Core 21:9, Game 33:14, 30:37, Summary 40:2, 17, 42:3-5, 22 43:38-39*

**Warrior Week.** A part of the Wake Up Warrior Academy, Warrior Week was at the end of a 6-week training program that incorporated the learnings from the 5 weeks of online work and conference calls and put it into a boot camp for life, in which the Warriors faced physical obstacles and tackled emotional issues amongst others in the Brotherhood. The 4 A's for Warrior Week are: *Access, Action Plans, Accountability,* and *Association.* It is for this reason that Wake Up Warrior Academy is specifically male oriented; it incorporates the Core 4 in a masculine way in order for the Warrior Kings to awaken and come forth. *Game 39:24*

**Weaponization.** A term inside Warrior on creating one's own personal body as a weapon or tool to handle whatever obstacle he may face in Core 4. The foundation of creating the body as a weapon starts physically, but requires all 4 parts of the Core in order to truly become weaponized. *Core 17:14, 18:6, 23, Keys 29:14, Game 37:30*

**Weekly Targets.** This metric-based process is done inside the General's Tent every week as a way to step-by-step make our way to our 90-Day Outcome inside the Key 4 of Business. Hitting these act as many targets in a way to maintain the path for the Quarterly Game. See Section 6: Game Chapter 36 for further explanation.

**What, Why, Lesson Apply.** This sequential format in asking and then answering questions has an iambic pentameter to it in order to help those in Warrior remember what order to do the steps as found in the Section 3: Warrior Stack under Production Focus, Chapter 15. It is linked with the Core 4 Body, Being, Balance and Business.

**What Do You Want?** This is the first question asked in the Key 4, under the mantra What? Why? When? How? When we are clear about what we want, even if we don't know all of the specific particulars in how to get there (that's later on in the Keys with How), we are able to establish an outcome to be attained. It is our Why that drives us to see it all through. *Code 8:28-29 (28-37), 10:13, Keys 28:1-5 (throughout chapter), 31:6, 8, 32:7, Game 34:6*

# X

**X Factor.** This is the unique skill set that you bring to the environment. Whether it's part of business or life, it is your own individual talent that you bring to the table which makes you stand apart from others. It's your own personal capital in a situation. *Keys 31:27-30, 32:10, Game 36:14*

# Z

**Zazen Meditation.** A technique used in meditation to bring the individual to a place of "zen" or ultimate peace. It is the study of the self, so therefore it requires frequent and lifelong learning, as an individual is always in a changing state, or at least he is once he becomes aware of his state. It is a simple practice most easily defined as seeing the body, mind and breath as one, therefore they are all connected and work together. This self-awareness brings great empowerment and opportunities for expansion by listening to the Voice and following the path that is specific for you. *Appendix Resources: Meditation*

**Zones of Core 4.** There are 4 Zones in which we can accomplish our Core 4 in throughout the day:

- Zone 1: Before 0800 hours
- Zone 2: 0800-1000 hours
- Zone 3: 1000-1200 hours
- Zone 4: 1200-2400 hours

The first Zone is the most ideal to accomplish the majority if not all of our Core 4, as it sets the stage and lays the foundation for the rest of the way we operate throughout the day. *Game 37:17-25*

# BIBLIOGRAPHY

Covey, Stephen R. *The 7 Habits of Highly Effective People.* Provo, UT: Franklin Covey, 1998. Print.

Dyer, Wayne W. *Getting in the Gap: Making Conscious Contact with God through Meditation.* Carlsbad, CA: Hay House, 2003. Print.

*The Power of Intention: Learning to Co-create Your World Your Way.* Carlsbad, CA: Hay House, 2004. Print.

Ford, Debbie. *The Dark Side of the Light Chasers: Reclaiming Your Power, Creativity, Brilliance, and Dreams.* New York: Riverhead, 2010. Print.

"Green Goddess Smoothie - Happy Food, Healthy Life." *Happy Food Healthy Life.* N.p., 21 Jan. 2013. Web. 01 Dec. 2015.

Grover, Tim, and Shari Lesser. Wenk. *Relentless: From Good to Great to Unstoppable.* N.p.: Tantor Audio, 2014. Audible audiobook.

Halbert, Gary C., and Bond Halbert. *The Boron Letters.* N.p.: n.p., n.d. Print.

Henley, William Ernest. "Invictus." *Poetry Foundation.* Poetry Foundation, n.d. Web. 23 Mar. 2016.

Hill, Napoleon. Think and Grow Rich: *The Secret to Wealth Updated for the 21st Century.* Place of Publication Not Identified: Tribeca, 2011. Print.

Katie, Byron, and Stephen Mitchell. *Loving What Is: Four Questions That Can Change Your Life.* New York: Harmony, 2002. Print.

http://www.thework.com

Keller, Gary, and Jay Papasan. *The One Thing: The Surprisingly Simple Truth behind Extraordinary Results.* Austin, TX: Bard, 2012. Print.

Kiyosaki, Robert T., and Sharon L. Lechter. *Rich Dad, Poor Dad: What the Rich Teach Their Kids about Money— That the Poor and Middle Class Do Not!* New York: Warner Business, 2000. Print.

"Lesmcguire." *Lesmcguire.* N.p., n.d. Web. 24 Apr. 2016.

"Mastermind Summit – Tony Robbins." *Mortgage Mastermind Tony Robbins.* N.p., n.d. Web. 01 Dec. 2015.

Roberts, Sam. "Divorce After 50 Grows More Common." 20 September 2013. *The New York Times.* 11 February 2016. <http://www.nytimes.com/2013/09/22/fashion/weddings/divorce-after-50-grows-more-common.html?_r=0>.

"Strategic Coach® Starter Kit." *Dan Sullivan.* N.p., n.d. Web. 01 Dec. 2015.

Tolle, Eckhart. *The Power of Now: A Guide to Spiritual Enlightenment.* Novato, CA: New World Library, 1999. Print.

"Zig Ziglar: Defining Success." *SUCCESS.* N.p., 31 July 2010. Web. 01 Dec. 2015.

# QUOTES

<u>Albert Einstein:</u>
"The significant problems we face cannot be solved at the same level of thinking we were at when we created them."

<u>Doctrine & Covenants 11:21, LDS scripture:</u>
"Seek not to declare my word, but first seek to obtain my word, and then shall your tongue be loosed; then, if you desire, you shall have my Spirit and my word, yea, the power of God unto the convincing of men."

<u>"Invictus" by William Ernest Henley</u>
Out of the night that covers me,
    Black as the pit from pole to pole,
I thank whatever gods may be
    For my unconquerable soul.

In the fell clutch of circumstance
    I have not winced nor cried aloud.
Under the bludgeonings of chance
    My head is bloody, but unbowed.

Beyond this place of wrath and tears
    Looms but the Horror of the shade,
And yet the menace of the years
    Finds and shall find me unafraid.

It matters not how strait the gate,
    How charged with punishments the scroll,
I am the master of my fate,
    I am the captain of my soul.

## Luke 11:9, King James Version (KJV), The Holy Bible, New Testament:

"And I say unto you, Ask, and it shall be given you; seek, and ye shall find; knock, and it shall be opened unto you."

## Mahatma Gandhi:

"Be the change you wish to see in the world."

## Matthew 7:3, KJV Holy Bible, New Testament:

"And why beholdest thou the mote that is in thy brother's eye, but considerest not the beam that is in thine own eye?"

## Matthew 7:6, KJV:

"Give not that which is holy unto the dogs, neither cast ye your pearls before swine, lest they trample them under their feet, and turn again and rend you."

## Matthew 16:19, KJV:

"And I will give unto thee the keys of the kingdom of heaven: and whatsoever thou shalt bind on earth shall be bound in heaven: and whatsoever thou shalt loose on earth shall be loosed in heaven."

## Quote on Secretary's desk in Garrett's High School:

"Your failure to prepare does not constitute an emergency on my part."

## Zig Ziglar:

"Don't become a wandering generality. Be a meaningful specific."

### Quotes in the Beginning of Each Chapter

## Chapter 1: The Pit

"Through me you go into a city of weeping; through me you go into eternal pain; through me you go amongst the lost people."

**–Dante Alighieri**

## Chapter 2: The Painful Problem

"The Industrial Revolution has two phases: one material, the other social; one concerning the making of things, the other concerning the making of men."

**–Charles A. Beard**

### Chapter 3: The Possibility

"But when a long train of abuses and usurpations, pursuing invariably the same Object evinces a design to reduce them under absolute Despotism, it is their right it is their duty, to throw off such Government, and to provide new Guards for their future security."

**–Declaration of Independence**


### Chapter 4: The Path

"Two roads diverged in a wood, and I—
I took the one less traveled by,
And that has made all the difference."

**–Robert Frost**


### Chapter 5: The Code Overview

"If you tell the truth, then you don't have to remember anything."

**–Mark Twain**


### Chapter 6: Real

"Facts are stubborn things; and whatever may be our wishes, our inclinations, or the dictates of our passions, they cannot alter the state of facts and evidence."

**–John Adams**

### Chapter 7: Raw

"It matters not how strait the gate,
How charged with punishments the scroll,
I am the master of my fate,
I am the captain of my soul."

**–William Ernest Henley**

## Chapter 8: Relevant
"When you can't make them see the light, make them feel the heat."

**–Ronald Reagan**

## Chapter 9: Results
"Insanity: doing the same thing over and over again and expecting different results."

**–Albert Einstein**

## Chapter 10: The Code Summary
"Do you wish to rise? Begin by descending. You plan a tower that will pierce the clouds? Lay first the foundation of humility."

**–Saint Augustine**

## Chapter 11: The Drift & Shift Model
"You come to the point in your life when you can't pull the trigger anymore."

**–Evel Knievel**

## Chapter 12: The Dark (Release the Rage)
"Niemand ist mehr Sklave, als der sich für halt, ohne es zu sein."
"None are more hopelessly enslaved than those who falsely believe they are free."

**–Johann Wolfgang von Goethe**

## Chapter 13: The Drift (Power Focus, Part 1)
"Thoughts will change and shift just like the wind and the water when you're on the boat; thoughts are no different than anything else."

**–Jeff Bridges**

### Chapter 14: The Shift (Power Focus, Part 2)

"And, when you want something, all the universe conspires in helping you to achieve it."

**–Paulo Coelho**

### Chapter 15: The Lift (Production Focus)

"Become a possibilitarian. No matter how dark things seem to be or actually are, raise your sights and see the possibilities…always see them…for they're always there."

**–Norman Vincent Peale**

### Chapter 16: The Light (Revelation Road Map)

"When you think all is forsaken
Listen to me now (all is not forsaken)
You need never feel broken again
Sometimes Darkness can show you
The Light."

**–David Draiman**

### Chapter 17: The Core Overview

"Struggling and suffering are the essence of a life worth living. If you're not pushing yourself beyond the comfort zone, if you're not demanding more from yourself - expanding and learning as you go - you're choosing a numb existence. You're denying yourself an extraordinary trip."

**–Dean Karnazes**

### Chapter 18: Body (Fitness)

"To keep the body in good health is a duty… otherwise we shall not be able to keep our mind strong and clear."

**–Buddha**

### Chapter 19: Body (Fuel)
"Let your food be your medicine, and your medicine be your food."

**–Hippocrates**

### Chapter 20: Being (Meditation)
"Meditation makes the entire nervous system go into a field of coherence."

**–Dr. Deepak Chopra**

### Chapter 21: Being (Revelation)
"There is a voice inside of you
That whispers all day long,
'I feel this is right for me,
I know that this is wrong.'
No teacher, preacher, parent, friend
Or wise man can decide
What's right for you--just listen to
The voice that speaks inside."

**–Shel Silverstein**

### Chapter 22: Balance (Partner/Posterity)
"Being deeply loved by someone gives you strength, while loving someone deeply gives you courage."

**–Lao Tzu**

### Chapter 23: Balance (Power)
"Nearly all men can stand adversity, but if you want to test a man's character, give him power."

**–Abraham Lincoln**

### Chapter 24: Business (Discover)

"The size of your success is measured by the strength of your desire; the size of your dream; and how you handle disappointment along the way."

**–Robert Kiyosaki**

### Chapter 25: Business (Declare)

"Next to doing the right thing, the most important thing is to let people know you are doing the right thing."

**–John D. Rockefeller, Sr**

### Chapter 26: The Core Summary

"Don't you ever get the feeling that all your life is going by and you're not taking advantage of it? Do you realize you've lived nearly half the time you have to live already?"

**–Ernest Hemingway**

### Chapter 27: The Keys Overview

"The greater danger for most of us lies not in setting our aim too high and falling short; but in setting our aim too low, and achieving our mark."

**–Michelangelo**

### Chapter 28: What

"I know where I'm going and I know the truth, and I don't have to be what you want me to be. I'm free to be what I want."

**–Muhammad Ali**

### Chapter 29: Why

"There are two great days in a person's life - the day we are born and the day we discover why."

**–William Barclay**

### Chapter 30: When

"Once you have mastered time, you will understand how true it is that most people overestimate what they can accomplish in a year – and underestimate what they can achieve in a decade!"

**–Tony Robbins**

### Chapter 31: How

"When you bring your full attention to each moment, a day is a complete lifetime of living and learning."

**–Mark Divine**

### Chapter 32: The Keys Summary

"No one is free who has not obtained the empire of himself."

**–Pythagoras**

### Chapter 33: The Game Overview

"Each player must accept the cards life deals him or her: but once they are in hand, he or she alone must decide how to play the cards in order to win the game."

**–Voltaire**

### Chapter 34: Quarterly Challenge

"We all need people who will give us feedback. That's how we improve."

**–Bill Gates**

### Chapter 35: Monthly Benchmarks

"Some men give up their designs when they have almost reached the goal; While others, on the contrary, obtain a victory by exerting, at the last moment, more vigorous efforts than ever before."

**–Herodotus**

## Chapter 36: Weekly Targets

"The most deadly thing on a battlefield is one well-aimed shot."

**–Gunnery Sergeant Carlos Hathcock**

## Chapter 37: Daily Actions

"To be nobody but yourself in a world which is doing its best, night and day, to make you everybody else means to fight the hardest battle which any human being can fight; and never stop fighting."

**–e. e. cummings**

## Chapter 38: The General's Tent

"The time to take counsel of your fears is before you make an important battle decision. That's the time to listen to every fear you can imagine! When you have collected all the facts and fears and made your decision, turn off all your fears and go ahead!"

**–General George S. Patton**

## Chapter 39: The Game Summary

"I've missed more than 9000 shots in my career. I've lost almost 300 games. 26 times, I've been trusted to take the game winning shot and missed. I've failed over and over and over again in my life. And that is why I succeed."

**–Michael Jordan**

## Chapter 40: The Summary Game

"The good news is that the moment you decide that what you know is more important than what you have been taught to believe, you will have shifted gears in your quest for abundance. Success comes from within, not from without."

**–Ralph Waldo Emerson**

## Chapter 41: The Armory

"Language is the armory of the human mind, and at once contains the trophies of its past and the weapons of its future conquests."

**–Samuel Taylor Coleridge**

## Chapter 42: The Brotherhood

"Rise up, warriors, take your stand
at one another's sides,
our feet set wide and rooted
like oaks in the ground.
Then bide your time, biting your lip,
for you were born
from the blood of Heracles,
unbeatable by mortal men,
and the god of gods has never turned his back on you."

**–Tyrtaeus**

## Chapter 43: The Leap

"One small step for man, one giant leap for mankind."

**–Neil Armstrong**

# ADDITIONAL RESOURCES

*Compiled by Natalie C Martin*

## America's Founding Fathers

Biography on who we consider to be America's Founding Fathers

http://www.biography.com/people/groups/founding-fathers

Transcript of The Declaration of Independence:

http://www.archives.gov/exhibits/charters/declaration_transcript.html

The Founding Fathers, Delegates to the Constitutional Convention

http://www.archives.gov/exhibits/charters/constitution_founding_fathers.html

Transcript of The Constitution and Bill of Rights:

http://www.archives.gov/exhibits/charters/constitution_transcript.html

http://www.archives.gov/exhibits/charters/bill_of_rights_transcript.html

For a glimpse into the mentality behind the driving force of our Founding Fathers, John Adams is an excellent source. Below is a link for the HBO series and Pulitzer Prize winning book it was based off of by nationally acclaimed author David McCullough:

http://www.hbo.com/john-adams

McCullough, David G. John Adams. New York: Simon &

Schuster, 2002. Print.

## Bucket Fillers
A children's book with the simple concept of filling up another person's bucket with kind words, adapted Warrior Style with our Daily Deposits of Honor, Appreciation and Love.

McCloud, Carol, Katherine Martin, and David Messing. *Fill a Bucket: A Guide to Daily Happiness for Young Children.* Northville, MI: Ferne, 2009. Print.

## Business Tools
In *Rich Dad, Poor Dad*, there is a game called Cash Flow that provides a foundation for making more money in business (which is not needed when using the Key 4 module through Warrior, but still a good reference):

https://www.richdadworld.com

Cash-Flow 101 Game, to purchase:
http://www.amazon.com/Distribution-Solutions-4098375-CASHFLOW-101/dp/
B0002R5IKI

The Gary Halbert Letter is a newsletter collection of published articles and information for the marketplace. Gary Halbert is known as the Godfather of Direct Response Marketing. The content he shares is GOLD. To learn more about its origins and download the articles now available online for FREE, go to:

http://www.thegaryhalbertletter.com

SANG, a huge networking event for Business people and entrepreneurs with speakers like Tony Robbins and Jack Canfield:
http://sangevents.com

Verbal Judo, or the art of gentle persuasion, is what we call Strategic Seduction here in warrior:

http://verbaljudo.com
Thompson, George J., and Jerry B. Jenkins. *Verbal Judo: The Gentle Art of Persuasion.* New York: Quill,
2004. Print.

The Wealth Factory is a business created by a former strategic partner of Garrett's (whose name is ALSO Garrett), Garrett B Gunderson:
https://wealthfactory.com

## The Feminist Movement
Timeline of the Feminist Movement in America:
http://www.pbs.org/independentlens/sistersof77/timeline.html

Second Wave Feminism, which took place during the 1960s-70s in America:
https://tavaana.org/en/content/1960s-70s-american-feminist-movement-breaking-down-barriers-women

## Fitness
CrossFit:
https://www.crossfit.com

In Chapter 22 Garrett mentions Chippers, a brutal CrossFit workout routine:
http://www.muscleandfitness.com/workouts/workout-routines/chipper-hardest-workout-crossfit-history

IronMan:
http://www.ironman.com/

Garrett participated and completed in the 2007 Championships in Kona, Hawaii, which required pre-qualifications through participating in other competitions, and is said to be the most difficult race in the world.

Sealfit:
http://sealfit.com
Kokoro, a 70 straight hour-long training camp designed by Mark Divine as a pre-training for the Navy Seal program BUD/S which also allows civilians to participate in:

http://sealfit.com/sealfit-events/sealfit-kokoro-camp/
Kokoro 37, which Garrett participated in and accomplished:
https://www.youtube.com/watch?v=aKDg45gpb5g

Ultramarathon Training:
http://www.runnersworld.com/ultramarathons/the-ultimate-ultramarathon-training-plan

## The Great Depression
http://www.history.com/topics/great-depression

The Great Depression: Crash Course US History #33
https://www.youtube.com/watch?v=GCQfMWAikyU
The New Deal: Crash Course US History #34
https://www.youtube.com/watch?v=6bMq9Ek6jnA

## The Great War
BBC: World War I documentaries and clips.
http://www.bbc.co.uk/programmes/p01nb93y
http://www.bbc.co.uk/schools/worldwarone/index1.shtml

Trench Warfare:
http://www.firstworldwar.com/features/trenchlife.htm

## Green Smoothies
A quick Google search for "green smoothies" will pull up thousands of recipes and resources, which you can also customize thousands of different ways.

For regular, up to date information by the Green Smoothie Goddess, Liz Phalp, go to: https://www.facebook.com/GreenSmoothieGoddess/

The basic formula for making a green smoothie is:
- 1/3 Greens
- 1/3 Fruit
- 1/3 Water

For variation, Phalp also provided a formula for warm, "green" smoothies which can be found at: http://lizphalp.com/warm-smoothies/

There's also programs for healthy eating, such as Food trainers that pieces together the puzzles of a person's lifestyle and body metrics by focusing on the food aspect FIRST then moving out to other areas of the body like fitness: http://foodtrainers.com

## Gutenberg Press

The invention of the printing press changed the whole structure of how information was sent and utilized in all of Western Civilization.

http://www.history.com/topics/middle-ages/videos/mankind-the-story-of-all-of-us-the-printing-press

## The Hero's Journey

Joseph Campbell's description of the monomyth, or hero's journey, is explained in detail within his book, *The Hero With A Thousand Faces*. Campbell's approach emphasized common themes throughout literature and cultural myths, while here at Warrior it is a path that we see the modern man in the pursuit of having it all also embarks upon, in his own symbolic way:

http://www.thewritersjourney.com/hero's_journey.htm

Campbell, Joseph. *The Hero with a Thousand Faces.*
Princeton, NJ: Princeton UP, 1972. Print.

## The Industrial Revolution

Documentaries and specific areas within society affected by the Industrial Age.

http://www.history.com/topics/industrial-revolution

Brief Encyclopedia description of the Industrial Revolution's inventions and shifts within society.

http://www.britannica.com/event/Industrial-Revolution

More Revolutionary books from the Industrial Revolution that brought change:

A collection of photojournalism depicting the reality of tenement living and overcrowded cities, especially in areas with a high immigrant ratio:

Riis, Jacob. *How The Other Half Lives: Studies Among the Tenements of New York.* Kessinger Publishing, 1890.

A book that revolutionized the safety and sanitation conditions in meat packaging companies based off of Chicago Meat Packaging Plants:

Sinclair, Upton. *The Jungle.* Dover Thrift Edition, 1906.

## Meditation

The Power of Intention is a principle developed by Dr. Wayne Dyer that stems from the Law of Attraction as an action of allowing, or giving yourself permission to attract what you are. One way to do this is through meditation. The following article explains this principle in more depth: http://www.drwaynedyer.com/press/power-intention/

*The Ascendant: Ishaya Monks*

http://www.ishaya.com

According to Ishaya Monks, when a man is able to do away with his carnal state, he is able to ascend into the Divine found within.

This is similar to reaching the peak in Maslow's Hierarchy of Human Needs, or self-actualization:

*Japa Breath Meditation:*

Mantra techniques for a clear mind: http://www.clear-mind-meditation-techniques.com/japa-mantra-meditation.html

*Transcendental Meditation (TM):*

Official website: https://www.tm.org

Medical benefits of TM: http://www.webmd.com/balance/guide/transcendental-meditation-benefits-technique

*Zazen Meditation:*

Finding Zen: https://zmm.mro.org/teachings/meditation-instructions/

## The Progressive Era
Stage in American History between the 1890s-1920s establishing entrepreneurism:

https://en.wikipedia.org/wiki/Progressive_Era

Child Labor Laws:

*Walter Trattner, Crusade for the Children: A History of the National Child Labor Committee and Child Labor Reform in America* (1970).

http://www.history.com/topics/child-labor

## Revelation/Religious Script

## Western Religious Text:
*The Holy Bible, which consists of the Old and New Testaments, King James Version:*

http://www.kingjamesbibleonline.org

*The Book of Mormon, another testament of Jesus Christ which takes place in the Americas:*

https://www.lds.org/scriptures/bofm?lang=eng

## Eastern Religious Text:

*Bhagavad Gita,* Hindu scripture as part of the epic Mahabharata, English translation:

http://www.bhagavad-gita.org

-Article on Arjuna's journey:

http://reluctant-messenger.com/bhagavad-gita.htm

-Article by Charles Eisenstein about the War against the Self and the World:

http://charleseisenstein.net/the-war-against-the-self-and-the-world-2/

And also by Charles Eisenstein:

Eisenstein, Charles. *The Ascent of Humanity: Civilization and the Human Sense of Self.* Berkeley, CA: Evolver Editions, 2013. Print.

-Mahatma Gandhi Biography:

http://www.history.co.uk/biographies/mahatma-gandhi

Gandhi, and Mohandas Karamchand (Mahatma) H. Desai.

*Gandhi's Autobiography: The Story of My Experiments with Truth.* Washington, D.C.: Public Affairs, 1948. Print.

*Dhammapada, which are principles from Buddha's Path of Wisdom, English translation:*

http://www.accesstoinsight.org/tipitaka/kn/dhp/dhp.intro.budd.html

*Tao Te Ching, written by Lao Tzu, classic Chinese text. It is referred to as the Laozi and is also known as Daodejing, Dao De Jing, or Daode jing, English translation:*

http://www.taoism.net/ttc/complete.htm

*Torah, Jewish religious text which is also known as Pentateuch, English translation:*

http://www.jewishvirtuallibrary.org/jsource/Judaism/The_Written_Law.html

*Qur'an, the central religious text of Islam composed in Arabic, which Muslims believe to be a revelation from God to the prophet Muhammad, English translation:*

http://quran.com

## World War II

Timeline and events:

http://www.historynet.com/world-war-ii

Brokaw, Tom. *The Greatest Generation.* Toronto: Random House, 1999. Print

There were many influences in society before, during and after WWII, one of which was about women within the workforce:

http://www.history.com/topics/world-war-ii/american-women-in-world-war-ii

http://womenshistory.about.com/od/warwwii/a/overview.htm

In the article "World War II's Effect On A Generation of Men" there is a podcast and book covering how history influenced men:

http://www.npr.org/templates/story/story.php?storyId=4828744

Mathews, Tom, and Thomas Richard Mathews. *Our Fathers' War: Growing up in the Shadow of the Greatest Generation.* New York: Broadway, 2005. Print.

# INDEX

*Compiled by Natalie C Martin*

# E

# F

# X

# Y

# Z

# ACKNOWLEDGEMENT

Nothing in the game of life is easy and the TOME that you hold in your hands is no different.

This WarriorBook Warrior's Way Doctrine has come on the wake of literally 20,000+ hours of blood, sweat and tears.

It has come on the backs of hundreds of men proving that the concepts of Having It All were more than just concepts.

First, I want to acknowledge GOD who without His constant guidance in my darkest nights, none of this would have been possible.

Second, I want to acknowledge my wife and my children for the sacrifices they have made over the past 15 years. Within the past seven years especially as we have perfected this doctrine and belief system within our home. You believed in me when I was lost and you stand with me now as a KING.

Next, I want acknowledge the FOUNDING members of the Warrior Brotherhood who believed long before it was popular to believe, long before the books, software, Apps, TV shows, Movies and large events with thousands of men. You were required to follow the VOICE at a level that men today will not be required to and I honor you for this.

I want to acknowledge Jeremy Finlay, my "Wedding Son," and the original believer in me. The WAY your sacrifice will never be truly known to anyone but me and who has taken a stand to broadcast this doctrine to the whole world.

I want to acknowledge Sam Falsafi my "Personal Body Guard" and my Persian brother who is as loyal and passionate about this doctrine then anyone who has ever come in contact with it. With courage, commitment and superhuman power he protects the CODE that we live by as Lead Trainer of Wake Up Warrior.

I want to acknowledge Michael G Isom, the first and longest standing brother of the Wake Up Warrior Brotherhood. My Brother, you and I have come miles from where we were a decade ago and I love, honor and appreciate your commitment to PROVE the Warrior's Way could work in another man's life and not just mine.

I want to acknowledge Natalie Martin, my backbone with all things written with Warrior and the curator of my transcribed words into the masterpiece that has become *WarriorBook.* Your willingness to listen to the Voice over the last two years while guiding this editing process has been nothing short of Inspired.

I want to acknowledge the Warrior Global Brotherhood who have grabbed hold of the Warrior's Way and who live it with passion. You're the reason we exist, YOU are the reason we are where we are and without your work this BOOK would mean nothing.

Finally, I acknowledge YOU, the reader of this great work, for finding this book and for your desire to learn to live the Warrior's Way to having it all in your life.

Welcome to a journey that will change your life forever.

The End.

Garrett J White
Founder, Wake Up Warrior